Searching for Justice

Searching
for
Justice
Fred Kaufman

KEY PORTER BOOKS

First published in 2005 by the University of Toronto Press.

Library and Archives Canada Cataloguing in Publication

Kaufman, Fred, 1924–
Searching for justice: an autobiography / Fred Kaufman.

ISBN 978-1-55470-189-6

1. Kaufman, Fred, 1924–. 2. Judges—Québec (Province) —Biography.
3. Québec (Province). Court of Appeal—Biography. 4. Governmental investigations—Canada.
I. Title.

KE416.K39A3 2009   347.714'0334   C2009-902049-1   KF345.Z9K39 2009

The publisher gratefully acknowledges the support of the Canada Council for the Arts and the Ontario Arts Council for its publishing program. We acknowledge the support of the Government of Ontario through the Ontario Media Development Corporation's Ontario Book Initiative. We acknowledge the financial support of the Government of Canada through the Book Publishing Industry Development Program (BPIDP) for our publishing activities.

Key Porter Books Limited
Six Adelaide Street East, Tenth Floor
Toronto, Ontario
Canada M5C 1H6

www.keyporter.com

Text design: Sonya V. Thursby
Electronic formatting: Sonya V. Thursby

Printed and bound in Canada

09 10 11 12 5 4 3 2 1

In memory of my parents, Richard and Alice Kaufman,
who gave **me life** and love and the will to succeed.

[contents]

[preface]

This book has been almost forty years in the making. In the early 1970s, at the suggestion of my wife and children, I started to jot down a few reminiscences of my early days in Vienna, my brief sojourn in England, and the rather unusual facts surrounding my arrival in Canada. I later expanded this to include my time as a reporter on the Sherbrooke *Record* and the *Montreal Star*—the word "journalist" was not then in general use—and my transformation into a lawyer. Of course, once I got that far, I couldn't stop, and although my writing was frequently interrupted, I finally managed to cover my years at the Bar.

I went to the Bench in 1973, and the expansion of my memoirs had to wait. But when I elected to become a supernumerary judge in 1989, my case load diminished, and even though I spent most of my evenings and weekends over the next two years taking an Executive MBA, I found a few hours here and there to bring the story up to date.

I retired as a judge in 1991, and for a few weeks I actually had the leisure to edit what I had written, correct mistakes (memory can play strange tricks!), and write additional material. But soon clients came to seek my counsel and, before I knew it, I was back in full-time practice. Governments called on me to conduct inquiries, companies and individuals sought me out to arbitrate disputes, and lawyers asked me for advice on pending cases. And so, once more, the book had to wait.

In 1993, on the advice of my good friend and agent, Michael Levine, I asked a professional editor, Sara Browser Barney, to read and evaluate what I had written. She did so in an admirable thirteen-page report, which concluded that, "published or not, the end product will be ... archivally meaningful—and, of course, wonderful for your family for generations." She added that mine was "a unique piece of history." That was encouraging, but what she found missing were insights into my personal life—my feelings, my thoughts, my social and domestic life, "bits of colour for the general reader." The book, she concluded, needed "opening up, a more personal stance, a less distanced tone."

This was not easy for me. I am a private person by nature, an observer of facts, not a communicator of feelings. But I realized that Sara was right, and with the help and love of my wife, given generously and unstintingly with this as with everything else, a better product emerged that eventually passed muster and was considered fit for publication.

I thank Donna for her precious assistance; Michael Levine for his encouragement throughout; our children, Leslie and David, for making many helpful suggestions; and many others, friends as well as strangers, who gave me excellent feedback as well as constructive criticism after the hardcover edition was published in 2005.

There have been a number of developments since 2005, which are included in this new edition. The *Truscott* case was heard by the Court of Appeal, and five judges unanimously acquitted him on the charge of murder, a crime for which he was sentenced to death at the age of fourteen. It took forty-eight years to clear his name, and when his nightmare was over, he would say only, "They finally got it right." The government of Nova Scotia settled with employees who were falsely accused of abusing children under their care—the end of an unfortunate chapter in the province's history. My recommendations in *Morin* continue to be applied throughout Canada. The Ontario Centre of Forensic Sciences has re-established its reputation: under new direction, it is once again a leader in the field.

Most chapters have been revised, some errors have been corrected, and new information has been added. With the help of Jane Warren, my editor at Key Porter Books, I hope the finished product will make "a good read."

—Toronto, March 10, 2009

[1]
In the Beginning

In my living room in Toronto hang two old Viennese etchings. On a bookshelf are two tattered children's books: *Stoffel und die Bösen Buben* and *Peters Reise*. In a drawer are two tiny moth-eaten slippers. These are the only tangible souvenirs of my early childhood.

I was born on May 7, 1924, in Vienna, the ancient capital of what was once a great empire. But by the time of my birth, the glamour and richness of the *fin de siècle* era was gone, and people were struggling for survival. The Great Depression was not yet upon us, but Vienna had already lost its lustre and it was drab and lifeless. Yes, there was opera and theatre, concerts and recitals. But, as Paul Hoffmann writes in his brilliant book *The Viennese: Splendor, Twilight, and Exile*,[1] "Austria's economy was a shambles and government ministers were shivering in their unheated offices." It was, as Lord Weidenfeld recalled in his autobiography, "a time of introspection, poverty and misery."[2]

My father was born in 1879 in Mährisch-Kromau, a small town in Moravia, now part of the Czech Republic. His father, Jacob; his mother, Charlotte Weiner; and their four children moved to Vienna at the turn of the century, where his parents made a modest living in a small grocery store. The language of the household was German, but all could speak Czech as well, which was useful in a cosmopolitan city like Vienna.

My father didn't tell me much about his childhood years in Mährisch-Kromau, but when I was ten or eleven he took me once to see his birthplace. It was an exciting adventure for us both, and I am grateful for the experience. Roots seem more important today than they did then, but this was something that my father felt he wanted me to see. Most of the images have faded, but I remember the town square, with a fountain in the centre. And I remember my father holding my hand tight in his, as though I was a much younger child and he foresaw what was to come.

When my father was three, his mother became one of the founders of a German-language kindergarten, and I have a certificate appointing her, "in the name of the Imperial and Royal School Board," a patroness of the new kindergarten. It is addressed to her in beautiful handwriting as the *Wohlgeboren Frau Charlotte Kaufmann, Hausbesitzergattin*. The *Wohlgeboren* is an archaic form of address meaning "Madam." A *Hausbesitzergattin* is the wife of a property owner. I knew nothing of this, but the honour must have been a source of great pride for my father to have kept it among the very few papers he brought to the United States some sixty years later.

While I know from local records that my paternal forebears settled in Moravia in 1809, I have no idea where they came from. Nor do I know when they adopted the family name, but I would suspect it was some time before that. According to the archives of the Nahum Goldman Museum of the Jewish Diaspora in Jerusalem, it is probable that some Jews who lived in German-speaking parts of Europe assumed the name of Kaufmann—it means merchant or shopkeeper in German—to denote their occupation. But there is another, more romantic explanation, which finds its origin in the biblical name Yaakov (Jacob in English) which, in time, became Yakovman, later spelled Yakofman. This was then shortened to Kofman, and eventually emerged as Kaufmann, perhaps to hide the Hebrew origins. My grandfather's given name was Jakob (the German version of Yaakov) and this became my Hebrew name, with the result that my "real" name is actually Jacob Jacob.

That my paternal ancestors should have settled in Moravia is not surprising. Jews in the Czech lands owed a remarkable degree of freedom—for the times— to Emperor Joseph II who, in 1782, proclaimed an Edict of Toleration which spoke of his desire "to ensure that all Our subjects, without distinction of nationality and religion, should share in the public prosperity which we hope to increase by Our care." This "gracious intention," the edict said, "cannot be reconciled with the existing laws against the Jewish Nation in our Hereditary Margravate of Moravia," and the so-called Jewish Edicts would, therefore, be modified.

And so they were. While Jews still had to live in the ghetto, they now were allowed to pursue a university education, and by 1788 two Jewish physicians had graduated from medical school in Prague. Gone were the restrictions that required Jews to stay off the streets until noon on Sunday lest their presence give offence to Catholics going to Mass, or the prohibition against Jews visiting places of public entertainment. Indeed, Jewish dignitaries could now wear swords to indicate their rank.[3]

There was, however, a *quid pro quo*: "The maintenance of mutual trust," the emperor wrote, "demands the abolition of the Hebrew language, as well as of the mixture of Hebrew and German, the so-called Jewish language." The emperor could not resist a warning: since the Jewish nation—the emperor's words—would now be treated as "almost equal with other foreigners of related religions," it behooved Jews not to abuse "Our Favour and the freedom that has accrued to them," for any heinous deed on their part would be severely punished and the offender banished from the emperor's lands. As Helen Epstein observes in *Where She Came From: A Daughter's Search for Her Mother's History*:

> The heart of Joseph's program was linguistic. He understood that language encodes culture and Germanized the educational system, in which the language of higher learning had been Latin. He threw out the Jesuits... and with the same aim in mind, he Germanized all record keeping, so that Jews who had been keeping their personal, community, and business records in Hebrew characters now had to use Latin ones. Any Jew who wished to marry had to certify that he had completed a German elementary school. Any man who wished to serve as a rabbi had to obtain a degree at a German university. Anyone who did not have a surname was obliged to adopt a German one.[4]

Czech Jews viewed this new order as progress and readily adopted German as their day-to-day language. But Jews in the more eastern parts of the empire—the *shtetl* Jews—resisted such assimilationist moves and Yiddish remained their secular language, a split that continued until the Second World War.

As I said before, the family name was Kaufmann. That is the German spelling—two *n*'s. But that is not how I spell my name today. When my parents entered the United States, an immigration officer said to my father: "In America we spell Kaufman with one *n*." And so my father, who probably had not understood a word of what the officer told him, said "yes," which was about all the English he knew. The result was that from that day on my parents used the Americanized version, while I continued with the original. Since I had no strong feelings on the point, I dropped the second *n* later on and that is now the spelling of my name.

My mother's family, the Singers, came from the north end of Slovakia, where it now borders on Poland, but at the time of her birth, in 1896, her hometown, Saybusch, was in Galician territory. This didn't matter much at the time, since both

Slovakia and Galicia were part of the Austro-Hungarian Empire, but it took on significance more than forty years later when my parents applied for visas to enter the United States and my mother fell under the Polish quota, which had a longer waiting period than the quota for persons born in what was then Czechoslovakia.

Her family's first language was Hungarian, and she went to school in Zilina (known in German as Sillein), where she learned both Czech and German. When she was sixteen, she took a one-year commercial course in Trautenau in Bohemia. By then she was fluent in German, because that was the language of instruction, and she got the highest possible marks in all ten compulsory subjects. She also got an A in English, but had to be content with a B in French. Her "comportment" was *löbenswert*—commendable—and her "diligence" was *ausdauernd*—persevering.

My maternal grandfather, Hugo, managed the local brewery in Zilina, but he died relatively young. Unfortunately, I don't know much about him, but family lore has it that as a young man he and two brothers moved to the United States. His brothers remained, but he returned to his native country to marry and raise a family. One of his brothers settled in New York, the other, with a yen for adventure, went west in search of his fortune. The fortune eluded him, but he found work as a deputy sheriff in Alaska, where he died at the turn of the century.

Meanwhile, the brother in New York prospered, married an Irish girl named McMahon, and soon became the patriarch of the American branch of the Singers. Their children were raised as Catholics and his son, the only American Singer I know, is a prominent lawyer in New York whose principal client is the real estate department of the Roman Catholic Archdiocese of New York.

My mother was twenty-six when she married my father, who was forty-three, which, by some coincidence—though others may not call it that—is also the age at which I married. They met when my father visited friends in Zilina. They had a brief courtship, married, and my mother moved to Vienna. They remained devoted to each other for forty-five years through some of the most difficult and heart-rending events imaginable.

My grandmother, who had remained in Zilina, eventually remarried, this time to a Viennese merchant named Markus Mittler. She too moved to Vienna, as did my mother's twin brothers, Karl and Walter. The Mittlers' was a traditional, though thoroughly emancipated, Jewish home, where major holidays were celebrated but dietary laws were not observed. The language of the household was German, but my mother and her brothers would sometimes lapse into Hungarian.

My grandparents lived in an apartment near the Mariahilferstrasse. It was furnished in the style of the times: large, heavy pieces of furniture; thick Oriental carpets; and dark, voluminous drapes. Since Grandfather Mittler smoked cigars—the same kind as the emperor, he told me with some pride—there was a heavy odour of smoke trapped in the drapery, which still lingers in my memory. We used to visit often, sometimes for afternoon tea (we called it *Jause*), at other times for dinner. I liked my grandmother's cooking, and since I was her only grand-child (my uncles had no children), she catered to my whims, which were many. Of course, in the best tradition of a Jewish grandmother, she also overfed me, but in those days I could eat all the cake and drink all the coffee I wanted, with heaps of sweet whipped cream on both, without gaining a pound, a luxury that I can no longer afford.

Grandfather Mittler thought that I was a beautiful child with a wonderful dis-position. But he was also highly superstitious and worried that evil spirits might destroy my happiness and rob me of my good looks. Fortunately, there was a way to prevent this, by tying a red ribbon to the inside of my clothes. I remember nei-ther my grandfather's concern nor the ribbon, but my mother referred to it often and told me that I wore it for a number of years. I suspect that it was easier for her to pin the ribbon on my clothes than to argue with her stepfather—and in any case she was not prepared to tempt fate!

The origin of this deterrent to evil spirits is found in Eastern European Kabbal-istic writings dating back many centuries, which suggest that a red string tied around the wrist will ward off the "evil eye." Interest in this mysticismic movement re-emerged in the late sixties, when Rabbi Philip Berg opened a Kabbalah Centre in Jerusalem. There, in the words of the writer Charlotte Edwardes, "an individual might escape the confines of organized religion and become a better person."[5] Since then, the current movement has spread beyond the borders of Israel and counts among its followers a number of celebrities, including Elizabeth Taylor, Barbra Streisand, Winona Ryder, Gwyneth Paltrow, and Madonna, who changed her name in 2004 to the more biblical-sounding Esther. The latest convert to the movement, according to Edwardes, "is Victoria Beckham, who has adopted the Red String ... after revelations of her husband David Beckham's affair with Rebecca Loos." Beck-ham, the famous English soccer player, has also taken to the string: he was pho-tographed, head in hands, after missing a fateful penalty kick in the Euro 2004 soccer competition; prominent on his left wrist is a red woollen string.

I doubt that my grandfather was steeped in the teachings of Kabbalah, but word must have gotten around. Was a ribbon—even pinned on the inside—just as effective as a woollen string? Who knows, but I did grow up without much trouble from the evil eye.

Sometimes, on warm and sunny days, we met my grandparents in a park across from the *Rathaus*. I hated these occasions because I was obliged to be on my best behaviour for the benefit of their friends, who pinched my cheek and asked silly questions. I was expected to smile and answer politely when I would much rather have been elsewhere.

When my parents married they settled in a two-bedroom apartment in the heart of Vienna, Gonzagagasse 12; this was the only home we ever had. Located a block or two from the Danube canal, a project undertaken in the nineteenth century to provide the inner city with a source of water to fight major fires, the apartment was comfortable. It was on the third floor and there was no elevator, but that was a minor inconvenience. There was hot and cold running water in the bathroom, but drinking water came from a common tap in the hall, although in later years this could be had in the kitchen. Laundry was done in the attic. Since we did not have a washing machine, it was all done by hand. This required big wooden tubs with washboards in them and it was extremely hard work to scrub everything clean. When the task was done, the sheets and towels and clothes were hung up on clothes lines in the back of the attic, which was constructed of wood. The humidity was unbelievably high and things took forever to dry. A pungent odour, caused by the damp wood and strong soap, made my eyes water and my nostrils sore.

There was a concierge in a small lodge near the entrance, and the main door to the building was closed at midnight. On rare occasions when tenants came home late, they had to ring the bell and wait for the old man to shuffle out of his cramped quarters and open a door within the door, for which he was, of course, entitled to a tip. In the centre of the building was a large courtyard and during the day itinerant musicians would often come and play their instruments or sing, to be rewarded with a few coins thrown from the windows.

There were three flats on each floor, two with doors near the staircase, the third, like ours, with a door at the end of a corridor. This passage had windows that looked into the courtyard on one side, while the other side had correspon-ding windows that looked into the kitchen and another room of one of the other apartments. Without this arrangement, these two rooms would have been with-out a source of natural light and that was unacceptable. The apartment with these windows belonged to the Oppenheims, who had a daughter named Lia. She was about my age and a good friend.

Once in a while, Mr. Oppenheim would see me in the corridor and ask me to go and get him a bottle of beer. He always let me keep the change so I was happy to oblige, and whenever I passed by his windows I hoped he might be in need of my services. He owned a store where he sold fabrics for men's coats and suits. He was well educated, with a good knowledge of Latin, and he would often tell me how he and his friends would gather at his place of business and hold a conversation in Latin.

I have less pleasant memories of our other neighbours on the floor, a widow and her son. I suspected the son of being a secret Nazi because I had once seen a small Nazi flag in his room, and my suspicion was soon borne out: when the Germans moved into Austria, he proudly sported a swastika button. Afterward, we remained outwardly polite toward each other, but the relationship clearly had changed.

The only other neighbours I remember were the Morgensterns, who lived a floor above us. They were great music lovers and, since we did not have a radio until the late 1930s, they would sometimes invite me to spend an evening with them listening to broadcasts from the Vienna State Opera. They had no children and they enjoyed having a child in the house. I remember one evening in particular. There was great excitement and anticipation because it was the premiere in 1934 of Franz Lehar's *Giuditta* and the lead role was sung by Richard Tauber, the well-known and highly popular Viennese tenor. I remember the sheer pleasure of hearing the music—a pleasure that I still feel when I am surrounded by music, at home, in my office, and in the concert hall.

Mr. Morgenstern died some years before I left Vienna. One day I saw two strangers in black uniforms navigating with seeming disinterest a long wooden box down the four flights of stairs. I didn't realize at first what had happened and when I found out I was deeply upset. It was my first experience with death and I had lost a friend.

On the ground floor of the building was a pub with a side entrance from the lobby. Occasionally I would be allowed to go down and get a treat—sliced knockwurst with chopped onions and vinegar was my favourite. When the season was right, the owner, an elderly woman, would give me a glass of new white wine, which tasted like grape juice and wasn't much stronger. But it had the appeal of forbidden fruit, as this was something just between us, not to be mentioned to my parents. Across the street was a barbershop. If the owner cut your hair, you didn't give a tip; that was reserved for employees. In those days, barbers still gave a lot of shaves, and the regulars came in every day, but I wasn't concerned about shaving just yet.

◆◆◆

My father loved to read me stories, and after a time I memorized them all—not only the words, but also where a new page began. By the age of three I was eagerly turning pages at the right time so the flow of his words would not be interrupted. I suspect—although, deep down, he knew better—that there were times when he actually persuaded himself that I had learned to read, but that, of course, wasn't so. I had just memorized all these wonderful stories!

At age five I was sent to a kindergarten. I have only one memory, though a vivid one, of this experience: on my first day I learned to tie my shoelaces. Although it likely wasn't the only thing I learned that year, I was proud of my achievement. I also met a life-long friend, Hans Segal, who, with his parents, later moved to Cleveland, Ohio. "Hank," as his new American friends quickly called him, served with distinction in the U.S. Army in Europe. On his return, he studied political science, with emphasis on the Middle East. He taught for many years at Cleveland State University, where he quickly established himself as a popular lecturer and much sought-after speaker. I don't remember how, but we "found" each other after the war and we have been in touch ever since.

My years in elementary school were uneventful. The school was located at Börsegasse 5 (which means Stock Exchange Street), a fifteen-minute walk from home. School started at eight in the morning and finished mid-afternoon. My class teacher, toward the end, at least, was Beatrix Briedl, a portly middle-aged lady. There were no girls in the class. There also were no sports, but neither worried me unduly: I never was much of an athlete and, as for girls, I didn't give them much thought until many years later.

Once a week, a small woman with a dour face, wearing black metal-frame glasses—the kind that once again are popular, but this time with the younger set—came in for an hour to teach the Jewish pupils our religion while the Catholics got a lesson in catechism. It wasn't a great course (or maybe I didn't pay much attention), but I remember that one day she mentioned a synagogue, and I asked her what that was—our family went to a temple, not a synagogue—a distinction she failed to explain. She also taught us how to pray: bow your head and hold the palms of your hands together, but never cross your thumbs; that was reserved for Catholics.

On July 7, 1934, after passing the required exams, I was promoted to the *Mittelschule*, which was the equivalent of grade 5. My last report card shows nine As (in "deportment" and "diligence," among other subjects) and three Bs—in religion, German, and writing. I don't have a certificate from the *Mittelschule*, but I must have done all right because at the age of 13 I entered a *gymnasium*, which might be described as a classical high school, with heavy emphasis on Latin and Greek.

Again there were no girls, but there was also a new restriction: the class was entirely Jewish, with parallel classes for non-Jewish students. The official explanation was that this simplified the running of the school, but since most of the Jewish students observed only three major holy days—two for *Rosh Hashanah* and one for *Yom Kippur*—the excuse didn't hold. In truth, it was rank discrimination, and no one took it for anything else. But the teaching was excellent, and so was the company, and the fact of segregation was accepted in pre-Nazi Austria without much protest.

I remember only two of my teachers in the *gymnasium*, Professors (that was their official title) Sabbath and Pollack. Professor Sabbath taught math and physics, and when he talked about Isaac Newton, the celebrated English physicist, we all presumed he must be Jewish because we couldn't imagine a non-Jew being christened Isaac. In pre–World War II Austria, certain biblical names, like Abraham, Isaac, and Israel for men, and Sarah for women, were almost exclusively borne by Jews, so much so that, when the Nazis arrived in 1938, all Jews were forced to have their documents amended with Israel or Sarah added as their middle name in order to clearly identify them as Jews. I don't recall what Professor Pollack taught, but I know that he managed to escape after the *Anschluss* and found refuge in Australia. The fate of Professor Sabbath eludes me.

George Clare, who wrote *Last Waltz in Vienna*,[6] went to the same school. He calls it "one of Vienna's top gymnasia," which it was, but his years there, he writes, loom "as gloomily in my memory as the corridors and classrooms of the school," and that is my recollection too. The *gymnasium* was a little further from home than grade school. It, too, started at eight, and that meant leaving home at about 7:30. Breakfast—coffee or hot chocolate and a fresh bread roll, stuffed with a generous helping of sweet butter—was prepared and vigilantly supervised by my mother, so there was no sleeping in and sneaking off without eating. We all brought lunch and ate it in school, but once in a while my parents would give me money to buy my lunch on the way. Those were special occasions because I could play grown-up and choose what I wanted. I have remembered for well over seventy years that one such occasion turned into disaster. I was given a single coin, which was enough to pay for a sandwich and a bottle of chocolate milk. I carefully selected beforehand the store and the menu: a thick slice of Hungarian salami in a kaiser roll. All the way, in delicious anticipation, I played with the coin by tossing it into the air. As I reached the store, just before going in, I gleefully tossed it particularly high, but this time I failed to catch it. It dropped to the ground, balanced precariously on an iron grate, and just as I bent down to pick it up, it fell between the slats and disappeared into the sewer. I was devastated.

When I was ten or eleven, my parents decided to experiment with summer camp. In North America, these are well-established institutions, but they weren't nearly as popular in Europe and I often wonder what possessed my parents to give it a try. I suspect that it was their desire to give me a few weeks of country air, which was considered very important. When I was little, we had spent part of every summer in a *pension* in Bad Ischl, a beautiful resort on a lake in the mountains, but the Great Depression brought an end to this luxury and maybe camp was a replacement.

The experiment was not a success. The first camp was not far from Vienna and I shared a room with a boy who lived across the street from us. A few days after we arrived, my friend took ill and I was told that he had been sent back to the city. Later that day, my parents arrived with the family doctor, who gave me a thorough examination. I was quite mystified by this, but my questions went unanswered, which didn't help the situation. At the end of the examination, my parents, who seemed greatly relieved at the doctor's findings, told me that they would like me to leave camp and go back with them. I readily agreed because I didn't like it anyway. What I didn't know then was that my roommate had contracted polio. A few days later he was dead.

This whole, sad episode was clouded in mystery. Someone—a doctor, a teacher, or a well-meaning but misguided friend?—had told my parents that I was too young to deal with death, and so I was told that the family had moved to America. This struck me as curious, but I was so glad to leave camp that I didn't ask questions. Still, I couldn't help but wonder why my roommate would not at least have said goodbye. But that is what I was told and that is what I believed until I returned to school in the fall and found out the truth. I felt hurt that my parents didn't consider me sufficiently grown up to comprehend and mourn the loss of a friend. It took me a long time to accept that they had meant well and wanted only to shield me from these exigencies of life.

The second camp, a year later, was a rustic place in the mountains, but I got homesick and wanted to leave. I called my parents and told them, no doubt with false bravado, that if they didn't pick me up within twenty-four hours I would leave on my own. Of course they did, as I knew they would, and that was my last experience with summer camp.

Until I was twelve or thirteen, my father almost always walked me to school. He told me that he was concerned I wouldn't pay sufficient attention to traffic, and perhaps he was right, but I suspect the real reason was that he wanted to protect his only, precious, much-loved child from every known—and unknown—danger. This was a source of great embarrassment to me, and I finally convinced him to let me go alone.

♦ ♦ ♦

My father always carried a briefcase filled with order forms and samples of imported silks. He was the agent for a large German silk mill and he sold their wares to retail stores throughout the city. Most of his customers were in the bedding business and it was fashionable in those days to use down-filled comforters with silk on the outside. The larger stores ordered whole bolts, which were shipped to them directly from the factory, but many of the smaller stores bought only what they needed at the moment, and to accommodate them my father kept a supply of the more popular fabrics in a large armoire at home. When he got an order, he spread out the bolt on the dining room table, carefully measured what was needed, and even more carefully cut the required length. Cutting silk is tricky and I eagerly learned to help him with the task. I was excited when he let me make the first cut, but deep down I was scared and it took me a long time to gain sufficient confidence to measure the length, take the large shears, and cut the silk with even strokes.

Sometimes, when I was not in school, my father took me with him on his rounds. We would start about nine and almost every place we went to offered refreshments: coffee and cake in the mornings, candies in the afternoon. Of course, I had my favourites and I remember one store where the owner always had a supply of rose-flavoured gumdrops. I took a modest number—don't be a little pig, my father would say—and sucked them one at a time to make them last longer. They were delicious, and I can still taste and smell them. It was part of the day's outing that my father and I would have a mid-morning snack, a *Gabelfrühstück*, in Viennese parlance. Sometimes it would take the form of a small dish of goulash with a dill pickle on the side in a restaurant; on other occasions we would stop at an outdoor stand in one of the markets and have a *Burenwurst*, a spicy sausage, with lots of mustard and a thick slice of freshly baked bread. I remember my father once bought a lovely red tomato, cut it in half with the pocket knife he always carried, and offered to share it with me. I had never tasted a raw tomato before—although home-made ketchup was one of my mother's staples—and I demurred because I was afraid of the unknown. But, with a little urging, I bit into it and I have enjoyed raw tomatoes ever since. As we ate these hearty snacks, we had the sense of being somewhat naughty co-conspirators: we shouldn't really do this because we knew that a delicious meal would await us at home. Still ...

My father did all the typing and bookkeeping himself, often late into the evening. It was a modest operation, but for many years his business gave him an income sufficient to look after the family's needs. In fact, we even had a live-in maid, who slept on a folding bed in a corner of the kitchen. But with the advent of synthetic fibres, which were cheaper and more durable, silk became a luxury item that only wealthy buyers could afford, and even they curtailed their spending in the dark days of the Depression. My father's income fell, the maid was let go, non-essentials were discontinued, clothes were made to last longer, my mother put her sewing talents to work, and we struggled through the early 1930s. Still, we were among the fortunate, for we had decent shelter and sufficient food. Others, of course, did not fare as well. Social assistance, as we know it today, didn't exist, and a large part of the population had to rely on handouts from friends and charity. False pride (but who am I to say that it was false?) made people hide their poverty. It somehow wasn't "nice" to be in that position, and many lived on starvation diets rather than ask for help. Unfortunately, even worse was to come.

◆◆◆

One of my father's customers was an Orthodox Jew. His business was in his home in the Second District, the *Leopoldstadt*. Many Eastern European Jews, seeking refuge from the atrocities at home, had settled there. Most were first-generation immigrants and Yiddish was their *lingua franca*. Since Yiddish is based in part on medieval German, they picked up German with relative ease. Certainly, in a place like Vienna, where many accents could be heard, this was but a further variation.

For the Jewish "establishment," however, these immigrants were a source of embarrassment and even irritation: they spoke with a strange accent, their manners were different, they were observant Jews who closed their stores on the Sabbath. Men wore skull caps in public and women dressed distinctively. And, to add further to the rift, these people fervently believed that the only hope for Jewish survival was the creation of a Jewish state. This was anathema to the largely assimilated Jewish population, who thought of themselves as Austrians who happened to practise the Jewish religion. As Henry Grunwald, a refugee from Vienna who eventually became editor-in-chief of *Time* Inc., observes:

That attitude went together with snobbery. Jews who gloried in the German language and culture, devotees of Goethe and Wagner, looked down on "Eastern Jews"... especially those who wore long earlocks and had heavy accents. It was those Jews, the theory went, who really caused anti-Semitism, not we respectable and, yes refined ones. This in effect meant accepting the cliché uttered by so many anti-Semites: "Ah, but if only all Jews were like you ..."[7]

Hermann Broch, an astute observer of the scene, links this uneasiness to the "inner antisemitism" of assimilated Jewry,[8] and Robert S. Wistrich, in *The Jews of Vienna in the Age of Franz Joseph*, gives examples of the tendency "to rely on facile secondhand Christian stereotypes concerning Jewish occupations, manners, and linguistic peculiarities."[9]

In retrospect, this sounds absurd and it was. But I remember endless debates among my parents and their friends about the virtues of Zionism, and in the 1930s this issue split the community. Elections to the state-sanctioned Jewish representative body, the *Kultusgemeinde*, were conducted along party lines, Zionists on one side, assimilationists on the other. (There was also a small Jewish monarchist party, made up mostly of veterans from the First World War.) This bickering didn't end until the *Anschluss* in 1938, when emigration to Palestine became an attractive option even for the most ardent non-Zionists. I hate to say this, but it took Hitler to unify the Jews of Vienna. In my own case, I think that it was my encounters with my father's Orthodox customer that allowed me to put a human face on Jews recently arrived from Eastern Europe, about whom I had heard such venomous stories. He was a good, hard-working man, devoted to his family, and what we had in common was much more fundamental than the things that separated us.

Jews had been flocking to Vienna since the Middle Ages, with the greatest influx, from the far-flung corners of the empire, in the nineteenth century. As the Jewish population increased, so did, albeit slowly and grudgingly, official recognition of their presence. In 1849, Emperor Franz Joseph, recently acceded to the throne, received representatives of the Jewish community of Vienna and accepted their "expression of the true devotion and loyalty which you extend to me in the name of the Israelite community." Three years later, the authorities gave "provisional recognition" to the by-laws of the *Israelitische Religionsgemeinde*—the Israelite religious community—the forerunner of the *Kultusgemeinde*. But all was not clear sailing thereafter.

The by-laws of the *Kultusgemeinde*, which now had the official blessing of the state, created a governing body composed of five executive members and fifteen councillors. These twenty officials had full power over the affairs of the Jewish community and, as Wistrich points out, "could regulate all matters of religion according to their judgment." Rabbis and preachers were excluded from this function, although they could give "advice" to the board. All officials, executive members and councillors, were elected, but—and here was the catch—only Jews who had paid a stipulated religious tax could vote. Since the tax was expensive (though not compulsory), the number of voters was small and all attempts to widen the franchise were fiercely opposed by those in power. Indeed, the government itself got involved, and in 1890 a bill was introduced in the Upper House to widen the franchise and give the rabbis a greater say in the affairs of the community. Once again, the establishment rallied and, mobilizing all its political influence, defeated the measure.

There were other complications as well. Orthodox and Reform Jews did not see eye to eye, and this, too, had political overtones. The executive members and councillors of the *Kultusgemeinde* tended to be closer to Reform and therefore more liberal in their outlook. But this didn't sit well with government officials, who believed in the old order and were suspicious of change. "Liberal," in that era, was virtually synonymous with "liberal-democratic," and from there it was but a short step to "revolutionary"—a fact that made the government uneasy. Orthodox Jews, who felt alienated from this "representative" body, eventually made common cause with the government, and both sought to curb its powers. The *Kultusgemeinde* survived these struggles, but lost some of its importance in the community following World War I, even though it had become more representative. It remained, however, the keeper of registers of civil status (similar to the situation in Quebec in the not too distant past, where religious communities were in charge of registering births, marriages, and deaths), and my birth certificate bears the seal of that body.

◆◆◆

I had a traditional *bar mitzvah*. It was held on April 17, 1937, at the *Seitenstettengasse Tempel*, the "see," if one might call it that, of the chief rabbi, who officiated.[10] This was of particular significance to my grandparents, as he had also officiated at their wedding. I remember three things in particular. The first is that while I knew my Torah portion fairly well I stumbled once or twice, which brought sounds of disapproval from the rabbi, accompanied, at the same time, by words of encouragement from the *shammes*, or beadle, who had joined the group in the sanctuary. Of course, the good man, I found out later, was entitled to a gratuity for his services, and I can only think that his praise, which was so clearly misplaced, was designed to make my father think more kindly of him.

I completed my portion despite the conflicting commentary, and when I turned around to look at my grandfather, who sat in the front row, I was shocked: there he was, dressed in a morning coat and striped trousers, a gold chain across his waistcoat, and a starched white shirt, but no tie. My grandfather was an elegant gentleman, always impeccably dressed and always correct and a tie was most certainly *de rigueur* on all occasions, let alone one as solemn and important as this. Yet there he was, the stud button of his shirt exposed. I found out later that he had put on a bow tie, the kind with an elastic, but it had snapped and fallen off. No one mentioned it to him and I can only imagine how he must have felt when he got home and looked in the mirror.

The third thing I recall—or fail to recall, rather—is the reception at the apartment. I know that we had invited the family and a few friends, but I got a violent headache and the party went on without me. I recovered in time to open my presents, mostly books and fountain pens, and I still have three: a book of poems by Chajim Nachman Bialik; *Der Kleine Brehm*, a book about animals; and an alarm clock that, alas, no longer functions. All bring back memories. The book of poems came from a friend of the family, the clock from one of my father's customers, and the animal book from one of my classmates, Richard Reich (who eventually settled in California, where he became Richard Rich). Somewhat prophetically, it was inscribed by him *Im ewigen Andenken*—In everlasting remembrance—and I thought how prescient that was when I picked it up not long ago: we've been out of touch for over sixty years.

My grandmother, already ill with abdominal cancer, was with us that day. *Oma* or *Omama*, as I called her, was a wonderful woman who had a kind word for everybody. She listened patiently to whatever I had to say, and often, having found such a good listener, I went on and on. She also was a great cook, and I remember festive meals when the table was laden with all my favourite foods, some traditional, others not, but always delicious. She adored me and I felt very close to her.

She died later that year, ravaged by the disease, and was buried on November 1 in the Jewish section of the city's large *Centralfriedhof*. This was All Saints' Day, a holy day on the Catholic calendar, and thousands went to the cemeteries to pay their respect to dead. This didn't affect the Jewish section, of course, but all roads leading to the enormous burial ground were clogged with masses of people, and it seemed to take forever to get there. Since no one in the family—except my rich uncle in America—had a car, we went by taxi, a form of conveyance we used rarely because of the cost.

The coffin, in keeping with custom and tradition, was a simple box made of pine. I remember that my father was given the task of identifying *Oma's* body, as required by law, since neither her husband nor her children wanted to do so. They preferred, as I did with my own parents many years later, to remember her as she was while alive. I was afraid for my father—he was always given the tasks that no one else wanted to do—but he did what was expected and never complained. It was my first funeral, and while I was terribly sad (and more than a little bit scared) I tried to act grown-up and not burst into tears.

I didn't know it then, of course, but the large plot of land that had been purchased by the Jewish Community in the 1920s to provide adequate burial grounds for the ever-growing population was destined to remain largely unused. As the writer Daniel Mendelsohn put it after a recent visit to the cemetery, the sight that greeted us was one largely of emptiness, with only a relatively small portion filled with graves.[11] He then added:

> We stared at this for a while until we realized that the new Jewish Section was largely empty because all of the Jews who, in the normal course of things, would have been buried there had, in fact, died in ways they hadn't foreseen, and if they'd been buried at all, had been buried in other, less attractive graves not of their choosing.

[2]
Storm Clouds on the Horizon

The mid-thirties were years of great unrest. Clashes between the left and the right in Vienna were frequent, and twice in my memory they involved bloodshed on a major scale. The first of these events occurred in February 1934, when socialists openly fought with government forces. It didn't last long, but the results were traumatic. The heart of the city, where we lived, was not directly affected—the fighting was mostly in the suburbs—but steel-helmeted police and troops were everywhere. Eventually, the socialist forces were crushed, with a heavy toll of dead and wounded. I was ten years old, and even if I didn't understand the full implications of all that was going on around me, I was tense and uneasy. News that a friend of my father's had given shelter to an injured civilian who subsequently died in his home didn't help, particularly when we learned that civic authorities had refused to remove the body while the fighting continued on the streets in the vicinity.

The second major upheaval was the assassination of Chancellor Engelbert Dollfuss, an attempted coup orchestrated by Austrian Nazis. I was away at the time, visiting family friends in Ilava, a small town just past Bratislava, which now is the capital of Slovakia. It was an idyllic summer, carefree, with kids of my own age and the freedom to just lounge around in rural surroundings. I remember that one of the main attractions for us was a large prison, and curiosity drew us to the walls again and again to catch glimpses of guards and prisoners. I don't know what we hoped to see—it all seemed quite mysterious and forbidden— but the simple answer is probably that there wasn't much else to do.

I returned to Vienna a few days after the attempted *Putsch*, and once again the city resembled an armed camp. Of course, for a twelve-year-old, this had a certain excitement, particularly after my friends discovered that to go to school I had to cross a checkpoint near the stock exchange: barbed wire (razor wire had not yet been invented), with a gate for cars and pedestrians, covered by machine-guns. To cross, I needed two pieces of identification, one from the school, the other to establish where I lived. This both thrilled and frightened me, but, most important, it made me quite popular with my friends, most of whom lived near the school and didn't have to cross a checkpoint.

The unrest lingered on and life never again returned to normal. By 1937, it was clear that Hitler's expansionist policies would soon include Austria, but in ostrich-like fashion the well-established, largely assimilated Jewish community clung to the hope that somehow this would not happen. After all, was ours not a civilized country?

As I reflect on these attitudes, I can conclude only that, for the great majority of our community, hope, however misplaced, was a more potent force than the harsh reality. Add to that a mix of understandable inertia, the inability to understand what was to come, a fear of the unknown (as life in a foreign country would have been), and the unwillingness to part with some worldly possessions, and one begins to understand why so many who could have been saved failed to act until it was too late. As Ron Chernow writes in *The Warburgs*—and this applies equally to their co-religionists in Austria—"the German Jews weren't cavalier about the Nazis. Rather, they would hesitate, procrastinate, and rationalize inaction for far too long."[12]

Of course, even then, if one had decided to leave, a move would not have been an easy matter. Few countries would accept Jewish immigrants, particularly those without significant funds, which was the majority of us. But before the *Anschluss*, immigration to another country was still feasible, though not always to one's country of choice. The fact is that, when settled, people do not move lightly, and I remember endless debates among my parents and their friends about what should be done. The conclusion always was the same: let's wait for now. But wait for what? How could they have been so blind? The persecution of Jews in Germany was already well under way, but, as close to home as it was, it seemed far away. And so we, and almost 200,000 others, procrastinated.[13]

There were, of course, exceptions, and some had the foresight to leave while it was still relatively easy to do so. My cousin Fred David, an aeronautical engineer who had worked for Heinkel in Germany, took refuge in Japan. When the Japanese established military links with Nazi Germany, he moved on to Australia, where he became the chief engineer at Commonwealth Aircraft Corporation. Three days after the Japanese attack on Pearl Harbor, he sketched a drawing of a single-seat fighter, using the most powerful engine available in Australia and as many components of aircraft as were then in use, to allow for the rapid production of new fighter aircraft for the Royal Australian Air Force, called the Boomerang. The fuselage of one of the 250 Boomerangs built is now on display at the Australian National Aviation Museum, and an explanatory note points out that the first detailed design was started on December 21, 1941, and by May 29, 1942, the first aircraft had been test flown: "a staggering period of little over 22 weeks." While this frantic activity took place, David, not yet a naturalized Australian citizen, was considered an "unfriendly" alien and was required to report to the police every fortnight. As the museum's note points out, "it is ironic that the development of Australia's 'stop gap' fighter was due to the efforts of a man technically treated as the 'enemy.'"

Our rude awakening came on March 12, 1938, when German troops marched into Austria. I well remember the day. A weak government had capitulated, but in truth it had carried out the will of the people. Unlike the fall of Paris, where grown men cried as German soldiers marched down the Champs Élysées, the Viennese turned out by the hundreds of thousands and cheered as wave after wave of German aircraft flew overhead. It was a horribly depressing sight and worse was to come. Austrians welcomed Hitler as a liberator, a leader who would restore the country to power and glory, part of a new, great empire, the pan-Germanic dream come true.

Whatever doubts we may have had about the need to get out were abruptly dispelled by the *Anschluss*. Closet Nazis, like our neighbour, came into the open and proudly wore their uniforms. Jews lost their jobs and livelihoods, and many were made to endure unspeakable indignities. The chief rabbi of Vienna (who had officiated at my *bar mitzvah*), together with hundreds of other Jews, was forced to scrub the streets with a toothbrush, while a large mob stood by and laughed. As David Edmonds and John Eidinow write in their fascinating book *Wittgenstein's Poker*, "the oppression of the Jews in Austria began at once and was more ferocious than in Germany proper—as if the Austrians were trying to make up for lost time."[14]

The unanswered—and, perhaps, unanswerable—question, as recently put by the American Nobel Laureate Eric Kandel, is what brought about this sudden release of such great viciousness in so many people. "How," asks Kandel, "could a highly educated and cultured society, a society that at one historical moment nourished the music of Haydn, Mozart, and Beethoven, in the next historical moment sink into barbarism?"[15] Kandel, whose older brother Lewis was a classmate of mine at the *gymnasium*, offers one conclusion— a conclusion that, he admits, is "troubling to an academic like myself." It is that a society's culture is not a reliable indicator of its respect for human life. But this "rather simplistic conclusion," as he calls it, raises a question: how can values within a society become so radically dissociated? In his view, "the Viennese achieved this dissociation by shifting their frame of reference. By defining Jews in racial rather than religious terms, they were able to exclude Jews from the "more highly evolved European Aryan race," the race they believed to be responsible for the rise of Western civilization." Others have different explanations, but in the end it doesn't matter: life for Jews in Austria had become intolerable.

Attendance at school became not only uncomfortable but also irrelevant: Latin and Greek were not good passports for escape. Fortunately—and I am deeply grateful for this—my father insisted that I learn English (although he himself did not), and so I went to classes in the evening. He also thought that I should learn a trade, in case some sympathetic country might admit semi-skilled labourers. I did that, too, and learned the basics of making small leather goods, such as wallets, handbags, and fancy cosmetic kits. I have always been good at doing things with my hands and, to be truthful, I liked this much better than school.

"Councils of war" of friends and relatives were held almost daily: someone had heard that Argentina would admit refugees; another "knew" that one could go to France; yet another said that the thing to do was to get something called an "affidavit" from a friend or relative in the United States. All rumours were checked out, but there was always a catch. Yes, some countries would take Jewish refugees, but only if they had money to invest. Others, such as the United States, would accept sponsored immigrants, but a strict quota system, based on one's place of birth, often meant years of delay.[16] And, as for Canada, as we now know, "none was too many."[17] And so it went, one heartbreaking disappointment after another. Henry Grunwald describes this frantic search for salvation:

> A new word began to dominate our lives: visa. The word signified escape, survival, safety. The search for countries willing to accept refugees from the Nazis became increasingly desperate. Crowds besieged Vienna's foreign embassies and consulates, especially that of the United States.[18]

Early in 1939 we heard about a scheme to provide homes in England for refugee children. My father applied at once, for the gut-wrenching decision had already been made that we would split the family if nothing else materialized. By this time, we had applied, with thousands of others, to go the United States. My mother's two brothers had settled in Detroit in the mid-1930s, and they provided the necessary guarantees, but the quotas were small, and our turn was unlikely to come in time. And so, when we got word in June that I was among the lucky ones chosen to go to England, we moved at once to get the necessary papers: German bureaucracy, already in place, required that certain formalities be followed even to emigrate. As Ruth Kluger recalls in *Still Alive*, "Vienna was a city that banished you and then didn't allow you to leave."[19]

◆ ◆ ◆

The *Kindertransport*, as this great rescue mission became known, had its origins in a meeting held on November 15, 1938, between Prime Minister Neville Chamberlain and a deputation of prominent British Jews, including the chief rabbi, Dr. J.H. Hertz; the Zionist leader (and first president of Israel), Dr. Chaim Weizmann; and Viscount Samuel, a former high commissioner to Palestine. They asked the government to permit the temporary admission of children from Germany, Austria, and Czechoslovakia, who would go to school or learn a trade in the United Kingdom and then would re-emigrate to other lands. The Jewish community would give the necessary guarantees that none of the children would later become public charges.

As David Cesarani recalls in his introduction to *Into the Arms of Strangers*,[20] the cabinet discussed the question the following day. The home secretary expressed fears that the admission of more refugees could provoke a backlash, but the foreign secretary, Lord Halifax, argued that "an act of generosity might have a knock-on effect and cause the United States to open its doors wider." In any case, the cabinet committee on refugees decided that Britain could accept unaccompanied refugee children under the age of seventeen. Originally, a figure of 5,000 was discussed, but after the Colonial Office turned down a request from the Jewish Agency to allow the admission of 10,000 children into Palestine, this number was accepted as an appropriate goal for admission to Britain.

Within a very short time, the Movement for the Care of Children from Germany—later renamed the Refugee Children's Movement (RCM)—sent representatives to Germany and Austria to set up the necessary mechanisms for the selection and subsequent transportation of the children. On November 25, just ten days after the matter was raised with the prime minister, Viscount Samuel broadcast an appeal for sponsors. Five hundred families answered the call, and many more followed later. It was a remarkable response to a desperate situation.

The first train left Berlin on December 1; the first transport from Vienna departed ten days later. In March 1939, after Hitler's troops moved into Czechoslovakia, arrangements were made to include children from that country as well. It was, as one author recently called it, "a sort of miracle."[21]

Cesarani takes up the story from there:

> By the end of 1938, children were pouring into Britain and straining the resources of the RCM. The earliest arrivals tended to be older teenagers who were at risk of arrest, but most families wanted to take in young children. So there was urgent need to find a temporary holding centre. Two summer holiday camps were located, one at Dovercourt near Harwich and the other at Pakefield near Lowestoft, both situated on the wind-swept, low-lying coast of East Anglia. Due to flooding, Pakefield had to be abandoned shortly after it was opened. Dovercourt was quickly filled to capacity with some 1,000 Jewish children and teenagers of all ages and backgrounds. Conditions at first were chaotic.[22]

Despite an appeal for funds by Earl Baldwin, a former prime minister, money was a constant problem, but a broadcast by the BBC Home Service from Dovercourt brought more prospective foster parents to the scene. Yet, as Cesarani tells it, it was difficult to soften the effects of the "cattle market" that took place every Sunday. It was then that prospective foster parents arrived to look over the children and select those that caught their fancy. Inevitably, the cutest and youngest children were picked first. Brothers and sisters were separated. Teenagers who were overlooked felt even more rejected. In the end, many of them had to be placed in hostels run by the RCM.

By a stroke of good fortune, I was spared this arrangement. A few days after I was accepted into the program, we were told that I would be taken in by a family in the northeast of England, and this was quickly followed by a letter from a Mr. and Mrs. John Fell, who said they were looking forward to having me with them. They had a farm on the outskirts of Darlington, in the County of Durham, called Oxen-le-Fields.

My father was very impressed by the name. To him, anyone who owned an "estate" with a name like that must at least be of the nobility, and he was pleased that I would be safe with a "good class" of people.

The Fells already had four children, with another on the way, and that was all they could handle. Yet they were anxious to help save the life of a Jewish child.

The solution was to sponsor an older boy who could work on the farm. Luckily for me, I looked bigger and stronger in the picture that my father had sent out with the application than I actually was, so I got picked.

It was the greatest break of my life.

[3]

Safe Haven

I left Vienna on July 25, 1939, barely six weeks before the outbreak of World War II. It was a few weeks past my fifteenth birthday, and while I was overcome with a mixture of sadness and guilt for leaving home without my parents, I must confess I also felt a certain excitement. A whole new world lay ahead and, rather than fearing the unknown, as older and wiser persons might have done, I looked forward to a fresh start in life. If this seems contradictory, it was. But somehow, in the short time available, my parents had prepared me for this moment, and the good front they put up—"Don't worry, it won't be for long"—buoyed my spirits and the three of us pretended that it was so. Two friends, a dentist and his sister, had joined us at the railway station, but they discreetly stood at a distance and left us alone in our last few moments together. Many years later, I learned what great support they were to my parents after the train had pulled out.

Others were not so lucky. Ruth Kluger's mother learned about the scheme but wouldn't apply for her daughter: children, she reasoned, belonged with their parents. Another child, Lory Cahn, was accepted and went to the station with her parents. She got a seat next to the window, which her father opened so she could lean out and say a final goodbye. But as the train started to leave, her father asked her to let him hold her hands. As Cahn recalls, "I held out my hands, and I said, 'I have to let go. I have to let go.'" Her father, overcome by the emotional strain, said, "No, no, no, no. I don't want you to go. I don't want you to go," and as the train moved on he held on to her hands and pulled her out of the window. Remarkably, both children survived the Holocaust.[23]

The leaders in charge of the transport were full of instructions: do this, don't do that, keep an eye on your suitcase, be nice to the others. I don't remember all the details, but one admonition addressed to the girls stands out: be careful, for on a previous transport a teenage girl was raped. It may seem strange in today's context, but I had no idea what that meant and knew better than to ask. The German word for rape—*Vergewaltigung*—still stands out in my mind.

We travelled most of that day and then all night, first along the Danube and then down the Rhine. We stopped in Cologne, where German soldiers looked at our papers, and a few hours later we crossed into Holland and to freedom. I remember Rotterdam and the Hook, where a large ferry stood by. It was a British ship, and one of the officers asked if anyone spoke English. I put up my hand with pride and he asked me to translate a few remarks he made about the ship: where to go, what to do, and, even more importantly, what not to do.

We crossed the Channel overnight and early the next morning we arrived in Harwich. From there we were taken by train to London and assembled in a large hall in the station. Periodically, names were called out, and when my turn came I was led to a man who identified himself as Mr. Fell from Darlington. I don't remember much about our first conversation, but he seemed kind and understanding. He took me to a nearby hotel where he had booked two rooms for the night, and the first thing I did was to get a picture postcard to send to my parents. I marked an X on the window which I thought was my room and asked Mr. Fell to mail it. I then cleaned up and off we went to meet one of his friends, a clergyman named Canon Lindsay, who awaited us in that most English of all institutions, a gentleman's club.

Having grown up in Catholic Austria, where priests wore cassocks even on the street, it seemed strange to me that a preacher should be dressed in a grey business suit. But I said to myself this is a different country, with different customs, and perhaps here priests were different too. Much more immediate was my concern about how to behave in this forbidding atmosphere: a large lounge with overstuffed leather chairs, fine paintings on the wall, well-dressed elderly men quietly drinking, talking, or reading the papers. A uniformed steward came to take our order for drinks, and Canon Lindsay and Mr. Fell looked at me and said, "Well, what shall it be?" This was a moment of sheer terror and I was afraid that I might say the wrong thing. Judging from those around me, this was not the time or place to ask for hot chocolate or some soda pop. Luckily, I thought of lemonade, and this seemed to satisfy the situation.

Canon Lindsay spoke a little German and he tried it out on me, but since Mr. Fell didn't speak the language, the conversation was mostly in English, and it consisted of basic questions about me, my family, Vienna, and the current situation in Austria, a country that Canon Lindsay knew well. They listened attentively and I quickly gained confidence and let it all pour out. I didn't realize it at the time, but there was so much pent-up emotion in me that it felt good to have someone to talk to. Then, after a lemonade or two, we moved on to a restaurant which Mr. Fell had picked with great care: it featured Viennese dishes and I had a hearty meal. Such was the nature of the man that he made every effort to make me as comfortable as he could on my first day in a new country.

I slept well that night, and after a hearty breakfast at the hotel—my first English breakfast, with bacon, eggs, stewed tomatoes, and home-fried potatoes—we went to King's Cross Station shortly before 10:00. *The Flying Scotsman* was about to depart for Edinburgh and Mr. Fell thought that I would like to see this famous "name train." I didn't know what this was all about—it certainly seemed a funny name for a train—but the sheer size of the locomotive impressed me. I didn't know then that I would often watch the famous trains of the London and North Eastern Railway go by our farm on their way to and from London. The small town of Croft, where I would be staying, was almost exactly halfway between the two cities, and the northbound and southbound trains, which left at the same time, would pass within a few minutes of each other. On the first full day of World War II, September 4, 1939, the "name trains" would stop running, as a fuel-economy measure, and I would wait in vain for them to pass—a harbinger that nothing would ever be the same again.

We took the regular northbound train, which left a few minutes later, and arrived in Darlington just before dinner. We ate at the railway station in the first-class restaurant, where the price for the meal was half a crown (a strange measure of money for a newcomer like me). We had steak and kidney pie, something I had never tasted before. But it was good and I was hungry and I enjoyed this little interlude. We then went off to Oxen-le-Fields, where I met Mrs. Fell and their children. They lived in a large, rather plain but spotlessly clean farmhouse and I was given a room on the second floor. It seemed luxurious to me, and so it was: much bigger than my room at home.

I wrote long letters to my parents, describing in minute detail my new circumstances, and I also heard from them on a regular basis. This came to a halt when war was declared, but for the first five or six weeks we communicated regularly. My parents' letters were cheerful, but that was for my benefit, and I later found out that life had become very difficult for them soon after my departure. My mother's stepfather, then in his seventies, was arrested by the Gestapo—no one knew why—and sent to a concentration camp. My mother had one letter from him in which said he was fine—I am sure he wasn't allowed to say anything else—but after that she never heard from him again. My mother kept that letter, and I now have it, but I cannot bring myself to read it. The pain starts when I hold it in my hand and so, unread, I always put it back into a file.

My father lost his job, and for many years I was burdened with feelings of guilt that I was responsible for this. It goes back to an incident in 1938 that I never disclosed to my parents. One afternoon I passed by a movie theatre. At the entrance were stills from the picture then playing. It was very enticing, and even though Jews were prohibited from going to the movies, I might have bought a ticket if I had had sufficient money. But I didn't, and so I lingered and enjoyed the stills. When I left, two young thugs—perhaps two or three years older than I—followed me. I walked faster and so did they. I finally started to run, but they caught up with me and pushed me into the doorway of a building. They asked if I was Jewish and I said yes. "Don't you know Jews can't go to movies?" they said, as they landed a few blows on my head. I protested that all I had done was look at the photos, but this fell on deaf ears. They then asked for my name, my father's name, and where he worked. Terrified, I told them and after a few minutes they left.

I was angry, upset, and, above all, ashamed: I had betrayed my family. And so I said nothing. The axe fell after I left, and the thought that my father had lost his job because of my weakness haunted me for a long time. To my great relief, my father told me many years later what had happened, and it had nothing to do with me. It was an edict of the German government—the head office of the company he represented was in Germany—as well as pressure by some local clients who were uneasy about having a Jewish salesman visit them, that had caused the firm to dismiss him. He was pleased that one of the owners had come to Vienna to deliver the bad news in person. It was the decent thing to do, and it helped preserve what little dignity was left for a Jew in those times.

At this point, with no further income, my parents had to give up the apartment and move into a room. All around them people disappeared and no one knew who would be next. I can only imagine what they were going through, how they must have felt about having sent away their only child and losing all financial security. Many years later, with the greatest reluctance, my mother and father would sometimes speak of those difficult times. Life must have been hell and it is hard to imagine how they survived in such a hostile and uncertain world, with next to nothing. They sold whatever they could, but those who bought paid ridiculously low prices. My mother traded her few pieces of jewellery for food. She realized that they had sold "everything" and still didn't have enough to eat.

Then they really sold "everything"—their gold wedding bands. When that money was gone, they had to ask for charity, but they survived. What gave them courage was the hope that I was safe and that one day we would be reunited.

August—my first month away from home—was a busy time on the farm, and I helped as much as I could. Certainly, on a farm there is always something to do, but only once did I realize my ambition to drive the tractor. The occasion stands out in my mind because it almost led to disaster. I knew how to start the machine, but no one had told me how to stop it, and as I drove I searched in vain for the answer. In desperation, I drove around the yard in circles, much to the amusement of everyone present, until a farmhand jumped on board and showed me how to turn off the engine.

I often went with Mr. Fell to purchase cattle and sheep. This was mostly at auctions, and even though I quickly became fluent in English, the language of the auctioneers remained forever unintelligible to me. Nor did I know that purchasers often indicated the price they were willing to pay by signals; it all seemed rather chaotic. One day Mr. Fell bought a cow, and there was some question about delivery. He was anxious to have the animal as soon as possible, but the seller would not accommodate him. With no other solution at hand, Mr. Fell asked me if I thought I could take charge of the situation, and of course I said yes.

And so I found myself on the outskirts of Darlington, about three miles from the farm, with an impertinent brown cow, singularly uninterested in obeying my orders. A few men around me had walking sticks with which they prodded their animals, so I picked up a piece of wood and started to urge on my cow, which took the hint and ambled off at a leisurely pace, though not always in the right direction. It probably took me three or four hours, but I did manage to drive the cow home along a busy highway, and I was proud of my achievement. I must admit, however, that I did not go out of my way on subsequent occasions to offer my services for similar assignments. Many years later, Mr. Fell said that it still troubled him to think of the incident. It was an error in judgment, he said, even to suggest that a boy of my slight build and with no experience could do the job.

I learned to milk cows, both with and without machines, and how to take care of cattle. I even learned how to help a cow deliver a calf. For a city boy, this was quite an experience, and I enjoyed such tasks. Yet, being somewhat small and not very strong, I couldn't help with some of the harder work on the farm, and by the end of August the Fells had decided that I should go to school. The nearest high school was in Darlington—the Grammar School of Queen Elizabeth—and I was enrolled in my age-appropriate class. The headmaster was a Dr. Hare, who led the assembly in prayer every morning, and I soon learned most of the hymns in the Anglican Hymnal.

School wasn't easy, not so much because of language, but because of differences in the curriculum. I was weak in English history, my knowledge of English literature was non-existent, and, as for sports, cricket seemed a very strange game to me. On the other hand, I was well ahead of my fellow students in Latin and mathematics, and this helped. There was, of course, a great deal of curiosity about me, but everyone was kind. The teachers made a special effort to help me integrate, and from time to time the headmaster would ask me about my progress. As long as the weather permitted, I bicycled to school each day, four miles each way, but with the onset of winter I took the bus. For lunch I went to a restaurant in a nearby department store, Bainbridge & Barker's, where I had a simple but nutritious meal. My favourite dessert was English trifle, which I consumed in great quantities, and even now, so many years later, I still order it whenever I find it on a menu. Regrettably, it never tastes as good as B & B's.

The Fells went to the Methodist church every Sunday, and I often went with them. However, when the time rolled around for the Jewish High Holy days, Mr. Fell made arrangements for me to attend services at the Darlington synagogue. It was a small congregation, quite Orthodox in custom, and my previous religious training had not prepared me for this. My Hebrew was woefully inadequate, although I could follow some of the prayers, provided the rabbi didn't read them too quickly. Of course, anyone who has been to a Jewish service knows that most prayers are said at breakneck speed, for custom demands that large portions be read on certain occasions. I was lost most of the time, but I did prepare myself to be given the honour of saying the blessings before and after the reading from the Torah. I had learned these for my *bar mitzvah*, and when the elders of the congregation did give me that chance, my blessings were so well memorized that everyone admired my proficiency.

Sending me to synagogue was typical of the Fells: kind and considerate, ever ready to help someone in need. They had agreed to take a refugee child at the suggestion of the Spielmans, a wealthy Jewish family who lived on a large estate a mile or two down the road. Claude Spielman was the managing director of a large manufacturing company in Darlington. His wife, Margaret, was active in community affairs. Both were highly respected. When the opportunity came to sponsor refugee children, they not only signed on themselves, but also canvassed some of their friends and neighbours, the Fells included. To my knowledge, they found places for three children: in their own home, with the Fells, and with a family in Darlington. All did their best to make us feel welcome.

Many years later, I found out that, in fact, the Spielmans had done a great deal more. Their elder daughter Joan spent several months in Vienna in 1937 and 1938, and in her letters home described the desperate situation in Vienna and begged her parents to do whatever they could to help people escape. In her autobiography[24] she wrote: "My mother was busy organizing the Mayor of Darlington's appeal for refugee children, which brought over some twenty Austrian children, and settled them in families. We took two of them ... We also got my dressmaker from Vienna, Mrs. [Ella] Rose,[25] over as a sewing maid with her daughter..." The daughter was placed in a boarding school. Later, Peggy, as Mrs. Spielman was universally known, helped Mrs. Rose establish a thriving dressmaking practice in Darlington. And, as Peggy's children recall, she helped many others during this critical period. Truly a remarkable person.

Others were not as lucky as I. Hedy Epstein, a fifteen-year-old refugee from Germany, was placed with a family on the outskirts of London. Her daily diet consisted of toast and butter and tea, served three times a day, with an extra cup of tea and a cookie on Sundays. While her hosts ate, she was sent out of the house. A transfer to another home was later arranged.[26]

Mr. Fell worked hard on the farm. He was highly knowledgeable about the latest developments in agriculture and quite prepared to innovate. I recall one particular incident. He had read in one of the many magazines that came to the house that cattle will not cross a ditch which is covered with pipes, placed an inch or two apart. So out came the main gate (which had to be opened manually whenever a car or truck wanted to enter or leave), a six-foot-wide ditch was dug, and in went the pipes. No half-measure here: they were anchored in concrete. The article was absolutely right. Cows went to the very edge, looked at the pipes, and turned around. Other farmers soon copied the idea.

Mary Fell was in charge of the house. They had four children when I arrived, all younger than I. A fifth child was born while I was there. So there was plenty to do. In addition, most of the farmhands had to be fed. Paddy, an Irishman with a big heart, was the chief herdsman. He lived somewhere else, but he arrived every day with a round loaf of currant bread, wrapped in a red handkerchief, and that was his lunch. Mrs. Fell was a gentle soul. She never spoke an unkind word or raised her voice. She was firm with the children (and with me), but while we sometimes argued, we all looked up to her since she was almost always right.

At 11 a.m. on September 3, Prime Minister Neville Chamberlain read a statement over the BBC declaring that Britain was at war. The first visible change, as

I said, was that the "name trains" stopped running. The second sign I remember is that barrage balloons were put in position to protect major industrial concerns from attacks by enemy aircraft. These were large captive balloons, not unlike small dirigibles, and they were strong enough to support steel cables that were anchored to the ground. This meant that aircraft had to fly above them, with the result that bombs were less likely to hit their targets. The army also had a more visible presence, and anti-aircraft guns were quickly put in strategic positions. There was talk of rationing food and fuel.

England's youth flocked to the colours, and there was hardly a household that didn't have someone in the armed forces. We all worked longer hours on the farm to make up for those who left, and those unable to join up pitched in wherever they could. We also learned aircraft spotting, and every time a plane flew overhead we tried to show off our knowledge. Spitfires were easy, with one wing painted white, the other black; we took great pride in seeing them on their manoeuvres.

Despite the war, I had a happy ten months in England. I was extremely fortunate to be surrounded by such kind and good people, and I genuinely liked my life. Regrettably, this was not destined to last.

[4]

Guest of His Majesty

The day was May 12, 1940, Whit Sunday, the seventh Sunday after Easter. The weather was sunny and mild, the grass had shed its winter hues, and peonies had just come into bloom. The news, however, was terrible. Germany had invaded Holland and Belgium, the road to France was clear, and Allied troops were in retreat. Worse was yet to come, and all of England seemed to sense this.

Churchill had taken over the government two days before and that gave people hope. Immediately on assuming office, he formed a high-level Home Defence Committee, charged with devising ways to deal with the threatened invasion. The committee met at once, and on the evening of May 10 it recommended to Sir John Anderson, the home secretary, that every male alien between sixteen and seventy, living in areas where German paratroopers were likely to land, be interned. Anderson, despite strong feelings expressed previously against arbitrary acts by the state, felt obliged to acquiesce. And so, on the morning of May 11, he told a cabinet committee that he would give the necessary order. The matter of the internment of enemy aliens came up again later that day before the full cabinet, which approved it but with one change: the maximum age would be sixty not seventy. Cabinet was fully aware that the net was cast wide: "No doubt 90 per cent of such aliens are well disposed towards this country," Sir John Dill, vice-chief of the Imperial General Staff told the assembled ministers, "but it was impossible to pick out the small proportion of aliens who probably constitute a dangerous element."[27] Thirty-one counties were affected, from Hampshire in the south to Nairn in northeast Scotland. Durham, where I lived, was one of the thirty-one. The cut-off date was May 12. I had turned sixteen on May 7, just five days before.

Telegrams were sent on the evening of May 11 to the chief constables of the thirty-one counties, instructing them to detain, beginning at 8:00 the next morning, all male Germans and Austrians between sixteen and sixty and hand them over as soon as possible to the military authorities. The telegrams, reflecting what Sir John Dill had said to cabinet, urged the police to show "every consideration ... to persons detained," since "the majority are well-disposed to this country and their temporary internment is merely a precautionary measure."[28] No one knew how many potential internees there were in the coastal counties or where they would be sent.

My turn came mid-morning on the 12th. Superintedent Huitson of the Durham County Constabulary knocked on the door and, quite apologetically, told us that he had a most unpleasant duty to perform: Would I please pack a few things, enough for two or three days, and be ready for him in an hour to go to the station? In the meantime, he said, he had two similar missions nearby, and he would pick me up on his way back to Darlington.

Huitson knew both me and the Fells, and this may explain why he left me unsupervised until his return. He also knew that, only a short time before, I had been classified "C" by one of the special tribunals that the Home Office had set up: "Refugee from Nazi oppression, not subject to internment." I was given an appropriate piece of identification, complete with photograph, signatures, and stamps, and that seemed to be the end of the matter. But, as I said, some nervous people in high places soon overruled the tribunal's considered opinion, and the short-lived security I felt was brutally shattered.

Dr. Moses Aberbach, a Hebrew scholar and later a professor of history and literature at the Baltimore Hebrew College, suffered a similar fate. In an article written forty years later and published in the London *Jewish Chronicle*, he analyzed "the tragedy" of Britain's internment policy. "In policy, as in strategy," he wrote,

> the Government continued to fight the First World War. To most Britishers, it was an old-fashioned national war against Germany, not an ideological war against Nazism. Jewish refugees from Central Europe were not seen as ideological allies, but as enemy nationals whose sympathies must be presumed to live with their fatherland. If the facts manifestly contradicted this theory, it was just too bad for the facts.[29]

The minutes of the war cabinet show that not everyone shared this view. As mentioned before, Sir John Dill, for instance, was fully aware that the vast majority of these "enemy aliens" were well disposed to the country that had given them refuge. Others, outside cabinet, were even more vocal, and (in Aberbach's words) "roundly condemned a policy which professed to defend human freedom, while denying it to the victims of oppression."[30]

And so, five days after my sixteenth birthday, small bag in hand, I waited with the Fells for the superintendent's return. We didn't say much, but there was gloom in the air. It was no more than an hour. He returned with two young men— teenagers would be a better word—each with a satchel. We drove to Darlington, where we stayed at the police station for a few hours, waiting for other detainees. The three of us had met before, though not very often, but our common plight quickly established a bond between us that was of help in the tribulations to come. By late afternoon, there were enough detainees to fill a small bus, and off we went to Newcastle-on-Tyne in neighbouring Northumberland. There we were duly delivered, as required by cabinet, into the hands of the military.

If memory serves me correctly, it was the armoury of the Northumberland Fusiliers, an old and well-known regiment. We were lodged in the drill hall, given food and mattresses, and told to wait for "developments." These "developments" came five days later, when the Newcastle group was sent to Huyton, on the outskirts of Liverpool, where the government had commandeered an uncompleted housing development. Rubble was everywhere, and so were people, who continued arriving by the trainload. But soon the bureaucrats—the military has bureaucrats too—took over. Most of us were assigned twelve to a house; the remainder were put in tents, which leaked when it rained—as it did often. Human beings are adaptable creatures, and one quickly learns to make the best of what can be had: cold showers, no soap, and no towels. But at least we stayed clean, though clean clothes were quite another matter. I don't remember much about the food, but it was certainly sufficient. And, as for exercise, one could walk within the compound, and walk we did, though it was difficult with the construction material that had been left on the site.

Some years ago, a fellow internee (and future Nobel Prize winner), Max Perutz, writing in the *New Yorker*, recalled that the camp commander at Huyton (whom I do not remember) "was a white-mustached veteran of the last war; then a German had been a German, but now the subtle distinctions between friend and foe bewildered him. Watching a group of internees with skullcaps and curly side-whiskers arrive at his camp, he mused, 'I had no idea there were so many Jews among the Nazis.'"[31]

How does one feel in a situation like that? Angry? Upset? Resentful? The answer is a mix of these and similar emotions, but worst of all is the slowly dawning realization that nothing can be done: the state has spoken and no one is prepared to listen to us. We know we are innocent; we know this is a horrible error; we cry out but there is no one to hear us. Many years later, when I was called upon by the Ontario government to inquire into the wrongful conviction of an innocent person on a charge of capital murder, I could understand the accused's agony: *he* knew that he was not guilty of the horrible crime, but no one in authority believed him.

Those of us who had been cleared by the special tribunals at least had hope; surely the government would quickly recognize its error. An administrative mistake, a bureaucratic mix-up. Certificate in hand, I went to see those in charge, first at Newcastle and then at Huyton. The answer was always the same: "Don't worry, you won't be here long. Your 'papers' will come soon." Oh, how I came to hate the word "papers."

Dr. Aberbach (who was at Huyton longer than I) recalls an event that, without disrespect, I cannot help but call amusing. A group of Orthodox internees were concerned with the biblical injunction against work on the Sabbath, which included (in the Orthodox tradition) a prohibition against carrying anything, such as books and other articles. This was, of course, an inconvenience, but there was an escape: the prohibition did not apply within one's home, and that was defined as any place within a perimeter surrounded by a fence, a wire, or even a piece of string—an *eruv* in Hebrew—so long as the enclosure belonged to the people within.

Laymen consulted the rabbis and a plan soon emerged: if the internees could "buy" the barbed-wire fence that surrounded the camp, an *eruv* would be in place and the problem resolved. And so a delegation went to see the camp commander and, as Dr. Aberbach describes it, "in their halting English, they asked him to sell them the barbed-wire fence for a token shilling. The commandant, a Colonel Blimp type who was not endowed with excessive intelligence even at the best of times [it was he who had expressed surprise that so many Jews were Nazis!], was convinced that this was a plot of sorts, either to cheat the Government of its barbed wire, or maybe even an excuse to escape by cutting open the barbed-wire fence once it 'belonged' to us."

It should not come as a surprise that the request was refused despite three attempts to negotiate the "purchase," which, it was explained to the puzzled commandant, wasn't really a sale in the strict sense of the word, but only an accommodation, much like the "sale" of bread by Orthodox Jews to non-Jews by way of cleansing the home of leavened goods before Passover. But, as Dr. Aberbach notes, "Talmudic logic was not a suitable topic for a British Army officer," and Huyton never got an *eruv*.

The stay in Huyton was short, a week or two, and then we went by ship to Douglas on the Isle of Man. The date was June 14, the day Paris fell to the Germans. As Sir Michael Kerr, a fellow internee, recalls in his autobiography, "sailing on an internment ship from Liverpool to the Isle of Man on the day when Hitler danced in Paris and France surrendered felt like existing in a vacuum."[32]

In Douglas we were lodged in boarding houses that had been commandeered for the purpose by Whitehall. This was a big improvement over Huyton: hot and cold running water, clean beds in comfortable houses, and the odd walk on the beautiful beach, albeit under guard.

I don't remember the other internees in my house, but in the mid-1950s, when my parents moved to an apartment on West 73rd Street in New York, they became friendly with a Viennese couple who lived a floor above them. One day the man happened to mention that, before coming to the United States, he and his wife had spent some time in England and that he had been briefly interned in 1940. My parents and their new friends soon established that the man not only knew me but also had been billeted in a room right above mine in Douglas. We had a happy reunion shortly thereafter.

By the time we arrived on the Isle of Man, the Battle of Britain had started. Night after night, we could hear, halfway across the Irish Sea, exploding bombs on the west coast of England. I still shudder when I remember the eerie sound. Since neither radios nor newspapers were permitted, the rumour mills worked hard, but on occasion a sympathetic soldier or civilian would bring us the latest news. The only bright spot was that the evacuation of Dunkirk had not been followed by the feared invasion of Britain. All other news, however, was bad, and life was very depressing.

Once again, the sojourn was short. On July 4 a large contingent, myself included, was taken to the harbour, put aboard a ferry, and sent off in a northern direction, destination unknown. After some hours at sea, we docked in Greenock, on the outskirts of Glasgow, alongside a modern ocean liner, the *S.S. Sobieski*. This was an 11,000-ton Polish ship, taken over "for the duration" by the British Admiralty. She had been built in England and commissioned in June 1939, and now was used to carry troops and, by exception, internees and prisoners-of-war.[33]

War Office records show that she sailed later that day with 1,530 Germans and Austrians, their guards, and, of course, a full crew—a total of well over 2,000 persons. Nine hundred and eighty-two of the passengers were refugees and 548 were

German prisoners-of-war. This was a dangerous mix, but by then those in charge had realized that the internees were friendly aliens and so the two groups were segregated on the ship. This avoided the hostility encountered on another ship, the *S.S. Ettrick*, which had left a day earlier, and on which vicious fights had broken out between two similar groups.

Three other ships carrying refugees left the United Kingdom during that time: the *Duchess of York*, the *Arandora Star*, and the *Dunera*. The first two were bound for Canada, the last for Australia. The *Duchess of York* was hopelessly overcrowded and no attempt was made to separate civilians from German prisoners-of-war. As Eric Koch notes in his definitive book *Deemed Suspect: A Wartime Blunder*, for the refugees to be surrounded by a majority of Nazis was an extremely painful experience.[34] During the voyage, a German soldier was shot dead by one of the guards, and this made an already tense situation even worse. A plot was hatched by the pro-German contingent to seize control of the ship, turn it around, and sail to Germany. Fortunately, nothing came of this plan.

The *Arandora Star* was less fortunate. It was torpedoed a day out at sea and nearly 600 internees, soldiers, and crew drowned before help arrived some four hours later. The survivors were taken to Greenock, where escorts awaited the internees and prisoners-of-war. But their sojourn on dry land was not to last. All, save for those who had been taken to hospitals, were put aboard the *Dunera* later that week and once again shipped out—a needlessly hurtful exercise of authority. Koch, who interviewed some of the *Dunera* passengers many years later, tells us what happened next:

> While in the Irish Sea, close to the spot where the *Arandora Star* was sunk, the *Dunera*, too, was attacked. But thanks to luck and to the captain's skillful maneuvering of the ship, the torpedo glanced off the hull and a disaster was avoided. There was a tremendous noise; many prisoners banged on the locked doors in panic, and even the troops guarding them were afraid. The experience must have been particularly frightening for the survivors of the *Arandora Star*.[35]

The passage to Australia took fifty-eight days under deplorable conditions. Internees and prisoners were subjected to physical abuse, and most of their meagre belongings—wallets, rings, and watches—were "confiscated" by their guardians. After the matter was aired in the British House of Commons, two courts-martial were held. The commanding officer was found guilty of failure to conduct a proper inquiry into an act of violence against an internee. A regimental sergeant-major was found guilty of ten charges of misconduct and sentenced to one year in jail and dismissed from the force. A sergeant was "severely reprimanded" for disobeying a superior officer "by not providing an alien with blankets and water."[36]

En route to Greenock, the three of us from Darlington had stuck together. But, moments before we were to board the *Sobieski*, one of my friends, Alfred Parnes, went below deck in search of water. When we boarded, he wasn't there and we sailed without him amid much speculation as to his whereabouts. It wasn't until 1959, on a visit to England, that I tracked him down and resolved the mystery. It seems that someone had miscalculated the number of passengers the *Sobieski* could carry and too many people had been sent from the Isle of Man. It was a case of first come, first served, and by the time my friend reached the gangplank, boarding had stopped and he and a few others were sent back to the Isle of Man. His subsequent internment was relatively short—his "papers" did catch up with him—and soon after his release he joined the British army and served with distinction until the end of the war. He subsequently settled in London, where he managed a Lyons Tea House and later the Cumberland Hotel.

There was a great deal of confusion on the *Sobieski*, but I succeeded in getting an upper bunk in a room that held perhaps forty or fifty persons, and soon after boarding we set sail, once again to an unknown destination. By dawn we were at sea, with a destroyer escort and a Royal Air Force Sunderland flying boat circling above. There were also two other passenger liners in the convoy, but we could not make out their names.

The sea was rough, and for two days, in addition to missing my parents and my home in England desperately, I was terribly seasick. The smell of vomit was all around me; people were moaning and groaning. Finally, on the third day, a friend (a friendly stranger, really) came to my bunk and literally dragged me out of bed, up the stairs, and onto the deck. I was convinced I would die—and not unhappy about it—but the fresh air did wonders, and within an hour or two I recovered. In fact, I actually looked forward to the next meal. After that I was fine, and toward the end of the voyage I would stand for hours near the bow of the ship, look down, and measure the waves as we bobbed up and down. By then, the escorts on the sea and in the air had left us, and there we were, three ships alone in the U-boat-infested Atlantic. From time to time, depth charges would be dropped, but we never knew if this was "for real" or just practice.

On the fifth day the convoy suddenly slowed down. There was a furious exchange of semaphore signals among the three ships, and an hour or two later we watched in disbelief as the other two ships steamed away, getting smaller and smaller on the horizon, until there were merely wisps of smoke. I felt terribly alone that day. Later, I learned that the *Sobieski* had developed engine trouble and couldn't keep pace. To stay together would have put all three ships in jeopardy, with a combined human cargo—the other ships carried civilian evacuees—of more than six thousand souls. And so the commodore decided to split up the convoy and leave the *Sobieski* to fend for herself.

For two days, we slowly zig-zagged across the waters—and then, quite suddenly, as if out of nowhere, a wonderfully welcome sight: a Canadian destroyer, sleek, fast, efficient. At top speed, it could literally run circles around us, which it did, and what a great feeling of confidence this inspired. Another surprise followed a few days later. That morning, I awoke with a start. The engines were silent and the ship didn't move. I raced to a porthole and there, looming large, almost in front of me, was a city built on a hill. It was St. John's, Newfoundland, the closest port for the liner. And what a safe haven it was, with the narrow entrance to the basin guarded by cannons built at strategic points close to the sea. Many years later, when I climbed Signal Hill and looked down at the narrows, the gun ports could still be seen, although the long-barrelled cannons were gone.

Repairs were made and we sailed a day later for Quebec, where we arrived on July 15. We docked below the Plains of Abraham, near the slopes that Wolfe and his men had climbed in 1759 to surprise the French forces. We were searched before disembarking, and I was forced to surrender some innocuous items, including a pair of small scissors that, I suppose, might have been used as a weapon. Then we went straight from the ship onto a train, which took us to Trois-Rivières, some ninety miles to the west. We arrived there later that day, and I remember the march from the railway station to the Exhibition Grounds, which was to be our home for the next few weeks. Curious citizens lined the streets, for here was a strange spectacle: several hundred men, ranging in age from sixteen to sixty, marching in decidedly non-military fashion, with soldiers on the outside of the column. Among the group was a small number of Hasidic Jews, dressed in their traditional black garb and large-brimmed hats, with side curls—*payot*—on their cheeks. I think it's fair to say that this was a sight the good Trifluvians had never seen before, and there must have been much speculation about who these people were.

We got to the Exhibition Grounds some time before supper, but I don't remember the meal, nor do I recall where meals were taken. I do remember, however, that we slept on mattresses filled with straw, which I got used to with time. We were mostly left alone so long as we didn't stray from the compound. There was a severe shortage of toilet facilities, and in the morning lineups were particularly long, with the result that almost any secluded space—remember these were agricultural exhibition buildings—was used for emergencies of this kind.

It was in Trois-Rivières that I saw my first baseball game. I had read about this strange game that North Americans played, but I knew nothing of the rules and, without someone to tell me, I had to use my imagination. That worked for most of the players, but when it came to the catcher—of course, I didn't know at the time that the player with the face mask and the shin protectors was a catcher—I was totally lost, particularly when he instructed the pitcher to give the batter an intentional walk. This was beyond my comprehension.

The games were played on a field adjacent to the building where we lived, and in order to watch we had to put two tables on top of each other, and then a chair on top of that, because that's how high the windows were. It was a hazardous undertaking, but for a sixteen-year old this was good fun. I visited the ball park many years later, and it looked like any other small-town field. Somehow, the magic was gone.

I now know from Koch's book that the camp in Trois-Rivières held 715 internees, who were there from July 15 to August 12, 1940. The commandant was Lieutenant-Colonel C.O. Dorval, but I don't recall ever seeing him. Koch recounts that, when the first internees reached the Exhibition Grounds, they realized that part of the arena was already occupied by German prisoners-of-war, and they refused to enter the compound. A hasty conference was arranged between a spokesman and the commandant, who appeared unsympathetic. But a short time later a barbed-wire fence was erected to keep the two groups separate. However, while the internees occupied the arena, the Germans were in charge of the kitchen, and there was great fear that food sent to us might be poisoned. The problem was even greater for the Orthodox Jews, who would not eat non-kosher food. Some attempts were made to accommodate them, but, as a report cited by Koch points out, "the question of kosher meat is being dealt with by feeding the Orthodox Jews fish, or letting them go without."

Trois-Rivières was, in fact, a holding operation, and on August 12 we boarded a train that headed eastward, once again destination unknown. It wound its way along the Gaspé peninsula and then veered south into New Brunswick before finally coming to a stop in the middle of a forest, near a relief camp left over from the Great Depression. It was called Little River (or sometimes the Ripples Camp) and was about twenty miles east of Fredericton.[37]

The official designation was Camp B and the commanding officer was Colonel A.T. McLean, a veterinarian from Moncton, New Brunswick. It is said that when he met the train and saw his new charges, he shielded his eyes and said: "Oh, what children have they sent me!" The colonel wasn't wrong: of 711 "men," 280 were between sixteen and eighteen years old. The camp covered a total area of fifty-six acres, fifteen of them fenced in and used as the prison compound. It was completely isolated, and while the barbed-wire fence had been completed, the dining hut was still under construction and the hospital and recreation huts were only partly finished.

The internees were quickly put to work in the surrounding forest. To keep the camp's hundred wood stoves burning, 2,500 cords of wood had to be cut that season, transported, and stowed. For most of us, this was a new experience, and while the work was hard it was healthy and, above all, it helped pass the days. It also paid twenty cents a day, enough to buy some treats in the canteen. I soon learned how to chop down trees, and to this day I can handle an axe. Of course, this took a lot of practice, but since there was no shortage of trees to be cut, my skills developed quickly. So, of course, did callouses and blisters on my hands, but that is something one gets used to, and after a while you don't mind. As winter approached, however, the woods of New Brunswick became very cold. We were dressed in prisoner-of-war clothes—blue denim with red stripes on the side of the pants and a large red circle on the back of the jacket. We were also given heavy sweaters, thick socks, warm mittens, and regular army boots. A blue peak cap completed the uniform, which on most days was quite sufficient.

The most spectacular thing I remember about my days in New Brunswick is the northern lights. Night after night, nature put on magnificent displays, awesome, ever-changing hues of green, jumping in the sky. I stood for hours and watched, unable to let go. It was a sight I had never seen before and it thrilled me beyond belief.

The last of the refugee internees left Camp B in mid-1941, and preparations were made to receive a larger and more diverse group of prisoners, including German and Italian merchant seamen as well as a number of Canadians who were interned under wartime regulations. The most prominent of the civilian internees was Camillien Houde, the flamboyant mayor of Montreal, who was opposed to the war and whose agitations were considered a threat to the country.

After the war, the fifty-two buildings on the site were sold to individuals and businesses in the surrounding towns and villages. A small number of these buildings continue to be used as homes and summer cottages in the Minto and Grand Lake areas. The camp is now gone, but in the early 1990s Ed Caissie, a school supervisor with an interest in local history, gave a group of students the task of constructing a replica of the camp. Old plans were found, artifacts were excavated, and people who had memories of the camp were interviewed. The project took on a life of its own, and an exhibit was organized that was shown in twenty-three locations in New Brunswick and seen by more than 20,000 visitors. In September 1995, the New Brunswick Internment Camp Heritage Committee was organized, and a year later the committee placed a commemorative sign at the camp site. The following year the village of Minto provided a home for the growing collection of mementos, and the Internment Camp Museum was opened on June 22, 1997. It houses 600 artifacts and is host to many visitors.

In 2008, St. Thomas University in Fredericton established a Holocaust Centre, and as part of its education and research program it will support the Camp Museum. At the time of writing, Dr. Michael McGowan, professor of Human Rights and director of the new centre, had begun collecting oral histories of former inmates of the camp, and I was happy to tell him of my experience. Regrettably, with the passage of time, there are not many of us left.

I have never returned to Little River, but I am told that today there is a forest where the trees grow in straight lines, equidistant from each other, as one might expect in an orchard. This oddity is the result of the reforestation program undertaken in 1940 and carried out with great precision by the German and Austrian internees.

I left New Brunswick in early 1941. The destination was Sherbrooke, Quebec, where the government had recently acquired two abandoned railway shops that were to form the nucleus of a new camp. Koch, who had been transferred to Sherbrooke from Farnham, Quebec, recalls that when he arrived there on October 15, 1940, "the railway tracks and oiling pits that ran through the sheds were filled with black water. Soot was everywhere [and] the place had six old-fashioned lavatories without ventilation, two urinals and seven low-pressure water taps which also had to serve the kitchen."[38] Conditions were truly appalling, as noted by the commandant, Major S.N. Griffin, in his journal, and it is not surprising that, in Griffin's words, "a considerable amount of severe trouble" was encountered. What turned the tide was the arrival of the assistant adjutant, Lieutenant J. Alex Edmison, a Montreal lawyer and an active member of the Council for Christians and Jews. Edmison understood the feelings of the men and his pleas for patience were heeded.

By the time my group arrived in Sherbrooke, the situation had improved somewhat. Life in the camp followed a certain routine. The internees had organized, spokesmen had been chosen, and a *modus vivendi* had been worked out. Cultural activities flourished—lectures, drama, music—and a camp school was in full swing. I quickly enrolled, and what an extraordinary experience it turned out to be: chemistry taught by Max Perutz, the "father of molecular biology"; courses in advanced mathematics given by a former professor from the University of Vienna; English literature, presented by a teacher from one of England's better public (that is, private) schools; classes in art appreciation given by Max Stern (later the owner of Montreal's Dominion Gallery); courses in music, with recitals by John Newmark, perhaps the world's leading piano accompanist of his time, Helmut Blume, destined to become the dean of music at McGill, and Gerhard Kander, a superb violinist. We also benefited from the instruction of the young Emil Fackenheim, an ordained rabbi from Berlin, who went on to study philosophy at the University of Toronto, where he received a Ph.D. in 1945. He joined the faculty three years later and quickly established himself as "the world's foremost philosopher of how Judaism and Jewish existence could remain meaningful in the shadow of the death camps."[39]

The principal of the school was William Heckscher, a budding academic and later professor of fine art at Duke University. The secretary was Charles Cahn, a future professor of psychiatry at McGill University and director of the Douglas Hospital. Heckscher's contributions to the world of education were recognized by McGill in 1981, when it conferred on him an honorary doctorate. He was introduced at convocation by Walter Hitschfeld, vice-principal of research and himself a former pupil at the camp school, who recalled that Heckscher, "through a toughness of spirit, allied with soft-spoken good humour, through consumate tact and devotion, but above all through his patent love of learning ... led and inspired his boys."[40] It was a rich and busy life and I am grateful for that opportunity born of adversity.

I had made up my mind early on that I would make the best of a bad situation. I also decided that I would not allow myself to be demoralized, either physically or mentally. Toward that end, I always dressed as well as circumstances would permit—a shirt and tie, for instance, even if they had to be worn with prison denims. I took some ridicule for that, but it helped my morale and that was important to me. On Yom Kippur I fasted and felt good about it.

Saturday afternoons were dedicated to the Texaco opera radio broadcasts, and on Sunday afternoons many of us gathered in a large hall to hear the New York Philharmonic. The most remarkable of these broadcasts was on December 7, when the program was interrupted with the announcement that Japan had attacked the U.S. fleet at Pearl Harbor. Other memorable broadcasts, though in a different vein, were Churchill's famous wartime speeches. Having heard it live, who can ever forget his speech to a joint session of the Parliament of Canada on December 30, 1941, which included this famous line: "When I warned [the French government] that Britain would fight on alone whatever they did, their general told the Prime Minister and his divided cabinet, 'In three weeks, England will have her neck wrung like a chicken.' Some chicken! Some neck!"

[5]

The Paradigm Shifts

Toward the end of 1941, some of the internees had started to be released for work or study in Canada, and I began to hope that I, too, might soon join this lucky group. This change in attitude by the authorities was brought about by a number of factors, among them the unceasing efforts of a small group of concerned Canadians, headed by two remarkable women, Senator Cairine R. Wilson and Constance Hayward. Both were active in humanitarian causes, and they took on this new cause as well. They were strongly supported by Saul Hayes, an official with the Canadian Jewish Congress, who forsook a legal career to heed Montreal businessman Samuel Bronfman's call to lead the struggle for more enlightened policies in Canada concerning Jewish refugees.

Hayes, whom I got to know well in later years, was perfect for the job: intelligent, urbane and, above all, persuasive. Indeed, the greatest compliment to his accomplishments came from his fiercest opponent, F.C. Blair, the director of immigration, who wrote in 1941 that getting rid of Hayes would be the best way to prevent increased assistance to Jews.

Help also came from a more unexpected quarter—Alexander Paterson, commissioner of prisons in England, who had been sent to Canada by the home secretary to try to straighten out the bureaucratic mess that now confronted the two governments. Paterson, a truly great figure in the field of corrections, was appalled by what he found and he worked hard to right some of the wrongs. His principal mission was to facilitate the return to the United Kingdom—as free men—those internees who wished to go. This was no easy task, and it meant hundreds of interviews in many locations, dealing with each case on a personal basis. Eric Koch recalls a conversation he had about Paterson with Hayes. "I had the greatest admiration for him," Hayes told Koch. "There weren't enough hours in the day for him. He used to stay in the Windsor Hotel in Montreal. Our office was on St. Catherine Street between Peel and Stanley. I could see him from my window as he walked toward us in the cold winter, without an overcoat. We became good friends. He liked to drink pink gins."[41]

Since much of the documentation was missing, Paterson frequently had to decide for himself who was a genuine refugee and who was not. He also dispensed friendly advice, and this was particularly helpful to those who hoped to immigrate to the United States or other countries in the western hemisphere. To them he said, "Stay put and it may happen." Of course, at the time, the possibility of settling in Canada did not yet exist, and with Blair at the helm at Immigration, a change in attitude did not appear likely.

Paterson's labours soon began to bear fruit, and by Christmas the first 287 internees were sent to Halifax for the return voyage to England. Other groups followed throughout 1941, but passenger transport across the Atlantic was scarce, causing lengthy delays. Koch estimates that almost 80 per cent of those interned in Sherbrooke who had not volunteered to go back to England had, at one time or another, applied for visas to enter the United States; now, with the added proximity, they were anxious to renew the applications. Many, like myself, had relatives in the United States (my uncles in Detroit) who were anxious to help, but the American authorities, as a matter of policy, would not issue a visa to someone who had to attend the consular office accompanied by soldiers with fixed bayonets. Canada, on the other hand, would not withdraw the guards until the visa was issued. It was an frustrating dilemma, a classic Catch 22. Yet we were powerless to change the situation.

Even those who already held valid visas faced a dilemma because an obscure regulation, now invoked by the U.S. Department of Justice, forbade the entry of aliens from territories contiguous to the United States unless they had themselves paid for the passage to that territory. Of course, we, who had come courtesy of His Majesty's government, failed this test and so, once again, there was stalemate. It was this regulation that prevented Hermann Bondi, the distinguished physicist and mathematician, from being released to join his parents in the United States. As a result, Bondi returned to England where he was soon released to work on major scientific projects, for which a grateful country conferred on him the honour of a knighthood. Bondi was not the only ex-internee to be knighted. So was Klaus Moser, later the chairman of Covent Garden, and Michael Kerr, who became a judge of the Court of Appeal in London, and there may well have been others.

Paterson also tried to improve the lot of those who could not yet be released. The customary prisoner-of-war uniforms were replaced by ordinary working clothes, radios and newspapers were provided, and conditions generally improved. Finally, on July 1, 1941, three camps were officially designated Refugee Camps (as distinct from prisoner-of war camps), and a director of refugee camps was appointed, thereby diluting the strictly military control.

For those of us who secretly harboured the hope of remaining in Canada, a significant breakthrough had occurred in July. Prime Minister Mackenzie King, in reply to a plea from Ruth Draper, the famous *diseuse* who had given a dramatic monologue at a Red Cross benefit in Ottawa, used his influence to obtain the release, by special order-in-council, of an internee whose parents Draper had known in Europe.

Until that point, only two internees had been allowed to "enter" Canada, Kurt Swinton, whose mother lived in Vancouver, and Charles Wasserman, whose mother was a psychoanalyst in Ottawa. Swinton, an electrical engineer, after some initial rebuffs by private employers, was commissioned as a second lieutenant in the Royal Canadian Signal Corps, and by the time the war ended he had been promoted to lieutenant-colonel.

Another remarkable person who worked hard on behalf of the refugee-internees was Chaim Raphael, who had been sent to Canada by a group of Jewish organizations in the United Kingdom. It was he who had urged Ruth Draper to press the matter of her friend's son's release with the Canadian authorities, believing, as he later wrote, that "if we could get him treated as a 'special case' it might start everything."[42] Raphael worked closely with Paterson and Hayes and Hayes's assistant, Stanley Goldner, a young lawyer fresh out of law school.

The efforts of all these good people, and undoubtedly others, began to bear fruit in the spring of 1941, when the federal cabinet decided that carefully selected internees could be released for residence in Canada if sponsors were found to guarantee their maintenance. Three categories were given priority: students, those qualified for war work, and agricultural workers. With that, the search for sponsors was on.

Luck played a role in some cases. Alfred Bader, who was interned at a camp on Ile-aux-Noix on Lake Champlain south of Montreal, had left Vienna on the first *Kindertransport* in December 1938. In England, distant relatives on his mother's side arranged with a Mrs. Wolff to pay a guinea a week for his room and board with a family in Hove, near Brighton. As he recalled many years later in his autobiography:

One or two Sundays a month I made my duty visits to Mrs. Sarah Wolff, who paid my board at the Scharffs. She was very deaf and I had to shout into an ear trumpet that looked like a large funnel. She urged me many times to become a rabbi—what a failure I would have been!—and told me in boring detail about her son and six granddaughters in Montreal. What interest could I possibly have in strangers living on the other side of the world?[43]

What interest indeed, until one day in August 1940, when the wind blew some scraps of newspapers from outside the wire fence into the camp. With papers and radio banned, the internees scrambled to retrieve this veritable windfall, and Bader happened upon a page from the Montreal *Gazette*, which he read eagerly. Imagine his surprise when he saw an obituary of Mrs. Irene Wolff, daughter-in-law of Mrs. Sarah Wolff of Hove, England. She was survived by her husband, Martin, and their six daughters. Bader wrote at once to Martin Wolff, but his early letters were stopped by the censors. Later, however, when conditions eased, he managed to establish contact with Mr. Wolff, who sponsored his admission to Canada and welcomed him to his home in Westmount upon his release in November 1941.

Bader, who had matriculated while still in camp, was refused admission to McGill because the Jewish quota had already been filled. He was subsequently accepted at Queen's University in Kingston, where he found a warm welcome. Many years later, when he had prospered as a chemist, he repaid this kindness by donating to his alma mater not only large sums of money but also an ancient castle in England where students could stay while pursuing studies in Europe. In 1998 he was made a commander of the Order of the British Empire, and at last count he was the holder of nine honorary doctorates.

Word that the government was now willing to permit sponsored internees to remain in Canada also spread quickly on the outside. At that time, Sherbrooke had a small Jewish community, perhaps fifty or sixty families, many of them well established. One of the leaders, Sam Vineberg, organized a committee to see if there was sufficient interest to sponsor one or more internees. The response was overwhelming and the decision was made to give the necessary guarantees for three internees. One would live with the Vinebergs, another with the Miller family, and the third with the rabbi, the Reverend Abraham Mittleman. But how to pick the three?

Fortunately for me, the committee decided to ask for the three youngest inmates, which got me in—or rather out! The youngest was my friend from Darlington, Walter Riese, whose birthday preceded mine by a day. I came next, and the third was Felix Weiss, who was a few days older than I. Riese went to live with the Vinebergs, whose son, Morty, was then a prisoner of war in Germany. He left Sherbrooke after qualifying for an honours degree in mathematics at Bishop's, took graduate studies and became an actuary. He later moved to Ottawa, joined the civil service, and finished his career as Canada's Chief Actuary. He died in 2007. Weiss joined the Miller household and eventually married one of their daughters and embarked on a commercial career.

My sponsor was Rabbi Mittleman. Of course, there were the usual formalities, with their attendant delays, but the gates of the camp opened for me on March 13, 1942. Nearly twenty-two months had passed since Superintendent Huitson of the Durham County Constabulary had knocked on my door in Croft and told me to pack enough for "just a few days."

♦♦♦

While means had been found to release the remaining "accidental immigrants,"[44] as we were sometimes referred to, our legal status in Canada remained in doubt. This was finally settled by two orders-in-council, the first in 1943,[45] the second two years later.[46] The preamble to the first set out the legal conundrum:

> Whereas the Acting Secretary of State for External Affairs reports that there are present in Canada a number of refugees who were transferred to this country from the United Kingdom, and who have been allowed to take up employment or to pursue studies in this country under prescribed conditions; and
> That it is desirable to make provision with regard to their immigration status in this country, and to render their position similar, in essential respects, to that of enemy aliens in general in Canada.

In other words, here were almost 1,000 refugees, all of them technically enemy aliens, yet free from "such restrictions [in the words of the order-in-council] as are placed by the Defence of Canada Regulations or any other Orders or Regulations upon any enemy alien ordinarily resident in Canada." A bureaucratic nightmare, if you will.

As I mentioned, the solution was a two-step process. By 1943, virtually all internees had been released by means of temporary ministerial permits, a process authorized by the law then in force. Henceforth, all relevant information about persons so released—or to be released thereafter—would be forwarded by the director of immigration (still the notorious F.C. Blair) to the registrar general of enemy aliens, who would now be in charge. Ministerial permits would be valid for one year, prior restrictions or conditions were waived, and all persons in this category would from here on be subject to the provisions of the National Selective Service Regulations "in the same manner and to the same extent as any other person in Canada." This meant that these friendly "enemy aliens" could now join the Canadian Armed Forces, as many of us wanted to do. As Eric Koch notes in his book, the order-in-council was a tremendous step forward and it paved the way for ultimate naturalization.

However, before this could happen, our status had to be changed, and this was done when the second order-in-council (entitled *Re Status of Refugees*) was passed by the federal cabinet. It was all-encompassing and it applied to approximately 3,500 refugees from enemy countries and from enemy-occupied territory who came to Canada during the war under non-immigrant status. This, of course, included us.

It is of interest to look at the reasons given by cabinet for the order:

That many of these refugees had become stateless and escaped from the country of their birth and citizenship prior to the outbreak of the war, others succeeded in leaving their homes prior to invasion by enemy forces, the majority having been deprived of their property and possessions;

That many have attained prominence in their professions, others being skilled artisans and technicians;

That those qualified to do so have rendered valuable service to Canada in the prosecution of the war; and

That it would be neither practicable nor equitable to compel all such refugees to return to their countries of former residence, nor is it in the best interests of Canada to defer indefinitely the determining of their status under the provisions of the Immigration Act.

As a result, immigration officers-in-charge at a port of entry were authorized to "grant a landing in Canada to any refugee who entered Canada as such under non-immigrant status subsequent to September 1st, 1939, provided the said refugee establishes to the satisfaction of the Immigration Officer-in-Charge that he is of good character and can comply with the provisions of the Immigration Act in all other respects." Of course, we hadn't entered Canada as refugees—about 2,500 others had and the order-in-council was really intended for them—but the wording was deemed sufficiently wide to cover the "accidental immigrants" as well. And so, on December 12, 1945, I took the short trip from Lennoxville to Rock Island, on the Quebec–Vermont border, and reported to the immigration officer-in-charge, who satisfied himself that I was of good character (as required by the order-in-council) and thereupon gave me a letter stating that I now was a landed immigrant.

◆ ◆ ◆

The "official" number of interned "friendly aliens" who remained in Canada is 952. In fact, as recent studies show, the real figure was somewhat higher—972. Many blended into the Canadian landscape and cannot be traced. Some changed their names. Others returned to England or moved to other countries. But, as Barbara Moon wrote in *Maclean's* in 1962, while many could not be located, "a number of them are almost impossible to miss in Canada."[47]

In 1996, Helmut Kallmann of Ottawa, co-editor of the *Encyclopedia of Music in Canada*, wrote a mimeographed "Ex-Internees Newsletter" that he distributed to all who could be traced. In the eight years that followed, he published nine more newsletters. Sadly, as the years passed by, obituaries soon began to fill more pages than news about the living, but Kallmann's chronicles make interesting reading.

Let me give you some examples. In his first newsletter, Kallmann noted anniversaries and deaths. For instance:

Fritz Bender ... celebrated his 90th birthday in Ottawa on August 19, 1996 together with Franz Dammers (known to us as Franz Spanier) who was born the same day and year. Franz lives in New Jersey. Fritz had a distinguished career with the Government of Canada as a wood chemistry expert. Both had escaped from Holland in the same rowboat, along with others.

George Shindler (Hans Georg Schindler from Leipzig) died at 72 in England ... Senior resident judge of the Inner London Crown Court 1987–1992 (when he moved to Norfolk) he was described as a "most humane" judge, a "compassionate and contemporary mind" and "a great supporter of the underdog."

Six months later, in his second newsletter, Kallmann brought news about forty-four ex-internees. Among the items noted:

Gregory Baum from Berlin studied mathematics, then theology and obtained a Th.D. from Fribourg in 1956. He is the author of at least seventeen books and numerous articles and continues to be associated with McGill U's Department of Religious Studies ... By 1990 he had received seven honorary degrees.

And a few months after that:

Ernest L Eliel has received the $20,000 National Academy of Sciences (USA) 1997 award for Chemistry in Service to Society "for his seminal and far-reaching contributions in organic stereo-chemistry and for his wise and energetic leadership in professional societies." Eliel was president of the American Chemical Society in 1992.

The newsletters kept on coming. More achievements, more deaths reported. In his final newsletter (the *Epistula Ultima*, as he called it), sent in February 2004, Kallmann noted that a number of ex-internees had stayed in touch with each other; most were in their eighties and nineties.

It was a remarkable group, with many remarkable people. When we were first identified in 1941 for what we were—friendly aliens—F.C. Blair said: "What we have to do, is protect Canada against the release of these people here."[48] Sixty years later, writing in *Maclean's*, Sonja Sinclear observed:

No doubt Blair would be surprised to learn what became of "these people" after the government released them from the internment camps in Quebec, Ontario and New Brunswick two to three years later ... more than seventy became university professors, including two Nobel Prize winners, and collectively they received more honorary degrees than anyone has cared to count. Of the nearly 1000 who chose to remain in Canada, dozens have contributed to Canada's cultural life as authors, musicians and scientists, and at least nine have been named members or officers of the Order of Canada ...[49]

Altogether, an interesting event in Canada's history!

[6]

Freedom Regained

It was cold and bleak, but the ride from the camp into Sherbrooke, a matter of ten minutes, was like a voyage of discovery into a world hitherto carefully hidden. I had a lot of questions, and so did my benefactors, and it was all marvelously exciting. Our first stop was Rosenbloom's on Wellington Street, a venerable men's store, where I was fitted with a brown three-piece suit, shirts, socks, and underwear. From there we went to my new home, a comfortable house with a large verandah on Portland Avenue, near the corner of Quebec Street. There, Rabbi Mittleman's wife, a warm and gracious woman, and their daughter Eta, who was a year older than I, greeted me with big hugs and an even bigger meal, my first home-cooked meal in almost two years. But I fear I didn't do justice to the feast because I was much too excited to eat. I was thrilled to be free, and the anticipation of things to come made it impossible for me to sleep later that night. If only my parents, whom I last saw three years ago in Vienna, could know how happy I was.

The Jewish community had strained its resources to have us and we received a warm and generous welcome. Regretfully, as Louise Abbott noted in the Montreal *Gazette* some years ago, "the Jews of Sherbrooke ... were a small but vibrant community. Now there's just the cemetery."[50] The first Jewish resident, Reuben Hart, had arrived in Sherbrooke before the census of 1863. By 1881, twenty Jews were registered. As the pogroms in Russia emptied the *shtetls*, the community grew, and by 1907 it was large enough to engage a rabbi, obtain a charter for a congregation, and rent premises for services and other communal activities. In 1921, Jews numbered 265, roughly 1 per cent of the population. But ten years later the number had slipped to 152. According to Abbott, "the Great Depression was one factor in the exodus. The search for Jewish spouses was another."

The slide continued after World War II. Soon it became impossible to constitute a *minyan*—the traditional quorum of ten males over the age of thirteen required to hold religious services. Many a time did I receive a call requesting my presence at the synagogue "to be the tenth" so that a congregant could say *kaddish*, the prayer for a dead relative. Of course, I never refused. The service was early in the morning, well before school, and it didn't last very long. Custom dictated that, at the conclusion, all who attended were invited to partake in "refreshments" furnished by the person who had requested the constitution of the *minyan*. To refuse would have been impolite, but it took me some time to get used to downing a generous shot of Geneva gin before breakfast.

In the years after I left, the congregation continued to dwindle and in 1983, after much soul-searching, the painful decision was made to sell the synagogue on Montreal Street. The building now houses a Pentecostal church.

The day after my arrival Mr. Mittleman took me to the Sherbrooke High School, a few blocks away, where I was interviewed by the principal, a kindly man named W.W. Wright. He pondered where I would best fit. I was almost eighteen, but my formal education had stopped in the middle of grade 9. Yet camp school had advanced me almost to university level in mathematics and, to some extent, physics. Mr. Wright thought that the wise course was to put me into grade 9, but after a few days I was moved up to grade 10, which I finished with good marks that June. Not surprisingly, I excelled in math, and whenever the teacher had some difficulty with a problem, he would turn to me to give him a hand. Although I was the object of some curiosity, the students had obviously been briefed by Mr. Wright and the teachers, and my fifteen months at Sherbrooke High were happy and carefree.

I completed grade 11 in June 1943, and I am proud to say that the class chose me to give the valedictory address. I wrote my speech and memorized it, but when the time came for delivering it, I became flustered about halfway through and my mind went blank. After an interminable pause—much longer to me, I am sure, than to the audience—during which I gathered my thoughts, I improvised and finished the valedictory to much applause. It taught me a valuable lesson and I have never since memorized a speech; I now use notes. I was upset at the time, but this was greatly surpassed by my joy at having my parents in the audience, who had come from their new home in New York City.

Theirs had been a long and arduous journey to the United States. They were so reluctant to speak about the many indignities they suffered after I left Vienna that I didn't hear the story until many years later. And even then, they spared me the most painful details. First they lost the apartment where we had lived since I was born. They moved to a room in a Jewish friend's home, and later, when all their money was gone, they shared accommodations with another couple. While many of their non-Jewish friends helped in the beginning, they were afraid of the consequences; contacts with them became less frequent and eventually stopped. All around them, people had started to vanish, sent off to concentration camps. Every knock on the door was a potential calamity.

Their break came in 1941 in the form of two United States visas, together with steamship tickets from Lisbon to New York, courtesy of my two American uncles. However, to get from Vienna to Lisbon was no easy matter, since it involved travel through Vichy France. Somehow—I was never told the full story—they made it: from Vienna to France (through Switzerland or Italy, I don't know which), from there to Spain, and then to Portugal, where they arrived a few days before their scheduled departure. Then disaster struck in the form of a thief who stole their tickets. Cables went back and forth across the Atlantic. New tickets arrived at the last possible moment and the voyage began, from Lisbon to New York by way of Cuba, a trip of almost three weeks. But freedom was at the end of the journey, and that was what mattered most.

They settled in New York, first in a one-room apartment in mid-Manhattan. They later moved further north, first to West 80th Street and later to a two-room flat in a brownstone on West 73rd Street. With help from Jewish organizations, both found work, but since my father spoke very little English, job opportunities for him were limited. His first job was in a clothing factory where he worked for a number of years. Later he got a job as a cloak-room attendant in a hotel not far from his home. But his health began to deteriorate and he had to stop working, which was a heavy blow to him. A proud and elegant man, he resented his illness and it hurt him that my mother now had to look after him. He spent his last two years in a wheelchair, often on the sidewalk outside the building where he and my mother lived, watching the world go by. He was eighty-eight when he died, and by then all his friends had predeceased him.

My mother, being seventeen years younger, managed to learn English fairly quickly, and, although she spoke with an accent, she became quite fluent. She had a few malapropisms, about which we teased her, but she didn't mind. Week-days, for instance, were "weekly days." To have a busy day, in her vocabulary, was to be "under the go." It was all perfectly understandable though.

She, too, began to work as soon as they were settled, first in a factory, and later (when her English improved) as a waitress in the dining room of a residential hotel. The guests were mostly Europeans, and they loved her for her good nature and devotion to her job. In 1970, three years after my father's death, we brought her to Montreal, where she made new friends. But, above all, she was near us and her grandchildren, whose visits gave her much joy. In 1983, a few months after a fall in which she broke her hip, she passed away.

I first heard of their rescue while still in camp in Sherbrooke. One of my uncles in Detroit wrote to say that they would soon be in New York, and a few days later a letter arrived from them, full of joy and hope. Until my uncle's letter I lived with the dreadful fear that they, like tens of thousands around them, had been deported, never to be heard from again. The relief was indescribable and I ran to tell those around me. But I quickly stopped when I realized that others were not so lucky and that my joy only cut deeply into their wounds.

During the time when I was uncertain of my parents' fate, they knew I was in Canada, interned but safe. The Red Cross provided mail service for prisoners-of-war, and this was extended to internees, and so I wrote. Miraculously, some of my letters, heavily censored, reached them in their new home in Vienna. What was left intact by the Canadian censor was meagre but sufficient. I was in North America, out of harm's way. The details didn't matter. And so, in June 1943, I had the thrill of having them with me in Sherbrooke.

I had applied for admission to Bishop's University in Lennoxville, not far from my new home, but fees and other costs were a serious problem. Fortunately, when the matriculation results were published, I stood near the top and Bishop's offered me an entrance scholarship that covered most of the tuition. I also qualified for a bursary offered by the IODE —the Imperial Order of Daughters of the Empire—but the committee decided it wasn't appropriate to make the award to a foreign-born student and so I had to do without it. Nevertheless, I was delighted to accept the scholarship and, after some discussion with a faculty adviser (who had administered a rather primitive aptitude test), I registered for courses leading to a Bachelor of Science degree in math and physics.

The student body at the time was about 200, less than a quarter of them women, and math and physics honours attracted only two students. As a result, classes were sometimes held in the professors' homes, often at tea time, with sherry as a welcome substitute for tea. Steeped in tradition, Bishop's had been founded in 1845 by George Jehoshaphat Mountain, the first Anglican bishop of Quebec, and it retained strong affiliations with the Church of England until the mid-1960s. Even today, the two official "visitors" are the Anglican bishops of Montreal and Quebec, a symbolic reminder of the university's origins.

My good friend Alex Paterson, who was at Bishop's some years after me, loves to recall the time one of his classmates climbed the bell tower one night and stole the clapper from the bell. The next morning, when the porter tried to ring the bell to summon faculty and students for matins in the chapel, there was an ominous silence. The principal ordered an immediate investigation, which failed to find the culprit. By then, I had moved to Montreal and worked as a reporter for the *Star*, and the mystery of the missing clapper made for a couple of good stories, which the students loved, but that the administration found less than amusing.

Most students at the time—this was 1943—had deferments for enlistment in the armed forces, but military training was strongly recommended and all of us joined the Bishop's contingent of the Canadian Officers Training Corps (COTC). The unit was commanded by Major Howard Church, a strong but fair disciplinarian, who personally conducted most of the classes and all of the field training. He was assisted by a couple of faculty members who had been commissioned as lieutenants, and by three senior students who were second lieutenants. We also had a company sergeant-major, who was in charge of the parade-ground drill and who made sure that boots were shined and buttons polished.

I liked the military, but there were two things I couldn't do in the beginning: swing my arms while marching, and hit the target with a service revolver. As to the first, I still recall the booming voice of Sergeant-Major Fuller shouting across the parade ground: "Kaufman, your arms." The embarrassment was sufficient to make me do it properly. As for the second, practice paid off, and I soon became a good shot with Bren guns, .303s, and standard Smith and Wessons, a skill that stood me in good stead twenty-seven years later when I was obliged to carry a loaded revolver while prosecuting members of the *Front de libération du Québec*. My favourite military exercise was the field trip, where a small group of cadets was taken in the back of a closed truck to a secluded spot in the countryside with instructions to pinpoint the location on a highly detailed army ordnance map. I never failed, and my map-reading skills have never left me.

As the end of first year approached, I was promoted to lance corporal. I also qualified in signals, which I liked. By then I was twenty, and the war in Europe was still going strong. I was restless and frustrated and felt that my place was on active service. University could wait.

I decided that the air force would be to my liking, and on April 20, 1944, I wrote to the recruiting office in Montreal requesting an interview. Two days later—mail was faster in those days—I got a reply from Squadron Leader F.W. McCrae, commanding officer, No. 13 Recruiting Centre, Royal Canadian Air Force

(RCAF), suggesting that I report to his office on the second floor of the Post Office building at Bishop and St. Catherine Streets at 9 a.m. on April 25. "If you will do so," he wrote, "all necessary tests and interviews can be completed in the one day, and you will be able to return to Lennoxville the same evening."

I took the early train from Sherbrooke and presented myself at the office at nine on the dot. To my surprise, Squadron Leader McCrae decided to interview me himself, a process that took about forty-five minutes. In the midst of the interview, a woman officer burst into the room to tell McCrae that a military aircraft had just crashed in Griffintown in Montreal and that some houses were on fire. McCrae quite calmly turned to me and asked: "Do you still want to join?" I assured him that I did. I later learned that the ill-fated plane was an RAF bomber that had taken off from Dorval Airport a few minutes earlier. Five crew members and ten civilians died in the crash.

The interview was followed by a series of tests, which determined that I had the aptitude to qualify for training as a pilot or navigator—exactly what I wanted. Then came a thorough medical, which I passed, flat feet notwithstanding. As promised, I returned to Lennoxville that night.

Squadron Leader McCrae had told me that the file would have to be reviewed by Ottawa—I was not yet a Canadian citizen—and that I should get word within a few weeks. That suited me well, since the final first-year exams were about to begin and I thought I might as well finish the year. When no word came by the middle of May, I grew impatient and wrote to McCrae, who told me that my application was still under consideration "at Headquarters." So I wrote to Ottawa, and on May 31 a group captain, writing "for Chief of Air Staff"—heady stuff for a would-be recruit—informed me that a decision had been made and duly communicated to the Montreal Recruiting Centre (channels are important in the military) and that, if I would again report to Bishop Street, they would tell me what had been decided. To make a long story short, I was told that my application had been deferred since recruiting for the RCAF had been stopped. Should the need for recruits revive, I would be called. In other words, the application was on hold.

By then it was June and all the good summer jobs were gone, but I did find employment in Lennoxville, and I spent the next three months unloading bales of wool from freight cars and sorting the wool according to the length of the fibre. It was hard work, but the pay was good and it certainly put me in excellent physical condition.

I returned to Bishop's in the fall for my second year, and continued training with the COTC. One day, while out on the rifle range, the instructor needed something from the office on the campus and I was ordered to get it—on the double, of course. It was a hot and humid day and I wore standard battle dress with shirt and tie and a steel helmet. On the way, as I ran, I first took off my helmet. Then I unbuttoned my tunic, and when that didn't help I loosened my tie and opened my shirt collar. Imagine my horror, just as I turned a corner near the office, when I literally ran into a small group of officers, including a brigadier with lots of red on his cap and lapels. I tried to salute as smartly as I could, but first I had to put the helmet on my head—in the Canadian army one doesn't salute without headgear—and while I did that I tried to hide my bare neck. It wasn't a very successful manoeuvre and I got some curious stares, but even though I was recognized no one took me to task. It was, as I said, a blisteringly hot day.

I got my second stripe around that time, and when the sergeant of my platoon moved on to bigger things, I replaced him with the rank of acting sergeant, the apex of my career in the army. I also got a notice, duly addressed to "Cpl. Kaufman, F.," to report for active service. I still have the notice, and it's amusing to look at it so many years later:

DEPARTMENT OF LABOUR, NATIONAL SELECTIVE SERVICE, MOBILIZATION SECTION. PLEASE READ CAREFULLY

INSTRUCTIONS CONCERNING ROUTE MONTREAL TO NO. 4, DISTRICT DEPOT, JACQUES CARTIER BARRACKS
Go to the corner of Ontario and Bordeaux streets by tramway from where you will take a bus to your destination.

WHAT TO BRING WITH YOU: YOUR RATION BOOK
The army will supply you with practically everything you require during your training period. It is useless to bring personal belongings which will not be needed. A parcel well tied with a strong string is the most practical—travelling bags, valises, etc., take up too much space.

In the parcel you should have
1. Toilet necessities:—razor, shaving soap, tooth brush, tooth paste or powder, hair brush and face cloth.
2. Necessaries for sewing and cleaning material—such as:—sewing thread, needles, buttons, safety pins, scissors, black shoe paste and shoe-brush.
3. Socks:—two pairs—the army supplies you with socks, but a few extra pairs will always come in useful.
4. Handkerchiefs:—six.

5. Pyjamas or night-shirt.
6. Bath and face towels: two.

Do not wear an overcoat, wear a "windbreaker" or cardigan. A cap instead of a hat, it takes less room. An old suit is recommended for travelling to camp. The Department of National Defence accepts no responsibility for damage to or loss of your civilian effects.

BRING JUST ENOUGH AND NO MORE[51]

I was surprised to be drafted because science students were exempt from conscription, and so I took the notice to Major Church, who told me to disregard it. I don't know what he did, but I never heard from the National Selective Service (the Canadian draft board) again, which pleased me since I was still on "hold" by the RCAF and hopeful that I would be accepted soon.

Victory in Europe came on May 7, 1945, my birthday. *The Campus*, the student newspaper of which I was cofounder and current editor, printed a special edition, classes were cancelled, and just about everyone went to Sherbrooke where an impromptu parade soon wound its way along Wellington Street. It was a day to remember—a huge outpouring of pent-up emotions and great joy.

My third year at Bishop's was uneventful and I got my degree.[52] By that time the war in the Pacific had ended as well.

[7]
Newspaper Days

I graduated from Bishop's in June 1946 with a Bachelor of Science degree in math and physics. In those days three options were open to mathematics majors: teaching, working for Bell Telephone (where long-distance tariffs were calculated by people good with figures), or a job with the Dominion Bureau of Statistics (DBS), the forerunner of Statistics Canada. Since I didn't want to teach (which, in any case, would have taken an extra year of teachers' college, which I couldn't afford), I applied to Bell and the DBS. But Bell wasn't hiring, and while the DBS was, and I had successfully written the required civil-service exams, preference for veterans worked against me and I didn't get the job. So what to do?

I stayed in residence as long as I could after convocation, but the bursar finally gave me an ultimatum—leave or be evicted. I found a nice clean room in the home of an elderly couple on Clough Street in Lennoxville. The move was accomplished with the help of a friend and a taxi. My room at Bishop's was on the second floor of the Old Lodge, on the road leading to Divinity House and the principal's residence. I had hired the cab by the hour, so we had to move quickly, and this we accomplished by throwing all my clothes out the window onto a small lawn on the edge of the road. I did the throwing and my friend completed the process by piling everything into the back seat of the cab. When we arrived at my new home, my friend, anxious to get going, opened the back door of the taxi to grab the first load. Unfortunately, it was the wrong door, and all the stuff that had been piled up against it tumbled out and came to rest in the gutter. My landlady confessed to me later that, at that moment, she had serious doubts about her new boarder.

The move made, I set out to look for a job and my first stop was the Sherbrooke *Daily Record* where I had worked the previous summer. I intended to speak to Don McMahon, the city editor, but even before I could see him I ran into John Bassett, the owner and publisher. We exchanged a few pleasantries and Bassett asked me what I was doing. I told him that I hoped McMahon might find a spot for me and Bassett said, "No need to see Don, we can use another reporter." The pay was $18 a week and one could live on that—not well, of course—in 1946. I started work the following morning.

Until that point, I hadn't seriously considered a career in journalism. I had enjoyed my work on the *Record* during the previous summer, but since I was trained in math and physics, it seemed a waste to give it up. Still, with the scarcity of jobs in that field, work as a reporter appeared a reasonable alternative, and rather than consider it a stopgap, I gave it all I had. It was a good decision.

My first assignment was to rewrite the long and tedious news releases that various organizations had sent in the day before. From that I moved to news submitted by a slew of local correspondents—every town and village in the region had one—which had to be edited and put into publishable shape. The trick with this was to keep it short, but not omit any names: Barbara Jones entertained the local chapter of the Red Cross for tea, and the following were in attendance. As Don used to say, names are everything. It was the stuff of local papers, the *raison d'être* of small-town reporting. It didn't matter where the names appeared, since every name was of interest to the person whose name it was, his or her spouse, and at least one friend.

The ultimate in "names" was a funeral, and reporters would be dispatched to stand at the door of the church or the funeral home and ask all those who entered for their names. This sometimes caused line-ups, but experienced funeral-goers had their business cards ready, and this not only made for greater efficiency but also ensured that names would not be misspelled and that titles would not be omitted. Once in a while, someone would slip you two or three cards and whisper that the others were unavoidably detained and would you please include them. We usually did. Bill Weintraub, a former Montreal *Gazette* reporter, alludes to this practice in *Why Rock the Boat?*,[53] a not-so-fictionalized account of newspapering in Montreal in the 1940s. He tells the story of a young reporter who has just covered his first funeral. On his return to the newsroom, he seeks out the religion editor, who is in charge of this activity. What do I do with this, he asks, as he hands over a sheet of paper with three names typed on it. They couldn't attend, but they want to be included in the list. The wise and seasoned editor looks at the names and tells his young colleague that these three men are not only important executives but advertisers as well. In short, include them in the list.

To cover funerals properly, it was essential to get the names of officiating clergy and the pallbearers as well. One such occasion stands out in my mind. This was at the Roman Catholic cathedral in Sherbrooke. The sexton had the information I needed, but since he also doubled as the bell ringer he couldn't leave the belfry to get the list. And so we made a deal: I would ring the bell while he got the names. And I did and he did.

Another funeral that I recall took place some years later in Montreal. Two of us were told to go to Wray's funeral home, but there were two well-known establishments with similar names: Jos. C. Wray on Mountain Street, and William Wray a little further to the east. Unfortunately, we went to the wrong Wray, and while the basic facts in the report we wrote were correct—at least we had the right deceased—the names of those who attended, of course, were not. But no one made a fuss, and after that we took this particular job somewhat less seriously. Indeed, the practice of publishing names in funeral coverage stopped soon thereafter.

I did rewrites for a couple of weeks, waiting for a "big" story to break—a fire, an accident, perhaps an important visitor. And sure enough, while I sat writing my umpteenth local report on my ancient typewriter, precariously perched on an even more ancient desk, Don approached me and said, "I'd like you to go out and get a story." I was thrilled and eagerly asked, "What story?" to which he replied, "How should I know? Any story."

So I went out and wandered along Wellington Street and onto King Street South. No particular reason for this, but it seemed to be as good as any other route. There was a small crowd outside the bus terminal near the Canadian National Railway station, and the object of attention was a gleaming new bus. I soon found out that it represented the latest in technology and it had just completed its first run from Montreal. It made a story and it taught me that one can always find something to write about. There is an audience for almost anything.

I had been on the *Record* for three months when a fortuitous event changed my career: an offer to join the *Montreal Star*. This was the result of an article I had submitted to the Star—we were allowed to do some freelance work—which had tickled the executive editor's fancy. He not only ran it with two cartoons on the home page, but also paid me $10 and invited me to come and see him on my next trip to Montreal. I did so, no doubt with indecent haste, and he hired me for $30 a week. This was the big time—a newsroom spread out over a whole floor in the *Star's* old building at 245 St. James Street West, with dozens of editors, reporters, photographers and copy boys, teletypes along the wall, and a circulation of over

200,000. Tell anyone—well, almost anyone—that you represented the *Star* and doors would open. Big stuff for a reporter with just a few months' experience.

In my first story for the *Star* (it ran on July 27, 1946) I put some of my early training to work. This is how it began:

> I am a Mathematician. I have also studied psychology, theology, philosophy, economics and logic. But I still can't figure this one out: Why does the number of grooms in the Province of Quebec exceed the number of brides by .1 per cent? To make it simpler for you here is the same problem in a different form: Why are 1,001 men necessary to marry 1,000 women? Who knows—I'll bet my last shirt (and shirts are hard to get these days) that even the Dominion Bureau of Statistics, publishers of the 1945 Canada Year Book, hasn't got the answer—and they made the statement. But wait—that isn't all. Turn the page and examine the figures for the whole Dominion. You will make a startling discovery. There they tell us that in 1943, of every thousand grooms married, 754 were born in the province of their residence, 129 in other provinces and 116 first saw the light of the world outside of Canada. Add it up and reconsider the remarks you have probably by now made about my mental status. I don't know how you propose to solve the problem of the missing groom, but I have come to the conclusion that one husband in every thousand drops straight from heaven.

There was much to learn. In the first place, I didn't know Montreal that well, and I spent many hours with a map of the city, trying to memorize the location of Montreal's many suburbs, the names of streets and how to spell them, and how to get there by streetcar, the *Star's* favourite mode of transportation. The use of taxis was reserved for emergencies, and taxi slips and streetcar tickets were kept under lock and key by Etta Schwartz, an administrative assistant on the editorial floor. Even the owner of the *Star,* who ultimately paid the bills, could not have been more careful than Miss Schwartz. Walking was encouraged, but if that wasn't feasible, streetcar tickets were handed out two at a time. And as for taxis, as I said, it had to be a true emergency. Eventually, I worked out a system to get somewhere fast. I would grab my jacket, rush over to Miss Schwartz's desk and, on the run, shout ahead, "Emergency, emergency, I need a taxi." Once in a while, she would say, "What's the rush?" but more often than not I got a taxi slip and I was spared a long ride on the streetcar.

When I first moved to Montreal, I rented a room on St. Denis Street. My hope was that by living in the east end I would pick up French more quickly. That turned out to be an illusion since I spent little time at home. A cub reporter's hours were long: from early morning until late at night, weekdays as well as most weekends and no extra pay for overtime. I therefore abandoned the idea of learning French by osmosis and took private lessons to speed up the process. Of course, in the 1940s and 1950s, one could get by nicely with English only. Police broadcasts, for instance, were made in both English and French, since many officers were not proficient in both languages. That began to change in the 1960s and English-language police broadcasts ceased. But an ability to speak French was clearly an asset, and I worked hard to achieve a good degree of fluency.

With my shift to more formal lessons in French, I abandoned the idea of living in the east end and moved to Notre-Dame-de-Grâce in the western part of Montreal, where most of my friends lived. It worked out well and I stayed there for almost twenty years.

◆ ◆ ◆

Editing on the *Star* was tight and writing had to be too. With four deadlines a day, editors weren't prepared to rewrite copy that wasn't up to standard. We each had a small desk with a standard size Underwood. We wrote on flimsy paper, prepackaged by the office boys, with three carbon copies. As soon as a page was complete, you tore it out of your typewriter and shouted "copy" and in no time flat the original would be taken to the city desk, the first carbon to the executive editor's office, the second to the horseshoe-shaped copy desk, and the third put on a spike in case the others got lost. The city editor—Ted Murphy at the time I joined—speed-read the story. If he was satisfied with the basics, the copy editors took over, and that's where the real editing was done. Charlie Jacobsen led the group and little got by him: grammar, spelling, appropriate titles (the *Star* was strong on that), taboos ("rape" was always changed to "indecent assault"[54] and "abortion" became an "illegal operation") and, above all, no free advertising and no personal opinions. The last was pretty standard procedure for newspapers in the 1940s and 1950s. Pierre Berton's recollection, from his days at the Vancouver *News-Herald* and Vancouver *Sun*, are similar: "Like most newspapermen I was a prisoner of the cult of objectivity and conformity. Since you assumed that most readers would never get past the first paragraph, you told everything at the outset. Just the bald facts … You kept your own personality, your own feelings … out of the story."[55]

And then, of course, Montreal wasn't Sherbrooke—a different mentality, a different persona; in short, a total change. You had to know who was important, what institutions were sacred (for instance, McGill with the *Star*), and how to spell such seemingly exotic names as Chaboillez Square (near the old Bonaventure Station in downtown Montreal). You also had to know what to avoid, like pictures of F.R. Scott, the poet and great constitutional lawyer, whose photo was banned from the pages of the *Star* for reasons, I suspect, connected with his socialist leanings. I learned this the hard way when I came back one day from an assignment where a photographer had shot a picture with Scott in the middle. The photo wasn't used. My instructions were that in future, if we couldn't avoid photographing Scott, we were to put him on one end or the other so that the photo could be cropped. This senseless and offensive policy changed in the 1950s, but it was quite a jolt to discover that often news was considered news only when it involved the "right" people.

I worked hard in those days. Twelve- to fourteen-hour days were not uncommon. There was much drudgery, but there also was the excitement of a big story, the satisfaction of a scoop, the thrill of a byline. And often I met interesting people. In my eight years with the *Star,* I covered a royal visit (Princess Elizabeth and Prince Philip), a vice-regal tour by Lord Alexander, and visits by prime ministers, premiers, and politicians of all stripes. I don't remember them all, but some occasions stand out in my mind. The royal tour, for instance. Adrian Lunny, a staff photographer, and I had instructions to get a picture of the royal couple at McGill. Huge crowds lined the approaches to the university and photo opportunities were limited, so we needed a plan. We looked for a spot where the limousine—a sky blue convertible—would have to slow down, and the ideal place seemed to be the entrance to the university where the cavalcade had to make a turn off Sherbrooke Street. Easier said than done, since Adrian wanted a spot where he could point his camera downwards the couple, not too high and not too low. We found a notice board inside the Roddick Gates, just the right height, but quite unstable and almost impossible to climb. Still, we managed to get him up, and there he sat on his narrow perch as the limousine approached. He pointed his large camera toward the car, the royal couple looked up, and he got a gorgeous shot of a radiant princess.

The *Star's* management was delighted with the picture and it ran on the front page. A few weeks later, the executive editor called Lunny to his office and told him that Buckingham Palace had requested permission to use the photo on the couple's Christmas card. Lunny felt pretty good about this, and he felt even better when the editor told him that such an honour would not go unrewarded. Sure enough, a few days later an envelope arrived on his desk. It contained a cheque for $10. The *Star* was known to be frugal, but this pushed frugality to the extreme.

The vice-regal tour I covered was to the Eastern Townships. At one point, as we approached North Hatley, the motorcade made an unscheduled stop at an inn on the outskirts of town. The proprietor, taken by surprise, ran out to greet his unexpected guests, but even before he could finish a few words of welcome, a uniformed aide-de-camp pulled him aside and told him quietly but firmly to show His Excellency to the washroom. When Lord Alexander emerged a few minutes later, he walked over to the small group of reporters assigned to cover the trip and told us that the best piece of advice he had received on his appointment was never to stand when you could sit, never to sit when you could lie down, and never to miss a chance to go to the bathroom. With that, he climbed back into his limousine for the short ride to the town square where an eager crowd awaited him.

The next day we went on a boat ride on Lake Memphremagog, from Magog to Georgeville. It was a small ship and the reporters were asked to stay below deck where the caterer was in the process of preparing a sumptuous lunch for the official party. We hadn't thought about food until then, and as the day progressed so did our hunger, but there was nothing for us to eat—nothing, that is, until the used plates were sent down from the deck. As happens with most buffets, people had taken more than they could eat, and this was a windfall for us. The only problem was the lack of cutlery, so we ate with our hands—coleslaw, potato salad, cold cuts, and delicious Camembert cheese. Clearly not finger foods. This feast was so good, and we were so hungry, that we didn't notice the arrival of the Governor General, who had decided on a friendly visit with the press. We didn't even have napkins to wipe our hands clean, but this didn't bother Lord Alexander one bit. He simply said, "I guess they forgot you," and with that he ordered the chef to bring us plates of food and whatever else we needed.

Later that day, after a drive through Ayer's Cliff and Tomifobia, we ended up at John Hackett's estate on the highway near Stanstead. Hackett, a Conservative, had been appointed to the Senate by his old friend and fellow Eastern Townshipper, Louis St. Laurent, and the honour of entertaining the Governor General went to him as the Townships' elder statesman. It was the end of the tour, the atmosphere was relaxed, and soon we started telling funny stories about the trip. At one point, a photographer asked the Governor General if he would pose for a souvenir shot with the press, to which he readily agreed. That picture taken, he told the photographer to join the group, and he would take a shot of the press corps. He did, and a few days later we each got a beautiful picture from Rideau Hall with the sky over Stanstead and a group of heads at the bottom!

When Louis St. Laurent—"Uncle Louis" to the press—was picked to succeed

Mackenzie King as leader of the Liberal Party, he made a sentimental visit to Compton in the Eastern Townships, where he was born. The old farmhouse was still there, and so were friends and neighbours, many of whom remembered him from his youth. I was assigned to cover the event, but it was difficult to get sufficiently close to have a good view of the inner circle. Today, all this would be arranged for the press, but things were more primitive in the 1940s and so I was left to my own devices. As I looked around, the thought struck me that if I could get on the roof of the farmhouse, I could see and hear everything. I found a ladder in the back and climbed up to a spot where no one could see me, particularly the Royal Canadian Mounted Police (RCMP).

I got to the top all right. But as I descended on the other side, I lost my footing and started to slide down, heading directly for the prime minister, who had just begun his speech below. The noise on the roof attracted his attention, he stopped in mid-sentence, and turned to look up at me. In the very nick of time, I managed to grab the eaves trough on the rim, and there I balanced myself as Uncle Louis finished his speech. I later apologized for the commotion, but St. Laurent was more amused than angry, which is more than could be said of his organizers.[56]

One evening I was working at my desk in the *Star*'s city room when the phone rang. The voice at the other end asked if we might want to have a word with Joey Smallwood, the premier of Newfoundland. I said I thought we might and asked who was speaking. "It's Joey Smallwood himself," said the voice. He gave me his room number at the old Mount Royal Hotel on Peel Street and I went up with a photographer. Smallwood, a former newspaperman, was delighted to see us—I suspect he wanted company—and we spent a wonderful evening with the premier. He had been to Alberta, where he was made an honorary Indian chief, and in no time at all we had him posing for a picture decked out in his new ceremonial dress. "Wait 'til they see that back home," he said—which they did, since Canadian Press distributed the photo on its network. Smallwood was excellent company, a born storyteller, and it was a memorable evening.

While I had no particular beat at the *Star*, I acquired the reputation for being good at covering massive searches, usually for missing children, sometimes for older folk lost in the woods, as well as the occasional manhunt for criminals on the loose. I was well prepared for these events. I had a complete set of army ordnance maps for the province, and I knew from my days in the COTC how to read them. I also had a good compass, strong flashlights with spare batteries, rubber boots, and clothing suitable for such occasions. When a call came in, I'd grab a photographer and off we'd go.

It happened at times that the *Star* team became in effect the search master, particularly when we got there before the specialized police team arrived. We would organize the volunteers, suggest what equipment was needed, make provisions for food for the searchers, and comfort the relatives. There was great satisfaction in this and, of course, good publicity for the *Star.* Many searches had happy outcomes, but sometimes the inevitable happened and the missing person would be found dead. On one such occasion, in the mountains north of Montreal, Cy Woods, a *Star* photographer, and I found the body of the missing child in the shallow waters of a lake. With heavy hearts we went to tell the family, taking no pleasure in that scoop.

This "specialty" once got me a job offer. Alex Janusitis, who had worked at the *Star,* went west in search of fame and fortune. He got as far as Edmonton, where he became editor-in-chief of a new paper, the *Bulletin.* In February 1950 he wrote to me as follows: "I see by the byline that you are still chasing little boys and girls lost in the woods. It occurred to me that being an adventurous soul you might be interested in coming west. I have a spot open for a good reporter like you." I was flattered, but while the west sounded exciting, I decided to stay with the *Star.* And a good thing, too, because the *Bulletin* folded soon thereafter.

◆ ◆ ◆

Montreal in the 1940s and early 1950s wasn't what Montreal is today. Nightclubs flourished, and they ranged from sleazy beer parlours with a live act or two to the fashionable Normandie Roof in the Mount Royal Hotel. Name acts appeared regularly in the better establishments—Edith Piaf, Charles Trenet, Milton Berle, Sophie Tucker, Sammy Davis, Jr., Dean Martin, and Jerry Lewis. Even Christine Jorgenson, the first person to undergo a sex-change operation, presented her act. As Weintraub points out in his delightful book *City Unique,* "Montreal had night clubs aplenty—fifteen of them in 1948, all with elaborate floor shows, plus about twenty-five smaller 'lounges,' with more modest entertainment.... These," he notes with some degree of understatement, "flourished without ecclesiastical approval."[57]

These, too, were the years of Oscar Peterson, playing his jazz numbers at the Alberta Lounge, next to Drury's Chop House on Dominion Square, where the Marriott Hotel now stands. Peterson was born in Saint Henri, a working-class district west of Windsor Station. His father, like so many other blacks, was a sleeping-car porter, but he was determined that his children should have a better life. The way out would be music, and Peterson and his brothers and sisters were taught to play instruments at an early age. I don't know about his siblings, but Oscar soon developed a taste for jazz, and by the time he was fourteen he won a nationwide contest on the Ken Soble Amateur Hour, broadcast from Montreal. My wife, Donna, and I are particularly proud of his achievement because Ken Soble was Donna's father, and he took great satisfaction in the fact that many of the contestants who appeared on his show, like Peterson, went on to fame. Donna and I attended a Peterson concert at Place des Arts during the Montreal Jazz Festival in 1995. We went to see him backstage after the event, and he and Donna shared a few nostalgic moments when they reminisced about her father and the Ken Soble Amateur Hour, which was carried on the CBC.

Montreal also had its share of lovable eccentrics. Reginald Plimsoll, QC, was the city's deputy fire commissioner, a sinecure conferred on him by his friend Maurice Duplessis in recognition of his services to the *Union nationale*. As Bill Tetley recalled in a memoir in 2006:

> Plimsoll was visible and recognizable from a mile away. Slim and six feet four inches tall, he always carried an elegant silver topped walking stick, wore a wing collar and hand-tied bow tie, a bowler hat, spats in winter and chequered woollen suits in bright, almost gaudy colours. He advised all and sundry that he had seven different such suits, one of which he wore each day, so that they never wore out. He solemnly counselled young lawyers to follow his example.[58]

I might add that Reggie, whom I got to know well, never wore an overcoat, and that his only concession to cold weather was a long scarf wrapped around his neck. He had a small office downtown, where he received a few clients, but neither his clientele nor his duties as deputy fire commissioner kept him from going for lunch at the Bodega in the basement of the Transportation Building on St. James Street at 11:00 most mornings, where he enjoyed a largely liquid fare. Well read and highly erudite, he was good company, and the "war stories" he told were legion.

From time to time Reggie would phone reporters from the city's major papers and invited them to come and cover a hearing in his court. Unlike other officials who made similar calls, it wasn't because he wanted publicity. Rather, the cases he chose often had titillating aspects, not infrequently of a prurient nature, which he thought his audience would enjoy. He died in 1963, and his funeral, held at St. Patrick's Church, was crowded with friends and admirers.

These also were the years when the "reformers," led by Jean Drapeau and his sidekick, Pacifique "Pax" Plante, set out to clean up the city. Plante, a lawyer like Drapeau, convinced the chief of police, Fernand Dufresne, to appoint him head of the Morality Squad. Henceforth, he said, police enforcement would be serious: gambling dens would be shut down, "blind pigs"—unlicensed drinking establishments—would be put out of business, and nightclubs would be forced to close at 2 a.m., as required by law, and not whenever they wanted. Brothels, which abounded, would no longer be tolerated. Plante also promised that when a court gave the order, as it could, to "padlock" premises that housed illegal establishments, padlocks would be placed on *all* doors, and not just on a side door, as was the custom. In all, an ambitious program, and Montrealers, although used to a more relaxed attitude, took these promises in stride. They didn't know Plante.

His first raid was on a gambling parlour and, for once, the actual owner was arrested. Usually an arrest would involve a "straw man" who was paid to undergo the ordeal of an arrest, with possibly a few days in jail after a quick plea of guilty. Of course, the press, notified by Plante, was there, and soon Plante's picture made a regular appearance in Montreal papers. At first, Plante would call the press after a raid. But later he would do so in advance, and I recall racing to a given address and arriving there in time to watch the Morality Squad enter the premises. It made for good stories and even better photographs.

As Weintraub notes, for many Montrealers, Plante was going too far, even closing church-hall bingos, which had the support of Archbishop Joseph Charbonneau. "Plante," it was said, was "destroying the city's reputation as an easygoing place where people could enjoy themselves."[59] But, within a year, Plante had achieved what professional police officers had been unable or unwilling to do. This made him many enemies, including the newly appointed director of police, Albert Langlois, who detested Plante's flamboyant ways. In 1948 three constables of the Morality Squad admitted that, "in the course of their duties," they had slept with prostitutes. Sleeping with prostitutes to make a case was contrary to strict orders given by Plante, but it gave Langlois the opportunity to suspend Plante from his duties, and Montreal soon returned to its old ways.

Plante, however, had the last laugh. The Superior Court granted a petition organized by Plante and Drapeau to investigate the city administration and, in particular, the police department. Justice François Caron was appointed to head the inquiry, dubbed the "Vice Probe." After thirty-one months of hearings, reported in great detail by the local press, he gave his decision on October 8, 1954. The largest court room in Montreal's *Palais de Justice* was filled to capacity. By then, I was an articling student in Joseph Cohen's office. Cohen, who represented Director Langlois, was occupied in another room, so he asked me to be there and take notes. My friend Billy Wardwell, the *Herald*'s leading crime reporter, was there and, to do me a favour—good publicity never hurt—put my name on the paper's front page as representing the director. Of course, had anyone checked up on this, they would have discovered that I wasn't even a member of the Bar at the time!

Caron's findings devastated the police high command. Director Langlois was dismissed from his post; the former director (who had appointed Plante) was fined $7,000; seventeen police officers, some retired, others still active, were fined. The "reformers" had won, and the new spirit soon swept Jean Drapeau into the mayor's chair. Plante was appointed director of police. Gambling was no longer the city's second-largest industry, right behind the manufacture of women's apparel, the *schmatte* business. The city now was "clean," but it was also much less interesting.

A lot of fine people worked on the city's many papers. Writers like Brian Moore, Mavis Gallant and Bill Weintraub, all of whom were to achieve great success as authors, were toiling away at the *Star,* the *Standard,* the *Herald,* and the *Gazette.* And many others were terrific reporters who knew how to hold the reader's attention. Who, for instance, could resist reading a story, written by Bill Bantey in the *Gazette,* which reported the slaying of a local gangster who had been acquitted of murder just a few hours before? This was the lead paragraph: "The underworld's court of appeal today reversed the verdict of Mr. Justice Lazure and a jury ..."

Of the city's English-language papers, the *Herald,* a tabloid that was snapped up by the downtown lunchtime crowd, was the most daring. Stories that neither the *Star* nor the *Gazette* would have touched could be found in the *Herald,* short but accurate and written with verve. Longer stories, again deemed unsuitable for the *Star* and the *Gazette,* could often be found in the weekend *Standard,* written by reporters from other papers anxious to find an outlet for stories that they had found and that they knew would not be used by their own editors. Wally Rayburn, Gerry Clarke, Stan Handman, and a few others ran the *Standard,* and their doors were always open for reporters with ideas for stories. Their own staff—people, for instance, like Jackie Sirois, their star reporter—were often deployed to do in-depth reporting, and the paper was a good weekend read.

◆◆◆

I left the *Star* in 1954, and as I look back on some old clippings from my years with the paper, I am struck by the enormous variety of stories I covered. In 1947, for instance, the only year when I kept track,[60] I attended nineteen banquets, each featuring three or more speakers. At fourteen of them the menu consisted of chicken, mashed potatoes, green peas, and apple pie with ice cream. Eight speakers said that they "only [had] a word to say" and then took fifteen minutes to say it. Six others took ten minutes each to introduce a speaker "who needs no introduction," and two told the old chestnut—remember this was 1947—that their address would be like a woman's skirt: long enough to cover the subject, but short enough to be interesting.

That same year, which was my first full year with the *Star,* I covered twenty-four funerals; fifteen annual meetings of societies (learned and otherwise); a rabbit show, a dog show, and a horse show; and eight protest rallies, six against the price of milk, one against the price of bread, and one against everything. I shook hands with the man who won $100,000 in the Irish sweepstakes, and I interviewed the woman who had lost her life savings on a crowded tram. Assignments also helped me widen my horizons. In one month, for instance, I covered meetings of the Anglican Synod of Montreal, the Montreal–Ottawa Conference of the United Church of Canada, the Central Conference of American Rabbis, and the Summer School of Catholic Action at Loyola College. On the political side, I attended twelve meetings. Six featured Conservative speakers, two were sponsored by the Labour-Progressive Party, two were socialist rallies, one was a Liberal affair, and one was all-inclusive—in French, an *assemblée contradictoire*—with speakers from three parties on the platform. Floods kept me occupied three days, storms two days, squatters four days, and elections another four days. I was thrown out of a meeting once, threatened twice ("If you don't leave on your own, we'll do it for you"), and subjected to primitive forms of attempted intimidation ("If you print this we'll stop advertising in the *Star*") at least half a dozen times.

Of course, more often than not, each story had to be researched and written hastily, in time for a deadline, and all were exposed to the scrutiny of an inquisitive and often critical public. Yet, as I look back, many of these articles were pithy, most were accurate, and all were readable. I loved being a reporter, and it was wonderful training for my later careers.

[8]
The Asbestos Strike

The strike began on February 13, 1949. Collective bargaining had brought no solution, and Jean Marchand, secretary general of the Canadian and Catholic Confederation of Labour, told the miners at the Canadian Johns-Manville plant in Asbestos that only two options remained: submit to arbitration, as provided by provincial labour laws, or strike. A strike, however, would be illegal, and he urged the men, who clearly favoured this action, to give him forty-eight hours to meet with the minister of labour. This was refused, and as midnight approached, groups of workers left the church hall where the meeting was held to notify the night shift that a strike had been called. Why the reluctance to follow the law? The short answer is that the union had no faith in the process: arbitration had been tried once before and the chairman of the tribunal had endorsed the company's position without considering the arguments advanced by the union. This was Maurice Duplessis's Quebec.

Much has been written about the Asbestos strike of 1949. It lasted eighteen weeks, and by the time the 5,000 miners returned to work in the asbestos mines in Quebec's Eastern Townships, the face of the union movement in French Canada had changed forever. The workers, who wanted better conditions, higher pay, and certain fringe benefits, didn't get what they asked for but, in the words of Jean-C. Falardeau, head of the department of sociology at the Université de Laval in Quebec, the strike marked the movement's coming of age in the province. The leaders realized that their demands could no longer be stated in abstract, theoretical language, as they had in the past, but must be put *en termes concrets, en termes économiques et en termes d'une morale entendue au sens dynamique*.[61] This *dynamisme* was something new, and no one quite knew how to deal with it.

Picket lines were quickly set up, but maintenance workers were given special passes and permitted to remain at their posts. The company's general manager, however, was refused entry and his wife was told "to take good care of him," which she interpreted as a threat. The following day, the Asbestos town council authorized the chief of police to swear in special constables to help maintain order, but as an observer pointed out, there was an atmosphere of great calm throughout the town. Miners in other asbestos companies soon joined their colleagues at Johns-Manville, and by nightfall on February 15 the strike had spread to all but three mines.

The provincial government quickly condemned the strike. It offered to set up an arbitration board, but only if the workers returned to their jobs. It also threatened to "invite" the Labour Relations Board to decertify the union—no idle threat, since in the heyday of the Duplessis regime the board's independence was quite illusory.

Montreal's English press did not pay much attention to the strike in the beginning. Neither the *Star* nor the *Gazette* was good at reporting labour relations, and whatever stories appeared, mostly by way of Canadian Press, lacked depth and were devoid of serious analysis. It was only when the strike turned ugly that reporters were sent to the scene. Gèrard Pelletier, in a chapter entitled *La grève et la presse,* which he contributed to a book on the strike edited by Pierre Elliott Trudeau (then a law professor), describes this situation in his usual eloquent style. The *Gazette,* he wrote, was an English newspaper, directed to an English-speaking population, and this implied a certain distance, a certain superior tone, as well as an ignorance of the facts, told with much elegance. It was an accurate assessment, and the *Star* didn't do much better.

I was sent to Asbestos some time in mid-April "to see what's going on." The reason I was chosen was not because I had any expertise in labour matters, but rather because I knew the Eastern Townships well. I am not sure how this was supposed to help—others much better qualified could have found out how to get there—the decision to send me to Asbestos showed the lack of real interest by the owners and editors in covering a major story that turned out to be a pivotal event in Quebec's history.

In looking back on those events more than sixty years later, I realize how woefully inadequate my preparation was for this assignment. I know that I attempted to be fair, but good intentions are not enough, and I fear that the *Star*'s readers did not always get a balanced picture. This was exacerbated by the fact that union officials were not readily available for comment, while the companies' public-relations departments worked overtime. And, as Pelletier quite rightly pointed out in his essay, my reports were *assez ternes*, which, loosely translated, means "flat"—a fact that he ascribed, again quite rightly, to my lack at the time of fluency in French. At least, unlike other reporters whom he singled out, he didn't find bias, and I am content with this judgment.

Things heated up quickly as the strike progressed, and soon I spent more time in Asbestos than in Montreal. The pot was boiling, acts of violence were reported, and more police were sent in. This, in turn, fuelled the anger of the strikers and their families, and a vicious circle began. By early May, 2,000 strikers had virtually taken over the town, and police were said to number between 800 and 900, a gross exaggeration as it later turned out. Barricades were set up by strikers on all roads leading into the town, and almost all who tried to enter were turned back.

On May 4 I managed to negotiate a "clearance," and Doug Allen, a *Star* photographer, and I were allowed to pass through the barricade. But the excursion was short lived. Within minutes we were stopped by a large group of strikers armed with rocks, bats, and crowbars. Common sense dictated that we retreat, and we tried, but even before we could turn around, someone smashed the window on my side of the car, grabbed my glasses, and broke them in half. While this was happening on my side—I was the driver—Doug tried to reason with a group of men on his side, but his arguments came to an abrupt end when he was threatened with a crowbar. I finally managed to extricate us from the crowd and, badly shaken, we turned around and left.

By the next day, it was clear the police had lost control of the town, and the decision was made to take it by storm if necessary. Reinforcements from all parts of the province were ordered to converge on Sherbrooke, some forty miles from Asbestos, where a command post was set up in the court house on Wellington Street. By midnight, Norbert Labbé, the inspector general of the Quebec Provincial Police, briefed his men—"I don't want trouble," he said, "but if you're attacked you know what to do." As hundreds of curious citizens watched, a convoy of forty cars and a bus, with Allen and myself in the middle, left for Asbestos.

The parish priest (and union's chaplain), Father Camirand, convinced the men to leave the barricades. "You've done a good day's work," he told them, "now go home and rest." It was good advice: the police had tear gas and some submachine guns, and their mood was angry, since some of their colleagues had been roughed up by strikers.

By the time we reached Asbestos, the chaplain's advice had been heeded, but the mood was still ugly, and isolated outbreaks of violence fuelled rumours of a mass attack on the police. When a raid on the parish hall yielded a cache of crowbars, blackjacks, rubber hoses, and stones, the civil authorities, encouraged, I suspect, by the police, decided that sterner measures were needed. They convinced a justice of the peace that the strikers who had fled to the street when the police arrived at the church were, in the words of the Criminal Code, "unlawfully and riotously assembled together." Moments later, Hertel O'Brady, a very nervous justice of the peace from Sherbrooke, pushed his way through the crowd, mounted the steps of the church, commanded silence, and read, in French and in English, the words of the Riot Act:

> His Majesty the King charges and commands all persons being assembled immediately to disperse and peaceably to depart to their habitations or to their lawful business on the pain of being guilty of an offence for which, on conviction, they may be sentenced to imprisonment for life. GOD SAVE THE KING.[62]

There was a stunned silence, but the crowd did disperse, although some arrests were made later in the day.

The strike was settled a short time later, with negligible gains for the workers, but the trials arising from the events dragged on until the following year. I was assigned by the *Star* to cover the cases, and I became quite friendly with the lawyers involved. The defence was led by Alexandre Chevalier, a prominent Montreal criminal lawyer. His principal assistant was Jean Drapeau, an ambitious young attorney of eight or nine years' standing at the Bar.

In those days, the trip from Montreal to Sherbrooke took close to three hours—it now takes less than two on the Eastern Townships Autoroute—but Chevalier and Drapeau decided to commute and they invited me to join them, which I did most days. I learned a lot of strategy during those rides, since they spoke freely in my presence. They were assisted on occasion by a rising local lawyer, Carrier Fortin, who had practised law in Asbestos before moving to Sherbrooke.

The crown was led by special counsel Noël Dorion, assisted by Redmond Hayes, a crown attorney in Sherbrooke. Hayes, a bachelor, lived in the New Sherbrooke Hotel, and he was quite accessible to the press late afternoons and evenings, either in court or in the lobby of the hotel. I knew Hayes from my days in Sherbrooke, and he frequently told me in advance of the moves the crown was planning. Because I knew from my travel companions what the defence intended to do, this made me the proverbial "fly on the wall," and I tried to foresee how each side might respond to the other. It was a great game, played out in my mind, and it taught me long before law school that the work of trial lawyers involves a lot more than just "making your case."

One of the leaders of the strike was convicted of conspiracy by a jury in Sherbrooke and sentenced to a term of imprisonment. Others were found guilty of minor offences, but by the time the final case was heard, tempers had cooled, feelings had abated, and everyone was glad to close the book. Chevalier continued his legal career until illness forced him to retire. He was witty, wily, bright, and fast, and enormously successful with juries. Drapeau, as already recounted, made his name a short time later when he and a friend, Pacifique Plante, launched a crusade to "clean up" City Hall in Montreal. He ran for mayor in 1954, won easily, and held the post, with one interruption, until 1986. Fortin, a conscientious worker and a decent man, entered politics and served a term as minister of labour in the provincial cabinet. In 1969 he became a judge of the Superior Court. Nöel Dorion, too, entered politics and became secretary of state in one of the Diefenbaker cabinets. Soon after the Asbestos trials, Hayes became a judge of the Court of Sessions of the Peace, with Sherbrooke as his base.

As I said before, the Asbestos strike was a pivotal event in Quebec's history. It brought the labour movement into modern times, it launched the political careers of the "three wise men"—Marchand, Pelletier, and Trudeau (who had gone to Asbestos to support the strikers)—and it caused a crack, ever so slight, in Maurice Duplessis's hold on the province.

[9]
Law School

My favourite pastime is reading—newspapers, magazines, journals, and books of all kinds. I read quickly, and I retain most of what I've read (especially trivia, according to my children). My tastes are wide, but I do have preferences that change from time to time. It so happened that in the late 1940s I was deep into legal biographies, and the lives of two English barristers had a profound influence on my future career.[63]

Patrick Hastings and Rufus Isaacs represented the finest standards of the English Bar, and I devoured not only their biographies but also books about their famous cases and transcripts of the evidence in the British Notable Trial Series. This brought me some familiarity with the lives of other legal giants of the late nineteenth and early twentieth century. Soon I had read all the major works on the subject, but Hastings and Isaacs remained my favourites and I was greatly inspired by what they achieved.

By then I had started to cover, on an occasional basis, the "legal beat" and this, too, had its influence. Many a day I listened in awe to the great advocates in the criminal courts in Montreal: Lucien Gendron, Joe Cohen, John Crankshaw, Alex Chevalier. Each had his own style, each could spellbind a jury, and each loved the law. The seed was planted.

I first looked into attending law school in 1949 or 1950. The news was not encouraging. To be called to the Bar of Quebec required not only three years of full-time study at a Quebec law school, plus a year for Bar admission classes, but also, as the law then stood, a Bachelor of Arts degree with at least three courses in philosophy, earned *before* starting law school. These were daunting obstacles. I had a B.Sc., not a B.A., and this was unacceptable to the Bar; nor did I have the needed credits in philosophy. Above all, I didn't have enough money to quit my job and become a full-time student. So I couldn't pursue my dream. But the idea became an obsession and in 1951 I tried again. By then, McGill had a new dean of law, W.C.J. Meredith, who had left a lucrative litigation practice to accept the position. Meredith was an active supporter of Bishop's and a member of the university's executive committee (which many years later I was to chair). Since I covered Bishop's for the *Star*, I knew him well, so in late August I made an appointment to ask for his advice.

We had a good meeting and covered all bases. It wouldn't be easy, he said, but since McGill regulations allowed the faculty of law to accept students after two years of undergraduate studies, the absence of a B.A. would not be an obstacle. Admission to the Bar, however, was quite another matter. He probed extensively into my reasons for seeking a career in law at age thirty-two, which I would be by the time I had completed my studies, and that, in those days, was considered a very late start: was it a whim or genuine desire? We concluded by saying that we would each sleep on it.

Early the next day the phone rang. It was the dean and his message was brief: if I still wanted it, I was in. Since classes were scheduled to start the following week, would I please see his secretary to sign an application form. I was thrilled, took a street car from St. James Street to St. Catherine and Peel, and then ran all the way up Peel Street to the Faculty of Law before Dean Meredith could change his mind.

If this sounds extraordinary, it was. Of course, law school admission tests and similar current means of screening didn't exist in the fifties, but even then it was customary to apply early in the year with appropriate letters of reference and fully documented transcripts. I had none of these, and as I look back on those hectic few days, I realize just how far Meredith went out of his way to accommodate me.

Later that day I wrote a letter to A.J. West, the *Star's* executive editor, resigning my job. He called me in and asked if my decision was firm. I said it was, and he said he was sorry to see me leave. We shook hands and as I turned to go he said: "Well, if your mind's made up, good luck. And if you'd like a part-time job we'll work it out." And so we did: for the next three years I worked at the *Star* summers and every Saturday and sometimes on Sundays as well.

The next thing on my list of things to do was to get a B.A. so that I could, in due course, be called to the Bar. I first wrote to the principal at Bishop's and asked him if I could trade my B.Sc. for a B.A. since a math major, as mine had been, could have been taken in either stream. He wrote back to say that this was the most preposterous request he had ever received and that the answer was "no." I then went to Sir George Williams College (now part of Concordia University in Montreal) and enquired about part-time studies. The registrar evaluated my transcript and said it would take two and a half years to complete the necessary requirements. Too long, I thought.

Fortunately, I remembered that the Thomas More Institute for Adult Education, which had been founded a few years before, had recently been accredited by the Université de Montréal as an affiliate college. This meant that a student who completed the Institute's required course of study would be granted a B.A. by the university. I made an appointment to see Charlotte Tansey, the registrar, who listened to my story sympathetically. Together, we then saw the director of studies, Father Eric O'Connor, a Jesuit who taught mathematics at Montreal's Loyola College. He, too, was most understanding, and when all the calculations were made, he and Charlotte decided that if I were to take the maximum number of courses allowed each year—four full evenings a week—I could complete all but one course in two years. That one course, however, posed a problem, since in those early days Thomas More offered no classes in the summer, and this would have meant an extra semester, with an arts degree in 1954 rather than a year before.

This year was critical since the Bar insisted that candidates for admission who got their B.A. *after* enrolling in law school could not practise for a specified period of time—at least six months, but often longer—after passing their Bar exams. Therefore, a year's delay for my degree might well have meant an extra year before my call to the Bar, a luxury I couldn't afford.

Father O'Connor and Charlotte both felt that this was unfair and so a scheme was hatched. A course in "English expression" was a must for all students. However, if I were to submit a letter from the editor-in-chief of the *Montreal Star* saying that I was proficient in the subject, they would waive this requirement and I could have my BA in two years. I was delighted and quite overwhelmed by the generosity of these two kind and understanding human beings. (I am proud to say that I am still associated with the Institute, most recently as a member of the board of governors.) The letter wasn't hard to get. I went to see the *Star's* editor-in-chief, George Ferguson, told him what I needed, and then followed his instructions and drafted the letter myself. It was a good letter and it did the trick. Two years later I had the requisite B.A., with three courses in philosophy as required by the Bar.

A funny thing happened at graduation from Thomas More. The class was small, just twelve students, and we were told to wait in the wings of the D'Arcy

McGee High School auditorium until each name was called. While I waited, the other eleven were called and received their degrees, and the next thing I heard was the voice of Father Emmett Carter, the Institute's president (and the future cardinal archbishop of Toronto), who began to read his annual report to convocation. I had worked much too hard to worry about protocol. So I walked out and slowly advanced to the front of the stage. The audience was a little bewildered by this, and Father Carter soon perceived that something had gone awry. He stopped his speech, turned around, and quickly realized that someone had skipped my name on the list. But he was up to the situation. Without missing a beat, he told the assembly that this oversight was unfortunate not only for me but also for the Institute, whose success depended to a large extent on publicity in the Montreal media. "What a P.R. disaster," he said, "the one person with all the 'right' contacts is left out. We'll have to do better than that." He then led me to the seat of Paul-Emile Cardinal Léger, the archbishop of Montreal and chancellor of the Université de Montréal, who conferred on me the degree of Bachelor of Arts. I have a lovely souvenir of the occasion, a photograph of me shaking hands with a very amused cardinal, with an equally amused Emmett Carter looking on. I later had the picture autographed by the two cardinals and it is one of my prized possessions.

I had another lucky break in 1952. I had been doing some freelance work for the Canadian weekly *Saturday Night*, but a change in direction brought about a change of personnel and I received a polite letter from the editor-in-chief informing me that my services would no longer be required. This was a blow to me since the work had given me a small but regular income. That evening, on my way home, I decided to stop for a beer at the Montreal Men's Press Club in the basement of the old Laurentian Hotel at the corner of Dorchester and Peel. It was a good place to meet friends and catch up with gossip.

I joined Jim Conant, the bureau chief for *Time* and *Life* in Montreal, who told me that he was overrun with work and in need of a stringer. "Too bad," he said, "that you're tied up with *Saturday Night* or the job would be yours." I couldn't quite believe my ears and I quickly told Jim that I had been fired earlier that day. He hired me on the spot and I started with *Time* and *Life* (and later *Sports Illustrated* as well) a few days later—an association that would last until I was called to the Bar in 1955. It was a happy, fruitful, and lucrative relationship.

We had a conference call with the editors in New York and other *Time* correspondents in Canada every Monday morning at 10. Suggestions for stories, which had been submitted over the weekend, were discussed. Some were accepted, others rejected summarily. Since Jim travelled a lot, I frequently took these calls in our office in the Sun Life building. To get there in time from my 9:00 class at law school, I had a taxi waiting for me to drive me down the few blocks to Dominion Square. I never missed a call, and I derived great pleasure from suggestions that made it into print. Of course, what actually appeared did not necessarily bear much resemblance to what I wrote, but the way it worked was that correspondents in the field would write reams of material about the subject and send it by teletype to New York. There, a large and well-trained research staff would get to work to check the facts and, quite frequently, add additional material. This would then go to the writer, who condensed it into one or two columns, all written in *Time* style. For instance, during that period, obituaries almost always said something like this: "Death came, as it must to all men, to John Smith."

A number of assignments stand out in my mind. I had an early interview with Maureen Forrester, not yet famous but clearly an artist on the way up. The meeting was arranged by a friend, and Maureen and I met in an apartment in lower Notre-Dame-de-Grâce. She offered to sing for me, which she did beautifully, and what I wrote reflected the great impression that this unassuming and so clearly talented young woman made on me. The story made it into print, and I was told later that it was the first major recognition by the media of this great Canadian star.

On another occasion, *Life* asked me to assist one of their renowned photographers, the late Carl Mydan, to prepare a Christmas cover for the magazine. Carl had heard that a European marionetteer was in Montreal, and we arranged for a private performance at which he took stills. They were all beautiful, but one was outstanding and it made a wonderful cover.

When Emilie Dionne, one of the famous quintuplets, died in 1954 of an epileptic seizure, the editors in New York were on the phone within minutes. I was at the *Star* when the news came in mid-afternoon, less than ten minutes before the final deadline. All the bulletin said was that Emilie had died in her home in the Laurentians. I sat down and wrote from memory a story that made it to page one. It put Emilie's death into context—the long and sad saga of five little girls removed from their parents and put on display in a virtual theme park called Quintland.

As soon as I finished this task, I jumped in a staff car and drove to the funeral home in the Laurentians that was in charge of the arrangements. My task for *Life* was to try to get a picture of the surviving quints looking at the remains of their dead sister. I was authorized to spend $1,000—more than $10,000 in today's money—to try to achieve this, but I must say that my heart wasn't in it, and in any case not all of Emilie's sisters were there.

I had one other part-time job: Montreal correspondent for *The New York Times*. I was paid $2.00 for each inch of print, and the trick was to write stories in such a way that they couldn't be cut by the editors. This was a delicate operation, since a story that was judged too long might be dropped altogether, leaving me without compensation for my efforts. I soon developed a two-pronged strategy: write important stories of medium length (six to ten inches), which were likely to be published and unlikely to be cut (too much trouble), and write relatively unimportant stories of an inch or two. They made good fillers and required little effort on my part. The *Times* loved stories like that, and I was good at finding them. For example, a magistrate who had been tough on speeders died in Saint-Jerôme, the gateway to the Laurentians. One might well ask of what possible interest this event could be to New Yorkers. The uninitiated would say none. But those who are paid by the inch know better, and so I sent a few lines to the *Times*: "Eugene Lafontaine, remembered by many American tourists for imposing heavy fines for speeding on the Laurentian highway, died today after a short illness." It wasn't quite an inch, but with its American slant it ran and I collected $2—enough to buy a decent dinner in those days.

As I look back on those years, I sometimes wonder if, knowing what I know today, I would do it all over again. The answer is yes, absolutely. It was interesting, it helped me enormously, and, more often than not, it was fun. True, I rarely got enough sleep, no moment was ever wasted, and I certainly didn't have an active social life. Law school during the day, B.A. classes at night, and a job in between didn't leave time for much else, which was just as well since I couldn't afford anything except an occasional movie. Still, my three part-time jobs gave me an adequate income and every day brought me that much nearer to my goal.

◆ ◆ ◆

In the 1950s, the Bar laid down the curriculum and every law school in the province taught the same subjects. There was no choice; everyone took everything. This has now changed, and I sometimes wonder if the pendulum hasn't swung too far. I am all for having electives, but not when core subjects are dropped to make time for more esoteric studies.

I never skipped classes and always took good notes. I also had the benefit— as did everyone else in my class—of Joe O'Brien's transcription service. Joe was proficient in shorthand and each week he produced a complete set of mimeographed notes. The price was $5.00 a month, which doesn't sound like much today, but in 1952 a double feature at a neighbourhood theatre cost thirty-five cents. Joe died in 1996. His contribution to the class of '54 was recognized by his colleagues and friends, who donated a games table to the Faculty of Law. It stands in the common room and bears a plaque that says: "In memory of Joseph E. O'Brien, without whose notes B.C.L. '54 might not have existed." It is a fitting tribute.

My friend and classmate Dave Kirshenblatt, who worked for British United Press while going to school, also took good notes, and every weekend he and I would prepare a set of typewritten notes for each course, which served us well at exam time. This method had the advantage of giving us a weekly review of the work, and nothing went into the typewritten set unless we thought we understood it. With Joe's notes as a backstop, we overlooked little.

Dave and I did most of our work on weekends, often late into the night. We lived close to each other so we didn't have to waste much time on travel. Neither of us had a car when we started—newspaper salaries didn't permit this luxury—but during our first year at McGill we convinced ourselves that streetcars and buses were inefficient and that an automobile would solve all our problems. We looked for something inexpensive and finally found an ancient and well-used four-cylinder Austin for $275. It was small, it didn't have much power, and in the winter it often wouldn't start, but as proud owners of an automobile, we felt we had come up in the world.

We devised a system in which each of us had the car for three days a week—the days were negotiable—but since both of us wanted it on Saturday night, our one free evening, we decided that the only equitable solution was to double-date. This still left the question of whose date was taken home first. Or, to put it into a better perspective, who had the car with his date last. But that, too, we settled on an amicable basis. We had the "Green Hornet," as we called it, for three years and when we sold it we got almost as much as we paid for it.

Law school in the 1950s was a far cry from what it is today. The largest classroom at McGill had ninety seats, with room for another ten or so on the windowsills. Since the rule was that ten to fifteen students wouldn't survive the Christmas exams, and that two out of three would not make it into second year, the shortage of seats for the first few weeks was not of major concern. My class—the class of '54—is a good example. We were ninety-six on the first day of school. By January, we were down to eighty-five, and by the end of the year this number had been cut in half. Thirty-five made it to graduation. The old saw—look to the right and look to the left; two of you won't be here next year—was perfectly true. It was a scary prospect.

Christmas exams in first year were orals. Five or six students at a time were invited to a professor's office and told to sit on chairs facing the dean and two or three professors, who put forth a series of questions on subjects taught up to that point. We sat in alphabetical order and I was the first in line in my group. Professor Stuart LeMesurier, who taught criminal law, asked me about the legal significance of the trial of Queen Caroline.[64] I had read the case a few days before, but I couldn't recall the point in issue—a piece of legal minutia unlikely ever to occur in modern practice.[65] I did, however, remember most of the details surrounding the trial, so I began by telling the dean and his colleagues that this was a major state trial, that it took place in the Palace of Westminster, that the lord high chancellor presided, with all the lords spiritual and temporal in attendance—I was stalling for time—and that it occurred in 1820. I also recalled that most of the evidence concerned allegations of adultery committed by Caroline, while Princess of Wales, in a tent on the deck of a steamer that travelled from Jaffa to the continent. Her lover's name was Bergami, an Italian count, then in her service. And that's as far as I got, although, had I needed more time, I could have added more of the prurient details, most of which were still clear in my mind. But at that point, the dean, clearly impressed by what he took to be my thorough knowledge of the case, said, "Excellent, excellent, now will the next student please tell us what the court held." I got a dirty look from my neighbour, who didn't know much more than I, but both of us passed that first test with distinction.

The faculty in those days was small, perhaps eight or ten permanent professors and a dozen or so downtown practitioners who came in for two or three hours a week to teach the more practice-oriented subjects. The most exciting lecturer was Frank Scott, the great constitutional lawyer, who held the class spellbound with stories of past battles fought in the Judicial Committee of the Privy Council in London, which at the time was Canada's final Court of Appeal. Scott, a leading socialist, was the co-author, with David Lewis, of *Make This YOUR Canada*,[66] a blueprint for Canada's economy should the Co-operative Commonwealth Federation (CCF)—the forerunner of today's New Democratic Party—ever gain power. He was highly irreverent, particularly when it came to the law lords in England. In his view, they misunderstood the nature of Canadian federalism, and he ridiculed many of their decisions, maintaining that they gradually eroded the power of the central government. Students loved him, and he was by far the most popular teacher.

He also was a great poet, and an anthology of his poems was published in 1981.[67] But what we liked best were his one-liners. For instance, when he returned from the Supreme Court of Canada where he had successfully argued that *Lady Chatterly's Lover* was not obscene,[68] the students organized an impromptu party to celebrate his victory. When he got up to speak, he said: "I went to bat for Lady Chat." When my former partners sent him birthday greetings one year, they said, "Best wishes, Yarosky and Fishes." He replied: "Thanks a lot, F.R. Scott."

On occasion, Scott asked Bora Laskin to replace him. Laskin's teaching style was similar to Scott's and his lectures were stimulating and highly informative. Laskin and I became good friends many years later, and I recall a memorable dinner at our home when our guests were the Laskins—he had become chief justice of Canada by then—the Scotts; Lynn and Alan Gold, a future chief justice of the Superior Court; and Senator H. Carl Goldenberg and his wife, Shirley. All were old friends, and all had played a major role in Canada's evolving constitution.[69] As it turned out, Scott, quite ill at the time, hadn't seen Laskin for many years and they had an emotional reunion. Our children, still young, passed nuts before dinner, and while they did not then appreciate the impact these giants of the law had on the country, they did so in later years when they pursued their legal studies.

◆ ◆ ◆

As I said earlier, the Bar was difficult for people who hadn't followed the regular stream, and those with late B.A.s were heavily penalized. This policy, happily long since abandoned, seems as absurd today as it did then. But since the Bar Act laid down the requirement, only an act of the provincial legislature could cure the deficiency, and that was the last obstacle to be overcome.

I was told to consult Charles Coderre, the Bar's popular secretary-treasurer, who was always ready to help students. He told me that nine others (with B.Com.s and B.Sc.s) were in the same position that year, and he gave each of us the list of names with the suggestion that we get together and make a joint application to the Legislative Assembly for a private bill to facilitate our admission to the Bar. There had been private bills before, but never a joint one, and there was great concern about how the Council of the Bar would react. On the other hand, with ten people sharing the cost, we could afford to hire an experienced and well-connected lawyer, and we chose Mark Drouin, a prominent Quebec attorney and speaker of the Senate of Canada. Drouin was wise in the ways of the legislature and he undertook to guide the bill through its various stages. His fee was $2,000, a big sum at the time.

It was customary to write a clause into such bills for a voluntary delay of six months before entering practice. In the past, the Bar had been satisfied with this undertaking—a penalty in everything but name for flaunting the Bar Act's inflexible rule about B.A.s and courses in philosophy. Drouin thought the whole idea was ludicrous, but he advised us to follow the custom and so we did.

However, lobbying was not a prohibited activity, and by the time the bill reached the Private Bills Committee of the House, Premier Maurice Duplessis, Attorney General Antoine Rivard, and Minister of Labour Antonio Barrette were fully briefed on the matter. Why the minister of labour? The answer is simple: he was a friend of Phil Cutler, one of the group, who had been a successful union organizer before his career at the Bar. Phil explained the matter to Barrette and Barrette briefed Duplessis and Rivard. Others, I discovered later, including Maurice Jacques, a future colleague of mine, had also lobbied hard.

Our worst fears were realized when the bill was called and the chairman of the committee asked if anyone opposed it. Achille Pettigrew, counsel briefed by the Bar, rose to say that his clients did. When asked why, he replied that the Bar was concerned about the ever-increasing number of candidates who sought admission by way of private bills. At this point, Duplessis, who sat next to the chairman and effectively controlled the proceedings, cut in and told the hapless lawyer that the Bar ought to be ashamed of itself for trying to block ten hard-working and outstanding students from practising their chosen profession. That was the end of the Bar's opposition and the bill was referred to the House for second reading and approval in principle.

But it got even better than that, and when the bill was read the second time, Rivard asked the bill's sponsor why there was to be a delay of six months before entering practice. Told that this was the custom, he snorted and moved that the clause be struck, which it was without dissent.[70] Many years later, when I became a judge of the Court of Appeal, Rivard, by then a senior member of the court, graciously welcomed me to the bench.

The last hurdle had been cleared and I could now concentrate on my Bar admission course. The system then in force—it changed every year or two, and still does—required students to spend mornings with a law firm in fulfillment of their *stage* (their articles) and then attend lectures in the afternoon, which were given at McGill. Some classes were useful, others were not, but attendance was compulsory, so everyone was there, at least in person if not in spirit. One of the courses was accountancy, which could have been interesting, but a lecturer had been recruited at the last moment to fill a sudden vacancy and he was deadly dull. He carefully prepared his lectures, then put it all on index cards and read them to the class, one by one, without any further comment or elucidation.

Dealing with him was a challenge for his students, and so a plot was hatched. One day, in the middle of the lecture, a messenger came in and told the lecturer that there was an urgent phone call for him. He excused himself and went out, making the fatal mistake of leaving the cards on the table. As soon as he was gone, a bold spirit went up to the desk and shuffled the cards. When the poor man came back—the call had been a ruse—he started to read where he thought he had left off. Of course, it made no sense and he quickly realized what had happened. Without saying a word he put the cards in his pocket and walked out. We never saw him again.

I finished the Bar admission course in April 1955. It was, perhaps, a reflection of my relief that the end was in sight that I did so well in the course that I stood first and got the gold medal. But Bar exams still had to be written, a 15-hour ordeal spread out over two and a half days. These were closed-book exams and all the major articles of the Quebec Civil Code and the Code of Civil Procedure had to be memorized. In those days, one could always recognize law students: they went nowhere without their codes, and their spouses, partners, or dates in the weeks preceding exams were quite used to spending evenings and weekend, asking questions like "List fourteen ways to extinguish an obligation."

We wrote the exams during a heat wave in June in the Arthur Currie Gymnasium at McGill. There was no air conditioning and the windows were shut to keep out the noise of the traffic on Pine Avenue. The temperature soon reached 100 degrees Fahrenheit. It was sheer torture, but when the results were posted a week later on the doors of the Old Court House, my name was on the list of those who had passed.

On June 25, 1955, I paid my fees and was called to the Bar in the presence of my parents, who had come from New York to be with me on that memorable occasion.

I had climbed a steep hill. But, as with the mountaineer who reaches the crest of Mount Everest, exhaustion quickly gave way to exhilaration and joy. I had achieved my goal and I was ready for a new beginning.

[10]

A New Career

There was a strong feeling at McGill in the 1950s that lawyers should develop their writing skills while still at law school. Therefore, as part of the course, each student had to write a mini-thesis on a topic assigned by the dean. However, permission could be requested to write on a different subject, provided a member of the faculty agreed to supervise the project. I had done well in criminal law—in fact, I got the prize for standing first in the subject—and I decided to approach Joseph Cohen, the legendary Montreal criminal lawyer, who had taught me criminal procedure and evidence. The topic I proposed was "The Admissibility of Confessions," and Cohen agreed to be my supervisor.

This was a "hot" subject, and despite the fact that judges had to deal with it daily, no book had ever been written in Canada on this specific topic. As a student, I wasn't particularly aware of the gap, but my good friend Harold Poitras, who had covered the courts for the *Montreal Star* for decades, suggested I tackle the issue. Harold encouraged me in every way, and when I graduated he presented me with the autobiography of a great American preacher, Rabbi Stephen Wise, with an inscription that read: "To my friend Fred Kaufman (Q.C.), meaning quite courageous." It was a much appreciated gesture. Harold's older son Lawrence (Larry) took up law a short time later, and for a couple of years he and I ran the *Star*'s city desk on Saturday mornings while we were both in law school. Not only did Larry become a distinguished lawyer, but also his father lived to see him appointed to the Superior Court of Quebec. Larry later became the court's popular and efficient chief justice, and I know what great joy this would have given Harold.

I put a lot of work into my thesis, and my supervisor was sufficiently impressed by the finished product that he gave me a very good mark. This encouraged me to ask if I could article with his small firm even though I knew the odds were against me because he had never before hired a student. When I first broached the subject, Joe was quite noncommittal. "Let's think about it," he said, but the tone of his voice suggested that he wasn't going to think very hard. I was surprised by this because we had worked well together on the thesis and I knew he needed help in his office.

Despite Joe's lukewarm reaction, I tried again, and this time he said, "Let me tell you a few facts of life." I had no idea what was coming, but I soon found out that his reluctance to hire me was based on his belief that I wasn't Jewish—the subject had never come up—and he felt that in the mid-1950s in Montreal even an early association with a Jewish lawyer might harm my later career. I put him straight on that and he hired me on the spot.

Joe's concerns may sound far-fetched today, but the legal profession in Quebec in those days had three solitudes, French, English, and Jewish, and while there was some crossover between the French and English sectors, neither was prepared to hire Jewish lawyers. The result was that a disproportionate number of Jews became sole practitioners, often in "boutique" fields such as bankruptcy, divorce, and criminal law. This also accounts for the emergence of all-Jewish law firms, a phenomenon that lasted well into the 1960s. Many "reasons" were advanced for the exclusion of Jews, high among them that the clients "wouldn't like" the presence of Jewish lawyers. It was a lame excuse. The truth was that Jews were not wanted by the big firms, and if they wanted to be lawyers they should be content to look after "their own." Later, when the winds of change came, overt discrimination against Jews generally lessened—a trend reinforced by the growth of Jewish-owned commercial firms whose business the non-Jewish law firms wanted.

This was not just a Montreal phenomenon. As reported some years ago in *Canadian Lawyer*, "large, successful [Toronto] firms such as Goodman & Goodman, Goodman & Carr, Minden Gross, and Fogler Rubinoff, can trace their roots to a time when their firm's founding fathers were kept out of the corridors of power in the 'established firms' of WASP Canada."[71] George D. Finlayson, a former justice of the Ontario Court of Appeal, speaks of this in his "Appreciation" of his mentor, John J. Robinette:

> Toronto had a large and vibrant Jewish community in those days and some of its members were leaders of the legal profession. But when I received my call ... there were no Jewish judges at the senior level, and Jewish lawyers were not admitted into the Toronto Lawyers' Club. I articled at McCarthy & McCarthy in 1951, and there

were no Jewish lawyers there despite the fact that Senator Hayden had a substantial Jewish clientele. Several of the senior lawyers were anti-Semitic. One refused to permit Professor Bora Laskin's seminal work on Canadian constitutional law to be in the firm's library.[72]

This slight of Laskin did not hurt his career. He not only taught thousands of students, but also later went to the bench and rose to be Chief Justice of Canada. But the discrimination was real—and it was not confined to Jews alone; blacks also suffered. When Lincoln Alexander, a classmate of Finlayson, was called to the Bar, he could not find a job with a Toronto law firm. But he, like Laskin, persevered and was able to become a member of parliament, a minister of the crown, and the lieutenant-governor of Ontario.

Like so many lawyers in the criminal field, Joe Cohen was essentially a loner. He had a partner, Ezra Leithman, but he did civil work only. While their offices were small, they had a good library, which became my office. I had a desk and a telephone, but no windows and no fresh air. The fact that Joe smoked cigars—up to ten House of Lords a day—didn't help. But I was young and eager to learn and no one ever had a better teacher.

In those days it was customary for young litigators-to-be to accompany their senior to court and learn by watching the master. It also meant carrying the senior's briefcase, taking notes of the evidence, doing research and, in general, making sure that all functioned smoothly. And that included getting lunch, taking shirts and wing collars to the laundry, and running all sorts of errands. But we all did this happily and felt privileged to be in a "good office."

This led to a funny incident one day. Joe had been engaged to act for one of four accused charged with the murder of a well-known local restaurateur. The trial was held in the formal setting of the Court of Queen's Bench,[73] the jury box on one side, the prisoner's dock on the other, and counsel and journalists in between: crown in the first row, defence in the second, press in the third. Five heavy leather-covered chairs stood in each row. Joe, as senior counsel, sat on the far left. To his right were the lawyers for the three co-accused, and I took the chair on the far right, next to the dock. At one point, about noon, Joe got up, bowed to the judge, and walked around the last row of chairs to where I sat. He whispered a few words to me and then returned to his seat. A friend of mine happened to be in the audience, and when I met him a few days later he said to me: "That was pretty impressive. Here you are, just out of law school, and Joe Cohen comes and asks you for advice." I mumbled something incomprehensible—how could I tell him what

Joe had really said: "Get me an egg salad sandwich and a glass of milk and be sure to be back by twelve thirty."

My thesis had been well received, and word soon got around that a text was available and people phoned for copies. I was happy to oblige even though making copies was not as quick and easy as it is today. Two choices were available: re-type the text, using thin paper and making as many carbon copies as possible, usually a maximum of six, or use a wet-process to copy the existing text, which was even slower. So we opted for the former and tried to keep the requests to a manageable number. One day, a year or two into practice, I was walking on Adelaide Street in Toronto when I saw a sign that said "Carswell's," the law publishers. On the spur of the moment I walked in and asked to see the editor. I told him that I had a manuscript that he might like to consider. He was receptive to the idea and assigned Boris Krivy, one of his editors, to help me put the book into shape.

I worked hard at expanding the thesis. My experience as editor-in-chief of the *McGill Law Journal*[74] helped me in this task, but even so, much of the work was drudgery: sources had to be verified, which involved research in two superb law libraries, Osgoode Hall and Harvard, and I had to track down a number of unpublished judgments. One great thing about the legal fraternity is that everyone is generally helpful, particularly for a project like this. Since word processors were not yet invented, each addition to the text required retyping one or more pages, all of it by me, since I couldn't afford the cost of a typist. I couldn't even do a "paste and scissors" job since, as I said before, copying was done by a wet process, a page at a time, with a quarter-hour or so to dry the product. What a relief when the first Xerox arrived!

The book was published in 1962[75] and it sold very well, even though one critic thought the price ($5.75) was outrageously high. But good reviews helped sales in Canada and abroad, and judges at all levels soon began to refer to it in their judgments. This, in turn, brought a flood of invitations to speak at conferences across the country and I accepted as many as I could. Giving such talks was hard work but good for my practice, since lawyers like myself, who work in narrow fields, have to rely to a great extent on other lawyers for referrals.

This was heady stuff for a young practitioner and it was a proud moment for me when a majority of the Alberta Court of Appeal (sitting as the Court of Appeal for the Northwest Territories) adopted a theory I had advanced in preference to a well-established line of jurisprudence. The case was *R. v. Brown (No. 2)*,[76] and it concerned the admissibility of evidence given by Brown at a previous trial on the same charge. Brown had been charged with murder and convicted of the lesser offence of manslaughter. However, the Supreme Court of Canada set aside the verdict and directed a new trial on a charge of manslaughter.

Brown had testified at the first trial, and the crown tried to introduce this evidence as part of its case at the retrial. No reason was given for the unusual procedure, but I presume that the crown found some corroboration for its case in the answers then given by Brown, especially in cross-examination. As often happens, two theories of law were in conflict. The first is that the accused cannot be compelled to testify against his will. By introducing the accused's previous evidence, the crown, as the chief justice pointed out, accomplished indirectly what it could not do directly. On the other hand, there also was the rule, equally sound and well-established, that evidence given by an accused under oath in a judicial proceeding is admissible against him in subsequent proceedings. It was a classic case of right versus right, but I had argued in my book that this type of evidence should be excluded. Canadian case law, I suggested, was based on a misapprehension of the issue.

I therefore was thrilled when Chief Justice Smith, supported by two of the other four judges, adopted my view. Alas, my pleasure was short lived, because a few months later the Supreme Court of Canada reversed the Northwest Territories Court of Appeal in one pithy sentence: "For the reasons given by Mr. Justice Johnson, of the Court of Appeal for the Northwest Territories [who had dissented], with whom we substantially agree, the appeal is allowed and the conviction restored."[77] *Sic transit gloria ... !*

Nineteen years later, with the advent of the Canadian Charter of Rights and Freedoms, the problem was definitively resolved by the inclusion of section 13, which provides that "a witness who testifies in any proceedings has the right not to have any incriminating evidence so given to incriminate that witness in any other proceedings, except in a prosecution for perjury or for the giving of contradictory evidence." Today, my theory is vindicated and Brown would win his case.

◆ ◆ ◆

I was offered a permanent job in Cohen's firm after my call to the Bar, but space was still scarce. My office remained in the library until we moved to larger quarters, when I finally got an office with windows.

Traditionally, young lawyers cut their teeth on small cases in the lower courts and I was no exception. In criminal law, this meant appearing in the municipal courts throughout the province and sometimes in minor matters in the Court of Sessions of the Peace. In Montreal, the Municipal Court (then called Recorder's

Court, an old English term) sat in two grandiose courtrooms on the second floor of a building on Gosford Street that also housed Police Headquarters. It had five full-time judges appointed by the province after consultation with the mayor. They were "magistrates" within the meaning of the Criminal Code, and this gave them jurisdiction not only over by-law cases, but also certain criminal offences such as assault, non-support, drunk driving, gambling, and solicitation by prostitutes. Their writ was enforced by bailiffs who wore blue uniforms and police-style caps with the letters HCR emblazoned in gold. This stood for *Huissier Cour du Recorder* (Bailiff of Recorder's Court), freely translated into English by jokesters as "Have Cash Ready," since one of their tasks was to collect fines.

Recorders had to deal with a huge volume of cases, but since most accused pleaded guilty, they managed to keep up to date. There was a *barême*—a tariff— for most sentences: $50 for driving while impaired, $500 and up for keepers of disorderly houses, depending on the number of previous convictions, and so forth. But once in a while a judge would get tough, often with an eye on the press, and increase the going rates with appropriate pronouncements thrown in for good measure. The story is told of a former recorder-in-chief who liked to play with some of the hapless creatures who appeared before him. On one occasion, a householder had pleaded guilty to leaving garbage exposed in a bin. This called for a stern lecture from the bench, with the admonition that "I could send you to jail for your negligence." There was silence in the court, interrupted only by a voice from the rear: "Be careful, he's mean enough to do it!" But most of the judges weren't mean, and they often tried to help people by asking private agencies such as the Salvation Army to be of assistance. It was an imperfect, makeshift social-welfare system, but quite effective in an amateurish sort of a way, and it helped keep people out of jail whose lives might otherwise forever have been marked by the experience.

My first appearance before a Montreal municipal judge occurred while I was still a student. The keeper of a house of ill repute was up for sentencing, and I was sent to ask for a postponement because my senior couldn't be there that day. I made whatever lame excuse I could, but the recorder, Emmet J. McManamy, one of the old-timers (who came from Sherbrooke and knew me from my *Star* days) wouldn't hear of it. "No," he said, "I'll sentence her today, but of course I'll be glad to hear anything you may have to say in mitigation."

I asked for a few minutes to look at the file, which included a copy of the *feuille de route*—the record—of the accused. I didn't like what I saw, but I had to proceed. It was a memorable start to many pleas of mitigation in the future. "My

Lord," I said—in Quebec we used the appellation freely, if incorrectly, even for justices of the peace, who loved it—"despite my client's fifty-two previous convictions for similar offences ..." and that's as far as I got. Everyone laughed, McManamy held up a hand and said, "That's enough. $500 or 30 days in jail." He then turned to the accused and with a straight face told her that she was lucky to have been so well represented.

My first trial was the defence of a man charged with dangerous driving. He had struck a child on a street in one of the larger suburbs, and the trial took place one evening before the local recorder, a practising lawyer who sat once a week. I had spent many hours preparing and I must have had about twenty books with relevant cases. This was in the days before photocopiers, so I packed the books in a suitcase, which I could barely carry, and at the appointed hour I declared that I was ready to proceed. The trial lasted about an hour and after a short argument the accused was acquitted.

Before leaving the bench, the recorder asked me to meet him in his chambers, and when I entered he said, "You know, no one ever pays me the courtesy of bringing law books to my court, let alone a suitcase-full." I said something about the equal importance of all courts, when the boy who had been knocked down walked in. The judge greeted him warmly and then introduced him to me with the words: "Meet my nephew." I took the news calmly, but I must say that it was a while before I fully recovered from the initial shock.

In those days, the mid-1950s, courts in Quebec were pretty informal. Lawyers walked in and out of judges' chambers, cases were "settled" in the corridors, and anyone who wanted a postponement, crown or defence, could generally have it. And, of course, there was a great deal of plea bargaining, actively encouraged by the crown and the judges.

The chief judge of the Court of Sessions was Edouard Archambault, the former head of the Quebec Liquor Commission. Archambault was an amiable man, very accessible and ever ready to "clear the decks" by nudging lawyers to make deals for their clients. He had a large corner office on the second floor of the New Court House, and all "regulars" were welcome to come in and sit down and watch the proceedings. There were abundant chairs, and good conversation—lawyer talk, though not necessarily law—was the order of the day. This was interrupted from time to time by appearances, motions, and other routine proceedings, but such matters weren't allowed to disturb the prevailing *bonhomie*.

The lack of formality had judicial repercussions in the Supreme Court of Canada, when some of the procedures followed in the chief's office were challenged in *Korponey v. A.G. Can.*[78] Justice Antonio Lamer, speaking for the court, noted the existence of a practice particular to the District of Montreal that did not comply with the provisions of the Criminal Code but which, he said, when understood by all concerned, did not cause prejudice to the accused. Most judges in the Court of Sessions were happy to bless plea bargains made by the lawyers, so long as the suggested sentences were not outrageous. These were the days before probation was recognized by the Criminal Code, and it was not unusual for a judge to take a plea of guilty and then postpone the passing of sentence for six months to a year "to see how the accused would do." If he or she stayed out of trouble, that would be the end of the matter; if not, it was jail. Many young offenders benefitted from this unofficial form of probation, even though some of the sentences, such as "time served," were, technically speaking, illegal.

Two judges pioneered this system. Justice Wilfrid Lazure of the Court of Queen's Bench was the first to release prisoners on their own recognizance after conviction and prior to sentence to give them a chance to rehabilitate themselves. In the Court of Sessions, Judge Irenée Lagarde followed this system with good success and other judges soon adopted it. It may have been primitive, but it worked.

Judge Lagarde was a crown attorney when he was named to the bench of the Montreal Municipal Court. A few years later he was promoted to the Court of Sessions, and his early reputation was that of a very crown-minded judge. But he soon changed and became the court's severest critic of police excesses. Crown attorneys often tried to avoid him, particularly in cases where the only evidence was a confession obtained by the police. In those cases he would embark on a very detailed inquiry of all the circumstances surrounding the taking of the statement—as indeed a judge should, though not all did—and the slightest irregularity would suffice to reject a confession. Prosecutors and police protested loudly but in vain, and the Court of Appeal rarely intervened in a judge's findings of facts.

I recall one case in particular, in which the police had arrested a young man for writing cheques that later bounced. His mother called me as soon as he was taken away, but my attempts to locate him at a police station proved fruitless: no one admitted to any knowledge of the case. This was strange, since the custom was to take a prisoner to the nearest station and then transfer him to headquarters downtown. A paddy wagon made the rounds every hour or so, and in the normal course of events, even if I missed a client at the station, I would catch up with him a short time later in the "holding tank" on Bonsecours Street. But two or three hours passed and still no sign of the accused.

In the 1950s and 1960s it was possible to get an order for bail from a judge by telephone, and so I called Judge Lagarde at home (I rotated among the judges, at least among those who would entertain such motions by telephone) and explained to him that the police appeared to be playing games by hiding the accused. This was not an unknown practice and it was based on the premise, regrettably true, that the longer the police could keep counsel away from a suspect, the more likely it was they could extract a confession. The normal remedy—a writ of *habeas corpus* took too long—was to involve a judge of the Court of Sessions, by telephone if necessary.

Predictably, Judge Lagarde was angered by the very suggestion that the police were hiding the accused, and he asked me to have the officer in charge of the detention quarters call him at home. The officer did, but since he had neither the file nor the prisoner, there was little that could be done at that point. However, a short time later, I got another call from the mother of the accused, who told me that her son had sent her a message that he was now in a suburban police station. I phoned the station and verified his presence, but they were not prepared to give me any further details. So back to Judge Lagarde, who set bail at $100, a decision that he communicated by phone to the police.

The mother immediately went to the station with sufficient cash to post bail, but she was told to wait. About an hour later, her son walked out, happy, of course, to be free, but somewhat troubled by the fact that he had made an incriminating statement to the local chief. "Why did you do that?" I asked him the next day. "Well," he replied, "the chief told me that I was young and that I had no previous convictions, and if I'd tell him what happened, he'd let me go. So I told him." Of course, as soon as he had signed his declaration he was charged and told to be in court the following morning. A check of the record showed that all this had taken place *after* Judge Lagarde had ordered his release on bail.

I was not, therefore, displeased to find that by coincidence Judge Lagarde presided in Arraignment Court the next day. I told the duty crown attorney what had transpired the night before, and he said, "Let me talk to the police." He returned a few minutes later and said that they "want to drop the charge and I have no objection." And neither did I or my client.

◆◆◆

Most of the judges who held court in those days were easygoing, always accessible, and even if some were not great students of the law, they had compassion and understood that some things were not black or white. I have fond memories of many of them.

One judge, Marcel "Hank" Gaboury, a former chief of the provincial police, sold tickets for the Irish sweepstakes to his friends. He had a contact in Ireland who had supplied him with tickets for many years, and he saw no reason that he should stop the practice just because he went on the bench, despite the fact that lotteries were still illegal.

Another judge was indecisive. Once, at the end of a preliminary hearing, he turned to me and said: "If you were me, what would you do?" Not an easy question to answer, particularly after I had spent the previous hour trying to demonstrate that the crown had no case. A third judge, Gerry Laganière, was a well-known Conservative—a *bleu* in Quebec parlance. He was appointed by a Liberal attorney general, a rare occurrence in those days. When the time came for him to order his judicial robes, wags in the courthouse said that his gown shouldn't have the usual red stripes on the front: in his case, one should be red, the other blue. And talking of red stripes, they didn't come to Quebec until the 1960s, when the Judicial Council decided that it should follow the example set by other provinces. That was the official explanation. But the real reason, courthouse regulars joked, was that the stripes were needed to help the wearer tell if he was coming or going.

Lawyers, particularly those who appeared in the criminal courts on a regular basis, were given great leeway in those days. Myer Gross, who represented many nightclub performers, was once engaged to defend Fawzia, a belly dancer who had performed for King Farouk in Egypt, on a charge of obscenity. Since there was no clear definition of the term—as one judge said, "I know it when I see it"—Myer argued that Judge Gerry Almond, who was assigned to hear the case, would have to see his client's act in order to decide if it went beyond acceptable standards. Almond, whose father was a canon in the Anglican Church, agreed and a date was fixed for Fawzia to dance in his court. At the appointed hour, all business stopped in the courthouse as lawyers, functionaries, and anyone else who happened to be there crowded into Court No. 5 to watch the proceedings. As Fawzia performed her act near the bench, Gerry leaned over and said, "Dance to the judge," and she did. He also warned spectators not to applaud. It was all over in a few minutes. Her performance, the judge ruled, was art, not obscenity, and Fawzia, followed by her admirers, triumphantly left court.

Joe Cohen, my mentor, once had a client accused of conducting an illegal gaming scheme. It was a three-card monte game, a variation of the old shell game but played with cards. The dealer invites the participants to guess in which of three places, after a rapid shuffle of three cards, the designated card reposes. If anyone ever guessed correctly, it was likely a matter of luck rather than skill, although some players steadfastly insisted that their superior powers of observation gave them the needed advantage.

The judge, who had never seen a three-card monte game, agreed that the accused should give a demonstration in court, and a table was set up near the bench for the purpose. The accused produced his stock-in-trade—three ordinary playing cards—and held up one, which the judge would have to point out at the end of the shuffle. Wonder of wonders, the judge was right. And so he was the second time and the third time. "This is clearly a game of skill, not one of chance," he ruled and the accused was duly acquitted. Within hours, three-card monte parlours (where the game was played much more quickly) sprang up all over town, and, as a member of parliament later told the House of Commons, three-card monte experts soon were pillaging the unsuspecting citizens of the town at an appalling rate.[79] The result was that Parliament decided to amend the Criminal Code by adding three-card monte to the list of games which, by definition, were deemed to be games of chance. This became known as the "Cohen amendment," and it is still on the books today.[80]

Those were the years when women first began to be appointed to the bench. Traditionally, men wore shirts with wing collars and white bands—as they had for over a century. But in Quebec, in contrast with their counterparts in other provinces, women felt something more feminine was required, and Réjane Laberge Colas, the first female High Court judge in Canada, sported a blouse with a soft collar, adorned by lace, and everyone seemed pleased. When the next woman was appointed, Judge Colas presented her with the appropriate lace, and this lovely tradition continues.

The advent of female judges in the Superior Court caused an administrative problem because there were no toilet facilities for women within the space reserved for their chambers. They were therefore obliged to use the public washroom, an inconvenience to say the least. One day, closeted in a cubicle, a judge overheard a conversation by two women. One said to the other, "What are you here for today?" and she replied, "For my divorce." "Will that be difficult?" asked the first, and the answer was, "No, we'll just tell the usual lies." Since the judge in the cubicle was assigned to hear divorce cases that day, this posed a problem, but she took the wise course of ignoring bathroom conversations and deciding by the evidence. However, the incident helped Chief Justice W.B. Scott (Frank Scott's brother) to convince Public Works to make the necessary renovations.

But I digress. As I said, a story—in some cases many—can be told about every judge of the criminal court. One collected pillows. All kinds of pillows, big ones, small ones, in every conceivable fabric and colour, all gathered on his travels and now displayed in his chambers. Another judge left many of his tasks, including the drafting of judgments, to his attendant. Once, when a lawyer entered the judge's chambers and saw the attendant at the judge's desk, he asked him how he was. "Not bad," was the answer, "if only His Honour would help me once in a while."

One judge—a good judge with a tremendous capacity to recall even the most obscure cases in the jurisprudence—was almost totally blind. Transcripts were read to him by his wife and he memorized the details. When he had to deliver a judgment, he would do so with the sketchiest of notes, written in letters an inch high, which he could barely see. Yet his decisions were invariably long and detailed, and he almost never misstated the facts or the law. I once had a complicated fraud case before him, in which the trial had lasted a number of days and the arguments of counsel took another two days. He listened intently, ordered the evidence transcribed, and in due course delivered a six-hour judgment from the bench. He started at ten, and when the court broke for lunch at 12:30 he had just reviewed the facts and neither my client nor I had any inkling which way the case would go. He resumed at 2:00, and it was not until the final minutes late that afternoon that we learned what the outcome would be. It was a masterly performance given almost entirely from memory. Since I knew him and his wife well, I sent his wife, who undoubtedly had spent many hours reading the transcripts to him, a bouquet of flowers with a card that said, "For service beyond the call of duty." It was greatly appreciated. Incidentally, I lost that case, and while the Court of Appeal overturned the judgment and acquitted the accused, the Supreme Court restored the conviction.

Sometimes, in deserving cases, judges would try to help an accused, but help of this kind was not always welcomed by the lawyers. I once defended ten or twelve members of the Kiwanis Club who had held a fundraiser for a well-known and worthy charity. Unfortunately, it involved a minor game of chance of the spin-the-wheel type, and an ambitious constable laid charges against all for running an illegal gaming operation. The crown attorney was highly uncomfortable—the press had loudly deplored the arrests—but he had a job to do and he couldn't find a decent reason to drop the charge. I knew from the judge's initial comments (he was the judge who sold lottery tickets) that he would gladly acquit given a proper hook on which to hang his judgment, and luckily (I thought) I found an error—a little error, to be candid—in the drafting of the charge and so I moved to quash the accusation. The crown made a feeble attempt to oppose this but, as I said, his heart wasn't in it and we both looked forward to a speedy end to the proceedings.

But it was not to be. "There are much better reasons to dismiss the case than the one you proposed," the judge said to me, and with that he proceeded to develop a theory that both the crown and I thought was unsustainable in law but on the strength of which he acquitted all accused without any further argument. A good result, but the reasons were so bad that the crown was afraid to let the ruling stand, lest it be cited in future cases, and so was forced to appeal. The Court of Appeal, a few months later, made short shrift of this "entirely new" theory of law and quashed the charge for the reasons I had advanced in the first place.

The informality that reigned in those days didn't survive for long. For one thing, the move to a new courthouse—a seventeen-storey glass and steel structure—created a new atmosphere. Judges' chambers were no longer as accessible to lawyers as they had been before, and judges now used inside passages to get from their chambers to the courtrooms. But I also suspect that the increase in criminal litigation, and with it the increase in the number of judges and lawyers, had something to do with it. Before, almost everyone knew everyone else. It was, in some respects, a club: you either belonged or you didn't. This was good for the regulars, of course, but not so for outsiders, and opportunities for abuse were great. Still, it was fun while it lasted.

◆ ◆ ◆

Every courthouse in Quebec has a robing room, and regulars keep their court dress in lockers assigned by the sheriff. The only exception was the New Court House (not all that new, but less old than the Old Court House across the street), which housed the criminal courts[81] Finally, in the early 1960s, the administration gave in to entreaties by defence counsel and designated a small room on the second floor to be the *vestiaire*. It was an improvement—before that we had to gown across the street in the Old Court House or in the corridors or public washrooms—but it lacked the usual amenities. First, it was "unisex," a word then unknown; men and women dressed together, but frankly no one cared. More serious, it was too small, it didn't have a toilet, and lockers were at a premium. I didn't get my own locker until a few years later when Roger Ouimet was appointed to the Superior Court and, being next on the list, I got his.

In Montreal, crown attorneys had office space on the third floor, so they gowned in the privacy of their offices. But in rural areas, where crown attorneys often were part-time appointees, they shared the robing room with all the other lawyers, and many a bargain was struck as crown and defence were getting ready for court. One case stands out in my mind. My client was charged with capital murder. His trial was aborted when the judge declared a mistrial, believing that the remarks of a police officer might conceivably have prejudiced the jury. Well and good, but that was in the District of Terrebonne, where the criminal assizes sat but once a year, and the accused would now have to wait twelve months before a new trial could take place. And so, just about a year later, I was in the robing room at the courthouse in Saint-Jérôme. The crown attorney who had pleaded the first case had recently been appointed to the bench, and his assistant was now in charge of the case. He, too, was in there getting ready.

After some lawyerly chit-chat, I said to him: "Roger, can we settle this case?" To my surprise, he said "yes." The deputy attorney general had authorized him to accept a plea to the reduced charge of manslaughter, should it be offered. And so I said, "Let's do it, but what about the sentence?" His instructions were to seek a long term of imprisonment, which, in the circumstances, was entirely reasonable. We haggled a bit and settled on fifteen years. Courtesy required that we tell the judge that there would be a plea, a matter entirely within the discretion of the crown. So we went to his chambers, and my friend said, "Good news, judge, we won't need a trial."

That is where he should have left it; however, my friend, in his enthusiasm, added that not only would the accused plead guilty, but also that we had decided what the sentence should be. Not surprisingly, the judge took a dim view of that and very sarcastically said, "Isn't it great to know that in the District of Terrebonne judges are no longer required. The lawyers now run the courthouse, they decide on the outcome of cases, and they even sentence the accused. I can't stop the crown from accepting a plea to a lesser offence, but the two of you get into court and say what you have to say about sentence in public." This we did and, after a two-hour hearing, the judge pronounced sentence: "Eighteen years." I asked if I could have the court's indulgence to say one more thing. Graciously, the judge agreed and I told him that in Montreal, his colleague Justice Lazure (whom he knew well, of course), often said to an accused, "My intention was to sentence you to 20 years, but just to let you know that justice is not only just but also merciful, I'll make it 19." To which the judge in Saint-Jérôme replied: "All right. Make it 17." Not as good as 15, but certainly better than the death penalty, which could have resulted had the case gone to trial.

◆◆◆

Although a major part of my practice involved litigation, from time to time I was asked to write opinions on a variety of questions. For instance, a company might ask if it had sufficient grounds to prosecute a supplier for fraud, a not-infrequent occurrence. I would examine the facts and give an opinion. Sometimes the answer was "yes, there was fraud, but you won't be able to prove it in court." While unsatisfactory to the client, my advice saved time, money, and protracted aggravation. Other times, of course, I could recommend that a brief be prepared for the crown, suggesting that a prosecution be commenced. One may well ask why a victim would retain private counsel rather than go to the police. The simple answer is that most police forces are understaffed and overworked, and non-violent crime is low on their list of priorities. For instance, it would not be unusual for someone to call the fraud squad with a complaint only to be told that a detective might be available to investigate in two or three months' time.

By having private counsel prepare the file, often with the assistance of a trained investigator, the process could be speeded up and, as I said before, a brief could go straight to the crown, bypassing the police altogether. And from the crown's point of view, a well-prepared presentation was always welcome, particularly where the facts were complicated and expert evidence was required to prove the case. Financial institutions—banks, trusts, and insurance companies—often resorted to this procedure and it was a lucrative part of my practice.

Occasionally, I would be forced into cases I didn't want but couldn't refuse. An example of this was a suit for slander arising out of a political meeting. A woman had presented herself for election to the council of a riding association. Her candidacy was opposed by another woman who, in the course of a heated argument, called her opponent *une femme de rien*, a nobody. A few days later, the insulted candidate consulted a lawyer who advised her to take action immediately and a suit was launched in the Superior Court. It lingered there for over a year, but a few days before the date fixed for trial, the plaintiff's lawyer, who had been so eager in the first place, backed out and said that he was no longer interested in the case.

This was a clear breach of professional ethics, and the client had to scramble to get herself new counsel. Witnesses for the defence—more than a dozen—had already been summoned, but not a single subpoena had been sent out on behalf of the plaintiff. The riding association, where peace had reigned since that fateful event, dearly wished the matter would simply go away. Desperate, the riding president called me and said, "You have to help us out." And so I met with my new client, the plaintiff, and after some discussion she agreed that an apology would settle the matter.

Easier said than done: the defendant was adamant that she would not recant. "Let's go to trial," she told her lawyer, who was as anxious to settle as I was, "and I'll prove that what I said was true." Of course, she was perfectly entitled to have a judge hear the case, but her lawyer was obliged to tell her that, as the law then stood, truth was not a defence to slander and that she might well be condemned to pay damages as well as costs.

The final negotiations took place in the corridor of the courthouse, minutes before the case was to be called. Since we needed more time, we went to see the judge, who was more than happy to delay the proceedings. "Take all the time you want," he said, "and try and settle. This case does not belong in court. No one will win, no matter what the judgment." As an old politician, he knew what he was talking about. But the defendant remained adamant that *she* would never get up and apologize. The stalemate didn't last long, and we quickly worked out a compromise: the defendant's lawyer would send me a letter stating that the incident was most unfortunate and his client deeply regretted that it had come to this. It was a face-saving device for the defendant—the words were deliberately ambiguous—and my client graciously accepted the regrets.

I was reminded of this case when I saw an editorial in *The Globe and Mail* entitled "Say It to Nobody." This is what it said in part:

> To quote the old spiritual, nobody knows the trouble I've seen. But a driver in Italy may be leery about singing that song after he landed in trouble for calling somebody a nobody.
>
> According to the Reuters story, a man ... got into a dispute with an attendant over a parking space and, in the course of the argument, yelled, "You are a nobody!" The attendant promptly sued him for slander, evidently to show that nobody could treat him that way. The court ruled that saying "you are a nobody" was equivalent to saying you are a nonentity [and] to state that a person is a nonentity is certainly offensive ... because it is damaging to the dignity of a person.[82]

It seems to me they, too, should have settled!

Speaking of Italian courts, I was once asked by the Italian embassy to investigate the possibility of extraditing a Canadian resident who had been found guilty of murder by an Italian court. The trial had been held *in absentia,* and that created a problem since the idea (save in very particular circumstances) is alien to our system. But even if that could have been overcome—for instance, by an undertaking to retry the accused on his return to Italy—there were further roadblocks. I still recall the colourful language of the judgment, written in a style reminiscent of Lord Denning, which began as follows: "It was a sunny day in Tuscany and the accused was riding his donkey on the road into town." So far, so good, but what followed was based entirely on hearsay, all of it inadmissible in Canadian courts, and I was obliged to inform the embassy that extradition would not likely be granted on the basis of this document.

Extradition is a tricky matter, and in my eighteen years of practice I acted in many such cases, almost all of them to or from the United States. One stands out in my mind, because bail was granted on a sidewalk on Craig Street, not far from the Old Court House. An American had moved to Canada where he obtained employment as a Hebrew teacher in a private Jewish school. A year or two later, a federal grand jury in Brooklyn indicted him for fraud, an extradition warrant was issued, and he was arrested late one afternoon in Montreal. His employer called me and said they couldn't do without him, and hoped to get him released on bail.

The Extradition Act provides that a Superior Court judge can release an accused pending the hearing, and I called the crown attorney, who agreed that there was little likelihood that the accused would abscond and that he would not oppose an application. It was after 5:00, and by the time I got to the courthouse, all judges had left. On my way back to the office, I spotted Justice G.B. Puddicombe on the street. His Lordship, a gentleman of the old school and courteous to a fault, agreed at once to hear me on what I termed "an urgent application concerning the liberty of a subject." This is the ancient English formula, and by tradition judges give preference to this type of application over all other cases. And so, as traffic whizzed by, I explained the facts of the case. Since Judge Puddicombe was unfamiliar with extradition matters, he sought my assurance that he had jurisdiction to make an order for the release of the accused, and he quickly fixed a cash deposit. I called the crown attorney, who was satisfied, and the police who held the accused, and by nightfall he was back with his family.

Of course, bail was but an interim measure, and the accused soon had to face not only the extradition hearings but also an inquiry by the Immigration Department to see if there were grounds for deportation. This is frequently used as a shortcut to extradition, since a deportation order is sometimes more easily obtained than a warrant to extradite. I don't recall the details of that investigation, but the upshot was that the accused was declared an undesirable alien and he and his family were ordered to leave within a stated period. This finding could be appealed, and so it was. I took the late Hy Soloway, a distinguished Ottawa lawyer, as my counsel, and in due course we appeared before a panel of the Immigration Appeal Board, with a retired army officer in the chair.

Our principal argument was that this person was needed by his employer, that Hebrew teachers were scarce, that the accusation against him was minor and would likely be settled in due course, and that his wife and children would unnecessarily suffer if his deportation was ordered. In short, the appeal was based on compassionate grounds, and the argument went back and forth between us, the crown, and the bench. At one point, the chairman turned to me and said, "I have a question. Is the accused's wife working?" I had no idea, so I went to the back of the courtroom where my client was sitting and asked him. But nothing is simple in life. He looked at me and said: "Is it better she should be working or better she doesn't?" I can see why he asked, but I needed a straight answer, and as he was pondering his reply, the chairman said, "What's taking so long? It's a simple question." I felt like saying, "You don't understand," but of course I didn't and I finally transmitted the answer I got, which was: "Sometimes she does and sometimes she doesn't." The deportation order was upheld, the extradition hearing was cancelled, and we quickly made a deal with the U.S. authorities for the accused to surrender, which he did. He pleaded guilty to a reduced charge and got a minor penalty.

I mentioned the old English phrase concerning the liberty of a subject. It isn't used that much anymore to gain precedence, but I couldn't resist invoking it on one more occasion. A client of mine had his bail revoked somewhat arbitrarily in the course of a preliminary hearing. Only a Superior Court judge could remedy this, and the only judge I could find was in the midst of hearing motions in civil cases. Undeterred, I rose when there was a short break in the proceedings and announced in a loud voice—well, not that loud—that I had an application to make concerning the liberty of a subject. It worked like magic. "Please proceed," the judge said, which I did quickly and successfully. Some of my colleagues, who had already waited a long time to be heard, were not amused, but such is life at the Bar!

[11]
Insanity and Other Matters

For more than fifteen years, the criminal assizes in Montreal were presided over by Justice Wilfrid Lazure, a quiet, ascetic-looking man with a broad knowledge of criminal law. He was stern, but not without compassion. I remember one case in which he was about to sentence a young woman who, with her brother, had been found guilty of a particularly brutal crime. He started with the brother and sentenced him to imprisonment for life. Their mother, who was in the courtroom, collapsed on hearing the sentence, and her daughter, distraught at the sight, screamed, "*Ma mère, ma mère!*" The scene visibly upset the judge, who quickly sentenced the woman to ten years in prison. He later told a group of lawyers, "You know, I had every intention of giving her fifteen years, but when I saw her agony I just couldn't do it."

One day Justice Lazure's messenger found me in the lobby of the courthouse. It was mid-morning and he told me that His Lordship wanted to see me most urgently. I went at once, and the judge told me that he would like me to act for the defence in a murder case. This was in the days before legal aid and no lawyer ever refused a request such as this. I said, "Of course, when will the case come up?" "In an hour," he said. "That'll give you enough time to speak to your client." And so I did, and twenty minutes later we had picked a jury—no challenges by either side—and the crown called its only witness, a detective who produced a confession. The defence was insanity and, courtesy of the crown, I produced a psychiatrist who had examined my client shortly after she committed the offence. In the psychiatrist's view, there was no doubt she was so mentally disturbed at the time that she could not tell right from wrong, making her legally insane. The judge therefore directed the jury to find the accused "not guilty by reason of insanity,"[83] and they did so without leaving the courtroom. It was all over by lunchtime.

Unusual circumstances, but there was an explanation. When my client's case was called for the first time, she was declared mentally unfit to stand trial. She was placed in an institution and subsequently cured of her illness. Her doctors were anxious to discharge her since she no longer posed a threat to society. She had no lawyer, and hence the judge's request; he rightly felt that any postponement would only needlessly prolong her detention, and in fact she was released a short time later.

Another case, perhaps the strangest of all, was that of a German immigrant who was accused of killing his landlady. The problem was that after shooting her he had turned the gun on himself but survived, blinded and with part of his brain blown off. I was engaged by some of his friends and when I saw him in prison he said—and I believed him—that he had no recollection whatsoever of the incident. He accepted that he had, in fact, killed the woman, but he couldn't tell me why or under what circumstances. This made it quite impossible to plan a defence and I moved to empanel a jury to decide whether or not the accused was fit to stand trial.

Until that point, Canadian and English case law had always held that to be declared unfit to stand trial an accused had to be so afflicted by *mental disease* that he could not instruct counsel. It was clear, however, that my client was not unfit "on account of insanity" unless a wider meaning could be given to this phrase. Yet it was equally clear that I could not defend him properly without hearing his side of the story. And, what made matters even worse, the medical experts agreed that his memory would never return.

Justice Lazure decided to leave the matter to a jury, and in his instructions he stressed the importance of an accused person's ability to tell his side of the story, first to his lawyer and then, perhaps, to the court. Without that, he said, a trial would not be fair. The jury accepted my argument that the accused was unfit to stand trial and he was returned to jail. Of course, no one knew what to do with him there: the mental wing didn't want him since he wasn't insane, and the trial ward didn't want him since his case had now, for all practical purposes, been put on hold indefinitely. And the prison where convicted prisoners were kept refused to accept him since he hadn't been found guilty of any offence.

I don't recall how the authorities settled the matter, but when the case was called in the normal course six months later to see if the accused had by some miracle improved to the point where he now might stand trial—a formality, since we all knew he couldn't recover—the sheriff announced that he could not produce the prisoner. What had happened, he explained, was that the Immigration Department had classified him as an undesirable alien and, without further ado, had put him on a plane to Germany, where relatives had agreed to take care of him. It was a humane solution to a difficult problem, but it certainly raised the judge's eyebrows since the order of the court had been that he be kept in "close confinement" until such time as he could be dealt with according to law. I was involved in many cases where insanity was in issue, but this was the most unusual.

♦♦♦

In 1960 I was engaged to defend a man who was charged with theft in Frobisher Bay in the Northwest Territories (now Iqualuit, the capital of Nunavut). I applied for admission to the Territorial Bar, which in those days was regulated by the commissioner for the Northwest Territories. Upon satisfying himself that I was qualified for registration in the Barristers and Solicitors Register, he gave me permission to practise law in the Territories. The fee for the licence was $25, a bargain even then.

This was before jets flew to the far north, and the trip in a DC-6 took close to seven hours. It was a comfortable 40°F when we left Montreal on a sunny February day, but it was minus 32 in Frobisher. It also was windy, and an RCMP officer who met the plane rushed me from the aircraft into a waiting car because the wind-chill factor was such that even a minute's exposure could result in severe frostbite.

The case was called the following day. The accused pleaded guilty, and after representations by the crown and me, the magistrate (who had come from Yellowknife), sentenced him to three months "in the custody of the RCMP." This gave discretion to the local authorities to find the most convenient type of "custody," and it frequently meant, particularly in the case of Inuit, that the prisoner would be sent to stay with friends or relatives in nearby settlements. My client asked that he be sent to Ottawa to serve his sentence, and the RCMP agreed. However, there were only two flights a week out of Frobisher, and both he and I had to remain for an extra two days. Since he was in custody, he had to stay in the barracks. Later that day, the officer in charge of the detachment gave a party for the visiting lawyers, and I'm sure my client could hear from his cell the merrymaking in the mess hall on the other end of the building.

The next day I was invited to do a little sightseeing, which included a trip by RCMP aircraft to a remote settlement. At one point, the pilot pointed to something below, which was only a speck on the ice, but when we got closer I realized that it was a dog team heading for Frobisher. I found out later that the journey, which took us less than an hour by air, takes more than three days by dog sled.

A few years later I was consulted by a Montreal couple about the adoption of an Inuit child. I didn't handle many adoptions, but I recall telling my clients that they had come to the one person in Montreal who could act for them in the matter, for I was the only lawyer in Quebec licensed to practise in the Northwest Territories. That they had come to me, referred by a friend, was pure coincidence.

I filed the necessary documents, and in due course the matter came up for consideration before the sole justice of the Territorial Court, the late J.H. Sissons, who was not only knowledgeable but also very outspoken. He knew the couple, who had formerly lived in the Territories, and he thought that it was a sound application, but the material that I had submitted, sufficient in Quebec and probably in any other province, lacked a certificate signed by the superintendent of child welfare in the Department of Northern Affairs in Ottawa. Frankly, I hadn't been aware that this certificate was needed, but as Judge Sissons pointed out, even if I were to apply for it, "it might take some very considerable time" to obtain. Instead, he told me, he was prepared to treat the application as an adoption in accordance with "Eskimo custom." He considered this sufficient but, he warned me, the powers in Ottawa might not like his decision and therefore would likely appeal it. In a letter to me, the judge, in characteristic fashion, set out his views about Ottawa:

We are dealing with a very powerful Ottawa colonial bureaucracy swollen with its own authority and engaged in departmental Empire building and seeking to control everything but the Northern Lights and the Throne of God and particularly usurping the functions and powers of the territorial court and generally riding roughshod over the Rights of the Eskimos.

His Lordship added that this bureaucracy did not like to be thwarted, and if I wished "any general enlightenment on this angle," he referred me to two published cases that were examples of Ottawa's attitude.

My clients accepted the judge's offer with pleasure, and in due course they received a certificate attesting that the child had been adopted "in accordance with Eskimo Custom" and that the court was "satisfied of their ability to fulfil the obligations and perform the duties of parents toward the said child." For whatever reason, Ottawa decided not to appeal, and as far as I know, the couple and their child never had any problem as a result of this unusual process.

Judge Sissons cared deeply about the north and its people, and his biography describes his struggles with Ottawa.[84] He was a thorn in the side of the Department of Northern Affairs, but his people loved him. He was succeeded by Justice William Morrow, a well-respected lawyer from Alberta, who ably dispensed justice in the Northwest Territories but without the strains that marked the Sissons years. I remained a member of the Territorial Bar until my appointment to the bench. It was a small association, with fewer than twenty lawyers and no particular rules. Each year, in order of seniority, a member assumed the presidency, and I would have too, but my appointment intervened.

◆ ◆ ◆

In 1963 the crown charged Crush International with running a lottery. The facts were simple enough. Tokens were hidden at random in the caps of some bottles, and if you found a token you were entitled to participate in the contest. There were four types of tokens and those who could answer a "skill-testing" question could win from $1 to $100. Winners in the $1 and $5 category received a phone call from a company official, who asked the contestant to solve the following problem within one minute: divide 12 by 3, multiply the answer by 6, add 7, and then subtract 15. If you answered correctly, the prize was yours. Those who had tokens that gave them a chance to win $50 or $100 had to present themselves at the company's offices and answer correctly, within two minutes, the following question: multiply 72 by 7, add 168, divide by 12, and then subtract 19.

There was no question that this was a game of chance, but we argued, as was customary in cases of this nature, that in order to win one needed skill as well as good luck, and this removed the contest from the prohibited class. The question, then, at trial was whether or not the calculations put to the contestants were "skill-testing" or a sham.

The crown was represented by Kenneth C. MacKay, an astute prosecutor and later a judge of the Superior Court. I led for the defence, and I was joined by William S. Tyndale, a litigation specialist from what is now Ogilvy, Renault, and later a colleague of mine on the Court of Appeal.

How does one prove that the questions asked are so easy they could be called a sham? MacKay took a novel approach: he called his eight-year-old son as a witness and suggested that if the child could correctly answer the questions within the time allowed so could anyone else. This, he said, would clearly show that skill was not a serious ingredient. I objected on the ground that it was for the judge to decide whether skill was required and that a witness, no matter what age, could not enlighten the court on this point. In any case, the idea that a prosecutor could call his own son to give unbiased evidence was quite preposterous, and we suspected that Ken had made this proposition tongue-in-cheek. So, just for fun, Bill and I also stipulated that MacKay's son was an exceptionally bright child—a statement that the crown could hardly refute—and that his evidence would not therefore be that of an average person. The court agreed with this submission and refused to hear Ken's child, but all to no avail. Even without expert evidence, the judge was quite convinced that the questions were too easy and in due course the company was fined $200.

◆ ◆ ◆

By the early 1960s I had a good practice. I also was active in the affairs of the Bar, but clearly I was not yet what one would call a "senior" lawyer. I therefore was surprised when I got a call in early 1964 from the *bâtonnier* of the Montreal section of the provincial Bar[85] who told me that he had nominated me to fill a vacancy on the board of examiners. This was a prestigious body, and it was a great honour to be chosen. No one ever refused and I accepted with pleasure, even though it was an onerous task, requiring ten days in June and another ten days in December in order for the board to prepare the questions, invigilate the students, and mark the papers.

The rule was that any three members of the board could pass a candidate, but it took five to block someone. Once a candidate reached the required mark in a paper—there were different standards for different subjects—we stopped reading and marked it a "pass." Papers that didn't make the grade were sent to a committee of five to be reread. This was a second chance, a built-in appeal, and the original decision was frequently reversed, often after a lengthy debate to determine whether an ambiguous answer might suffice. It was an eminently fair process and, contrary to common belief among students, the examiners had no quota of failures to fulfil; nor did we derive any pleasure in failing a candidate.

When I joined the board its president was François Lajoie, a distinguished lawyer from Trois-Rivières (and later a valued colleague of mine on the Court of Appeal). François was an indefatigable worker who frequently scheduled the first meeting of the day for 7:00 a.m. The day ended when the work was done, and that meant fourteen to sixteen-hour days. It was no sinecure, and we were fully conscious that the candidates had much at stake. But it was fun and I made many solid friendships.

Inevitably, such close associations led to in-jokes and even pranks, and there are two that stand out in my mind. The first was that François had invented an imaginary character named Joseph Laderoute, and his name kept cropping up in practical questions in all sorts of improbable situations. Typical law school stuff, sometimes funny, often tricky, designed to test a student's knowledge of the law. Since this was a fictitious person, we didn't go to any great pain to make Laderoute more sympathetic. Imagine our surprise when one day we saw an obituary in *La Presse* announcing Joseph Laderoute's demise. François clipped the obit and sent it to all his colleagues with a note suggesting that a new character had to be invented.

The second in-joke, which, by the time I joined, had become a well-established tradition, was to "steal" the completed exams. The Bar's secretary-treasurer, Robert Levêque, also acted as the board's secretary and it was his particular task to make sure that questions didn't leak out and that completed papers be kept under lock and key until the marking was finished. To achieve this purpose, Bob had a sturdy suitcase that went wherever he went during the examination period: his bedroom at night; breakfast, lunch, and dinner; even the bathroom— it even once went to a nightclub in Quebec. We used to tease Bob about this and someone always tried to steal the suitcase. Being a good sport, he got into the spirit of things and one evening at the old *Cercle universitaire* on rue d'Auteuil in Quebec he showed up with the suitcase chained to his wrist in diplomatic courier style. This, of course, was a challenge we could not resist.

I asked one of the attendants at the club to try to find a pair of heavy-duty wire-cutters, which he did (for a price). The plan was to distract Bob while someone crept up from behind and cut the chain. Bob loved a good story and I was elected to keep him amused. The plan worked beautifully, and Bob was soon deprived of his treasure—a fact that he didn't realize until he threw up both hands to say, "What a wonderful story!" A search was organized by him at once and he personally inspected every room in the house. He opened every cubicle in the men's room, but one was locked and he apologized for disturbing whoever was in there.

It so happened that Jean Turgeon, the *bâtonnier général* of the province, was present that evening. Indeed, it was his party. But no one had briefed him and he was very upset. If the suitcase wasn't found, he said, the entire exam would have to be rewritten. And so we told Bob to go back in the bathroom and take a closer look at the locked cubicle, where the suitcase, its padlock still intact, rested in all its glory on the throne.

Examiners were paid $75 a day to compensate them in some measure for the time lost in their offices. It wasn't much, but a cheque for $750 was always welcome, especially to members of the Bar who were sole practitioners. Tradition demanded that, as the cheques were handed out on the last day, someone from a large office—"large," in those days, meant fifteen lawyers or so—would move that the money be turned over to the Bar's Benevolent Fund, since the honour of having served was compensation enough. No one, of course, had any intention of doing this, but it was always fun to see the faces of the "new boys" when the proposition was made.

[12]

A Future Prime Minister

I first met Pierre Elliott Trudeau when he was a law professor at the Université de Montréal. The occasion was a party given by a mutual friend, Douglas Cohen, and, to be perfectly frank, I was much more interested in Pierre's date, a very attractive young woman, than in Pierre.

The second time we met was a year or two later, but this time the circumstances were quite different. The date was May 20, 1960, and the time was 2:30 in the afternoon. The place was what was then called the New Court House, on Notre Dame Street in Old Montreal.[86] This building housed the criminal courts and it was a busy, often hectic, place. In those days, the duty crown attorney had an office on the ground floor, and one of his tasks was the screening of bail applications.

It was such an application that had brought me to the crown attorney's office. It was to be presented later that day before a judge of the Court of Queen's Bench, and Gabriel Houde, the attorney on duty, and I were discussing the details. Suddenly, we heard what sounded like an explosion, followed by loud voices and the sound of people running. We quickly realized that the noise had been a shot, and with our bodies cautiously protected behind a wall, we peeked around the corner. A man was lying on the ground, surrounded by officers and guards, flailing his arms and legs. As we approached, we saw that he was bleeding profusely from one leg. By then, Detective Sergeant Montpetit, a tall, heavy-set liaison officer with the Montreal Police Department, had pushed aside the onlookers and taken charge. In quick succession he took off his jacket and shirt, pinned down the man by sitting on his chest, and made a tourniquet out of his own shirt sleeves in an attempt to stop the blood from gushing out. Four or five constables, directed by Montpetit, held the man's arms and legs while the detective went about his task.

All this happened near the front door of the courthouse. At this precise moment in walked Pierre Trudeau and his friend Jacques Hébert.[87] Trudeau quickly took in the scene and at once walked over to Montpetit, tapped him on the shoulder, and asked what he was doing. Montpetit told him to bugger off (or was it fuddle duddle?). Incensed with the reply, Trudeau insisted that this was no way to treat an injured person.

Further words ensued between Trudeau and Montpetit, with the result that the detective told two constables to place Trudeau under arrest and take him away, which they did in short order. Hébert, enraged by what he had seen and heard, spotted me—we knew each other slightly—and asked me to intervene. By then, an ambulance had come, the injured man was taken away, and the crowd had dispersed.

It was clear to me that Trudeau's actions were based on his belief that the police had grossly overreacted, first by shooting the prisoner—by then we knew he had escaped from a courtroom—and later by having a 250-pound officer sit on his chest. Of course, what Trudeau didn't realize at the time was that much of the force had been necessary in order to put a tourniquet on the man.

I knew from experience that misunderstandings of this kind, when not resolved quickly, often escalate to unpleasant encounters in court. I therefore decided to explain the situation as quickly as possible to the highest-ranking police officer I could find. I located a deputy director of the Quebec Provincial Police in an office in the basement of the courthouse and, after hearing my explanation, he ordered Trudeau's immediate release. The issue was resolved and I thought that was the end of the matter.

However, six days later, an article appeared in *Le Devoir* under Jacques Hébert's byline denouncing the aggressive attitude of the police. According to Hébert, Trudeau's words to Detective Sergeant Montpetit had been as follows: "As you can see, the injured man does not resist any longer. He can't save himself. Could you put less weight on his chest?" This admonition was without effect, and Trudeau's arrest followed quickly. According to the same account, Trudeau said to the officers who were taking him to the cells, "I could sue you," to which they replied, "Just try, you can be sure there will be perjury." Hébert then recounted how I was instrumental in obtaining Trudeau's release.

But that was not the end of the matter either. On June 4, Montreal's *La Presse* reprinted Jacques Hébert's version and then added another—that of the prisoner.

This is what he said in answer to three questions put to him by a reporter:

Q. Were you mistreated by the police?
A. No, not at all.
Q. Did Detective Sergeant Montpetit hurt you?
A. If he did, it was my fault, because I was struggling.
Q. Did you have the impression that Mr. Montpetit tried to stop the bleeding?
A. I am certain he wanted to help me. If he hadn't done so, I would be dead.

This story found its way into public print a second time, shortly after Trudeau's election in 1968 to the leadership of the federal Liberal Party, when Robert McKenzie and Lotta Dempsey, writing in the *Toronto Star*,[88] recalled how "Trudeau dashed in and tried to get the officer off the bleeding man," only to be "grabbed ... and carted ... off to the cells."

Trudeau himself did not forget the incident. When he called me in 1973 to inform me of my appointment to the bench (more on this later), he said, "Since you got me out of jail once, I couldn't let this Order-in-Council go through without telling you of your appointment myself." And twenty years later, when he published his memoirs,[89] he inscribed my copy: "For Fred Kaufman. With all good wishes and the best of memories."

[13]

To be Hanged by the Neck

In 1955, when I was called to the Bar, there was only one kind of murder and the punishment for murder was death. In later years, when the tide started to turn against capital punishment, the law in Canada began to differentiate, first between capital murder and non-capital murder, and later between first-degree murder and second-degree murder. But in the 1950s and early 1960s, there was a real chance that an accused charged with murder would end up on the gallows. Of course, the crown, in appropriate cases, had the option of reducing the charge from murder to manslaughter; however, the attitude frequently was, "Let the jury decide," since they, too, could reduce a charge. All too often, particularly in cases that had attracted a lot of attention, the crown would not take the responsibility of charging manslaughter rather than murder—even if that would have been the proper course—in order to avoid any potential criticism by the press and the public.[90] Moreover, in a capital case, the judge had no choice in the matter of punishment. A jury might well recommend mercy—it did so in *Truscott*, for instance[91]—but the judge had no power to temper his sentence. It was prescribed by law, and only the mercy of the crown, exercised by the federal cabinet, could save an accused from this final and irreversible fate. It was a heavy burden on counsel for the defence.

The very idea that the state had the right to put a person to death revolted me. To me, this was simply wrong: we are not God's deputies, and even the biblical injunction of an eye for an eye and a tooth for a tooth could not justify this. Yes, it was said that a sentence followed only the unanimous verdict of the accused's peers; yes, there were legal safeguards; and yes, there were appeals. Of course, even then, there were some, myself included, who dared to think that mistakes might be made, but the idea seemed remote: was ours not a foolproof system? We know now that miscarriages of justice occurred and that innocent persons were indeed put to death. And we also know that commutations—the ultimate safety valve—were all too often hit-and-miss. So how could we continue for so long with so barbaric a punishment? The answer is that society was unwilling to tolerate people in its midst, even in prison, who had committed the ultimate crime.

It was an attitude inherited from past generations. As late as the nineteenth century, a whole range of crimes was punishable by death in the belief that this was a deterrent to others. Public hangings were then the mode, and what an occasion they were for pickpockets who plied their trade while onlookers craned their necks in order not to miss the slightest gory detail! So much for the deterrent effect.

Public opinion began to turn in the mid-1960s, and while capital punishment remained on the books a few years longer, cabinet almost routinely commuted every sentence to the point where the law was a sham and had to be changed. This was no easy matter, and the final compromise was to say that in a first-degree case—a murder that was planned and deliberate—"life" meant a minimum of twenty-five years in prison. That was balm to those who opposed the change, because, in the past, "life" had often meant ten years, which in many cases seemed altogether too short.

In my early career I was involved in a number of cases in which clients faced the stark reality that death was not only a possible but indeed the likely outcome. This was an unimaginable weight on them, but also a heavy burden on all the other players in a capital case—the judge, the prosecutors, the defenders, the witnesses, the prison guards, right down to the prison chaplain who had to comfort these souls on their final journey. The shadow of death pervaded the proceedings, and the accompanying rituals, remnants from a period past, served to underscore the solemnity of the occasion: the judge's tricorne and black gloves when pronouncing a sentence of death, the red and ermine robes of the judges in the Supreme Court of Canada (worn only on ceremonial occasions and when hearing appeals in capital cases), the prescribed formalities of an approaching execution. It is not surprising, therefore, that many participants in the drama sought an escape. This led to compromise—and often to perverted law as well. For example, a man stabs a co-worker in the course of an argument. He is indicted for murder. He may lack premeditation, and yet he may have intended to cause serious bodily harm. Enough, as the law then stood, to meet the criteria. His lawyer will tell him that he will likely be convicted. Of course, the jury may be kind and stretch the facts and bring back a verdict of manslaughter, inappropriate in law but more in keeping with reality. No reasons are given, just the verdict, but in this type of case a jury may well feel that hanging is too severe a punishment. After all, the first thing lawyers told the jury at the start of the final argument was usually, "Members of the jury, the accused before you stands charged with murder and the punishment for murder is death."

The result of this was that the lawyers would negotiate, the defence out of fear, the crown because of the uncertainty. In the end, they might agree that the accused plead guilty to a lesser charge, but that the sentence should be life. In other words, each side got something: the accused knew that he wouldn't have to face the gallows and the prosecution was certain that it would get a conviction, albeit to a lesser charge. The point is that, had it not been for the threat of hanging, the trial would have run its normal course, the verdict would have been in line with the facts as found by the jury, and the punishment would have been assessed by the judge after full and proper representations by counsel for the parties. In other words, the law would have been followed.

Most judges I have known dreaded the day when they might be called upon to sentence an accused to death. One judge, after pronouncing a sentence of death, returned immediately to his chambers. Minutes later, a bailiff found him in a dead faint on the floor. He had used every ounce of his strength to utter the required words and leave the bench, but once in the privacy of his room the pent-up emotion spilled out. He had carried out his duty with dignity and then was overwhelmed by what he had been required by law to do.

I recall another case in which a very experienced judge of the Quebec Superior Court aborted a trial for murder on the third or fourth day because a witness had made a remark that, by some stretch of the imagination, might have been prejudicial to the accused, but that I would not have objected to. Though both sides were quite prepared to continue, the judge declared a mistrial and bound the accused over to the next sitting of the court. Some months after the incident, I met the judge at a social event, and he said, "I suppose you wonder why I declared the mistrial." I said "Yes, I do," because, as lead counsel for the defence, I was totally satisfied that my client would have suffered no prejudice had the trial continued. "Well," said the judge, "I did it because I knew if he was convicted I could not have pronounced a sentence of death." So heavy was the ultimate burden on a judge in a capital case that he was forced to act perversely—not a good commentary on the system of justice.

George D. Finlayson, in his biography of John J. Robinette, recalls a somewhat similar situation. Robinette was defending a youth charged with murder. It was a bad case, and the best the accused could hope for was that the jury would find him guilty of the lesser offence of manslaughter. But how to get the judge to leave that verdict open to the jury? Robinette, who had given the case to Finlayson, suggested that Finlayson invite the judge to tell the jury that the accused and a co-accused had been engaged in a "joint venture for manslaughter." As Finlayson relates the story: "I said [to Robinette], 'What's a joint venture for manslaughter?' 'Never mind,' Robinette replied, 'just make sure the trial judge says this to the jury.'" And he continued:

> I still don't know what a joint venture for manslaughter is, and when I mentioned the legal proposition to my very experienced co-counsel and former Crown Attorney Norman Borins, K.C., he did not know what it was either. The trial judge, the Honourable Mr. Justice Aylen, looked blank when I insisted that he so instruct the jury, but he did so. Justice Aylen was a very kind man, and he had no enthusiasm for sentencing two teenagers to death by hanging. He jumped at the chance to give the jury an alternative verdict to murder. The reality of the situation of these two young men was that without this creative instruction of Robinette's, there was no foundation on the evidence for a verdict of manslaughter.[92]

♦ ♦ ♦

I quickly learned the heavy weight of capital cases. At first, as a junior, the burden was shared with counsel who led me, but soon it fell on my shoulders, sometimes at the trial stage, at other times in the Court of Appeal or in the Supreme Court of Canada. Let me tell you of an early case.

Marcel Descoteaux—I have changed his name to honour his request for privacy—was an eighteen-year-old of slight build and weak intellect. He was the youngest of eleven children. His mother and two sisters suffered from "nervous disorders," and Marcel himself, we were told, was "childlike in his attitude and tastes, rejoicing in games suited for ten-year-olds." He worked as a pin boy in a bowling alley, but after hours he visited night clubs and taverns, where he frequently drank to excess. Not surprisingly, he always was broke.

On October 21, 1961, Descoteaux worked his regular shift at the alley. He was paid at 11:00 p.m., went to a tavern, and then moved on to a restaurant. In the early hours of morning, he and some friends took a taxi to a club called The

Flamingo, where he had more to drink. It was his recollection later that, in the course of the evening, he had consumed two large bottles of beer at the tavern, two more with his supper, and then, at The Flamingo, two glasses of spirits, with four small bottles of beer on the side. He had no trouble walking but, as he said, *j'étais heureux*—I was feeling no pain.

Descoteaux left the nightclub in the small hours of morning, cut across a parking lot, and noticed a case of beer in the back of a car, an opportunity too good to be missed. He broke a window, stole the beer, and hid it on the verandah of a friend's house in the neighbourhood. That done, he decided to return to the club, but on the way he met Robert Lepine (again, the name has been changed), forty-eight, married, and employed as a pumpman at an oil refinery in east-end Montreal. Lepine invited Descoteaux for a drink at The Flamingo, but the doorman wouldn't let them enter because earlier that night Lepine had annoyed the staff and some female customers.

Not to be deprived of his drink with Lepine, Descoteaux went back to his friend's house and took two bottles of beer from the case he had hidden, which they proceeded to drink. It was at that point that Descoteaux decided to steal Lepine's money. He hit him on the head with a bottle, and Lepine hit him back with his fist in the stomach. It was a heavy blow, and Descoteaux fled. While he was running, he spotted a wooden plank on the ground. He stopped, picked it up, and returned to Lepine. A short fight ensued, and Descoteaux struck Lepine with the plank. Lepine collapsed and Descoteaux took his watch and his money, some five or six dollars. He disposed of the plank and the watch and went to sleep in a shack on a vacant lot nearby. Lepine was found later that night, on the sidewalk, in a pool of blood. He was taken to hospital where he died of his injuries.

Descoteaux was arrested two months later, and after a twenty-four-hour detention—there was a police ball that night and the detectives were too busy to question him—he made two declarations, the first to his brother-in-law (whom he had requested to see), the second to the police. Both were highly incriminating. After a brief preliminary hearing, he was committed for trial and he appeared before a judge and jury in the fall of 1962. He was defended by an astute and highly promising young lawyer, Claire Barrette, later a judge of the Superior Court. The charge was capital murder, and if convicted, that meant death.

The trial lasted three days (today it would have taken weeks). Both confessions were admitted in evidence and Descoteaux testified in defence. The sole issue left for the jury was to determine intention, an essential ingredient in the charge. Thus, if he was too drunk to know what he was doing, intent to kill or seriously injure would have been lacking and a verdict for manslaughter would have been proper. Alternatively, if he meant to injure but not kill, the jury could have reduced the offence to non-capital murder. Neither would have called for capital punishment.

Both defences failed and Descoteaux was found guilty as charged. But he was young and simple-minded, and the jury clearly felt that to be hanged by the neck until dead was punishment which didn't fit the crime, so they added a recommendation for "clemency by the court." But, as the law then stood, the judge had no discretion in the matter: there was only one sentence possible, and barring a reversal on appeal, the only hope for the accused to escape execution was through the exercise of an ancient royal prerogative, the mercy of the sovereign. And this, by constitutional usage, would be granted only if the solicitor general so recommended and cabinet agreed.

And so, in the late afternoon of September 21, 1962, in the stately, wood-panelled Court of Queen's Bench, Justice Maurice Cousineau mounted the bench, wearing a tricorne and black gloves, the traditional garb for a judge about to pronounce a sentence of death. Descoteaux was asked by the clerk if he had anything to say before sentence was pronounced. There was no answer.

The judge looked at the prisoner, who was surrounded by guards, and then addressed him as follows:

> Descoteaux, I regret that I must pronounce upon you the sentence which the law imposes in cases such as yours. The law obliges me to impose capital punishment after a verdict of capital murder. I hope that this may serve as a lesson for others who may be tempted to involve themselves in crimes such as this.
>
> The sentence which I now impose upon you, Marcel Descoteaux, is that you be taken to the common jail of the district whence you came and that on Friday, the 30th day of November next, within the precincts of the prison where you will then be detained, you will be hanged by the neck until you are dead.
>
> And may the Lord have mercy on your soul.

There was utter silence in the room as the prisoner was removed to the cells.

Descoteaux's conviction was appealed to the Quebec Court of Appeal. Four of the five judges found that there was no reversible error in the court below, but Justice Antoine Rivard, a former attorney general with some experience in criminal law, would have rejected the confessions because they were not "free and voluntary" as required by law. In his view, the detention for twenty-four hours before the statements were taken vitiated the accused's consent. It is noteworthy that Rivard's most famous case while in practice—*Chapdelaine*—involved the defence of a woman who was charged with murder.[93] The principal evidence against her was a confession obtained by the police after she had been held incommunicado for nine days. The trial judge rejected the statement and the Court of Appeal confirmed his decision.

At the time when *Descoteaux* was argued, the length of a detention considered sufficient to vitiate a confession had been whittled down from nine days to much shorter periods, but twenty-four hours was relatively short even then. To Justice Rivard, however, any detention longer than absolutely necessary was too long, and he reached back to his successful defence in *Chapdelaine*. I had written the leading text on the subject[94] and I agreed with Rivard's sentiments: all detention puts pressure on a suspect to confess, and the longer the detention the more likely that he or she might even confess to facts that are false. (If this sounds unlikely, I can say that it has happened in the past and is likely to happen again.) Still, despite his rejection of the confessions, Justice Rivard found that even without this evidence there was enough proof on which to convict. And so the appeal was unanimously dismissed.

To appeal the unanimous judgment of five judges of a Court of Appeal is not easy. Nevertheless, the partial dissent opened the door for a respectable argument before the Supreme Court of Canada, and Claire Barrette, who had carried the full load up to now, asked Claude Joncas (soon to be her husband and later also a judge) and me to appear with her before the highest court in the land. This was a legal aid case for which, in those days, lawyers were not paid, even though appeals such as this meant many hours of work and heavy out-of-pocket expenditures. We got to work at once—a real team effort—and spent hours poring over the transcripts to make sure that every conceivable point that could be advanced would be argued to the fullest. The fact that our client faced execution spurred us on even more.

Three avenues of approach emerged. The first was rather technical and it concerned a defect in the drafting of the charge. The second dealt with the intent of the accused, and the third was based on Justice Rivard's partial dissent in the Court of Appeal.

Preparation was well underway when we received a message from our client. It was short and pithy: "I killed and therefore I must die. Drop all proceedings." This was in contradiction to his earlier instructions, and we suspected that his detention on death row had affected his already simple mind. We therefore consulted the prison chaplain, who confirmed our suspicion. Descoteaux no longer thought clearly. Together, we decided to press on.

The appeal was heard on June 11, 1963. It was an exceptionally hot day, which added to the tension. The first of our arguments went nowhere, and after all these years I must say rightly so: the drafting was not a model of perfection, but we had to concede that the accused was not misled and suffered no prejudice because of this. The second point dealt with Marcel's intent. It was our submission that the lapse of time—a minute, perhaps—between the original fight and Marcel's return with the wooden plank indicated that what he wanted was revenge for the blows, not robbery, and that it was only later that he stole his victim's watch and cash. We argued that it was open to the jury to say that the fatal blow was not for the purpose of facilitating theft but rather an act of revenge. If so, it would not, as the law then stood, have been capital murder. It wasn't, I admit, a strong point, but it could decently be argued. However, this, too, gained no favour. Nor did the third point carry much weight, for, as Justice Rivard had pointed out himself, even if the confessions had been excluded, Descoteaux's admissions made in the course of his evidence had sealed his fate.

The appeal was dismissed from the bench. One feels no greater sense of finality than when one hears those fateful words pronounced by the presiding judge. It is the end of the road, and even though we were satisfied that we had put before the court all that could properly be argued, we were heavyhearted as we returned to the robing room. The date for execution was five weeks away, and the only hope that remained was that cabinet would commute the sentence. As a precaution, we had already sent the necessary documents to the solicitor general, on whose recommendation cabinet would likely rely.

Fortunately, the suspense was short lived. As we packed our bags and headed back to the hotel, Maurice Charbonneau, a lawyer from the Department of the Solicitor General, who had sat in on the proceedings, approached me and said that he was authorized to tell us that his minister would recommend to cabinet that, in view of our client's youth, the sentence be commuted to imprisonment for life. And so, a short time later, it was.

There is a postscript to the case. Descoteaux began to serve his sentence at Montreal's notorious St. Vincent de Paul Penitentiary. He was a model prisoner and soon he discovered an agreeable hobby: he learned to paint. A few months later, each of his three lawyers received a small painting with a letter of thanks. The last line touched me most. It said: "Your client Marcel, who is happy to be alive." Somehow this made it all worthwhile.

♦♦♦

In eighteen years of practice I either led or participated in the defence of forty-nine homicide cases, sixteen for murder, fifteen for manslaughter, seventeen for causing death by criminal negligence, and one on a charge of infanticide. In the murder cases, two accused were found unfit to stand trial and two others were found not guilty by reason of insanity. One, Descoteaux, had been convicted of capital murder and sentenced to hang, but his sentence was later commuted to imprisonment for life. All others were either acquitted or found guilty of lesser offences and sentenced to terms ranging from "time already served" to life.

All cases involving death are difficult, but the most draining was the infanticide, where a mother, in a moment of utter despair, drowned her week-old baby boy. When the police arrived to question her, she made a statement that was read in court by a veteran member of the homicide squad. He barely got beyond the first paragraph when he broke down and started to sob. The part he couldn't read was this:

> I wanted so badly to try and look after him as best as I could—but in my mind I was absolutely positive that I wasn't able to cope with it—I guess that hearing the baby cry so often must have been getting on my nerves too much—so I decided—I don't know what made me decide to drown him—but I thought he would be much happier if I did, and put him out of his misery, because I'm sure he is a little angel in heaven and is much happier there, than with the care I had been giving him after a few days at home.... I really loved my little infant—to me this is all a dream.[95]

Not surprisingly, the jury found her guilty but insane[96] and she was committed to an institution. After several months of psychiatric treatment, she was released and returned home.

Another case stands out in my mind. An elderly man had shot and killed his daughter's boyfriend, and now he stood charged with capital murder. The accused and his wife had strongly disapproved of their daughter's lover, leading to severe quarrels between the parents and the daughter and her boyfriend. One night, the father, whose bedroom was on the second floor of their house, heard a commotion outside. He got up, went to the window, and saw the boyfriend throwing stones at the windows. He told him to stop, but to no avail. He told him a second time, and the only response he got was a shower of verbal abuse.

Filled with rage, he went to a closet, got a gun, and told the young man that if he didn't go away he would shoot him. Again, the only response was further verbal abuse. A shot rang out and the boyfriend fell, mortally wounded.

The police arrived quickly, and within hours the accused made a statement describing his utter frustration with the situation: he was desperate to protect his daughter, who had resisted her parents' entreaties to end the relationship. When he got the gun, his intention was to frighten the boyfriend, not to harm him, let alone kill him.

The judge's charge was sympathetic to the accused, with a strong hint that manslaughter would be the appropriate verdict. After a short deliberation, the jury returned and the foreman said that they had a question: "What if," he said, "and I only say 'if,' we were to find the accused guilty of manslaughter, what would the sentence be?" To say the least, a highly unusual—and also highly improper—request. Sentence is the judge's domain, and while the court may give effect to a recommendation from the jury, clearly no verdict should be based on the eventual sentence. The judge and the lawyers knew this, of course, but the jurors didn't, and this had to be explained to them.

But the judge went one step further, and after telling the jury that sentence was his exclusive domain, he asked: "Why do you want to know?" The answer was, "We want to know because we want certainty." This was a cue too good to miss, and I blurted out, "If you want certainty you should acquit." That's when all hell broke loose. The judge, already angry at the jury, now turned his anger on me. He broke a pencil in two, threw it toward me from the bench, and said, "You had no right to say that." Now, with the passage of time, I am prepared to admit that he was right—in telling me off, not in losing his temper—but it shook me to the bone at the time because I couldn't see the harm in speaking out, nor did I like to be the object of judicial scorn. After all, what I had said only made sense.

While this little contretemps was in process, the jury was hustled back to their room, and a few minutes later they returned and found the accused guilty of manslaughter, with a strong recommendation for mercy. By then, the judge had calmed down and he was gracious enough to tell the jury that they had carried out their task well. I had apologized in the meantime and that, too, helped calm the waters. Before the crown and I could even begin to speak to the sentence, the judge ordered a pre-sentence report, to be filed a few weeks hence, and he released the accused on his own recognizance so he could return to his family. The report was highly favourable, and in due course the accused was given a suspended sentence. It was, said the judge, a case of a protective father driven to the brink.

While capital punishment still has its proponents, I can only thank God that it's been discarded in Canada. Never again, I hope, will an accused, no matter what the crime, be kept in suspense whether he or she will live or die while the gallows are tested a few feet from the death cell. Never again will a defence lawyer have to sit in his or her office the day before the scheduled execution and wait for that terse, fateful message which would announce the cabinet's decision. And where it was adverse, this is what it said: "Governor General in Council will not interfere with death sentence passed upon [John Smith] tried for murder." Seventeen words for a life. And always at the last possible moment.

The ritual for putting to death the condemned person was all neatly spelled out in a handbook published by the Queen's Printer for Canada: *Capital Punishment Procedure: Instructions by the Secretary of State.* Item One: two months must elapse between the sentence of death and the execution. But no executions on civic or religious holidays. And "sometimes it is inconvenient to fix a date of execution on a Monday." Why? Because the secretary of state knew that despite his suggestion that, "for the sake of uniformity," an execution should be carried out at 8:00 a.m., it almost always (in Quebec, at least) took place a few minutes after midnight to avoid the agony of yet another night for all those involved. Since an execution required much preparation, it was felt that Sunday needed to be kept free. And there was also another reason: it was not unusual for those in charge of the execution—the official hangman (always called Mr. Ellis), the sheriff, and the guards—to have a few drinks to help ease the tension, the danger being that by morning they might be unfit to carry out their functions, as indeed happened on occasion. Sunday drinking was thought to be inappropriate.

The manual went on: at the moment of execution, a black flag must be hoisted on a mast sufficiently elevated to be seen outside the prison; it is to remain flying for one hour; and the prison bell or, by prior arrangement, the bell of a nearby church, must be rung for fifteen minutes both before and after the execution.

It's hard to believe that this is recent history; hard to believe that anyone would want to bring it back; hard to believe that some whose lives were so irretrievably taken were perhaps wrongly convicted—a topic about which I have become very knowledgeable in recent years and about which I am now passionate.

[14]

St. Vincent de Paul

Spring did not come gently in 1963 to Montreal's ancient penitentiary. Overcrowded, primitive, devoid of modern facilities, St. Vincent de Paul, on the north shore of the mighty St. Lawrence, housed some of Canada's most dangerous convicts. Killers, robbers, and rapists filled the cells in the old stone buildings, frequently two to a room barely sufficient for one. Fights, often fatal, were frequent; discipline was tough; and access by inmates to seek relief in the courts was not encouraged by the authorities. The air was tense, and the pent-up resentment was ready to erupt.

On April 30, two prisoners, inspired by a successful hostage taking in British Columbia two weeks before, seized two guards and demanded transfers to other institutions. As they had in British Columbia, the authorities obliged. Clearly, the situation was out of hand. Some officials, perhaps unwisely, said so in public.

On May 2, at 3:50 in the afternoon, two more inmates, Marcel and Claude Marcoux, serving time for armed robberies, grabbed a guard and forced him into Marcel's tiny cell. They had homemade knives and their hostage was quickly subdued. They then hung a blanket behind the bars that separated the cell from the corridor and threw out a note demanding a transfer to New Brunswick. The reason, Claude Marcoux testified later, was that he was not allowed to work in the shops, that he was often framed by guards and sent to the hole by the warden, and that a gang of muscle-men was in charge of the prison. "Ask for an aspirin," he said, "and you might get it a week or so later."[97] Inmates were frequently beaten, morale was low, and a transfer seemed the only solution. His cousin Marcel, he added, felt the same way, and since a similar plan had already worked twice, they thought it might succeed again.

The guard's disappearance went unnoticed for some minutes, and when it was discovered, at about 4 p.m., the proper channels were followed: one guard told another, and together they went to the supervisor on duty. He, in turn, informed the deputy warden, who called the warden at his home. The regional director came next, and finally a call was put through to the top, the commissioner of penitentiaries in Ottawa.

What happened then is not entirely clear. But we do know that the warden arrived on the scene, assessed the situation, and informed the commissioner. They agreed that force should not be used unless absolutely necessary, and a dialogue began through the makeshift curtain. No progress was made and the Marcoux's patience quickly ran out. Shortly before 6 p.m., the warden and his aides became convinced that the hostage was about to be harmed. The regional director, who had by then joined the team, asked for volunteers among the guards, and the cell was taken by force. It was all over in seconds. But when the gun smoke cleared, the hostage was dead, shot by the guards. And so was Marcel Marcoux.

The following week, as required by law, the district coroner assembled a jury of five men—there were no women on juries in Quebec at that time—to hold an inquest into the deaths. They met in the small courtroom above the morgue in an ancient building on St. Vincent Street in Old Montreal. In those days, coroner's inquests were conducted by crown attorneys, who summoned the witnesses and questioned them before the jury. Other parties, including persons who might ultimately be held to blame, were entitled to be represented by counsel but, unlike counsel for the crown, lawyers for such "interested parties" were not entitled to cross-examine witnesses except by leave of the coroner. In most cases, such permission was readily granted, but the very fact that the Coroner's Act made distinctions between different categories of counsel created concerns about the inherent fairness of these proceedings. This was later changed, a direct result of this case.[98]

In keeping with custom, the crown called those who were present on that fateful day. If their stories differed at all, it was in detail only, and no one doubted that Claude Marcoux would be held liable. It had never occurred to federal authorities, however, that the actions of the warden and his men would be questioned, which explains why the commissioner failed to request the federal Department of Justice to have counsel assigned to the inquest.

The evidence was brief, and the jury, in short order, found that the death of Marcel Marcoux was "justifiable." In other words, no blame should be attached to anyone. But the death of the guard, they said, was due to criminal negligence, and blame was put on the warden because he gave the order to attack "hastily and without sufficient concern for the danger to human life." The two guards who had fired the fatal shots were also held to blame. In the words of the jury, "They were negligent, perhaps unwittingly so, in the manner in which they had fired the shots."

It would be an understatement to say that the commissioner and his officials were not pleased with the jury's findings, which the coroner sent to the provincial attorney general for further action. In particular, the commissioner believed that the jury had not been given the complete picture, and he pointed to the fact that had he been asked to appear, he could have provided information that might have altered the outcome. "I can only emphasize again," he wrote, "that this is a most unsatisfactory verdict in so far as the Penitentiary Service is concerned because its effects, if it remains unchanged, will be felt in every one of our institutions."[99]

The commissioner's complaint set off a bureaucratic process which culminated in a recommendation by senior officials in the federal Department of Justice to the minister, Lionel Chevrier, that efforts be made to hold a second, more complete inquest. The minister agreed, and on May 31, 1963, he wrote to the Quebec attorney general, Georges-Émile Lapalme, requesting that a new inquest be held with new jurors. This could be done in virtue of an obscure provision of the Coroner's Act that permitted the provincial attorney general, where he deemed it "necessary in the public interest," to set aside a verdict and order a new hearing. On June 6, 1963, Quebec acceded to the federal request, and a new inquest with a new jury was ordered. Lapalme also required that full standing be given to counsel representing the federal Department of Justice, and I was engaged by Ottawa to act for all federal officials involved in the event.

The new inquest was scheduled to begin in less than four weeks and there was much to be done: witnesses to be interviewed, photographs to be studied, an architect's plan of the scene to be prepared. I had the full cooperation of all parties, but my dealings with the provincial crown had to be delicate because, in its view, the original inquest had been complete. I had a number of meetings with Claude Wagner, who, as assistant chief crown attorney for the District of Montreal, had taken personal charge of the case.

Claude (a future member of parliament, attorney general, and judge) and I had a good working relationship, and he and his assistant, Jacques Ducros (later a justice of the Quebec Superior Court), and I agreed on the procedure to be followed. We decided that the inquest would open in the regular premises of the Coroner's Court in Montreal. It would then adjourn to the penitentiary, where

I had arranged for the boardroom to be transformed into a courtroom. Photographs and plans would be presented to the jury, and so would the witnesses who had already been heard. But, in addition, the commissioner, A.J. Macleod, would be called. Not only did I have to concern myself with legal matters, but it also fell to me to arrange for lunch to be served in the penitentiary to all participants so that time would not be lost by leaving the premises to go to a restaurant. It was not regular prison fare!

The inquest went well. The jury was impressed by the evidence given by the commissioner, who testified that he had instructed those in charge at the scene to try to keep the inmates talking but to make no concessions without his approval. He had also instructed his senior officials—the regional director and the warden—that if the inmates commenced to hurt their hostage, force was to be used "forthwith" to save the officer's life. The degree of force was not specified, but it was clear from MacLeod's evidence that, if necessary, firearms could be used for that purpose. The jury also visited the scene and this, perhaps more than anything else, demonstrated how very difficult it was to storm the cell without taking certain risks. The threat to kill the guard clearly outweighed the dangers of an armed attack, a judgment that had to be made on the spot and under pressure.

After a short deliberation, the jury returned with a unanimous verdict that exonerated the warden and his men. The key was the jury's conclusion that the guard's death was brought about by the criminal manoeuvres of the two inmates who had taken him hostage. The rest had followed. The jury also made three recommendations: first, that the number of guards be increased in the prison; second, that one or more physicians should be permanently attached to the prison; and third, that guards be given additional training in the use of firearms. I doubt if these were ever carried out.

◆◆◆

In Montreal in the early 1960s, juries were picked by the coroner and they were mostly "regulars." Their pay was minimal: $2.00 for each half-day, enough in those days to buy a decent meal. There was no shortage of men willing to serve, and on days when two or three inquests were held, the coroner could provide this small income to a dozen or more people in need. It was his private form of charity, and he made sure that the work was spread around.

I was involved one day in what I thought was an open-and-shut case: a homicide that was solved within hours with a confession by the suspect. There was no point in arguing the admissibility of the statement at that stage. That would come later. So, in Coroner's Court, the detective read the confession to the jury and the coroner said: "Well, it's pretty clear that this death was caused by culpable homicide and your task is not difficult." The jury retired at 11:30 and I was sure that they would be back in a matter of minutes. Not so. The coroner had invited crown counsel and myself to his chambers to wait for the verdict, and when I expressed surprise that it was taking so long, he said: "They'll be in with a verdict at 12:05." And so they were. The reason for the delay? If the case went beyond noon, they not only got an extra half-day's pay but also a free lunch.

Being a coroner's juror in those days was not very taxing. If recommendations had to be made, they were drafted by the coroner and "adopted" by the jury. Once in a while, a jury went beyond these suggestions and added a sentence or two, but that was rare. Indeed, the only unpleasant part of the job was that the Coroner's Act required the jurors to view the body, so a trip had to be made to the morgue in the cellar and what they saw was never pretty.

The morgue personnel, while generally kind to family members, had their own morbid sense of humour. I remember one occasion when a reporter from *La Presse*, Léo Lizotte, asked an attendant what the victim in a vicious slaying looked like. The attendant told him to wait in the lobby while he went downstairs to look. He returned a minute later with the victim's head, which had been severed by the killer. Léo asked for an immediate transfer to a different beat.

◆ ◆ ◆

A short time after the penitentiary inquest, I received a second major mandate from the federal government, this time of a more permanent nature. It came about when Pierre Lamontagne, a well-known Montreal lawyer, called me to ask if I would like to prosecute counterfeit cases on a part-time basis for the Department of Justice. Pierre, who had strong Liberal connections, had been asked by the minister of justice to recommend lawyers for various tasks of this nature, and he had thought of me.

I told Pierre I was interested and a few days later he informed me that the minister had approved the appointment "in principle," but that I would have to furnish a letter of recommendation from my member of parliament. What they wanted, of course, were my political credentials. This presented no problem and I called Eddie Asselin, the newly elected member for Montreal-Notre-Dame-de-Grâce, who wrote a fine letter (which didn't surprise me because, at his request,

I had drafted it myself). A few days later, I was appointed "standing counsel" to the RCMP in counterfeit cases. This meant that prosecutions of this kind would come to me directly, without the need for prior approval on a case-by-case basis. Pierre had opted for narcotics prosecutions, a choice that some years later gave him a lot of grief, through no fault of his own.

To prosecute successfully, I had to learn how counterfeiters worked. The "printers" usually occupied nondescript quarters, equipped with second-hand equipment, which wasn't quite up to the task. Nevertheless, the product appeared sufficiently genuine to fool the unwary. Experience had shown that busy merchants rarely took the time to examine smaller bank notes—from $20 down—with sufficient care to spot the fakes, and while illegal printers did produce some tens and fives, the twenty soon became the standard. Of course, this was long before automated bank machines dispensed $20 bills in huge quantities, but even with the smaller number of twenties then in circulation, a cost-risk analysis indicated to the counterfeiters that this denomination produced the largest profit.

To print these bills was one thing, but the more complicated issue was how to put them into circulation. This was achieved by selling counterfeit bills at large discounts to wholesalers or jobbers, who would then pass them on, with an appropriate mark-up, to retailers. The latter would then use them to pay for small items in stores, receiving change in legal currency. The average "take" of a retailer was 50 per cent of the face value of the counterfeit currency, and on a good day this could amount to a few hundred dollars. The risk of detection was relatively small, and even when caught, there was always the defence: "Gee, I didn't know this was a counterfeit bill."

To obtain a conviction, the crown had to prove that the "uttering" (the legal term for passing or distributing) was done "knowingly," which was a major challenge. Frequently, circumstantial evidence could make the point. For instance— and it always surprised me that experienced distributors weren't any smarter—when police searched a suspect, they often found the counterfeit bills in a separate pocket, away from the genuine money. Judges accepted this as *prima facie* evidence that the accused "knew" that these were counterfeit bills, and in the absence of a reasonable explanation a conviction would follow. At other times, police found that counterfeit bills, while mixed in with genuine bills, were folded in a different manner. Again, this called for an explanation.

To get to the source—the printers—police often made "deals" with those on the lower rungs, and most raids on print shops resulted from information so obtained. A major seizure would slow the counterfeit trade for a while, but fresh supplies, from different sources, would soon arrive and flood the market.

There was a brisk trade in Montreal in counterfeit United States currency as well. Again, the favourite denomination was $20, but these were harder to spot because merchants were less familiar with the foreign bills. In the summer, when thousands of American tourists were in the province, the incidence of counterfeit U.S. bills rose, and while I prosecuted these cases as well, they presented special problems because they required the attendance of experts from the United States Secret Service to prove the currency was fake. This often meant that cases had to be postponed to await the attendance of an expert, with many complaints, of course, from the defence.

While the Montreal-based Counterfeit Squad of the RCMP—a sergeant and eight to ten constables—worked around the clock and had a good arrest record, those convicted often received sentences that were insufficient to act as a deterrent to others. For instance, a person convicted of uttering a counterfeit $20 bill might be fined $50. The theory was that passing counterfeit money was analogous to fraud, and fraud of $20 was so low on the scale for punishment that even a fine might seem excessive. But this approach was fundamentally flawed, since the very essence of commerce is based on the assumption that payment for goods and services is made by legal tender.

As the number of counterfeit cases increased, some of the judges began to make the distinction. In one case, Judge Redmond Roche, in passing sentence, alluded to the fact that a few days before, when he tendered a $20 bill in payment for a minor purchase, the shopkeeper took the bill, studied it carefully, and finally held it under an ultraviolet lamp before giving change. This, said Judge Roche, was quite unacceptable: passing counterfeit bills was not just another form of fraud; it was an offence against society at large and had to be punished accordingly. This was the beginning of a movement toward more significant sentences.

Of course, I was conscious that a distinction had to be made between professional distributors and persons who had received a counterfeit bill and then tried to get rid of it by passing it on to someone else. In my view, the former deserved harsher punishment than the latter who, in a sense, were innocent victims trying to minimize their loss. Generally, they readily confessed, promised never again to be tempted to act in this fashion, and gratefully accepted a suspended sentence.

In the three years that followed my appointment, I prosecuted more than one hundred counterfeit cases, including one where I acted as special prosecutor for the City of Montreal. These cases were usually handled by the RCMP, but the city became involved when the municipal police raided the home of Martha Adams (at one time a well-known madam in Montreal) and found, quite unexpectedly, some counterfeit bills hidden under a cushion. Normally, a city attorney would have taken over the case, but the accused bragged shortly after her arrest that she could "look after things" with the city police. The city's chief legal adviser therefore decided, as a matter of prudence, to hire outside counsel, and I was recommended by the RCMP.

The principal argument of the accused was novel but legally flawed. Since the bills were in sheets not yet cut, her counsel submitted that it couldn't be "counterfeit money" as the term was generally understood. But the Criminal Code defined counterfeit money as "including" false paper money, "complete or incomplete," and the judge held that the word "incomplete" implied that even if the bills were not perfect, they nevertheless fell within the definition of the Code. She was convicted and sentenced to sixteen months in jail.

Adams later wrote a book that she dedicated to two of her lawyers and a mysterious "Monsieur George F."[100] It was part autobiography and part commentary on the laws of prostitution, while also offering reflections on various police forces she had encountered in the course of her life. The RCMP, she said, were gentlemen always. When they left her home, whether it was in Quebec, in the Maritimes, or in Ontario, after executing a search warrant, the house was spotless. Not so with the Quebec Provincial Police or the City of Montreal constabulary. They seemed to delight in leaving a mess. As for jails—and she confessed to having spent time in a few—the food was better in Quebec than in Ontario.

In those days, the incidence of uttering false bills was higher in Quebec than anywhere else in the country, yet sentences for those convicted were the lowest. My special assignment was to try to change this situation. I had compiled statistics to support my position when an opportunity presented itself to try to convince the Court of Appeal that counterfeiting was more serious than theft or fraud, because it jeopardized commerce, and therefore called for higher sentences. The opportunity arose in *R. v. Lacoste*,[101] a case from Joliette, in which a magistrate had sentenced an accused to three months in jail for the possession of 6,400 counterfeit $5 bills. I was instructed to appeal and the case was heard by a panel of five judges, presided over by the Chief Justice, Lucien Tremblay.

I referred to the statistics in the course of my argument, but was stopped by Justice Paul Casey who told me in no uncertain terms that if these facts were not in evidence (and they were not), I couldn't introduce them in my argument. He was quite right, of course, but just when I thought that I would have to save my statistics for another day, another member of the bench, Justice Edouard Rinfret, said: "These figures may not be in evidence, but I would like to see them anyway." Of course, I was only too happy to oblige, but as I handed the documents to the registrar, Justice Casey said, "I don't want them." The other three members of the bench remained silent. This put me in an awkward position, but fortunately the registrar had already taken the papers from me, and I could therefore say with a clear conscience (and great relief), "As the court pleases," and sit down. The problem now was his, not mine.

Judgment was given a short time later. Each of the five judges wrote reasons: two would have allowed the appeal and increased the sentence by adding an additional term of imprisonment for two years. Two others would also have allowed the appeal, but rather than increase the term of imprisonment, they would have obliged the accused to sign a bond to keep the peace for two years, with supervision during that time. The fifth judge—the one who had asked for the statistics—also would have allowed the appeal, but he would have increased the sentence from three months to five years. This caused some confusion, but the net result was that the accused was ordered to serve an additional two years. More important to me was the fact that, in his reasons for judgment, Justice Rinfret repeated the statistics, in addition to saying the following:

> Judges in general, and particularly those in the Province of Quebec, do not appear to attach all the attention they should to the intention expressed so clearly by the Legislature, and impose insignificant sentences which are more an encouragement to such conduct than true deterrent.
>
> In my opinion the statistics supplied by counsel for the appellant are ... revealing and call for severe corrective punishment.[102]

Thereafter, whenever I wanted to cite the statistics, I would simply refer to the report of *Lacoste*, and much use was made of these figures in subsequent cases. Indeed, within a year, sentences went up in Quebec and counterfeiting offences decreased significantly.

[15]

Of Heart Transplants and Other Things

Some years ago, in giving judgment in a contract case,[103] Justice Paul Casey, speaking for the Quebec Court of Appeal, examined the facts and found that, at a certain point, the plaintiff had had a "change of heart." No problem there, but the headnotes in the Quebec Law Reports are published in French, so the judgment was sent for translation, and when it finally appeared in print it told the story of a plaintiff who had undergone a *transplantation de coeur*, a heart transplant. Although somewhat amusing, no great damage was done, but it demonstrates the potential pitfalls of translation.

There are, of course, many occasions when judges and lawyers must rely on interpreters, and while most courts in the country have competent people to perform this difficult task, mishaps—sometimes funny—do occur. My favourite is the time I had a Chinese client who spoke neither English nor French and therefore testified with the help of an official court interpreter. It all went well in the beginning, but when we got to the heart of the matter, my client's answers in Chinese were much longer than the English translations. The judge first thought that the interpreter gave an abbreviated version and told him to translate what the accused said sentence by sentence. He did so for the next few answers, but soon fell back into his old habit. Finally, when the accused gave a very long answer that the interpreter condensed into a simple "no," the judge became angry and asked the interpreter if he had understood the witness. "Certainly," he replied, somewhat indignant that the court should doubt his competence, "but it was all hearsay and therefore inadmissible."

Another time I acted for a scrap dealer who got into a fight with a competitor. At first they shouted at each other, but as the battle heated up, my client pulled a knife out of his belt and began gesticulating wildly with the knife in his hand. He slightly injured his opponent, which surprised them both, but the fight stopped at once, and by the time the police came calm had returned. A few days later, my client was charged with assault causing bodily harm. We opted for a speedy trial and hoped that the judge might acquit or at least reduce the charge to a lesser offence. The crown's case was straightforward, but the accused, testifying in his own defence, said that the victim had provoked him and that he had lost all self-control. Not surprisingly, the judge wanted more detail, but the accused was most reluctant to expand. "He called me a bad name," he said. "So bad that it's not fit to be repeated in a court of law." But "bad names" do not shock judges, and after much urging the witness, who had testified in Yiddish, told the interpreter that the victim had referred to him as "Moishe Putz." This posed a dilemma for the interpreter, since idiomatic expressions are hard to translate. Finally, after proper reflection, he translated this as "Moses Prick," which is literally correct but devoid of any flavour or meaning. By then, the judge had had enough of the whole matter and he cut the proceedings short by finding the accused guilty of common assault and fining him $100, a result that satisfied everyone, the victim included.

One of the best-known interpreters at the time was Harry Schaeffer, who was a fixture in the criminal courts in Montreal for as long as anyone could remember. In the 1950s and 1960s, interpreters were paid $2.00 a case and volume was therefore important to them. Every morning, Schaeffer would scan the lists and hurry to the courtroom that had the largest number of accused with foreign-sounding names. Since he could speak five or six languages, his services were frequently required, but even when they were not—not everyone with a foreign name needs an interpreter—judges would often ask him to see how well an accused or witness could speak English or French, and even if he or she could do so perfectly, Schaeffer would get a voucher from the clerk to collect his $2.00. That way the judges made sure he made a decent, if uncertain, living.

Often Harry had to work hard for his money, and while he interpreted to the best of his ability, the modern world sometimes posed problems for him. I recall the case of a smuggler who was caught at the airport with a small bag of diamonds that he had failed to declare. A favourite method of smugglers in those days was to put such contraband goods into a condom, tie the open end with a string, and hide the condom and its cargo in his rectum. Schaeffer was called upon to interpret the arresting officer's evidence for the benefit of the accused, but the word "condom" stumped him completely. I suspect that it wasn't even a question of being unable to translate the word but rather that he didn't know what it was. So, for the rest of the trial, a "condom" became "the thing," and I sometimes wonder if Schaeffer ever understood the details.

Speaking of smugglers, I must recount my favourite case. It concerned a portly gentleman who passed through customs at the airport without incident, but then made the fatal error of starting to run as soon as he got to the "other side." The officers watched him with benign amusement as his speed diminished rapidly and after twenty paces or so he fell to the ground—brought down by the weight of four hundred watches tied to the inside of his coat. It was the easiest arrest they made in a long time.

◆ ◆ ◆

We always made a point of telling our clients to be appropriately dressed for court. Of course, this shouldn't be exaggerated, but I am quite convinced that judges and jurors take in the "whole" person and dress plays a part. It needn't be fancy, but suits and dresses should at least be neat and clean.

I once had a case in Sainte-Anne-des-Monts, a circuit town on the lower St. Lawrence just east of Rimouski. I had gone there to defend a group of strikers and their supporters, who had been arrested on a picket line. The charges ranged from disturbing the peace to assaulting a constable, and while the strike had by then been settled, the atmosphere remained tense. On the morning of the trial, every seat in the small courtroom was filled, and there was no doubt where the spectators' sympathies lay. Loud cheers greeted the accused and equally loud jeers were directed at the police. The judge, of course, told the crowd to be quiet, but he was a local man and he fully understood the feelings of the strikers and their families and friends.

One of my clients was the wife of a striker and she was charged with assault and resisting arrest. She was a young woman, perhaps twenty-five or so, and as she stood at the bar she was the picture of innocence: an angelic face, no make-up, her hair nicely arranged. She wore a blue dress with a white collar and no jewellery except a simple wedding band. The crown's evidence suggested that she was loud and abusive on the picket line, and when asked by a constable to calm down, she kicked him. When he decided to arrest her, she resisted, which is a criminal offence provided the arrest is lawful.

When I cross-examined the constable, he agreed that the picket line had been peaceful until the police arrived, but he wouldn't budge on the fact that the accused had kicked him and then resisted arrest. I must say, as we all looked at the accused, dressed as she was, it seemed unlikely that this vision of angelic innocence could have behaved in the manner described by the constable, but a defence had to be made, and so I called my client. Sure enough, she denied the allegations, although she agreed that perhaps, quite accidentally, she might have had some body contact with the officer which he might have considered an assault. Certainly, I thought, a clear case for a "benefit of doubt" acquittal.

When the crown attorney rose to cross-examine, his first question was: "Madam, would I be right in saying that on the day in question you were dressed differently than today?" "Yes," she said, "I was. You see," she added—and as she said it she looked at the judge—"this is what I wear to church, and I wanted to show respect for the court, so I put on my best dress." Of course, the judge was all smiles and he praised the witness for her commendable attitude. The crown attorney, too, added his compliments, but unlike the judge, he knew precisely where he was going and so he pressed on, politely but firmly. Would the witness like to tell the court just how she had dressed for the picket line? "Sure," she said, "in a sweatshirt and jeans." Once again, His Honour couldn't resist a remark: "That's very sensible," he said, and turning to the crown attorney, he added: "You certainly wouldn't expect her to wear her best dress on that occasion."

Still, the crown pressed on: "Was, by chance, anything written on the back of the shirt?" At that point I began to feel a little uneasy—that indefinable feeling of doom and gloom that defence lawyers get once in a while. "Oh, yes," she said, "the letters PP." And what did that stand for, crown counsel asked. "Provincial Police." "And was there anything else?" "You mean the arrow?" she replied. "That's what I mean, an arrow pointing downward." A smile came on her face as she answered: "I guess you don't know what that means," she said. "PP, Provincial Police, and they can kiss my ass!" Wild cheers in the courtroom, with only a feeble attempt by the judge to stop it.

The crown had no further questions and neither did I, and in a short judgment from the bench the judge expressed his considered opinion that the contest was a draw: the police had provoked the accused, but then the accused had provoked the police, and in any case, if there was an assault, it was insignificant, and the arrest might therefore not have been lawful. And so, he ruled, this was a case for benefit of doubt, a decision that clearly pleased the spectators.

◆ ◆ ◆

Sometimes lawyers are simply unlucky. I remember a case—by then I was a judge—in which a man had been ordered to support his former spouse, a lawyer, during a period of *recyclage*, perhaps a year or two, during which she would acquire the skills required to re-enter practice and take care of her own needs. Three years had passed with no results, a lapse of time that the husband found altogether too long and he now asked to be relieved of any further payments. His lawyer argued eloquently that although his client had been happy to support his ex-wife while she studied law the time had come for her to earn some money. Instead, he said, she now had the *rocambolesque*—"audacious" or "preposterous" in English—idea to go on for a master's degree to make herself an even better lawyer. And that at great cost to his client.

Of course, the unlucky lawyer didn't know that two of the three judges who heard the appeal (myself and Louis LeBel, now a judge of the Supreme Court of Canada) were married to lawyers with master's degrees. But he did have a point, although he might have wished that his language had been a little less colourful.

◆ ◆ ◆

In the late 1960s and early 1970s, the Rolling Stones topped all the rock charts. People lined up for days to get tickets and scalpers got astronomical prices. Everyone wanted to be at the concerts.

In the summer of 1972, the Stones were on their seventh tour of North America. They were booked into the Montreal Forum for the night of July 17. The *Gazette* called them "the greatest rock band in the world," and Dan Lanken, in a full-page feature two days before the concert, noted that fan enthusiasm had reached "fever pitch." "The Rolling Stones," he wrote, "are ... the ultimate masters of a musical form that's been developing for two decades and has captured and/or expressed the imagination of a generation."

I took the upcoming event in stride. Rock is not my favourite form of music, and I had no plans to be at the concert. Indeed, I made a mental note to avoid the vicinity of the Forum, where traffic was bound to be tied up for hours and fights were likely to break out between security guards and fans trying to crash the event. But all this changed with a phone call three days before the show. A lawyer from New York wanted to know if I would act for the Stones "in case my services were needed." This was a bit mysterious, but he explained that the Stones' managers were worried about incidents that might arise, and they therefore had a lawyer "stand by" in each city where the band appeared. Would I be their representative in Montreal?

I agreed and we arranged the fee—$100 and two tickets for the concert. All I had to do was be available in case of need. I invited my partner Harvey Yarosky to join me at the Forum. It was quite an event, and while it didn't change my taste in music, it was exciting. There were no incidents that evening, and the next morning I got a message that the Stones had left Montreal and now were in someone else's jurisdiction.

Apart from the fun and the fee, I also earned the admiration of my children when they reached their teens. The talk had turned to rock and I mentioned my experience. It had an electrifying effect. "You represented the Stones?" they asked in disbelief. "You must have been a very important lawyer." I didn't disabuse them.

There is an interesting sequel. Thirty years later, when the Stones, still going strong, performed in Toronto, the senior partner of my daughter Leslie's law firm, Austin Cooper (who had successfully defended Keith Richards on a drug charge many years earlier), was engaged to do what I had done, and Leslie got to make the necessary arrangements. But she proved to be a better negotiator than I, and the firm got six tickets rather than two!

♦ ♦ ♦

The *Dictionary of Canadian Law*[104] defines a "presumption" as "an inference or conclusion about the truth of some questionable fact which is drawn from another fact judicially noted, admitted or proved to be true." In plain language, this means that once a certain fact has been established, a court may presume the existence of another fact even though direct proof is lacking. For instance, in virtue of section 215(4)(b) of the Criminal Code, "evidence that a person has in any way recognized a child as being his child is, in the absence of evidence to the contrary, proof that the child is his child." Thus, if, for instance, I introduce a child as "my daughter," the law will presume (for certain purposes, at least) that she is indeed my child. Such presumptions are important because certain facts, such as paternity, are sometimes difficult to prove (although DNA testing now overcomes some of the hurdles). It is for reasons such as this that we have legal presumptions, but they do not always have the intended effect. Indeed, I recall two cases where presumptions actually hindered rather than helped. Now, with the passage of time, the incidents even seem funny.

Léonard Trépanier, an old-timer on the Montreal legal scene, was given on occasion to courtroom histrionics. For instance, legal lore has it that one day he cited an article from Quebec's Civil Code, only to be told by the judge that the provision was without significance. Without skipping a beat, Trépanier replied: "Very well, if your Lordship says it has no meaning, it shouldn't be there," and with that he tore a page out of the book. Another time, in the Court of Appeal—and this time I was present—Trépanier led off his argument with this startling statement: "My Lords, this case concerns a child which has two fathers." This may have been unorthodox, but it certainly caught everyone's attention, and a request to explain quickly came from the bench. And explain he did, for what had happened was that two men had been ordered to pay for the child's upkeep, one by a magistrate in a criminal case, the other by a judge of the Superior Court. And all because of presumptions.

This is the explanation. The mother of the child was married to A, but they separated and she moved in with B. The child was born a year or so later, but this union didn't last either and B disappeared. Neither man supported the child, and the mother was urged to prosecute B for failure to provide the child with the necessaries of life. B was located by the police, and at his trial the crown made proof that he and the mother had "cohabited" when the child was conceived. A presumption (which has since been removed from the Code to keep up with the times) kicked in and B was deemed to be the father and therefore found guilty as charged and ordered to support the child.

In the meantime, Trépanier's client, who was the real husband and therefore deemed in civil law to be the father, moved to "disavow" the child, but his action was dismissed because it was taken more than a year after he had heard of the birth, which was too late under the law that then existed. He, too, was therefore ordered to support the child, and hence the legal oddity that the child did indeed have two putative fathers, a conundrum that the Court of Appeal had to resolve. I don't remember how it was done, but a common-sense solution was found in the end.

The second case concerned a charge of drunk driving. The evidence showed that my client and a friend left a suburban golf course in the early hours of morning. The friend, who drove, failed to stop at the exit, crossed a busy highway, and ended up in a ditch on the other side of the road. Both were in a happy mood and neither was quite sober. Stuck in the ditch, they considered their plight, and the driver suggested that his passenger move into the driver's seat to steer the car while he, the driver, pushed the vehicle out of the ditch. Of course, it was a hopeless endeavour, but this is what he was trying to do when the police arrived a few minutes later. After a quick survey of the scene, the constables arrested my client, who sat behind the wheel, and took him to the station to be charged. The real driver, in the meantime, exhausted from his efforts, was gently put in the back of the cruiser and driven home "to sleep it off."

The uninitiated might say this is a case of mistaken identity. Not so, because the Criminal Code (in section 258(1)(a)) creates a presumption that whoever occupies the driver's seat of a car shall be deemed to have the care and control of the vehicle. This was sufficient to convict my client, but given the circumstances, he was fined a nominal amount. And since he didn't own a car, the mandatory prohibition from driving for three months caused him no particular hardship.

There is a postscript to the story. A few weeks after the event, I got a call from the judge. He seemed to recall, he said, that my client—the "deemed" driver—worked for the *Gazette* in Montreal. When I confirmed that he did, the judge asked me if, perhaps, I could ask him to use his influence to have the paper publish a photo taken at his nephew's wedding. I made the call, my client spoke to the appropriate editor, and a few days later the picture was printed.

[16]
The Tax That Wasn't

Most cases start with a phone call and this was no exception. The caller was the deputy attorney general of Quebec, and he found me in Montreal's ancient Bordeaux Jail, where I had gone to interview a client. He asked if I could be in Quebec City later that day to meet with the attorney general. The date was April 30, 1968. It was mid-morning. I said I could, and he arranged for transportation—the attorney general's Buick with a provincial police officer as driver. I saw my client in jail and then returned to my office, curious to know what the afternoon held in store. I had asked my caller, but all he would say was, "We'll tell you when you get here."

I suspected I knew what it was about. Some weeks before, the city of Montreal, short of money as always, had announced the institution of a "voluntary tax." The scheme was set out in flyers and newspaper advertisements throughout the province. "Become a VOLUNTARY TAXPAYER OF MONTREAL," the announcement urged. "A payment of $2 is valid for one month and gives you the opportunity of receiving one of the 151 MONTHLY PRIZES." There was one "grand prize" of $100,000 "in silver ingots," plus 150 other prizes, also in silver ingots, ranging in value from $100 to $1,000. The announcement then added this: "The selection of the 151 candidates whose names have been chosen for examination will be made publicly. They will be advised immediately of the time, day and place where they will have to answer, in public, questions related to the subjects printed on the reverse side of the official receipt. Having answered correctly, candidates will then be awarded their prize."

That, then, was the catch: a "skill-testing" question, designed, no doubt, to try to make it legal. But what if the "taxpayer" was too young or not available to answer questions? Not to worry—parents, or even others, could answer for the child, and if the taxpayer chosen for examination was ill, "a person duly authorized by the candidate" would be allowed to answer on his behalf. That's what the notice said. Questions about the plan's legality had already been raised. Could this be why I was called to Quebec?

I had by then acquired a reputation as an expert on lottery law. It started with a case I had in 1963 in the Supreme Court of Canada.[105] Buckley's Wholesale Tobacco conducted a mail-order distribution plan that, in effect, was a pyramid scheme: a group of individuals would receive an explanation of the company's operation, together with three cards; they could then sell the cards to friends and neighbours for $4.00 each. Purchasers would fill in their names and addresses in the appropriate space and give the card back to the vendor, who would return it to the company together with the $12 he had collected. Upon receipt, the company sent three cartons of cigarettes to the original vendor and three empty cards to each of the three buyers, and so *ad infinitum*. Certain safeguards were included in the scheme. For instance, if a person was unable to sell a set of cards, he could return them to the company and choose a premium from a number of items.

A magistrate found the company guilty of conducting a lottery scheme, but the Quebec Court of Appeal reversed the decision, holding that a carton of cigarettes did not fall within the definition of "valuable security," as required by the Criminal Code before a scheme could be declared a lottery. The crown was upset with this judgment—if it's a carton of cigarettes today, what might it be tomorrow?—and obtained leave to appeal to the Supreme Court of Canada.

The day the case was to be heard in the Supreme Court, I met the crown attorney in the robing room. He had never been to the Supreme Court before, and he asked me what to expect. I said it was very much like the Court of Appeal, only the number of judges would be larger, probably five or seven (the case wasn't important enough for all nine). They would be gowned in black. He, as the appellant's counsel, had to sit on the left—in the Court of Appeal it didn't matter where you sat—and, as a Queen's Counsel, he was entitled to sit in the first row, inside the bar, as it was called (and there actually was a bar!). As the respondent's counsel, I would sit on the right, but since I had not yet achieved the status of a Queen's Counsel, I would sit in the second row, behind the bar. The rest, I said, would be just like at home.

We were in our seats at 10:30 when the large oak doors behind the bench opened. An attended cried for "Order" and in marched nine judges dressed in red and ermine. My friend turned to me and mouthed something that I could only interpret as, "You little son of a bitch," and all I could say was that I was as surprised as he was at the spectacle. The mystery was solved almost immediately when the chief justice said, "We are here to welcome our new brother, Mr. Justice Emmet Hall."[106] Both the chief justice and the new judge then said a few appropriate words and the court was adjourned and the nine judges walked out. Five of them returned a few minutes later, led by Chief Justice Robert Taschereau, who invited crown counsel to begin his submissions. He started in the usual way—"My Lords, this is an appeal from the Quebec Court of Appeal, reversing the judgment of a magistrate finding the Respondent guilty of conducting a lottery scheme by mail."

All this seemed reasonable enough, but as soon as my hapless friend mentioned "mail," the chief justice interrupted him to ask if the crown had had any complaints from the postmaster general. It was meant to be funny, but "funny" remarks by judges are not appreciated by counsel, and while I, as the respondent, could afford to smile, to the crown attorney this was an irrelevant question, yet all he could say was "No, my Lord" and let it go at that. It did, however, set the tone, and a few days later a short judgment came down dismissing the appeal. It was duly reported, with my name as counsel for the respondent. And since most schemes of this nature are questionable, it quickly attracted all sorts of people with all sorts of schemes to get my advice on the subject. Most plans, of course, were hopelessly illegal, but by 1968 I had a thick file containing all the case law and all the written opinions I had given. I grabbed this file and read it during the three-hour drive to Quebec.

My hunch was right. The attorney general, Jean-Jacques Bertrand,[107] wanted to confirm his advisers' view that Montreal's scheme was indeed a lottery. He suggested I stay overnight to prepare an opinion. But, having studied the matter in the car, my mind was made up, and I told him then and there that I had no doubt that the scheme was illegal, a view that I supported with the relevant authorities. He was impressed, but slightly annoyed. Who, he wanted to know, had informed me in advance of the subject? I hastened to assure him that no one had done so and that I had taken a chance on the topic. He seemed satisfied with my answer.

Bertrand, who later became leader of his party and served one term as premier of Quebec, represented the best of the rural bar. He was a good, well-rounded lawyer, unfailingly polite and genuinely interested in the welfare of his community. His private office was a small one-storey house in Sweetsburg, now part of Cowansville, in the heart of Quebec's Eastern Townships. The courthouse (and the jail) were across the street, and his practice covered all facets of law. Country lawyers, unlike their city cousins, cannot afford to specialize. They must know something about everything, but frequently they know much more than that, and I have often marvelled at the very broad base of knowledge that they bring to their practice. Jean-Jacques Bertrand was of that breed, a man devoted to his family, his province, his country, and his profession.

I first met Bertrand in 1965, when we served together on the provincial Bar's Board of Examiners. This was a time-consuming job, as I've mentioned, and I asked him one day how, with a practice at home and a seat in the legislature, he could afford to spend twenty days a year setting and correcting papers. The question surprised him. "Mon cher Fred," he said, "when the Bar asks you to serve you do not refuse."

The meeting in his office lasted well into the evening. We all agreed—the minister, his senior staff, and I—that Montreal's "tax" scheme violated the clear provisions of the Criminal Code. That was the easy part. The hard part was to determine what the province should do. Some thought the crown should apply for a warrant to search city hall and seize all documents relating to the scheme. This plan did not appeal to me and I said so. After all, however illegal the "tax," it was unthinkable to me that the city, faced with the threat of prosecution, would destroy any potential evidence. Besides, the advertisements that the city had placed already told the full story.

As happens so often, there was also a political aspect: Would the population of the province, where the demand for lotteries was great, countenance a drastic step of this kind? Would the provincial authorities, warrant in hand, not look rather ridiculous invading City Hall and hauling hundreds of filing cabinets to a fleet of waiting trucks? It would be a media event, and what government needs that kind of circus, with a possible backlash in court?

I voiced my concerns and the idea was abandoned. Our thoughts then turned to the nitty-gritty of a prosecution. But who should be the accused? Some thought that it should be the mayor, Jean Drapeau; others were prepared to settle for the municipal corporation. I sensed that the minister was ill at ease with this advice. Again, the politics of the situation could not be overlooked. It was at that point that I suggested that a reference might be in order, and Bertrand liked the idea. In the provincial context, a reference is a question addressed by the cabinet to the Court of Appeal. This is done by order-in-council, and it asks the court to give its opinion on the legality of legislation, proposed legislation or, as in this case, an existing scheme. And so, late that day, Bertrand decided to ask his cabinet colleagues to authorize a reference.[108]

I returned to Montreal late that night, and I must confess that I was not displeased to read, two days later, an editorial written by Claude Ryan in *Le Devoir* which suggested that the province should test the legality of the scheme without, however, resorting to actions such as search and seizure.[109] My caution, I thought, had been vindicated. Soon, cabinet approved the plan, and a formal order-in-council was passed on May 8, 1968, referring the matter to the Court of Appeal.[110] The question put to the court was simple: Does the carrying out of the scheme by the city of Montreal contravene any provisions of the Criminal Code? The legal battle had begun.

A panel of five judges, presided by Chief Justice Lucien Tremblay, heard the case on June 20, 1968. Yves Pratte, later to become a judge of the Supreme Court of Canada, and I appeared for the province. The city was represented by Michel Côté, head of the Law Department, and a rising young lawyer, Antonio Lamer, who was to become the chief justice of Canada.

The five judges deliberated over the summer and their decision was released on September 24.[111] Three justices, Casey, Taschereau, and Owen, answered in the affirmative: the scheme was illegal. Chief Justice Tremblay gave a qualified "yes"—if the answer to the skill-testing question was indeed found on the back of the ticket, as the crown claimed. Justice Rinfret thought that the scheme might be saved if the answers required of a winning candidate were truly skill testing and not a sham. But this, he thought, would be known only once the scheme was operational.

It was a victory, of course, but not as clear-cut as we had hoped. The city found encouragement in the dissents and wanted to appeal. However, a decision given in a reference is not a "judgment"—it is advice to the crown—and there is no provision for an appeal. To overcome this obstacle, the government had early on introduced special legislation that, by a fiction of law, declared that the opinion to be given by the Court of Appeal on this reference "shall be deemed to be a judgment ... and an appeal shall lie therefrom as from a judgment in an action."[112] The way was thus paved for the city to appeal to the Supreme Court of Canada, and so it did. In the meantime, my colleague Yves Pratte had assumed the chairmanship of Air Canada, and the attorney general asked Claude Gagnon, the *bâtonnier* of Quebec (and, many years later, one of my colleagues on the Court of Appeal), to be senior counsel. Like Yves Pratte before him, Claude Gagnon was a pleasure to work with. Gracious, urbane, and highly skilled, he was in every sense a leader of the Bar and I looked forward to arguing the case with him.

But it was not to be. Some days prior to the hearing, Gagnon was called to Paris on urgent business for the Bar. A postponement could probably have been arranged, but both parties were anxious to have the issue resolved. The attorney general expressed his confidence in my ability to "go it alone" but offered to appoint senior counsel should I so wish. I declined with thanks. As it turned out, this was the right choice but, until the judgment came out, I often wondered if I had not been overly confident. The unanimous decision completely supported the view that this was not a tax but a lottery,[113] and the city was forced to abandon the scheme.

I had worked hard since the initial phone call in 1968, and my reward was not only the satisfaction of having concluded the case successfully (and, of course, collecting my fee) but also a letter from Gérald Boisvert, the associate deputy attorney general, congratulating me on the result and telling me of "the satisfaction with which the decision was received, not only by the Department of Justice, but also by the Provincial Cabinet."

[17]
The Computer Riot

Everyone that believes in justice,
let's get off your asses and take a stand for a change.
——SIR GEORGE WILLIAMS UNIVERSITY STUDENT URGING MASS ACTION.[114]

Judge Emmett J. McManamy thought it was "the work of experienced activists."[115] Angry Conservatives and *Creditistes* blamed the attack on "everyone from French Communists to Black Power Radicals and Chinese Maoists."[116] Others thought that the violence was but the climax of "the frustration that the Brothers experienced for nearly a year."[117]

Whatever the catalyst, the destruction of the Sir George Williams University Computer Centre on February 11, 1969, shocked the community. No one believed that this could happen in Montreal. And, of all places, at Sir George's, a university that had its roots in adult education, an institution that often accepted students not wanted by anyone else, a place where lack of funds never prevented anyone from obtaining a higher education, a university that, many years later, would accept me as an MBA student even though I was well past the normal age for admission.

To try to understand what happened on that fateful day, we must go back to April 1968. A complaint was made that a professor, Perry Anderson, systematically gave lower grades to blacks. An inquiry was launched by the university, but the hearing process broke down at the start when the parties involved could not agree on the composition of the committee being struck. Fired up by this "evidence" that the democratic process had not worked, the situation deteriorated quickly.

On January 22, 1969, eleven black students went to the office of Vice-Principal John O'Brien. Angry words were exchanged, and some of the students rifled through files looking for evidence that Dr. O'Brien had not been truthful in his public statements. The vice-principal and four staff members who were in the office at the time were not permitted to leave and a stalemate ensued. Ultimately,

O'Brien was forced to write a letter of apology for an alleged misstatement. Significantly, the last line read: "I do not make this statement under duress"—a clear giveaway that he had done just that. The occupation of his office then ended. The following day, acting on legal advice, the university charged three of the students with kidnapping and extortion. From that point on, the situation went rapidly downhill. A further hearing into the affair was held on February 1. It ended in chaos. Outraged students left the meeting, surged up the escalators, and invaded the Computer Centre. From there they issued five demands:

1. That the Hearing Committee and its subsequent proceedings be totally and publicly rejected;
2. That the Administration arrange a meeting of themselves, Professor Anderson and ourselves to settle the composition of a Hearing Committee, the procedure under which any such hearing will be conducted and the date and time of such a hearing;
3. That any such meeting with the Administration be held in an atmosphere free of all threats of reprisals and other primitive measures, judicial, educational or otherwise;
4. That due consideration be given to those Caribbean students who have lost study time due to their brotherly devotion to this case over the last few months;
5. That all criminal charges against black students be dropped immediately.[118]

Negotiations took place, but they were not fruitful. The occupation continued and in the beginning the university permitted occupiers to leave and return at will. They also permitted food to be brought to the centre. On February 7 a second occupation occurred. This time, it was the cafeteria and the Faculty Club.

Then, on February 11, violence erupted. Computers were set on fire, and IBM cards fluttered like snowflakes from the ninth floor windows to the street below. Smoke poured from the doors, leading authorities to believe that there was a clear danger to life, and so police and firefighters moved in. Ninety-seven students were arrested, photographed, and sent to police cells. Seven students under eighteen were taken to Juvenile Court. The others were kept in the holding cells at the Municipal Court, and arraignments on criminal charges began at 3:30 in the afternoon. The process lasted until midnight. At that point, I was an interested bystander and my office was not involved.

Inevitably, there was a great deal of confusion. Anxious parents milled about, many with lawyers. Bail was refused at that point, but some of the lawyers, realizing that their clients might otherwise have to spend the night in jail, bypassed the process in the Municipal Court and addressed themselves directly to the Superior Court to have their bail applications heard. Most were successful and in the end all accused were released.

The complaints against the occupiers were signed by an official of the university. The charges ranged from conspiracy to commit indictable offences to causing mischief to private property, and all of the adults accused opted for trial by judge and jury. This meant that preliminary hearings had to be held, and as the law then stood, counsel chosen and paid for by the university would conduct these hearings. After much legal wrangling, it was decided that the prosecution would proceed in one case, and that the evidence so collected would then be applied to the others. All were committed for trial. From this point on, the crown would be in charge.

My status as an uninvolved party changed abruptly on August 26, 1969, when I received a call from Louis Paradis, the chief crown attorney for the District of Montreal. The attorney general had decided that special counsel should be engaged to lead for the crown in the forthcoming trials and wanted me to undertake the task. After a quick consultation with my partners, I agreed.

I didn't know it then, but my involvement would ultimately last two years. The first task was to examine the voluminous files, and this I did over the next few days. Claude-Armand Sheppard and Charles Flamm, who had acted for the university at the preliminary hearings, also were given appointments as crown attorneys *ad hoc*, with the specific mandate to assist me, which they did effectively in the months that followed.

The first step in the trial process was to have the accused arraigned on the indictments, and this was done before Justice Maurice Cousineau in the Court of Queen's Bench on September 2, 1969. This alone took the entire day. Many, with the crown's consent, re-opted to be tried by a judge without jury, and this involved further appearances before the Court of Sessions.

In criminal trials, the crown has the privilege of deciding who shall be included in an indictment. In other words, it was our decision whether to proceed individually or by groups. I chose the latter route, mostly because individual trials would have involved lengthy delays. On the other hand, it is inadvisable to try too many persons at once. First, it may confuse the jury. But, equally important, it may involve too many lawyers since each accused is entitled to his or her own counsel. Because each lawyer may cross-examine every witness, including witnesses called by their co-accused, such trials can go on for months.

Choices therefore had to be made, and they had to be made quickly. It soon became clear that there were certain discernible groups. For instance, I received a telephone call from the high commissioner in Ottawa for Trinidad and Tobago, who told me that his government had engaged counsel for ten of the accused who came from his country, but that they could not afford to pay for more than one trial. I therefore agreed to put all ten in one indictment—an action for which I received a great deal of abuse from some who thought that I had picked ten black students on purpose. Regrettably, none of the three lawyers who acted for the defence saw fit to explain that I had drafted the indictment at the request of their clients' government and with the full consent of counsel, who not only were content to have their clients tried together but also requested that their case be the first to be heard, another action for which I was criticized in some quarters. I had to bear this criticism in silence because I considered it inappropriate at the time for the crown to comment on how these choices were made.

I later learned that, even though the government of Trinidad and Tobago had agreed to fund the students, the relations between the two groups—the government and the students—were tenuous at best. This was brought home to me in the course of the trial when Matthew Ramcharan, the high commissioner from Trinidad and Tobago, indicated his desire to attend one of the sessions. Since he was a distinguished advocate himself, I introduced him to the court and the judge invited him to take his seat in the well of the court that was reserved for counsel. This did not suit the accused, who considered the high commissioner to be part of the "establishment" and therefore hostile to their cause. Nevertheless, he took his seat, and apart from a few angry stares, the case proceeded without incident.

The trial of the Trinidad and Tobago Ten, as the group became known, began on January 19, 1970, before Justice Kenneth MacKay and a jury. It lasted nine weeks, at that point the longest jury trial ever held in Montreal. (This record has long since been surpassed, and it is not unusual today for complex cases to last many months and sometimes even years.) The accused were represented by Bernard Mergler, a veteran lawyer and frequent champion of left-wing causes. He was assisted by Juanita Westmoreland, a young and very able lawyer, who later became dean of law at the University of Windsor and subsequently a judge of the Quebec Provincial Court, and Robert Lemieux, who a few months later became deeply involved in what came to be known as the October Crisis.[119]

It would not be an easy case. Skirmishes between the crown and the defence (and sometimes the court) began almost at once when the defence wanted to put wide-ranging questions to prospective jurors. It is, of course, of the utmost importance that an impartial jury be found, but the law puts limits on the type of questions that counsel can ask. I had made up my mind that I would accept the first twelve jurymen called, and not a single challenge was made by the crown. The defence, however, rejected so many of the prospective jurors, either for cause or peremptorily, that the panel that had been summoned, already much larger than usual, quickly ran out. This does not happen very often, and the remedy is a writ by the judge to empower the sheriff to go on the streets and gather a sufficient number of persons so that the jury may be completed.

Justice MacKay quickly issued the appropriate order, and squads of Provincial Police went out to look for English-speaking persons of the age of majority on the streets of Montreal. These astonished people were brought to the court, four or five at a time, examined for their basic qualifications—ability to comprehend English and no criminal record—and they were then examined by the parties in the usual manner. We soon began to notice that this group of talesmen, as they are called, contained an abnormally large number of persons engaged in finance, insurance, and, in general, the business world. A few questions by me to the officer in charge of this operation soon solved the mystery: the squads of police had swept St. James Street and Victoria Square, then Montreal's financial centre, where the number of English speakers was likely to be higher than in other parts of the city. My favourite souvenir of this event is a cartoon that appeared the next day in *Montréal-Matin*.[120] It shows a fur-coat-clad, portly middle-aged man, cigar in mouth and briefcase in hand, walking along the street. Two constables, partially hidden behind a fence, swing a lasso in his direction as one says to the other (in French): "If that's not an Anglo, we got a problem."

We finally empanelled a jury of twelve men, and legal history was made when one of them disclosed, but only after he had taken the required oath, that he was not yet a Canadian citizen. Normally, that would have excluded him from jury service, but the rules for talesman differ from those that apply to persons normally summoned, and the judge quickly congratulated him on serving his new country in such an important function. He remained on the panel.

It is interesting to speculate on what might have happened had the police brought in a woman. In those days, in Quebec, women could not sit on juries, but the Criminal Code clearly provided (and still does in section 642) that the sheriff must bring in "as many [additional] persons, *whether qualified jurors or not*, as the court directs for the purpose of providing a full jury" (emphasis added). It would have been an interesting test, but I am sure it never occurred to the sheriff to do so, and with so much at stake I didn't quite dare to propose it. Women in Quebec finally acquired the right to sit on juries in the mid-1970s, and because I left practice in 1973, I never had the privilege to address a jury that included a woman.

As I said, the trial lasted nine weeks, and they were nine difficult weeks. I was in court all day and in my office all evening and sometimes part of the night. Computers were not yet in general use, and the daily transcripts of evidence had to be read, digested, and indexed. Today, this is done with the aid of sophisticated software, but then it was all done by hand. Finally, when it was my turn to sum up for the jury, I spoke for an entire day. I remember when I got home that night I was too tired to eat and too revved up to sleep. For the next two days, defence counsel addressed the jury, and then it was the judge's turn. My task was over for now, although many more trials loomed on the horizon. My wife (we had been married less than three years and had two small children) had been in court throughout the trial—my most loyal supporter and my severest, but always most constructive, critic.[121]

The jury deliberated for a total of four days, with frequent calls for transcripts of the evidence and explanations by the judge. In the end, eight of the ten accused were found guilty of conspiracy to commit mischief by occupying the Computer Centre, and one was found guilty of the additional charge of conspiracy to commit mischief by occupying the Faculty Club. The remaining two were cleared of all charges.

We expected that the judge would fix a date, perhaps a day or two later, for representations on sentence, but after a short adjournment he surprised everyone by announcing that he was ready to pass sentence then and there, and so he did by imposing fines ranging from $1,000 to $15,000. His reason for choosing fines rather than imprisonment, he said, was that the whole affair already had cost the Canadian taxpayer a considerable amount of money and he did not wish to add to the burden. He also recommended that the Immigration Department consider deportation, which didn't happen, although some of the students left voluntarily. Within a few hours, the government of Trinidad and Tobago announced that it would pay all fines and there was no appeal. A few years later, Dorothy Eber, who had written a seminal book on the Computer Centre affair,[122] published a follow-up focusing on the trial of the Trinidad and Tobago Ten.[123] In it is a short sentence that I cite with pride: "Kaufman was fair."

I prosecuted two more jury trials in the Sir George Williams case, both long and complicated, though not quite as difficult as that of the trial of the Ten. In the first of these, Brenda Dickenson-Dash, who was found to have played a minor part, was fined $2,000. Two of her fellow accused, Roosevelt (Rosie) Douglas and Ann

Cools, were said by the crown to have been ringleaders in the events. Both were convicted. Douglas was sentenced to two years less a day in prison and fined $5,000. He served sixteen months before his release on parole, but his freedom was short lived. Ottawa got a deportation order and, after an unsuccessful appeal, he left for Jamaica rather than return to his home in Dominica, where the government then in power was cracking down on reputed dissidents. He stayed six months in Jamaica and then spent some time in Cuba, but after a few weeks there he thought the time was ripe to go back home, where he immersed himself in social causes. First, he helped to organize the island's agricultural workers, including several hundred on his father's estate, an act for he was banished from the family home. Eric Sibling, writing in *Saturday Night*, takes up the story from there:

> In those days, Dominica was caught up in a political maelstrom that involved Rastafarians, colonials, independence-seekers, new leftists, and black power advocates. Added to the mix was now Rosie Douglas, who within weeks of his return helped organize supporters of independence to inundate the House of Assembly's visitors' gallery. The legislature soon backed the idea; independence from Britain was formally achieved on November 3, 1978. But, despite his success, Douglas faced an uphill battle to wrest power from the government, losing some elections, winning others, and, at one point, dividing his time between Africa and Dominica, his activities funded by Libya. His efforts finally bore fruit in 2000, when his party won and Douglas became prime minister of Dominica. That, too, was short lived. He died, at fifty-eight, later that year.[124]

Anne Cools, a native of Barbados, was sentenced to six months in jail and fined $1,500. On her release, she enrolled at McGill University and obtained a degree in social sciences. She became active in politics and ran, unsuccessfully, in the 1979 and 1980 federal elections. From 1980 to 1984 she was a member of the National Parole Board. She also taught at a community college and at what is now Ryerson University. In 1984 Prime Minister Trudeau appointed her to the Senate of Canada. She sat as a Liberal until 2004, when she crossed the floor to sit as a Conservative.

Throughout this affair, I also took charge of all cases in the Court of Sessions, but there most of the accused pleaded guilty. All were fined. Finally, toward the end of 1970, with seven cases still unresolved, I handed the file to Ray Schachter, a full-time crown attorney who, with skill and dispatch, completed the assignment. The truth is that I couldn't face another prosecution arising from the events at the Computer Centre. I was exhausted.

[18]

McGill Français

The handbills said *McGILL FRANÇAIS—manifestation—28 mars—8hrs—Carré St-Louis.* The year was 1969, and Montreal was scared. Bombs planted by terrorists had already exploded in buildings and letterboxes; two persons were dead and many more had been injured. Then came the incident at the Computer Centre at Sir George Williams University in February. The city was nervous and so was McGill.

Early "intelligence"—in non-police language we would say reports from informers and infiltrators—indicated that there would be a march on McGill on March 28, 1969, and that it would be violent. The plan, it seems, was for a group of 10,000 or more to walk toward the university and engage the attention of the police. In the meantime, a smaller group would create disturbances in other parts of downtown Montreal. It was also part of the plan that the great majority of those who would take part in the march would do so in good faith and complete ignorance of what the extremist elements had in mind. This, of course, was not an unusual pattern. In the past, radical groups had frequently turned peaceful demonstrations into scenes of violence.

The police had learned that a small group of persons, including at least one convicted terrorist, planned to seize key points at McGill, including the sensitive Data Centre. The plan was then called *Operation Cigare*; this was later changed to *Operation McGill* to attract outside supporters. However, there was yet another change in the name, and in the end the event became known as *McGill Français*, reflecting the organizers' aim that McGill be turned into a French-language institution. It was this new designation that attracted well-meaning demonstrators.

At some point in the planning, those who had peaceful intentions became aware that they were being used, and a confrontation occurred sometime in

February, when officials of the *Movement pour l'integration scolaire* insisted that violence be avoided. The ideological battle continued and more meetings were held. At one such meeting, the suggestion was made that demonstrators be equipped with helmets and placard sticks heavy enough to serve as weapons. Someone else suggested the use of Molotov cocktails. At yet another meeting, the use of .22 rifles was recommended to destroy searchlights used by the police. By then, the organization had grown in size, and it included two McGill groups, the Radical Students Alliance and the Social Action Council, as well as two highly activist university lecturers. Reports received by the police also indicated that some of the better known organizers had cut their hair and shaved off their beards to confuse those who might otherwise spot them.

With these reports in hand, civic authorities, in consultation with McGill, drew up a master plan. It divided the areas surrounding McGill into three zones, red, yellow, and green. Red was the campus, yellow a buffer zone between the university and Carré St-Louis, where the marchers were to gather, and green was the square itself. As a police official explained, it was like a traffic light: green for go, yellow for caution, and red for stop. Eight targets were identified, including the McLennan Library. Thirty-four private guards—all off-duty firefighters— were assigned to this building. The second target was the building housing French-Canadian studies. Then followed the Administration Building, the Data Centre, the Arts Building (which is at the very heart of the campus), the power house, the greenhouse (used as a storage building but vulnerable because of its glass cover), and finally the McIntyre Medical Sciences Building on Cedar Avenue. This building caused special problems because it was two blocks away from the campus, and police feared a diversionary attack.

Leading up to the day, all buildings surrounding the immense front lawn were equipped with nineteen mercury-vapour lights—the strongest lights then available—and they turned night into day. There were closed-circuit television cameras in strategic locations, and police with walkie-talkies were placed on rooftops in order to give constant reports to their superiors, who had gathered in a $400,000 trailer parked discreetly behind a building on the campus. This was the mobile command post, filled with sophisticated communications equipment, and its operators were in direct touch by radio and telephone with Police Headquarters, the Quebec Provincial Police, the RCMP, and Civil Protection personnel. Special radio bands were cleared to allow for on-site broadcasts uninterrupted by the chatter of regular police communications. Also hidden were four portable generators, in case the electricity was cut.

The police had decided that some of their power should be displayed, while reserves would be hidden. And so 110 riot-gear-equipped police stood at the perimeter of the university, with 900 more constables nearby. Out of sight, in the university library, were 300 provincial police officers, equipped with helmets and clubs, with another 100 officers, equally equipped, in another building not far away. Two hundred RCMP officers stood by in their quarters one mile away, and could be on the scene within minutes. A further reserve of 100 provincial police officers remained in the Justice Building on Parthenais Street, two miles east of McGill. Overhead, a police helicopter surveyed the situation and maintained radio contact with the command post. It was also equipped with two powerful searchlights.

The Montreal Fire Department was placed on stand by, with a deputy director in charge; Bell telephone had a crew ready in case wires were cut, and so did Hydro-Québec. At the Montreal General Hospital, 95 doctors—55 on regular duty and 40 brought in for the occasion—were in place, together with 45 nurses and technicians and 300 student nurses. Also on hand were 145 private security guards, 90 McGill janitors, 150 faculty members, 85 Civil Protection personnel, and 21 St. John's Ambulance workers. A lone McGill public relations adviser stood by in the principal's office.

There were rumours that the government of Quebec had requested that military personnel be held in readiness, but this was later denied by the solicitor general. However, *Hansard* reveals[125] that discussions had taken place between the deputy attorney general of Quebec and the deputy attorney general of Canada, "the usual type of thing that passes between officials," as the solicitor general later described it.[126]

My involvement in the event began on March 18, 1969, when Peter M. Laing, McGill's chief legal counsel and a member of its Board of Governors, asked me to join the legal team he was putting together to deal with the event. In addition to Peter and myself, the group included James K. Hugesson, now a judge of the Federal Court, and Antonio Lamer, then a rising star on the Montreal legal scene. Peter decided to set up a command post in his office in the heart of downtown Montreal on the 22nd floor of what is now La Maison Trust Royal on Boulevard René-Lévesque (then known as Dorchester Boulevard). This post was to be staffed by him, Jim, and me, while Tony Lamer would spend the afternoon and evening with Michel Côté, chief legal counsel for the Montreal Police Department (and later a judge of the Superior Court), in the trailer on the campus. Our function was to advise McGill, the private guards, and, if asked, the police.

Peter Laing had been a tank commander in North Africa, where he had served with distinction. He was severely wounded in action and lost both legs. He was a military strategist at heart, and I could not help but feel during the long hours of that night that he was reliving the war. I still have his plan, called "Administrative Arrangements for Lawyers." It is crisp and to the point. For instance, "alternative location [for the Laing Group] if forced to move for any reason without notice will be Queen Elizabeth Hotel, Laing's Room." Or, "air-conditioning has been laid on until 2:00 A.M. in the telephone zone and can be extended if necessary." We were also informed that "modest refreshments will be available from time to time." We even had the home address and telephone number of a Superior Court judge, should judicial intervention be needed. It was perfect planning for the uncertainties that lay ahead.

Administrative advice for university staff was given by Bob Shaw, vice-principal, administration, and it urged "all members of the University community to take no part in the demonstration or in any counter-demonstration which might cause a Franco-Anglo confrontation." Arrangements for the evening were set out in a twenty-one-paragraph memorandum, appointing eighteen deans and other senior personnel to be "in command in the areas specified." All staff members were urged to carry flashlights. Communications were to be by telephone, walkie-talkies, or runner. Buildings would be identified by numbers rather than names. Emergencies could be dealt with as follows: "If the security staff in any building feels that it is necessary to leave the telephone to investigate a suspicious condition, then he should first report by telephoning 4311 and advise that he will telephone again in a stated number of minutes. If this second call is not placed, it will be taken as a call for help."[127]

At the appointed hour, about nine thousand demonstrators gathered on Carré Saint-Louis, and the seventeen-block trek toward McGill began. As the marchers approached, they saw not only the visible presence of the police but also a group of 4,000 McGill students who milled about in the vicinity. Some had come to help defend their university; others simply wanted to see what would happen. Inevitably, scuffles began, two Molotov cocktails exploded on Sherbrooke Street, and stones, pieces of wood, ball bearings, and empty bottles were tossed at the police. The ball-bearings were particularly dangerous because people stepped on them and fell.

A serious fight broke out between a group of demonstrators and some students near the Roddick Gates, McGill's main entrance, and at that point the police commander called in the riot squad. The cast-iron gates were unlocked and the 110 policemen who had been kept inside the campus marched out in three platoons. They took heavy punishment, and seven men were injured, but after the event it was agreed that their discipline had been superb and that they had succeeded in breaking up the fight without excessive force. Soon thereafter the demonstrators dispersed, and less than two hours after this show of strength the event was over and city sanitation crews began to clean up the mess.

At McGill, life continued and so did minor confrontations in the months that followed. But these were to be expected in the age of contestation we were in, and most disputes were quickly and quietly resolved. It is worth emphasizing that this type of radical action met with strong disapproval from the public and that the agitation to make McGill a French-language university did not find universal favour. I quote from an editorial published in *La Presse* on March 19, 1969, written by Renaude Lapointe:

> McGill will continue to be an English language university, but with a strong and flourishing French presence on its staff and student population. And in the courses given within the daily life of the university, French will have a well-established place: this is the essence of the ambitious program which was put into force by Vice-principal Michael Oliver. This is a program which all Quebecers not involved with extremists are ready to endorse.[128]

I heartily endorse these comments. My wife, my children, and I are McGill graduates, and each of us received a great education: Donna, Leslie, and I in law, David in North American studies. We loved the prevailing atmosphere, and we appreciated the fact that many courses, particularly in the Faculty of Law, were offered in both languages. This attracted more francophone students, giving greater diversity to the student body. It helped bring the "two solitudes" together, without, however, changing McGill's character as a world-renowned, English-language university.

[19]

Apprehended Insurrection

It is difficult to recreate, almost four decades later, the atmosphere that existed in Quebec at the time of the October Crisis of 1970. In retrospect, it is tempting to say that the federal government overreacted. Certainly, the facts as we know them today seem to indicate that the "apprehended insurrection" was not as great a threat as the federal cabinet believed, but hindsight is, of course, 20:20. To understand fully the situation, one had to be there, and if the imposition of the War Measures Act sounds harsh today—and it was—remember that one of the greatest civil libertarians of all, the late Frank Scott, thought it was justified. And so did I, and I was intimately involved in the events.[129]

I first came into contact with *Le Front de liberation du Québec* (FLQ) in 1968 when I was asked to represent the son of a prominent French-Canadian family who had held up a bank. Nothing extraordinary in that except, as I discovered in the course of my preparation, he had done so in order to raise funds for terrorist activities. I don't believe that I had ever met a terrorist before, but if this young man was any indication of what was to come, I realized that we were dealing with zealots, convinced that freedom for Quebec could never be achieved by peaceful means.

My client and his friends were quite prepared to pay the price, and so he did when he pleaded guilty to robbery and was sentenced to a term of imprisonment. This was an early case of ordinary people in Quebec turning to crime for political reasons: destruction of property, theft, assault, and sometimes even murder. The courts dealt with these cases in the normal course, but for every person convicted and sentenced, others stepped in to fill the breach. The violence was creeping and insidious, and fear of the unknown—who would strike next and where?—gripped the city. The air was tense, and no solution seemed to be in sight. Finally, the pot boiled over.

Monday, October 5. It is 8:20 a.m. Two men ring the doorbell at the home of James Richard Cross, the British trade commissioner in Montreal. They tell the maid that they have a present for her employer, but once inside the door they force her to take them to the bedroom where they find Cross, still dressed in his pyjamas. At gunpoint, they force him to go with them. A third man, also armed, is at the door and a fourth is behind the wheel of a taxi outside the house on Redpath Crescent, a fashionable street on the slope of Mount Royal. By 8:28 they are gone and two minutes later the police receive their first call.

The anti-terrorist squads of three forces—Montreal, Quebec Provincial, and RCMP—spring into action. The island of Montreal is sealed off within minutes, known FLQ haunts are searched, taxis are placed under special scrutiny, but all to no avail. At 9:45 the news of the kidnapping is published. Forty-five minutes later, Mrs. Cross receives a phone call from a man, but all he will say is that further news will soon be sent by the FLQ to the media. And so the long vigil begins.

At 11:45 Jacques Payac of radio station CKAC receives a call telling him that four letters were placed in the Lafontaine Pavilion of the Université du Québec in downtown Montreal. He races to the scene, only to find that the police had received a similar call and beaten him to the punch. After a brief search, the envelopes are found: one for Payac; another for Pierre Pasceau of CKLM; the third addressed to *Québec Presse*, a Montreal weekly; and the fourth to the police. But what they say is not made public. All are seized by the authorities.

When the House of Commons meets at 2:30 that afternoon, Mitchell Sharp, the secretary of state for external affairs, assures members that the government will leave no stone unturned to find the kidnappers and secure the release of their hostage. Leaders of all parties express their shock and dismay that such an act of violence should have occurred in Canada. News is still scarce, but a short time later, in Quebec City, the provincial minister of justice, Jérôme Choquette, makes public the gist of the letters found earlier that day. They list six demands:

1. The publication by the press of an FLQ manifesto;
2. The release of certain political prisoners;
3. The preparation of an aircraft for a flight to Cuba or Algeria;
4. The re-hiring of a group of strikers fired some time before by the Post Office (commonly known as *Les gars de Lapalme*);

5. The placing of $500,000 in silver ingots on the aircraft; and
6. The government making public the name of an informer who had denounced the members of an FLQ cell who were arrested and charged.

Choquette refuses to elaborate, but he does say that the ultimatum has a forty-eight-hour deadline. He also tells the large crowd of reporters that Cross suffers from hypertension and that he hopes his captors will not jeopardize his life by withholding his prescribed medication.

By 7 p.m. the first arrests are made, but I suspect that this was truly a case (in the immortal words of the prefect of police in *Casablanca*) of "round[ing] up the usual suspects." Later that evening, the Quebec government announces that henceforth all actions will be taken jointly with the government of Canada. More arrests follow.

Tuesday, October 6. At 9:30 a.m. the full text of the kidnappers' demands is released to the media, and radio stations have it on the air within minutes. It is a lengthy document that stresses the need for "total independence." It declares support for the oppressed wherever they may be, and it "salutes" in particular the people of Cuba and Algeria. It concludes with the words "*Nous vaincrons*"— "We will triumph"[130]—the rallying cry of the movement. An hour later, the federal cabinet meets. At the conclusion, Sharp tells the press that, "needless to say," the demands of the kidnappers will not be met.

At 1 p.m. the senior officers of the Montreal Police Department meet with Jérôme Choquette in the police building on Bonsecours Street in Old Montreal. Two hours later, Robert Lemieux, a Montreal lawyer engaged to represent most of the FLQ members held in jails and prisons in Quebec, announces that twelve of his clients are ready to leave for Cuba or Algeria.

Throughout the day, extra security for public officials and diplomats is put into place and the number of uniformed officers patrolling the streets visibly increases. The premier of Quebec, Robert Bourassa, declares himself satisfied with the arrangements. That night, the scene shifts to Ottawa. An anonymous caller directs police to look for a letter in the bus terminal. It is written by hand and the message is short: the government must reply to the kidnappers' demands before 9:00 the next morning.

Wednesday, October 7. Nine o'clock comes and goes with no word from either the government or the kidnappers. At 9:30 the prime minister issues a brief declaration: a minority, he says, cannot impose its will on the majority by violence. The kidnappers' demands will not be met. Later that day, a lineup of suspects is held in Montreal, but the maid who opened the door cannot identify anyone.

At 1:30 p.m. a new *communiqué* is delivered to CKLM. It says that to show their good faith the authorities must arrange with *Radio Canada* (the French network of the CBC) to broadcast the complete FLQ manifesto between 8:00 and 11:00 that night. It must be read by a "responsible" announcer and a name is suggested. Also, all searches and arrests must cease. Attached to the *communiqué* is a letter from James Cross. It says:

1. I ask the Authorities to respond favourably to the demands of the FLQ.
2. It will be faster and easier for everyone if all the FLQ *communiqués* are published in full.
3. Please assure that I am well and receiving the medicaments for my blood pressure.
4. I am being well treated but the FLQ are determined to achieve their demands.

The errors in the letter indicate that Cross is not the author.

That afternoon, incensed by the events, the Liberal caucus in Ottawa urges the government to reinstate capital punishment. The members also suggest that a substantial reward be offered for information leading to the arrest of the kidnappers. Meanwhile, in Quebec City, Bourassa prepares to leave for a scheduled trip to New York where, ironically, he will try to convince Wall Street that Quebec is a safe place for investment.

A new session of Parliament is scheduled to open tomorrow, and tonight, as tradition demands, all members are invited to a ball at Rideau Hall, the residence of the Governor General. The mood is subdued and security is tight. That evening, even while the festivities are in progress, Mitchell Sharp takes to the air and tells the kidnappers that the government is ready to negotiate with them.

Thursday, October 8. The theme of negotiation is again taken up when the government offers to appoint a minister of the crown to lead the team. The FLQ's reply is yet another *communiqué*, sent to Pierre Pasceau at CKLM. The idea of mediaton is rejected. "We will continue to communicate in our fashion," the short statement says, "and we will not fall into traps set by the fascist police."

A report broadcast by *Radio Canada* declares that James Cross is dead. It is quickly corrected. Robert Lemieux, the young activist lawyer, holds yet another press conference, this one to say that the government's offer to negotiate is but a trick to gain time. At 9 p.m., a Court of Queen's Bench jury, after deliberating for seven hours, finds Robert Hudon, one of the persons whose release was demanded by the FLQ, guilty of conspiracy, robbery, and theft. An hour and a half later, on the

French network of the CBC, an expressionless announcer reads the FLQ manifesto. As he reads, the text is shown on the screen behind him. A major demand of the kidnappers has been met.

Friday, October 9. Two more *communiqués* from the FLQ and another letter from James Cross. Pierre Trudeau cancels a trip to the United Nations in New York. A direct telephone link is established between the Montreal office of Jérôme Choquette and his federal counterpart, John Turner.

Saturday, October 10. The "final" deadline fixed by the kidnappers is 6 p.m. and nothing has changed. At 6:18, three men armed with machine guns, their faces covered with masks, kidnap Pierre Laporte, Quebec's minister of labour, outside his home in St. Lambert, a quiet bedroom community near Montreal. As the minister's terrified nephew watches, they throw Laporte in the back of a 1968 Chevrolet and speed away. Two minutes later, another gigantic manhunt begins.

This is Yom Kippur, the Jewish Day of Atonement, a day of prayer, reflection, and fasting. Donna and I were invited to the home of friends to break the fast. Normally this would be a happy occasion, the beginning of a new year, the slate of sins wiped clean. But this year the mood is sombre, and there is only one topic of conversation. The news of the Laporte kidnapping hits us as we begin our coffee. And "hit" is not an overstatement. We leave almost at once, and as we drive from the town of Mount Royal to our home in Westmount, Donna turns to me and asks "Will we inevitably be involved?" And without waiting for a reply, she adds, "I hope not."

I understand what she means. I have just completed the taxing prosecutions that followed the destruction of the Computer Centre at Sir George Williams University, and I have not yet fully recovered from the strain. Other major cases are in the wings, and I am completely booked for the fall—a case in the Supreme Court of Canada, two important appeals, and a complex commercial fraud case, the aftermath of the collapse of a financial institution. It is a very busy schedule and I don't want any more. So I say, "Probably, but I hope not, too." But deep down we know that our hope is not realistic.

Thursday, October 15. The premier of Quebec formally asks that federal troops be sent to Montreal and Quebec to help protect public buildings "and the population," a request that is granted at once.[131] By late afternoon, the first soldiers, dressed and armed for combat, appear on the streets of the two cities. Other developments follow in quick succession. First, all police forces in the province (a total of 13,000 men and women) are placed under the command of the director of the Provincial Police. Then, a short time later, Bourassa releases a statement addressed to the kidnappers. It is a lengthy document and it makes certain concessions, among them an undertaking that, upon the release of the two hostages, the kidnappers will be given safe conduct to any country of their choice. This, says the premier, is offered after considering "the implications of the alternatives which may exist," whatever that may mean. By nightfall, 6,000 soldiers patrol Montreal. In the Paul-Sauvé arena in the city's east end, 3,000 students loudly declare their support for the FLQ.

Friday, October 16. At 3 a.m. the prime minister of Canada is handed two letters. One is from Bourassa, the other from Jean Drapeau, the mayor of Montreal. The province, they say, is "in a state of apprehended insurrection." An hour later, the federal cabinet, hastily summoned, decides to invoke the War Measures Act,[132] and the required proclamation is signed by the Governor General at 4 a.m. The document is rushed to the office of the Queen's Printer, which prepares a special edition of the official *Canada Gazette*.[133] It is 11 a.m. before the task is done, and this is what it tells a startled population:

Proclamation declaring that apprehended insurrection exists and has existed as and from the 15th October, 1970

ROLAND MICHENER
Canada

ELIZABETH THE SECOND, by the Grace of God of the United Kingdom, Canada and Her other Realms and Territories QUEEN, Head of the Commonwealth, Defender of the Faith.

To All to Whom these Presents shall come or whom the same may in anyway concern, Greeting:

DONALD S. MAXWELL
Deputy Attorney General
A Proclamation

Whereas the War Measures Act provides that the issue of a proclamation under the authority of the Governor in Council shall be conclusive evidence that insurrection, real or apprehended, exists and has existed for any period of time therein stated and of its continuance, until by the issue of a further proclamation it is declared that the insurrection no longer exists.

And Whereas there is in contemporary Canadian society an element or group known as Le Front de Liberation du Quebec who advocate and resort to the use of force and the commission of criminal offences including murder, threat of murder and kidnapping as a means of or as an aid in accomplishing a governmental change within Canada and whose activities have given rise to a state of apprehended insurrection within the Province of Quebec.

Now Know Ye that We, by and with the advice of Our Privy Council for Canada, do by this Our Proclamation proclaim and declare that apprehended insurrection exists and has existed as and from the fifteenth day of October, one thousand nine hundred and seventy.

Of All Which Our Loving Subjects and all others whom these Presents may concern are hereby required to take notice and to govern themselves accordingly.

In Testimony Whereof, We have caused these Our Letters to be made Patent and the Great Seal of Canada to be hereunto affixed. Witness: Our Right Trusty and Well-beloved Counsellor Roland Michener, Chancellor and Principal Companion of Our Order of Canada upon whom We have conferred Our Canadian Forces' Decoration, Governor General and Commander-in-Chief of Canada.

At Our Government House, in Our City of Ottawa, this sixteenth day of October in the year of Our Lord one thousand nine hundred and seventy and in the nineteenth year of Our Reign.

By Command

J.R. GRANDY

Deputy Registrar General of Canada

Attached to the proclamation are regulations that set out the new emergency powers. Among them are the following provisions:

* The FLQ is declared to be an unlawful association;
* A member of an unlawful association is guilty of an indictable offence and liable to imprisonment for a term not exceeding five years;
* Persons arrested in virtue of these regulations shall be detained in custody without bail pending trial unless the Attorney General ... consents to the release of that person on bail;
* A peace officer may arrest without warrant persons he has reason to suspect to be members of an unlawful association;
* Anyone so arrested may be detained without arraignment for seven days, but the Attorney General may issue an order that the accused be further detained until the expiry of a period not exceeding 21 days ... at the end of which period the person arrested shall be taken before a justice ... or released from custody;

- A peace officer may enter and search without warrant any premises ... in which he has reason to suspect that evidence may be found that a member of an unlawful association is present or that any person is being detained by the unlawful association.

Never before in peacetime were such extraordinary powers given in Canada to civil authorities.

By the time dawn breaks on October 16, and well before the special edition of the *Canada Gazette* becomes available, police begin their searches and arrests.[134] By 10 p.m., 250 persons are in custody and 170 premises have been searched. Masses of seized documents are stored in boxes, to be read—and found mostly useless—in the weeks to follow. Interrogations are conducted by teams of three, one each from the RCMP, the Quebec Provincial Police, and the Montreal municipal police. The questions are naive and show the lack of special training: "Are you a member of the FLQ?" "Do you know of anyone who is?" "Have you been to meetings of the FLQ?" Everything said is written down in longhand and put into files. Again, the information obtained is mostly useless.

That day, Donna and I are invited to attend a special convocation at Bishop's University in Lennoxville. It is held as scheduled, but the atmosphere is subdued and all talk centres on current events. A male student reads a poem of love— love thy neighbour, but love also thy enemy. It seems singularly inappropriate and we can't wait to get out.

We return to Montreal later that day, and what we find is a city under siege: police and soldiers everywhere, rumours of the most terrible kind, most of them false, but highly disquieting all the same. The population is scared, but there is comfort in the fact that the government has acted decisively. And if civil liberties have been suspended, that is the price to pay.

Today, almost two generations later, some tend to criticize this "overreaction." But, as Pierre Trudeau wrote in *Memoirs*,[135] "nothing like this had ever happened in Canadian history, and the sheer senselessness of it caught us off guard, which meant that we were badly equipped to deal with it." There is much truth to this, because the War Measures Act was all the government had. There was no "in-between" law.[136] And so it was all or nothing, and Ottawa and Quebec chose the former.

Saturday, October 17. The searches and arrests continue. The House of Commons is in extraordinary session, debating the regulations proclaimed under the War Measures Act. An anonymous caller tells the police that Pierre Laporte is being held in a medical building on Montreal's St. Joseph Boulevard. Two hundred soldiers and police surround the block and start a search. But there is no trace of the minister. Another anonymous call is received at 7 p.m. The message is brief: Laporte has been killed and the body is in the trunk of a car at St. Hubert Airport. But the call—there were hundreds that day—is not followed up. At 8:30 that night, the message is repeated, but once again there is no action. Finally, an hour later, when a third call with the same message is received by a reporter at CKAC, the caller is asked for more detail, and he tells the reporter that a letter with a description of the car has been placed in the lobby of Place des Arts, Montreal's main concert hall. This time, police race to the scene and the letter is found. It tells them where to go and what to look for.

A car that fits the description is located in the airport's parking lot. The trunk is pried open and Laporte's lifeless body is found. A cursory examination shows that he was strangled. The tragic news is made public at midnight. In Ottawa, all opposition to the imposition of harsh measures crumbles.

Tuesday, October 20. Arrests and searches continue. A state funeral for the murdered minister is held in Notre-Dame Basilica in the heart of Old Montreal. The prime minister, the premier, and the mayor of Montreal attend. Snipers with guns at the ready stand on surrounding rooftops and a helicopter hovers overhead. It reminds me of what I saw in Vienna in the mid-1930s. But this is Canada. How can this be?

Friday, October 30. It is mid-afternoon and I am at work in my office on Phillips Square. The phone rings and it is Antonio Dubé, Québec's deputy minister of justice. He tells me in a few words that his minister (who doubles as attorney general) has decided to engage special counsel to deal with persons detained under the War Measures Act. Four other lawyers in private practice have already accepted the mandate. Will I do so too? I tell Dubé that I would like to consult my wife and my two partners, Harvey Yarosky and Morris Fish.

I call Donna and I have a quick meeting with Harvey and Morris. All three confirm what deep down I already knew: I am a lawyer and a Canadian whose home is Quebec. My duty is clear and I cannot refuse. We agree that the weeks ahead will be difficult—an English-speaking Jew with a young family prosecuting the FLQ, but that is part of being a barrister. One doesn't always get cases that are pleasant or easy. I remember Donna's apprehension the night Laporte was kidnapped, but I know that, as always, she will support me and I will need that support. At 5 p.m. I call Dubé to tell him that I accept the minister's request. "Go and join the others at police headquarters," he tells me. "They are already at work."

I find my colleagues in an office in the Provincial Police's Parthenais Street complex: Jacques Ducros, a former assistant deputy attorney general; Gabriel Lapointe, a former crown attorney; Bruno Pateras, also a former crown attorney; and Yves Fortier, a litigator with a large downtown firm. A meeting is in progress. It is chaired by a regular crown prosecutor. Later, we are joined by a sixth crown attorney *ad hoc*, Jean-Guy Boilard.[137] The most immediate task is to examine the files of all persons still detained to see if charges should be laid. The chairman suggests that we keep minutes, but we reject the idea. Our task is to work quickly and efficiently and to get things done. There is no time for bureaucratic record keeping. We work late into the night, are driven home for a few hours of sleep, and start again early the next morning.

Saturday, October 31. We receive formal authorization from the minister to act on his behalf "in all matters arising from the imposition of the War Measures Act or any subsequent law which may replace it."[138] By noon, it is clear that our work is not progressing as well as it should, and the "special crowns" adjourn to Moishe's, the famous steak house on the Main,[139] to eat and to discuss the situation. We agree that we need an efficient coordinator, and our choice is Stephen Cuddihy, a crown attorney in nearby St. Jérôme.

Ducros calls Choquette at his home and the minister suggests that we come right over. After listening to us, he summons Cuddihy to be at his house as quickly as possible. Cuddihy arrives an hour later, and before the day is out, he has been promoted to the newly created position of coordinator for the Judicial District of Montreal. We return to our room at police headquarters with Cuddihy in charge.

Later that night, Choquette drops by for a visit. He tells us that an announcement of our appointment will be made the next day. I urge him to be positive: tell the public that our first task is to order the immediate release of those against whom there is no evidence of violations. He agrees. But when the announcement is made, it describes us as "prosecutors," and no mention is made of our function to release. That is a pity, because the great majority of those detained are, in fact, quickly set free.

Thursday, November 5. With the release forms signed, we turn to those still detained, and the job of drafting indictments begins. A mass arraignment for twenty-four accused is held in a courtroom usually used by the coroner in the police building on Parthenais Street. All indictments are signed by the attorney general in person—"preferred indictments" in legal jargon—bypassing the normal process and sending the accused directly to trial by a judge and jury without the benefit of preliminary hearings. The Criminal Code permits this procedure and its purpose is to speed up the proceedings; that is why it is used in this instance, particularly since all accused are held without bail.[140]

The atmosphere is highly charged, and both the presiding judge—Justice Ignace Deslauriers, the senior judge of the Superior Court—and the six special crown attorneys take a great deal of verbal abuse from the accused. All sorts of threats are hurled at us, and when the hearing ends the director of the Provincial Police, who has the overall command of all police forces in the province, tells us that he feels obliged to take protective measures.

I didn't take the director's comment too seriously. I didn't even tell Donna. But at 1 a.m. that night our doorbell rings, which, frankly, scares the hell out of us. When I look through the peephole I see a group of soldiers in the hallway. I open the door, and a young lieutenant tells us that he and his men have been assigned to guard us.

The lieutenant proceeds to examine the premises and quickly assigns two soldiers to the lobby of the apartment building, two more to the corridor on our floor, and a radio operator to be at our door to report all comings and goings. He looks out of all the windows and tells me that he is concerned about a tall, concrete structure not far away, at the corner of Dorchester and Greene in Westmount. "A sharpshooter from there could pick you off," he tells me solemnly, "so you'll have to keep the drapes closed at all times." I tell him not to worry: the building belongs to the RCMP.

Protection of this kind is comforting, but the novelty quickly wears off; besides, Donna and I are not convinced it is needed. Still, one doesn't argue in such situations, and we do our best to live for more than three months in a glass house with half a dozen strangers watching our every move. The low point is when I return one day and find our son, David, then barely two, on the floor in the foyer with a loaded rifle in his hands. One of the soldiers had come in to use the facilities and left his gun outside the bathroom. Some toy.

Fortunately, there were some funny moments too. We weren't allowed to leave home without an escort, and the Westmount Police Department had taken over this function. One Saturday morning we had to take our children to the pediatrician, Dr. Victor Goldbloom, for routine vaccinations. At the appointed hour, a police car with two officers picked us up and drove us to the doctor's office. We rang the bell and two Provincial Police detectives opened the door; as a minister in the provincial cabinet, Dr. Goldbloom was also being protected. A short conversation ensued among the four officers and it went something like this: "We brought the Kaufmans to see the doctor," our bodyguards said. "But who are you?" the doctor's guards replied. And so, before we could get in to see the doctor, the Westmount officers had to pull out their IDs and show them to their provincial counterparts, who then, in turn, showed their IDs to our guards. That done, we entered. As we prepared the children to be vaccinated, one of the officers, a tall, burly man, asked if he could wait outside: "I faint when I see someone get a needle," he said with some embarrassment.

There was another incident I found amusing. One night, about three weeks into the job, the seven of us—Cuddihy and the six special crowns—decided that we should invite our wives for a quiet dinner in a secluded place. None of us had spent much time at home, and it seemed a good idea to have an evening off together. We arranged for a private dining room on the top floor of the Reform Club on Sherbrooke Street,[141] and we ordered a simple meal with a few bottles of good wine. Of course, we all came with our bodyguards, but no one gave this a thought. To make a long story short, after dinner I happened to look out the window and there, on the street below us, was a very large crowd, attracted by all the police cars and officers milling about, waiting to see what was happening. So much for a quiet, intimate dinner.

When we were first engaged, the police suggested that it might be wise to be armed, and we were given permits to carry revolvers. I had an old .38 calibre Police Chief's Special at home that a client had once given me as a present. It was registered, but I never kept ammunition in the house and the gun was secure in its hiding place. When I got the permit to carry a weapon, I took it out, had it cleaned and inspected, and went for target practice at the police firing range. All I can say is thank God I never had to use it.

◆ ◆ ◆

The prosecutions that followed were long and arduous and not very successful. Most accused were acquitted of charges laid under the War Measures Act, although the crown later had better luck in prosecutions based on the Criminal Code. There were some guilty pleas that winter, mostly in cases involving charges that the accused had been a member of the FLQ. But some of the more serious cases seemed to go on endlessly, with legal arguments, many successful, at every stage of the proceedings. In one case, in which I was directly involved, Justice Roger Ouimet threw out an indictment for conspiracy because he considered the drafting unclear. We asked him to suspend his order until the afternoon to give us time to draft a new indictment and he agreed.

We quickly corrected the language, but the new document had to be signed by the attorney general in person, and when we tried to locate Choquette we were told that he was out of town and that the premier, Robert Bourassa, had taken on the portfolio during his absence. Luckily, Bourassa was in his Montreal office on the top floor of the Hydro-Québec building on Dorchester Boulevard. He agreed to receive us at once and we hurried over with the new document. He asked a few very appropriate questions and, after a brief consultation with his advisers, concurred with our suggestion that a new indictment be preferred. There was one hitch, however: he was concerned that the public would not realize that he had signed the indictment in his capacity as acting attorney general. The media, he reasoned, would fail to make that distinction, and the news would be broadcast that the premier had stepped into this highly charged atmosphere, so full of political overtones.

To resolve the dilemma, three cabinet ministers—a quorum—were rounded up, and they appointed, by order-in-council, another minister to be the acting attorney general. That done, the new acting attorney general signed the indictment and we raced back to the courthouse to present the new document to Justice Ouimet at the opening of the 2:00 session. Since the accused had been held in custody, they were quickly re-arraigned. This time, the indictment stuck. It was the busiest two hours of my professional life.

While preparing some of the cases, we realized that one of the accused was a police informer, but we didn't know who, and no one would tell us. In an attempt to find out, Yves Fortier and I, having obtained the highest security clearance, were sent to RCMP headquarters in Ottawa to examine a number of existing files. We were put in a small conference room and the door was locked behind us. On the table sat five thin files. All but one had a number of reports prepared by the anti-terrorist squad, which were of marginal interest. One had a single sheet of paper. It said: "For details, apply to the Commissioner." We had our answer.

One of the accused was Robert Lemieux, the young Montreal lawyer who had espoused nationalist causes and who had many members of the FLQ as his clients. I knew Bob well from practice, and while he was in jail he called me at home every evening to get information about his case. Our relations were cordial and correct. I saw no reason not to tell him what I thought he was entitled to know, and he appreciated the fact that he was able to reach me most of the time. Others, however, had nothing but contempt for the special crowns, and venom was part of daily life.

The shortest case I had was a jury trial of an accused who had painted "NOUS

VAINCRONS" on a sidewalk in Old Montreal a few hours after the proclamation of the War Measures Act. The terms of the regulations made this an indictable offence. It was a strange case because the accused was what Quebecers would now call an "allophone," that is to say, someone of foreign birth. Why he had painted the offensive words no one could ever find out, but inquiries by the police soon revealed that he had left a mental institution in Ontario a few days before, and a psychiatrist who knew him was prepared to say that at the time of the offence he was unable to appreciate the nature of his acts.

I called only two witnesses: the police officer who had arrested the accused and the psychiatrist. With that in the record, the judge, Justice Antonio Lamer, instructed the jury to acquit the accused, which they did without leaving the courtroom. A few hours later, this unfortunate victim of events beyond his understanding was returned to the only home he knew, the mental institution in Ontario.

◆◆◆

James Cross was finally found, exhausted but unharmed, in a house on Recollets Street in Montreal North. The date was December 3, 1970, and a deal was made with his captors to give them free passage to Cuba. The exchange took place on Expo Island, and I well remember the flotilla of helicopters that took Cross from the parking lot on the island to the Jewish General Hospital where he remained a few days for tests. Considering his ordeal, he was in remarkably good shape.

Three weeks later, Paul Rose, Jacques Rose, and Francis Simard, who had kidnapped Laporte, were found by police in a twenty-foot tunnel in St. Luc, a village near St. Jean, Quebec. They were tried and convicted and sentenced to long terms of imprisonment. All were eventually released on parole. I was not involved in these cases.

My assignment ended in the summer of 1971. It was a great relief to put away my revolver and return to my regular practice. But the events left a mark on all of us, and some years later, when I read a bedtime story to my children, I showed them a picture of a toy soldier with a blue tunic and red pants. "That's not a soldier," one of them said. "A soldier wears a green uniform and carries a gun." They, too, remembered.

[20]
The Art of Cross-Examination

Cross-examination is an advocate's most powerful tool, and can make or break a case. Confronted with a skilful examiner, a witness who is less than candid will soon be exposed. Of course, the law takes certain precautions to encourage the truth, such as an oath or affirmation, but as we all know, fear of punishment in the hereafter is not always a sufficient incentive to make a witness speak the truth.

In Quebec a solemn affirmation in lieu of an oath is a recent addition to the law. When I started practice in 1955, it still happened on occasion that in a civil case (where the rules differed from criminal cases) a lawyer would question a prospective witness whose evidence he wanted to avoid not only about his or her religious persuasion, but also about the witness's belief in a state of punishment or reward after death. As the law then stood, a witness who even expressed so much as a doubt about this dogma could not be sworn and therefore couldn't testify. Most practitioners frowned on this practice, but some did not, and sometimes a case would be won by depriving an opponent of a key witness. Fortunately, this has now changed.

A by-product of the old law was the presence in all Quebec courts of a large crucifix placed in a prominent position. The explanation usually given was that a witness could take the oath either by placing his or her right hand on the Bible or by facing the crucifix and raising his or her right hand. Either way, it had to be the right hand and the name of the deity was invoked by the concluding words, pronounced by the clerk, "So help you God." In all my years at the Bar, I never saw a witness take an oath by looking at the crucifix, but this is no longer possible since crucifixes were removed in the early 1970s, when Montreal's ultra-modern *Palais de Justice* was opened.

This move came at the suggestion of the chief judge of the Youth Court who thought that it was an inappropriate symbol in Quebec's new multiracial, multicultural society. His plea, made to his fellow chiefs, was met with some dismay, but a committee was struck to examine the matter. Advice was sought from the Archbishop's Palace, and I am told that the question was put to the *curia* in Rome, which ruled that there was no objection to the removal of the crucifixes. The government agreed, and flags now adorn Quebec courtrooms.

Oaths may take many forms. Jews will swear on the five books of Moses, Christians on the New Testament. Muslims, Hindus, Buddhists, and others each have their own form. The important point is that the oath be binding on the witness's conscience, and judges will sometimes conduct mini-inquiries to make sure that the form proposed by the witness fills this requirement. Certainly, the old-time strictures are gone, and we no longer have, for instance, seemingly endless arguments whether a Jew must cover his head while taking the oath. Some do and some don't and no one but the witness cares.

This reminds me of a story. Sometime in the 1960s I was engaged to defend a man who was charged with assaulting his neighbour. The accused had survived a German concentration camp and after the war found refuge in Montreal. His neighbour was a former member of the *Wehrmacht*, and he too had recently arrived in Montreal. The two lived in peace, until one day an argument arose about some trivial matter, and heated words followed, climaxing in a fist fight. In the ensuing trial, the prosecution led off with two witnesses, both of them Jewish, who covered their heads while taking the oath. When the German's turn came to testify, he entered the box, carefully took a handkerchief out of a pocket, neatly folded it, and placed it on his head. A puzzled judge asked him what he was doing. "Well," came the reply, "isn't this a Canadian custom?"

In later years, when I started to teach, I told my students again and again that the cardinal sin of cross-examination is to ask a question without knowing the answer. It's a lesson that many lawyers forget, but an illustration from my own practice helped drive home the point. I was defending a man charged under the Criminal Code with failing to provide the "necessaries of life" to his spouse. His explanation was simple: his wife, from whom he was separated, was a highly skilled secretary with regular employment and a good salary. Two weeks before laying the charge she had suddenly quit and now she was unemployed and without means. I thought we couldn't lose.

The trial came on before Judge Roland Lamarre in the Montreal Municipal Court. The complainant was a very attractive young woman, beautifully dressed, of perfect demeanour and with a voice to match. Her answers were short and to the point and the judge was all ears. As expected, she said that she now was destitute and, despite repeated requests, her husband had refused to support her. I got up to cross-examine and at first all went well. Was it not true, I asked her, that she was highly skilled in her field and that she had never had trouble in finding employment? Yes, that was so. Was it also not true that, quite of her own volition, she had abruptly quit her job two weeks before laying the charge? Yes, she said, that too was so. And that is where I should have stopped. But, being young and eager and quite inexperienced, I felt the cake needed icing, and so I asked one more question. "Is it not a fact," I said with great aplomb, "that you quit your job so that you could go to court and say you are destitute and have your husband charged with non-support?"

I had barely completed the question when the witness started to tremble. Tears rolled down her lovely cheeks and her voice seemed to have left her. The clerk gave her a glass of water and the judge ordered the bailiff to get her a chair. After what seemed an eternity—at least to me since I couldn't quite comprehend what had happened—she wiped away her tears, stood up, and in a calm voice said, "I quit because my father told me that day he had cancer and that he had only a short time to live. I wanted to spend every minute I had with him until the end." There was utter silence in court, broken only by the judge who turned to the accused and said, "Guilty, six months in jail." I quickly pointed out that we hadn't even made a defence yet, but this fell on deaf ears. "I don't care what you or your client might say," Judge Lamarre answered, "my mind is made up."

My client took a new lawyer (for which I couldn't blame him), and the Superior Court quickly quashed the conviction for "gross irregularities," notably the judge's failure to afford the accused an opportunity to make "full answer and defence" to the charge as guaranteed by the Criminal Code. I don't know what happened to him in the end, but I had learned a lesson that I never forgot. As my mentor used to say, if you absolutely must ask one more question, ask the witness if his mother had a cat. Whatever the answer, it won't hurt your case.

Of course, such advice is easy to give but hard to follow, and every advocate will sooner or later ask that one question too many. And it happens to the best. There is a well-known story about the famous Washington lawyer Edward Bennet Williams. As his biographer writes:

In another Transit Company case, he wanted to show that a pedestrian run down and killed by a streetcar was not an innocent victim but a drunken bum. The man's son had been seen at the scene of the accident bending over the body of his father. Williams felt confident that the boy had been removing a bottle from his father's back pocket. On cross-examination he closed in on the boy. "You leaned over him didn't you?" asked Williams. "Yes," the boy replied. "You were sniffing his breath for alcohol, weren't you?" "No, sir," replied the boy. "You were reaching into his pocket for a bottle, weren't you?" he pressed. "No, sir," insisted the boy. "Other witnesses have testified that they saw you bending over your father. Now why were you bending over him?" Williams demanded. "Because he was my father," said the boy, "and I wanted to kiss him good-bye." Williams immediately asked the judge for a recess, went to a pay phone in the hall and recommended to the insurance company that they settle the case.[142]

The legendary New York lawyer Samuel Leibowitz had a similar story to tell.[143] He was cross-examining a policeman who, his client told him, had beaten a confession out of him with a blackjack. Leibowitz asked the officer what he carried in his back pocket, hoping that he would say "a blackjack." He didn't. It was a medal. Surprised, Leibowitz shot back, "So you're a hero?" "No," said the cop, "not a hero—a Roman Catholic." As Leibowitz recalled the event, "with four Irishmen on the jury I could feel my face turning red. I'd trapped myself by going fishing in waters that held no fish."

When I tell these stories, no student ever forgets them. This doesn't mean, of course, that they heed them, for the temptation to ask "just one more question" is always great.

It's fair to say, however, that I won many cases on the strength of my cross-examination. Often, for instance, a witness will be much less didactic on cross-examination than when first questioned. That is perfectly normal, and an honest witness will not mind being asked for greater precision. What witnesses object to, and rightly so, is being badgered and roughhoused and having their words turned and twisted in an attempt to create doubt and confusion. That is not only unfair, but also usually counterproductive and sometimes downright dangerous, especially with juries who tend to identify with a witness harassed by counsel.

I can think of no finer example of the power of cross-examination than a manslaughter case in which the crown had relied to a large extent on the evidence of a medico-legal expert. It was a complex matter and it involved the determination of the precise cause of death. The expert, a pathologist, told the jury that he had found a certain type of infection in the victim's body. This, he said, he could tell from his observations during the autopsy. He then added that he also had grown a culture. And that is where he stopped.

I must confess that it never occurred to us—Joe Cohen and me—to cross-examine the doctor on this particular finding, backed up, as it appeared to be, by scientific proof. That evening, however, we received a phone call from a lab technician who was outraged by what the expert had done. "Sure we grew a culture," he said, "we always do. But the result was inconclusive." The next morning we received permission from the judge to re-examine the witness. And this time, knowing what the answer would be, we put the crucial question: "You said you grew a culture?" "Yes," said the witness. "And what did it show?" "Well," he replied somewhat sheepishly, "nothing, because someone had messed up the test."

Perry Mason used cross-examination to get a witness to admit that he or she, and not the accused, had committed the crime. That rarely happens in practice, but I did have one case in which the accused's nephew admitted on cross-examination not only that he had stolen certain articles which were later found in his uncle's house, but also that he had stored them there without his uncle's knowledge. Since the uncle was charged with both theft and possession of stolen goods, the charges were dropped with this new information.

In another case in which I was co-counsel with Claire Barrette (later Justice Barrette-Joncas of the Quebec Superior Court), I managed to elicit an admission from the crown's principal witness that his wound had been caused not by a shot fired by the accused (who was charged with attempted murder), but rather by a policeman who had fired at him earlier when he escaped from the scene of a crime. It was Claire's painstaking preparation that had given us the idea that this might have happened, and the witness, after some prodding, agreed that this was so. Such cases are rare, and they have a particular excitement.

Also fun, in a forensic sense, is the rare case in which careful planning and good strategy induces opposing counsel to ask a question that seems both safe and logical, even essential, but that destroys his or her case—a poison pill, if you will. I used this strategy once and it worked perfectly. I represented a juvenile, charged with a delinquency that I no longer remember. He had an alibi, supported by a friend, who testified that she had seen the accused in another part of the city at about the same time as the offence was committed. I had examined the witness in my office, and I was satisfied that her evidence was honest and precise. Of course, even an honest witness can be mistaken, particularly when the event in question happened some months before, as was the case here. And so I asked a lot of questions to make certain that the day on which she saw the accused was in fact the day on which the offence had occurred and not, say, the Thursday before or the Thursday after. Her explanation was compelling, but I thought that it would have greater impact if it came out in cross-examination. My strategy, therefore, was to leave a loose end; as my opponent was a very thorough lawyer, I knew he wouldn't let it go at that.

My questions to the witness were brief. Did she know the accused? Yes. Did she meet him some months before on the street? Yes. What street? Sherbrooke at the corner of Guy. Could she recall the time of day? Yes, a few minutes before four. And finally, could she tell the court the date? Certainly, it was Thursday, May 9th. I thanked her and sat down.

As I had hoped, my opponent thought that this was too good to be true, and so he moved in with a frontal attack. "Tell me, madam," he said, "how can you be so sure of the date so many months later?" "Simple," she replied, "there is a big red circle around that date on my calendar. You see, I had a doctor's appointment at four o'clock, and when I met the accused I couldn't even chat with him because I didn't want to be late." And with that she pulled a calendar out of her bag, and of course it had a big red circle in the right place.

That settled the case and the accused was acquitted. As we walked out of court, a student who was with me said, "You took quite a risk." I told him that I hadn't. In the first place, any good crown attorney would cross-examine the witness to test her power of recollection. Some might do so with more caution, but in the end the answer would be the same, although the impact would have been less. And even if the crown attorney's questions didn't give the witness the opportunity to pinpoint the date conclusively, I am sure the judge would have permitted me to ask the question myself on re-examination.

◆◆◆

Francis Bacon, advocate extraordinary and, from 1618 to 1621, lord high chancellor of England, had the gift of striking phrases that wittily and pithily made important points. One of the best remembered is his admonition to loquacious judges: "Patience and gravity of hearing is an essential part of justice; and an overspeaking judge is no well-tuned cymbal."[144]

I was reminded of Bacon's pronouncement when I was engaged in 1966 to lead the defence in an appeal against a conviction on a charge of indecent assault. The maximum sentence for the offence was five years, and that is what the accused got. So, for good measure, we appealed that too.

The facts, as often happens, were banal. A twenty-year-old woman accepted a male coworker's invitation to go after work to his apartment "to visit his cousin." When they got there there was no cousin, and from that point on we had two versions of what happened next: hers, that the accused tried to rape her; his, that she consented to his amorous advances. Apart from her say-so, the crown had a statement from the mother that her daughter had arrived home that evening in a most distraught state. The police were notified and, two days later, detectives arranged for the complainant's examination by a medico-legal expert. Why this was not done sooner was never explained. In any event, the doctor's report to the court was brief: "This young woman did not lose her virginity and the medical examination does not ... confirm that a sexual assault ... occurred." This, to some measure, corroborated what the accused told the police. And so it became a matter for the jury.

Even a quick perusal of the transcript confirmed the accused's claim that there had been "open hostility" between his lawyer and the judge. Insults were traded—politely, but insults nevertheless—and the atmosphere was far from serene. In fact, the air was poisoned, as reflected by the judge's imposition of the maximum sentence on the accused, who was without any prior conviction.

Clear and precise drafting of a notice of appeal is crucial, yet it often must be done quickly. Some generalities must, therefore, be included, but a notice that is too general will not inspire credibility. Nevertheless, we wanted to keep the notice as wide as possible and so we started with a broadside:

> That the trial judge, to the prejudice of the appellant, made certain remarks to counsel then acting for appellant, which remarks caused prejudice to the prisoner;
> That, taken as a whole, the trial of the appellant was unsatisfactory, and this to appellant's prejudice.[145]

The problem here was that the trial judge was highly experienced, with a good reputation as a very sound jurist. The errors that we alleged did not involve complicated points of law on which trial and appellate judges may reasonably differ. So what we alleged was a polite way of saying that the trial had gotten completely out of hand.

The appeal was heard some months later, and I was assisted by Harvey Yarosky, then in his fourth year of practice. Three judges heard the appeal: Justice Edouard Rinfret, a former minister of the crown and a future chief justice of Quebec; Justice Antoine Rivard, a former provincial attorney general; and Justice Elie Salvas (whom seven years later I would succeed on the court).

Harvey and I began our argument in the middle of the afternoon, and it soon became clear that the judges were somewhat disturbed by the trial judge's strong and continuous interventions. Fortunately, the court adjourned at that point, and we returned to the office to plan our strategy for the following day. The thought then struck me that a graphic demonstration was needed. And so we ordered sandwiches and coffee and got down to business. The trial transcript covered 722 pages, and in the course of that night we analyzed every question that had been asked—3,151 in all. Of these, we discovered, the judge had asked 562, an astonishing 17.8 per cent. And, at the judge's invitation, the jury had put another 380 questions to the witnesses. In other words, the judge and jury together had asked almost one-third of all the questions. This, I felt, would clinch the case, and so it did.

When we resumed the following morning, I led off with this information and it impressed the court profoundly. Justice Salvas spoke for the court:

> With all due respect, the learned trial judge contravened the rules [established by the jurisprudence], and ... in the course of this long trial he needlessly reproached counsel for the defence, he intervened on many occasions, particularly during the case for the defence, to cross-examine, sometimes at great length, the appellant's witnesses and even the appellant himself, and he made some observations which indicated to the jury that he believed neither the witnesses nor the appellant.[146]

Justice Salvas found examples of such judicial enthusiasm on seventy-nine pages of the trial record, more than 10 per cent of the transcript. He concluded that, without such interventions and remarks, the outcome of the trial might well have been different and his two colleagues concurred. The conviction and sentence were therefore quashed and a new trial was ordered.

But this was not to be. A few days later, crown and defence put their heads together and re-examined the evidence. At most, we concluded, the accused would be found guilty of having assaulted the complainant. And so, on February 29, 1968, he pleaded guilty to a charge of common assault and was fined $25.

[21]
Some Personal Notes

In the early 1960s, to add a little spice to life, my friend Seymour Machlovitch and I decided we should learn to fly. I don't recall what gave us the idea, but once the plan was hatched, we signed up for a course at Laurentide Aviation at the old Cartierville Airport in the north end of Montreal. "When can we start?" we asked the man at the counter, and he responded, "Right now." And so, a few minutes later, I climbed into the pilot's seat of a very small Cessna 150, with my instructor, Phil Rogers, on my right. We taxied to Runway 24, made a final check of the equipment, and Phil told the tower, "Ready for takeoff."

The controller cleared us and Phil said, "Push in the throttle." I did as I was told and the aircraft started to roll down the runway. My heart started to beat a little faster. "Now pull back the wheel," was his next command, and as I did the aircraft's nose gently lifted and we were in the air. By now, my heart was racing. But this was the easy part. As I found out half an hour later, getting airborne is a lot less difficult than landing.

From that moment on I was hooked. I went to bed at night wishing that morning would come quickly so I could have another lesson. I also dreamt night after night of taking off and flying to all sorts of places. Just two weeks after my first flight, as I came in for yet another "touch-and-go," Phil told me to stop the aircraft before going on. I did and he jumped out and said, "You're on your own, good luck." Before I could even contemplate my fate, the tower told me to get going and I did my first solo circuit over the airport. I was terrified but exhilarated, and by the time I landed I was drenched in sweat. Phil and Seymour pumped my hand and off we went to nearby Ruby Foo's to celebrate.

Seymour and I had kept pace with each other, and there was an unacknowledged race as to who would get a licence first. We did our written exam together, which we both passed, and all that was left was the required solo flying time. One of my first solo trips took me to Ottawa. I landed, parked the aircraft near the terminal, and ran to the control tower to have my logbook signed. That done, I raced back to the plane, climbed into the pilot's seat, and picked up the microphone and told the tower, "Ready for take-off." A bemused controller answered my call: "It would be better," he said, "to taxi to the runway first!"

As soon as I reached the magic number of hours logged, I hurried to the Department of Transport, logbook in hand, and applied for the licence, which I got on the spot. The number was ULP-5456. I didn't tell Seymour, but when I saw him the following day, even before I could boast of my achievement, he took out his brand-new licence with the number ULP-5457. When I showed him mine, he couldn't believe it: in order to trump me, he had sneaked out to the airport the day before to put in the final hour he needed, but when he went to get his licence, the clerk found an error in his logbook and he had to go back for one more "final" hour.

My flying days were fun. It cost $15 an hour to rent a two-seater and $18 for a four-passenger aircraft. So four of us would get together on weekends and fly for a few hours each day. We all had licences for daytime only—visual flight rules and no instruments—which forced us to return before nightfall. On occasion we would be a little late, so our favourite trick was to radio the Cartierville tower and give a location closer to Montreal than we actually were. For instance, we might say that we were over Repentigny while actually flying over Trois-Riviéres, about thirty miles further away. We played this little game with the controllers, who were quite tolerant because they knew that if they closed the small Cartierville airport, which had no lights on the runway, we'd have to go on to nearby Dorval, leave the aircraft there overnight, and return the next day to fly it back to its home base. This would have meant an extra fee for rental that we could ill afford.

I had two close calls in three years of flying. The first was when we took off from La Guardia in New York. I don't remember who was at the controls—it wasn't I—but Phil Rogers, my old instructor, who often joined us on these trips, sat in the co-pilot's seat. We were eight hundred feet in the air when the single engine conked out. The skyscrapers of Manhattan were ahead of us, the sea below. Phil took over instantly and tried one or two things, but no luck. He gave a "Mayday" and got an immediate reply from the tower asking what the emergency was and what we thought we could do. Phil told them that we had lost power and that we would try to make a gentle turn and glide in for a landing.

The turn went well, but we quickly started to lose altitude. Suddenly, the engine caught on, giving Phil a chance to set a proper course. But a minute or so later, we heard that awful silence again. The tower cleared all aircraft from the area, and all around us we could see commercial flights turning away from La Guardia. The pilot of one plane, a Pan Am, expressed the feeling of all: "Good luck, little fellow," he said, and then he was off. A controller asked if we wanted a blanket of foam on the runway to soften the impact. We had a quick conference, and someone said, "That's $5,000," so we said, "Negative." We simply couldn't afford it.

Phil was a superb pilot and brought the aircraft in for a near-perfect landing. Fire engines lined the runway and firefighters in asbestos suits stood by, ready to pull us out of a burning wreckage. As soon as the aircraft stopped, police came to take a report. Phil told an officer that we were headed for Philadelphia. I didn't hear that and I told another officer that we were returning to Montreal. That made us suspect, so further inquiries were made and I discovered the truth: it was my birthday and my friends had arranged to take me for a surprise dinner at a restaurant in Philadelphia. That cleared up the mystery and we were allowed to go. We spent the night at an airport hotel and the next morning Laurentide sent another plane to pick us up. The culprit, the mechanics discovered, was a defective spark plug.

My second emergency happened when I was flying between Glens Falls, New York, and Montreal. There is a point where high mountains in the area cause low-flying aircraft to lose radio contact and fall off the radar. We were in that stretch when the weather suddenly closed in and visibility went down to a few hundred feet. We could have climbed to 10,000 feet in the hope that radar from the Plattsburgh Air Force Base would spot us and guide us to safety. But small aircraft are not pressurized and lack of oxygen can be dangerous at that altitude.

Since it was nighttime, Phil was at the controls and I was the navigator. I looked at the chart to find a place where we could land and noticed an unattended airstrip near Ticonderoga, New York, on the eastern shore of Lake Champlain. This wasn't far and there was no danger of hitting one of the Adirondack peaks. We went down fairly low, saw the lake, and a few minutes later spotted lights on what appeared to be a runway. Phil made a good landing on the grass strip, but the nose of the aircraft tipped over, lifting the tail up in the air and giving us quite a jolt. We were all strapped in, however, so no one was hurt. We gingerly climbed out and saw a couple on a road nearby. We asked them for a lift into town and they were happy to oblige. On the way, I said, "How lucky for us you were here," and the man replied, "We saw you circle the field and we thought you might crash, so we stayed on to watch."

The next day we found out that the airport was maintained by the local Chamber of Commerce but that very few aircraft used it. We called the president of the Chamber to thank him, and he told us that each year there was a debate whether or not to continue to light the strip at night. "Now," he said, "that argument is over for a while."

I flew a few more times, but my interest started to wane. I came to the conclusion that this was not a sport for amateurs: one had to take it seriously or not at all and I was not prepared to spend sufficient time flying to be a really proficient pilot, so I stopped.

◆ ◆ ◆

In 1964, Seymour, another friend, Max Shenker, and I decided that a visit to Israel was long overdue and we booked a flight on El Al. Seymour's father was active in the Zionist movement, and he spoke to Sol Granek, who ran the Montreal branch of the Zionist Organization of Canada. Granek said, "Leave it to me," and when we arrived at Ben Gurion Airport near Tel Aviv, we were met by a car and driver who told us that he would be our guide for as long as we stayed, compliments of the state tourist office. His name was Mordecai and he spoke six languages, all of them badly. But he had a wonderful disposition and we quickly became friends.

Mordecai, like most Israelis, was a veteran of the army and he took pride in its accomplishments. Battle sites were of greater interest to him than archaeological digs, which suited us well. He also believed that good food should be on every tourist's agenda and with this, too, we agreed. We made a deal that when the weather was hot, as it was throughout our trip, we would spend some time each day on the beach. Our favourite spot was Herzliya, a beautiful resort on the shores of the Mediterranean, just north of Tel Aviv.

Mordecai's employer had given him a list of things we had to see, and we saw them all, but sometimes in abbreviated form. My finest recollection is my first view of Jerusalem. As we approached the Holy City, Mordecai stopped the car and pointed to the hills in the distance. "That is Jerusalem," he said, and as we drew closer we could see the ancient buildings in the heart of the city. It was a strangely moving experience, unlike anything I had ever experienced before, and I still remember my overwhelming feeling of awe.

At that time Jordan still occupied the eastern part of the city, and our movements were therefore restricted. On later visits, Donna and I, along with our children Leslie and David, spent time in the old Jewish quarter, with its narrow streets and little shops and tiny synagogues. I also went to the Wailing Wall, the only remnant of the Great Temple from biblical times, and although I am not particularly religious, I did leave a message for God in one of the cracks in the wall, as custom prescribes.

Mordecai was sometimes replaced by another guide, Paul Beer, a Viennese who had fought on the side of the Socialists during the skirmishes in 1934. He immigrated to Palestine while that was still possible and joined the Haganah, the Jewish underground force that protected settlements from attack and helped illegal immigrants gain entry despite the British ban on Jewish immigration. Later, when the state of Israel was proclaimed, Paul joined the Israel Defence Force, and by 1964 he had retired to make his living as a guide. He knew the country intimately, and his views of Israel, its politics, and its relations with its neighbours were well-balanced and highly informative. We enjoyed his company and he and his wife became our friends.

The airline ticket entitled us to break up the return trip with a stop in Europe, so after ten days in Israel we flew to France. We had budgeted a certain amount for the trip, but Israel had been less costly than we anticipated and we had a few hundred dollars left. We decided to spend it in Paris, with a suite at the Georges V and dinner at Maxim's. It was worth every penny.

◆ ◆ ◆

When we returned from Israel, Granek asked me if I would speak about Israel to some Jewish groups, and of course I was pleased to do so. As a result, he and I stayed in touch. One day, in the summer of 1966, he called me and said that a friend of his in Hamilton, Ken Soble, had asked him to be in touch with his daughter who was temporarily in Montreal. Granek interpreted this request as a mandate to arrange a blind date for Soble's daughter, Donna. "Have lunch with her," he suggested, "I hear she's very nice."

Donna had come to Montreal to organize coverage of Expo '67 for Hamilton's CHCH-TV, where she was executive director of public affairs programming. She was constantly travelling—Montreal, Toronto, Hamilton—and reaching her on the phone wasn't easy. But eventually I did and we agreed to meet at 737, a restaurant on the top floor of Place Ville Marie. Lunch was pleasant and I wanted to see her again, but as I found out later, Donna thought that I had invited her in order to apply for a job at her television station. She was somewhat reserved when I called to make another date.

I persevered, and we did get together a few times for coffee, but her hectic schedule made this difficult to arrange. Still, I was fascinated and intrigued by this attractive and highly intelligent woman, twenty years my junior but with the wisdom and knowledge of a much older person. Well read, up to date on current events, interested in politics and business, she was a joy to be with and I looked forward to our all-too-infrequent meetings.

On the evening of December 16, as I was about to leave my apartment to go to a party, I received a phone call from a woman who asked me if I was the Fred Kaufman who knew Donna Soble from Hamilton. I said I was and she said she was Donna's sister and she had terrible news. Ken Soble had died suddenly and the family didn't want to break the news to Donna on the phone. They could think of no one else in Montreal who could do so.

I had met Donna's father by chance in Montreal a few days earlier. The meeting took place over dinner at the Montreal Airport Hilton, since her father had to catch a flight to Ottawa later that evening. It was clear that a very special relationship existed between father and daughter. He told her about business matters, even asking her for advice, and I marvelled at the ease with which they dealt with complex issues. My presence didn't interfere. At one point, he turned to me and apologized for being so rude as to exclude me from the conversation. By way of explanation, he said that he and Donna had little enough time to talk, so every opportunity had to be used. I felt privileged that I was trusted to keep the conversation confidential.

I called Donna's apartment but she was not at home. I then tried to make a reservation for her on a late flight to Toronto, but no seats were available. I called an Air Canada vice-president I knew, explained the situation, and he sprang into action and managed to get her a seat. The only problem was that I still couldn't get in touch with Donna. I finally reached her at home and asked if I could see her. But she had company and told me it wasn't convenient. I said it was important. She sensed that this was not a ploy and said, "Come now." I later learned that she had had a premonition that her father would die and had, in fact, discussed it with him that very morning.

There is no easy way to break bad news. I did so quickly and suggested she pack a few things immediately. I then told her visitor, a woman she knew from Toronto, who volunteered to come with us to the airport. It's a road that I had taken at least a hundred times before, but with my mind on other things I took a wrong turn and we ended up on Mercier Bridge, far from the airport. I made a U-turn—I still don't know how—got back on the highway, and arrived at Dorval a few minutes after the plane was scheduled to leave. I stopped at the entrance and asked her friend to take care of the car.

We raced to the gate, and fortunately my friend from Air Canada had arranged to hold the aircraft until we arrived. At that point, Donna grasped my arm and said, "I won't go alone." Another seat materialized and I bought a ticket and went with her. It was in that hour in the air that we became very close, even though we had seen each other only a few times before. Her friend, after waiting for me for more than an hour, surmised what had happened and finally left the airport to return to her home.

I stayed in Hamilton until after the funeral. From then on, Donna and I were in touch almost daily and I returned to Hamilton on two successive weekends to be with her. Friendship blossomed into a wonderful romance and I realized that I was very much in love. On January 24, 1967, we flew together from Toronto to Montreal. I said to Donna that the following day was my father's eighty-eighth birthday and wouldn't it be nice if we could tell him that we planned to get married. Donna asked, "Is this a proposal?" I said it was. She immediately turned to the woman sitting next to her and told her that we were engaged. I think she thought we needed a witness, and I took that as an acceptance. We arrived in Montreal, went straight to the ticket counter, and booked seats on the next flight back to Toronto. Her mother was somewhat incredulous to have us back in Hamilton so soon, but when I told her that I had come to ask her permission to marry Donna, she happily said yes. I then called my parents and told them that I would be in New York the next day for lunch and that I would be bringing a friend.

The flight to New York arrived late and I called from the airport to say that we were delayed. My mother said, "Don't worry, lunch will be ready whenever you get here." And then she added: "We have your friend's picture in a nice frame." I told her quickly to put it away. Wrong girl.

We had a wonderful lunch and for dessert my mother produced an authentic Viennese *Kugelhupf* with lots of freshly whipped cream that a neighbour had prepared to celebrate the occasion. How did they know, we asked. Well, as the neighbour told my mother, I wouldn't bring a "friend" to meet my parents unless we planned to get married. And so she prepared. Incidentally, the woman who baked the cake was the wife of the man who had lived in the same house as I on the Isle of Man. Small world.

We were married in Hamilton on April 9, 1967. My good friend Len Poller, who was the rabbi at Temple Beth Sholom in Montreal, helped officiate. My mother came from New York, but sadly my father was too ill to travel; we did, however, stay in touch with him by telephone throughout the day. He died later that year and I am very happy that he met my wife.

I am happy, too, that I had met Donna's father that time in Montreal, a few days before he was felled by a heart attack at the very young age of fifty-five. Much later, I learned that when Donna's father spoke to her mother after the dinner, he said, "She's going to marry that man." I am glad he was right.

◆ ◆ ◆

A friend of mine who ran the Queen Elizabeth Hotel in Montreal had volunteered to assist me with hotel arrangements for our honeymoon. The first stop was an airport hotel in Toronto, and when we checked in after the wedding reception, the room clerk winked at me and said, "I hope you will enjoy your stay." What he didn't tell me, but what we found out a few minutes later, was that my friend had arranged for us to spend the night in the hotel's Maharaja Suite, a very large room, with a huge round bed on a raised platform. Neither of us had ever slept in a round bed before, and it took some getting used to, but it was a fun way for us to start our honeymoon. We left early the next morning for Jamaica, where we stayed at Montego Bay. It was a lovely spot, lots of sunshine during the day, dinner by candlelight in the evening, with music by a small band. On the first night, when the musicians played a nice, slow piece, I asked Donna to dance. It was the first time we had danced together, and neither of us will ever forget that moment. The song was "Lara's Theme" from *Doctor Zhivago*, and that is now "our song."

While there I received an urgent message from a client from Montreal who had gotten into serious difficulties in Spain. She was anxious to have me there as soon as possible to give her advice about her predicament. My client knew that I wouldn't be happy to leave my new bride at home, so she invited Donna to join me and I accepted the assignment. When we checked into the hotel in Barcelona a few days later, we were greeted with twenty-four magnificent roses and a bottle of exquisite champagne. We dubbed this our second honeymoon.

I managed to work out a settlement, and we left Barcelona a few days later. We intended to fly to Madrid, but when we got to the airport, the agent informed us that the tickets had been issued in error and there was no flight to Madrid that day. "Do you fly anywhere today?" I asked, and he said, "Yes, to Torremolinos." So we exchanged our tickets and went to Torremolinos, where we stayed for two delightful days. On the third day we rented a car and drove to Gibraltar. In 1967 one could still cross on foot from Spain into Gibraltar—the border was closed a few months later—and so we decided to do so. There was a long lineup of men outside the gate, and I suggested to Donna she stand in line while I looked for a place to park the car. When I returned a short time later, she had left the queue and said, "You'll never believe what you asked me to do." The line, it turned out, was for Spaniards looking for work in Gibraltar, and some of them had made fun of her because she didn't know better.

We entered Gibraltar without difficulty and hired a car and driver and arranged for a three-hour tour of the city. It was a Friday afternoon, and the driver told us that most of the shops would close early in honour of the Jewish Sabbath. (Gibraltar has an old Sephardi community, strong on tradition and very active in the life of this crown colony.) We therefore started our tour in the commercial district, and when the shutters came down in advance of sundown, our driver took us to the top of the Rock where we saw the famous Barbary apes.

We left Gibraltar that evening and headed for Lisbon. We had no hotel reservation, but we were confident that we would find a comfortable country inn on the way. I had mapped out a road that I thought was a shortcut, and it was, but it took us four hours to reach the first village. Night had fallen and we were cold, tired, and hungry. I drove around the village and found a small hotel. It wasn't very appealing, but it had a big sign from Diners Club, so I said, "How bad can it be when they take credit cards?" Whatever the answer, it was our only choice.

I went to the desk, rang the bell, and the hotel keeper's wife came to greet us. She spoke a few words of French and I managed to rent a room for the night. There was a crisis, however, when she asked for our passports: Donna's still identified her as Soble and our hostess wasn't prepared to let us occupy the room together. After much discussion in a combination of languages, accompanied by appropriate gestures, I convinced her that we were recently married and that Donna's new passport had not yet arrived. I think what finally convinced her was that an amorous unmarried couple would hardly pick a hotel like hers in the middle of nowhere. The room had one small bed, with the middle about six inches lower than the sides. We didn't bother to undress, but even with our clothes on and a thin blanket we froze overnight and couldn't wait for daylight. We paid the bill and retrieved our car from the "garage," which was a barn filled with straw, much of which clung to the car's exterior. We laughed about how everyone would think what a romantic stay we must have had at this old country inn in Spain, when in truth it was one of the worst nights on our journeys.

We arrived in Lisbon the next afternoon, had lunch in the lobby of the Ritz (the dining room was closed), and then went on to Estoril where we spent two days in great luxury. Unfortunately, Donna's grandmother had died the day before and when the news reached us we decided to take the first flight out, too late for the funeral but at least in time for the *shiva*. Donna loved her grandmother dearly, and as we made our way back to Toronto we recalled the only time I had met her. It was during our short engagement, and Donna took me up to her grandparents' apartment in Toronto. By then her grandmother hadn't spoken for some time and gave no indication she recognized either family or friends. Indeed, we were told there was little point to the visit. But, as always, Donna's instincts were superb. We went into her room. She was in bed, eyes closed. Donna said, "Grandma, I want you to meet the man I am going to marry." To our delight, and everyone's astonishment, she opened her eyes and said, "Welcome, son." It was a deeply moving moment.

By the time we returned to Montreal, Expo '67 was in full swing and Donna went back to work, doing features as well as daily broadcasts on CHCH. I was accredited as a "technical adviser," which gave me access to all exhibits without lining up. It was a good summer for us, but at the end of Expo Donna gave up her position because the constant commuting between Montreal and Toronto had become too much. Since most English television programs are produced in Toronto, Donna was unable to find similar work in Montreal, and so she switched to radio and freelanced for some time for CJAD and the English network of the CBC.

Our first child was born on October 28, 1968. In those days, fathers weren't allowed in the delivery room, but Dr. Crawford Lindsay, our obstetrician and friend, sent for me seconds after our baby girl was delivered, just as a nurse placed her on Donna's chest. It was the most thrilling moment of my life as we both held this amazing little person. She cried lustily, as babies are supposed to do, and so did we, full of happiness and joy. We named her Leslie Ann, after Donna's grandmother.

Our second child, David Richard, was born eleven months later. He bears the names of our fathers: David was Ken Soble's Hebrew name and Richard was my father's name. By that time, hospital rules had changed, and I was told to scrub and put on surgical clothes. At the last moment, however, Dr. Lindsay asked me to leave the delivery room, which I did. He had perceived a possible complication and didn't want non-medical personnel in the room. Fortunately, all turned out well, and a few minutes later a nurse came out, held out her hand to me, and said, "Congratulations, you have a child." If this sounds peculiar, it was—why not tell me if it was a boy or a girl? The answer was that that was the prerogative of the physician, and nurses weren't allowed to tell. However, the suspense lasted only a minute, because another expectant father rushed over to me and said, "You have a boy!" I was thrilled, but how did he know when I didn't? "Well," said the nurse who stood there with a big smile on her face, "the rules only say we can't tell the father, but there is no reason why I can't tell someone else."

In the 1960s, it was customary (and considered medically necessary) for mothers to remain in the hospital for four or five days after giving birth. But David's birth had been difficult, and Donna needed more time to recover. She also had to have all her wisdom teeth extracted under general anaesthetic—a procedure that the dental surgeon hadn't wanted to do while she was pregnant—so she and David stayed on until she had recovered from this procedure as well. This meant that David's *bris*—the ritual circumcision on a boy's eighth day—would have to be performed in the hospital, and the administrator made a small day-surgery room available for the procedure. The charge for the room was $10, and he suggested that I give the money to the nurse to avoid a lineup at the cashier's wicket when we checked out.

A few minutes before the ceremony was to begin, a nurse brought David from the nursery. I said "Thank you" and gave her a $10 bill. She looked at me sweetly and said, "That's very nice of you. Nobody has ever given me a tip for bringing a baby from the nursery." I didn't have the heart to tell her that it wasn't for her.

David was born on September 30, 1969. That created a problem because at that time in Quebec September 30th was the cut-off date to enter school, so he and Leslie would both be in the same school year. We took advice on this and were told that we should try to come to some alternative arrangement, and we did so by enrolling both our children in private schools, where the rules were more flexible. We are delighted that both had highly successful scholastic careers, vindicating the early choices we made.

◆ ◆ ◆

In the summer of 1979 Donna woke up one day and said, "I think I'd like to go to law school." This took me by surprise but I encouraged her to follow up. Within days, she had an appointment with a member of the admissions committee at the Faculty of Law at McGill University, my old *alma mater*. She had no undergraduate degree, although she had taken several university courses many years before. She had by then been out of school for over twenty years and we wondered if she could adjust to the life of a student.

This was a highly unusual situation, and the admissions committee suggested that she spend a year in arts and recommended what courses she should take. They also said, "Come back with straight A's and we'll consider your application." She took more than a full course load and earned straight A's. Her academic ability thus established, she was admitted to law, where she became a Faculty Scholar.

Donna's studies brought about a major change in our lives. Many days I would drop her off at the old Chancellor Day Hall on Peel Street and then go on to my office. Late afternoon or early evening, I would pick her up again, but I made a habit of parking my car and joining the students in the common room. I tried to put them at ease—by this time I was a judge of the Court of Appeal, and therefore placed on a pedestal in a law school—and after a while I developed a wonderful relationship with Donna's classmates and friends, as had she. We would sit around and talk, and since almost anything "reminds me of a story," I always had a good audience. Soon I was known as the "judge in residence," and I enjoyed this designation.

The children, more used to school than Donna was, pitched in and taught her how to be a student. We put an extra leaf into the dining-room table, and Donna took one end where she spread out her books and studied. At dinner time, we moved to the other end. While both of us still helped the kids with their homework, I now took on a greater share and I enjoyed my expanded role as a father.

Donna graduated with a Bachelor of Civil Law degree in 1984. A year later, concurrent with her Bar admission course, Donna completed the course work and a thesis for a Master's degree in public law from the Université de Montreal. It was quite an achievement. She later expanded her thesis into a book, *Broadcasting Law in Canada: Fairness in the Administrative Process*,[147] which she dedicated to the memory of her father, a legendary broadcaster, "whose vision," she wrote, "was an inspiration to many, but to no one more than to me."

Donna and I have been married forty-two wonderful years. We love each other deeply and we are each other's best friend and one can't ask for more. Both children, quite of their own volition, opted to study law, Leslie at McGill and David at the University of Toronto. We think they made good choices.

[22]

Politics

I first became involved in politics in the summer of 1945, when John Bassett, the owner of the Sherbrooke *Record,* returned from service overseas to contest the Sherbrooke riding for the Conservatives in the federal election. The whole staff was recruited (I had a part-time job) and while I don't recall what we did, it was fun and it whetted my appetite for more. Bassett won the advance poll—the first one to be counted—but as the results were tabulated throughout the evening, it all went downhill.

When I moved to the *Star,* I frequently was assigned to cover elections—municipal, provincial, and federal—and I found the task exciting. In the late 1940s, the *assemblée contradictoire* was still in vogue in rural Quebec. These meetings often took place on the steps of the local church, right after Sunday Mass, and they were taken very seriously. Each candidate would have his say, with many interruptions, some good-natured, some quite nasty, none exactly to the point. Exaggerations were the order of the day, the bigger the better, and great stories still are told. One of my favourites is about the part-time crown attorney, who was a candidate in a federal election, who boldly told the crowd that they should vote for him because His Majesty the King had picked him as his lawyer, and not to forget that the king could afford to hire the best. As the story goes, the would-be M.P. wound up his peroration by sharing a confidence with his listeners. "And do you know," he would ask, "how the king pays me? I'll tell you, by cheques drawn on the *Royal* Bank of Canada!" I don't know whether he won or lost, but I doubt if any politician today would be so entertaining. And the crowds loved it.

I dabbled in the backrooms of local politics, both provincial and federal, when I became a lawyer, and with relatively frequent elections I soon acquired some of the skills needed to help candidates and would-be candidates. For the former, the battle lines were clear: it was one party against another; but for the latter, who had to fight for their nomination, the situation was more delicate, since their opponents today would, they hoped, be their supporters tomorrow. This wasn't easy to achieve, but in many Montreal ridings nomination was tantamount to election, and so the real battle had to be fought at that level.

One of the fiercest contests I recall was in 1966 in the provincial riding of D'Arcy McGee, when Victor Goldbloom and Louis Ornstein fought for the Liberal nomination. I had joined Victor's team a few months before the convention, and the first task at hand was to sign up members for the riding association. We went out in teams of two to ring doorbells and sell memberships in the party for $2 each. Of course, that was only part of the task, since we also had to try to convince the people that Victor was worthy of their support and that they should come and vote for him at the convention.

My partner in the task was Stanley Hartt, a recent member of the Bar, bright, efficient, and fluently bilingual. So, night after night, Stanley and I knocked on doors, mostly in the Snowdon–Côte-des-Neiges area, to "sell" our candidate. We had a good product. Victor's father was one of Montreal's first pediatricians, with a wide practice and a superb reputation. Victor had followed in his footsteps, and by then he, too, was well established as a pediatrician. But his opponent also was well known. He was a good lawyer, active in the community, with particular support in the more orthodox Jewish circles, and that was important since D'Arcy McGee was a predominantly Jewish riding.

I well remember that campaign. At the end of each evening, Stanley and I would go to his house, empty our pockets, count the money, and divide by two. That way we knew how many new memberships we had sold. Of course, we also had receipt stubs and, with luck, they matched the tally. The convention was held in the Hussars Armoury on Côte-des-Neiges Road and close to 4,000 people showed up. Victor had prepared an excellent speech, and the night before the meeting he asked Mel Rothman and me to read it and make suggestions. Mel and I went to work in my apartment and we did have a few comments, which we passed on to the candidate. The convention the following night was a rousing affair. Victor won the nomination and then the election, and went on to a seat in the provincial cabinet.

This had not been Victor's first foray into politics. In 1965, when Alan Mac-Naughton decided to retire from the House of Commons, Victor sought the nomination, and it seemed that he had a good chance to succeed. This was the year that the Liberal Party had recruited the "three wise men" from Quebec, Jean Marchand, Pierre Trudeau, and Gérard Pelletier. A few days before the nominating convention, I ran into Trudeau in the Faculty of Law building at McGill, where he was waiting to met Frank Scott. It was a Saturday morning and I stopped for a chat. I remember asking Pierre where he intended to run and he told me that he had been asked to meet Guy Favreau and Louis Giguère in the Windsor Hotel at noon that day. "I suppose," he said, "they'll tell me then." And tell him they did, and the answer was Mount Royal, the very riding Victor planned to contest. It was clear that Trudeau had the party's full support, and when he got the nomination it was to no one's surprise. But the speech I remember best from the convention was Victor's—a first-rate performance that got the biggest applause and did much to establish him as a serious candidate for political office.

I worked in many counties: Notre-Dame-de-Grâce (NDG), Westmount, and St. Lawrence–St. George in federal elections, and D'Arcy McGee, NDG, Westmount, and Sainte-Anne's in provincial contests. I enjoyed them all: the excitement, the camaraderie and, not least, the "incidents."

I was a poll captain when Eric Kierans ran against Jeanne Warren in NDG in the provincial election in June 1966. NDG is a pretty civilized riding, where candidates speak politely of each other and where roaming gangs don't wreak havoc in committee rooms. Still, strategic tactics are legitimate, and I noticed one of these ploys in the late afternoon on polling day. Scrutineers named by the *Union Nationale* were told to require every voter to be sworn. This was an absolute right given to every candidate's representative and there wasn't much we could do about it. But the real purpose was to discourage voters from waiting to cast their ballots—taking an oath takes time—on the theory that Liberals were in the majority in the polls in that part of the riding. Therefore, every vote *not* cast would be a gain for the *Union Nationale*. However, that was not my only problem. With each ballot box came a Bible, but it was the New Testament only, and Jewish voters, perhaps 25 per cent of the population but solidly Liberal, quite rightly refused to be sworn on the Gospels. In those days it wasn't possible to make a solemn affirmation, which would have solved the problem, and so I looked for a solution. I immediately dispatched one of my runners to the Saint-Raphael Motel on Upper Lachine Road, not far away, to borrow some Gideon Bibles. But that would take time, and I could see good Liberal voters leaving the scene in disgust.

As I pondered the problem, I took a good look at the Bibles provided. They were New Testaments all right, with a picture of Jesus on the front cover. Quite by chance, I turned one around and there, in all its glory, was a map of the Holy Land in biblical times. I at once instructed my scrutineers to put the Bibles upside down, displaying a perfect map of Israel, which stopped all objections. By the time the *Union Nationale* observers found out what had happened, my man was back from the motel where, in his words, he had temporarily "liberated" enough Bibles to put one at every poll. The Bibles were returned, with apologies, at the end of the day. Kierans won by a large margin, and quite likely would have done so even without the map of Israel and the Gideon Bibles.

The provincial riding of Sainte-Anne was a different matter: downtown, rough, very diverse. Frank Hanley was the sitting member, an Independent with strong *Union Nationale* leanings, and George Springate, a police officer-turned-lawyer, was trying to unseat him. Hanley, a former flyweight boxing champion, was extremely well known in the riding—a part of the city that he had represented, mostly unopposed, for many years on city council. The party knew that the fight against Hanley would be tough and probably dirty.[148]

I knew Springate, and when an organizer asked me to help on election day, I accepted. As expected, it was tough all the way. The first problem was at some polls where we thought we could win: 9:00 came and went, early voters were there and so were the scrutineers, but no deputy returning officer (DRO). By 9:15 I had called the chief electoral officer in Quebec, and, as George recalls, I said, "I'll give you 15 minutes to open the polls. If you don't, we'll swear in DROs of our choice." I don't know how we might have accomplished this, since the ballots were locked in the box and only the appointed DRO had the key, but it worked, and by 9:30 all polls were open and functioning.

In working-class ridings like Sainte Anne's, the heaviest vote usually comes late in the day, and that's what happened. And with it we began to get reports of "trouble." Voters were challenged, and when they couldn't produce acceptable identification they were summarily rejected. This was in violation of the Election Act, which lays down the procedure to be followed. Worse, when someone complained, DROs (who are appointed by the party in power) would call a constable and have the "troublemakers" removed from the premises.

I had a number of lawyers armed with copies of the Election Act on standby, and I sent four to a nearby school that had ten or twelve polling stations, with trouble reported at all. Today they would have cell phones, but in the 1960s they didn't, so we had to rely on "Ma Bell;" this posed a problem, since it was altogether too easy for someone to tie up the single pay phone on the premises. By 4:30 or so, George got a terse message: all four lawyers were in jail. He was very upset and wanted action. But that's where experience helps, and I told George to forget it. "They'll be out at seven," I said, "and they'll have a good story to tell. But for now let's do nothing."

George was appalled by this seemingly heartless advice, but I knew what I was doing. Sure, almost any judge would have released them on their own recognizance, and I probably could have had them out in fifteen minutes. But first a charge would have had to be laid, and no matter how innocuous the accusation (and we didn't know the facts at that point), it's not a good thing for a lawyer to have on his record, even if the case is later withdrawn or dismissed.

As it turned out, my prediction was right. Polls closed at 7:00, and at 7:05 my four lawyers walked out of the station and joined us as we received the good news that George had won. By then, they were able to joke about the events, but as I listened to their story I knew that I had served them well, for in their eagerness to be of help they had transgressed some minor dictates of the law and had they been tried they might well have been convicted. Why were no charges ever laid? Simple: that was politics in Montreal. Live and let live, but put the culprit out of circulation until the polls close.

◆ ◆ ◆

In 1962 I lived on Mountain Street in downtown Montreal in the federal riding of St. Lawrence–St. George. My good friend and classmate Jim Robb thought that his colleague John Turner would be a splendid candidate for the Liberal nomination and so he organized a small group of lawyers to see what could be done. It was a tough fight, but John got the nomination, and with it an even tougher fight began. St. Lawrence–St. George was a big, diverse riding that stretched from Guy Street to the Main, and from McGregor (now avenue Docteur Penfield) in the north to the banks of the St. Lawrence. Its population is a mix of old and new, rich and poor, French and English, and it includes McGill and Chinatown. It's a tough riding to organize. John's opponent was Egan Chambers, the president of the Progressive Conservative Party.

John had the good sense to appoint John Claxton to head the campaign, and within days it was in full swing. There was a large empty lot at the corner of Sherbrooke and Peel, now the site of the *Le Cartier* apartments, where the committee erected a tent. This soon became the focal point of the campaign. Day after day, young and eager campaigners went forth from there to blanket the riding with posters, literature, and personal hard-sell to shore up believers, convince the doubters, and convert the Conservatives. It was a cause and it was fun.

A highly successful strategy was the "blitz." We would target some of the large apartment buildings, find an organizer in the building, send out some volunteers to help, and at the appointed hour the candidate would come and make his pitch. Turner was very good at this. He always was well briefed, he knew the issues, and he related well to people. Many a convert was made on these occasions. At one point, an advance party had scouted out a building in the heart of Chinatown, and the plan was to have John go from door to door and introduce himself. When he knocked at one door, a voice from within said, "It's open, come in." He did and a naked lady stepped out from the shower, looked at the candidate, and said, "Come back when I'm dry." I don't think he did.

The hard work paid off and John was elected by a safe margin. The press quickly dubbed him a "comer," and he had good coverage wherever he went. Of course, the publicity had to be nurtured and Turner made the best of this: he was always accessible, and his speeches were both highly quotable and always to the point. It didn't hurt that he was handsome—he was "the man who had danced with Princess Margaret"—and his conversation flowed as freely and easily in French as it did in English. In short, a feature writer's dream.

Soon after his election, John asked a few of us to be his "kitchen cabinet": John Claxton, Jim Robb, John deB. Payne, Emmett Kierans, Dino Constantino, Mel Rothman, and me, and from time to time a few others. We would meet every Saturday for lunch at the old *Chez son père* at the corner of St. Lawrence and Craig (now the site of the *Palais du congrès*) to discuss the week's events, make suggestions to the new M.P., help with speeches, and plan strategy for the future, for it was clear that he had every expectation of going far. The talk was uninhibited and no topic was sacred. Criticism was ruthless, but John was a good listener and these sessions were helpful to him.

So what should a bright, young member aim for? First a parliamentary assistantship, then a junior ministry, with subsequent promotion to a senior portfolio. And ultimately—and that was our aim—the very top. We didn't know it then, of course, but we had to wait more than twenty years for that event, and when it finally happened it lasted only a few short weeks. Such are the vagaries of public life.

◆◆◆

Since I lived in Turner's riding I had joined the local organization, and in 1968 I was elected president, just in time for his run at the leadership of the Liberal Party.

Once again, John's loyal supporters pitched in, but the Trudeau bandwagon proved overwhelming and the result is history. Donna was pregnant with our first child, but she joined us in Ottawa and one of her functions was to keep the people in Turner's box supplied with food. We often joked that if the child should have an aversion to hot dogs and Coke we would know why!

Later that year, I received a call from Liberal Party headquarters in Montreal to ask for help. A meeting was scheduled for the city of Laval that night, and the principal speaker had just told them that he couldn't be there. Would I take his place? Foolishly, I agreed to do so without a proper briefing. After all, one could always speak in generalities—or so I thought.

To make a long story short, I appeared and gave a general outline of the party platform. So far, so good. The audience listened politely, even with interest, and I thought I had it made. So, with the utmost confidence, I invited questions from the floor. The first two weren't too bad, but then someone asked what the Liberal candidate proposed to do about the railway station. I didn't have the slightest idea, but I thought I could deflect the question by telling the audience that Laval, which had recently been formed through the amalgamation of a group of municipalities north of Montreal, now was the third-largest city in the province (after Montreal and Quebec), and that the new member would surely bring the issue to the prime minister's attention. "And," I said with great bravado, "when the member for the third-largest city speaks, the prime minister has to listen."

I was quite proud of my reply—how to say nothing but say it well in two minutes or less—when my persistent questioner asked me to get to the point. "The railway station," he insisted, "what was the candidate's position on this contentious issue?" I thought for a moment and decided to go with the standard reply: if people ask for something, tell them they'll get it, and so I said my candidate would exert his full weight to see that a station was built. There was dead silence and the chairman quickly stepped up to the microphone and declared the meeting concluded. Pleased he was not, and I soon discovered why: a station existed, but the government had closed it a few months before.

St. Lawrence–St. George disappeared in a subsequent redistribution. We had a last meeting of the riding association at the Reform Club and I presented John with a copy of our minutes for "safekeeping." It was a sentimental evening, a lot of good friends and, of course, an abundance of war stories, some true, many exaggerated and, no doubt, a lot apocryphal. But no one seemed to mind.

[23]
The Bench

In 1971 the provincial government decided to increase the number of judges of the Quebec Court of Appeal from twelve to fifteen. Two of the new judges would be assigned to Montreal, the third to Quebec City. The proposed increase came at a time when I had begun to ask myself, "Where do I go from here?" I had just completed two long and complicated jury trials, the aftermath of the destruction of the Computer Centre at Sir George Williams University. Then, within weeks, I found myself prosecuting a series of cases arising from the imposition of the War Measures Act in 1970. And, in between, I carried on with my regular practice. I worked seven days a week, mostly fifteen- and sixteen-hour days, without any break whatsoever. I was exhausted.

In the winter of 1972 Donna and I finally managed to go to Florida for a week, and on a lovely day in February we packed box lunches, bought a bottle of California wine, and went to Fillippi Park on the shores of Old Tampa Bay. There, over a three-hour picnic, we came to the conclusion that life on the bench looked attractive.

Today, a lawyer who aspires to the bench applies for the job. But in the 1970s this process didn't exist and the custom was to try to bring one's "availability" to the attention of the minister of justice. This was done in a number of ways: directly, if one knew the minister or one of his assistants; indirectly, if one did not. One thing was certain, though, and that was that an aspirant could not simply sit back and hope for the best.

When John Turner had assumed the justice portfolio in 1968, he asked me to consider an appointment to the bench. At that point I was not interested, but I left the door open. Two years later, he asked me again, this time with a firm offer to fill a recent vacancy on the Superior Court. I still wasn't interested, but I took the occasion to tell him that if I ever decided that the bench was for me, my preference would be the Court of Appeal. This may sound audacious, and it probably was, but my very active practice in the courts made me feel that if I were to make a change, the greater tranquillity of an appellate tribunal would be more to my liking. However, since there was no vacancy on the Court of Appeal at the time, the question was academic and we did not pursue the matter. But John did suggest that I should think about the Superior Court judgeship carefully since he might not be able to renew the offer. I decided to take that chance.

During our lunch in the park by the sea, Donna and I decided that the time to leave practice was now and that we should actively pursue the idea of a judgeship. And so we did, but there were problems. True, the Court of Appeal would soon be increased in size, creating two vacancies in Montreal (the court held sessions both in Montreal and in Quebec City), but there was a strong feeling at the time that, in proportion, there were too many English-speaking incumbents on the court and this was the chance for the government to redress the imbalance.

By tradition, four of the twelve judges came from the anglophone community, while the remaining eight were francophones. Furthermore, of the four anglophones, again by tradition, three were Protestants and one was Irish Catholic. That left no room for a Jew—there had never been one on the court—and none of the three groups was prepared to give up a seat to which each believed it was historically entitled. So there were two strikes against me: language and religion. But by 1972 it was less a question, as it would have been even a few years before, of keeping a Jewish candidate out; rather, it was a question of where one would fit. And so the three new vacancies were filled by three well-known French-Canadian lawyers: Claude Gagnon, a former *bâtonnier* from Quebec City; Justice Marcel Crête, a Superior Court judge from Grand-Mère; and Jules Deschênes, a leading practitioner from Montreal. No one could quarrel with the quality of these appointments.

A few months after the three vacancies were filled, Don Maxwell, the deputy minister of justice, called me about another matter, and in the course of the conversation asked me if I was still interested in an appointment to the bench. I said yes, but I repeated that my preference still was the Court of Appeal. He said, "That's fine, but as you know there is no vacancy on that court."

The period of uncertainty during which I hoped to be appointed to the bench lasted more than a year and caused me a number of problems. Rumours of my "imminent" appointment began to circulate. In this sort of situation, it was natural for clients and potential clients to ask themselves whether it was in their interest to hire a lawyer who might not be there long enough to complete a case. Indeed, I was engaged in a major commercial fraud case during that period and at one point, when the hearing had to be adjourned for the summer vacation, the judge said to my client: "The adjournment will give you time to find a new lawyer." The client was taken aback—as, of course, was I—and he asked the judge why he would need a new lawyer. "Well," the judge replied, "we all know that Mr. Kaufman will soon go to the Court of Appeal." This was news both to me and to my client, and in any case the judge was wrong because the appointment did not come until many months later. The press, too, had started to speculate, and I still have two clippings, one from the Montreal tabloid *Photo-Police*[149] and the other from the more respected *Le Devoir*,[150] suggesting my imminent appointment. *Photo-Police* at least added a line: "This would be an excellent nomination."[151]

In January 1973 two judges of the Court of Appeal resigned, creating two unexpected vacancies, one in Quebec City, the other in Montreal. I wasn't even aware of this, and I was therefore quite surprised when, on the morning of February 1, Phil Vineberg, one of Canada's most astute lawyers and a good friend, called me to say that he had been in Ottawa the day before, and while this was a hard call to make, he would rather I heard the news from him than from the media: the Montreal vacancy would not be filled by me. I thanked him for the call and told my wife.

That afternoon I had a meeting with another lawyer, Meyer Gameroff, and our respective clients, brothers who were unable to settle differences that had arisen between them in their business. We thought that we would give it one last try to settle the dispute before going to court. I had left instructions not to be disturbed, but at about 5:00, our long-time receptionist, Toni Forget, called to say that the prime minister of Canada was on the phone. Toni warned me that it could be a prank, for my friend Irving Adessky, when anxious to speak to me, often would say, "It's the attorney general," or some official of similar stature, in order to be put through. However, he had never claimed to be the prime minister, and Toni thought it best not to take chances.

I excused myself and went from the boardroom to my office, and sure enough it was Pierre Trudeau. As I've already recounted, he said to me, "Fred, you once got me out of jail, and the least I can do is to tell you myself that you have just been appointed to the Court of Appeal." I had been chosen to replace Justice Elie Salvas, who was retiring; after all the concern about ethnic balance, in the end I replaced a French-Canadian judge, and there was no discernible murmur.

Indeed, *Le Devoir*, in commenting on my appointment later, was very complimentary.[152] Trudeau also told me that the second vacancy, in Quebec City, would be filled by Jean Beetz, a professor and former dean of law at the Université de Montreal and a well-known constitutional scholar. Trudeau was kind enough to say, "the court can use both of you," and he wished me good luck. He added that the minister of justice would officially inform me of the appointment the following morning, and he asked me to sound sufficiently surprised when the minister called. In the meantime, he said, I should not speak of this to anyone but my family. This posed an immediate dilemma, for down the hall I had a room full of people already annoyed that I had left them in the middle of serious negotiations. Therefore, despite the prime minister's admonition, I asked Meyer to come to my office and I told him of the appointment. He congratulated me warmly and said, "Leave the clients to me." I still don't know what he told them, but a few minutes later the boardroom was empty.

I called Donna and gave her the news and she was very excited, particularly after the disappointment just a few hours before. My partners, too, were most gracious. While they were genuinely sorry to lose their friend and partner, they were happy for me. Of course, there was some balm to their sorrow, since my share of the profits would now be theirs to divide, provided they could hold on to all our clients, which I assured them they could and that, in fact, they did.

When I came home later that day, in the middle of the living room, standing on a tall pedestal, was a beautiful bronze sculpture by the Italian artist Minguzzi. It was an archbishop, about two feet high, a maquette for the doors of the cathedral in Milan, and there he stood in all his glory. I recognized him at once for he was an old friend: many a Saturday, on our frequent excursions to art galleries, we had visited him at the Dominion Gallery, and now he was mine—Donna's way of saying *mazel tov* on my appointment, which thrilled us both. In addition to the archbishop, there was also a bottle of chilled champagne. Once again, despite the prime minister's admonition not to tell anyone, I called our friend and neighbour, Justice Roger Ouimet, who joined us with his wife Odette for an impromptu celebration.

Sure enough, bright and early the next morning, I had a call from Otto Lang, the minister of justice. He formally advised me of the appointment and I thanked him. He also phoned Jean Beetz, and told him, "You have been appointed to the Court of Appeal *in* Quebec." Jean thought that this was an odd mistake to make, for surely the minister meant the Court of Appeal *of* Quebec, but it slipped his mind until the following Monday, when both he and I went to see Chief Justice Lucien Tremblay to make arrangements to be sworn in. The chief justice said that my ceremony would be in Montreal and Jean's would be in Quebec. It was at that moment that Jean realized that he had been appointed to be a judge of the court with residence in Quebec, not Montreal. This was not to his liking, and after several phone calls he reached an agreement with the government that while he would for now fill the vacancy in Quebec, he would be transferred to Montreal as soon as possible. And so he was about five weeks later, when Justice Hyde retired and Jean became his successor.

Since Jean's elderly and ailing mother lived in Montreal, the chief justice allowed both Jean and I to be sworn in at a joint ceremony on March 2 in Montreal. Donna, the children, and my mother were there, and we have warm memories of an occasion that marked such an important point in our lives. I sat for the first time in Quebec City the following Monday, and Justice Antoine Rivard, the senior judge of the court in Quebec, made a gracious speech of welcome.

I had great affection for my colleague Jean Beetz, and so did my wife, who counted him among her closest friends. My children, too, enjoyed his company on the many occasions he came for potluck dinners at our home. Jean always had presents for the children, though not always age-appropriate—for instance, a dictionary when they could barely read. This was in stark contrast to our colleague Marcel Crête, who would often join us. Marcel, more used to children, would say, "Who would like to treat me to a concert?" and Leslie and David would race to the piano and play chopsticks, which was the extent of their repertoire. Marcel would thank them profusely and give each a quarter, which was so well received that both would ask almost daily if we couldn't have Judge Crête for dinner that night. As they got older, they also came to appreciate Jean's presents, many of which they still have.

Jean's stay on the Court of Appeal was brief. In December 1973, less than a year after taking office, he was appointed to the Supreme Court of Canada, where he served with great distinction until ill health forced him to retire in 1988. He died two years later, and I was asked by the *Ottawa Citizen* to write an "Appreciation." The headline tells it all: "It was a pleasure to know such a civilized man."[153]

◆ ◆ ◆

People sometimes ask, "What was your first case as a judge?" The plain truth is that I don't know. The first item of business after the speeches in Quebec City were motions, mostly routine, which required the consent of three judges. The first of these was presented and now, more than thirty-five years later, I can confess that I didn't have the slightest idea what it was all about. As the junior judge—*le benjamin*—I sat on Justice Rivard's left, and I tugged at his gown as politely as I could to attract his attention, and when he turned to me I whispered that I hadn't understood the nature of the request. His reply was short and to the point: "Don't worry, judgment has already been given."

Since my practice was almost entirely in criminal law, it would be an overstatement to say that my experience in civil and commercial law was limited: in fact it was non-existent, save for the odd judgment that I had read, and while I knew the basics, I was not familiar with civil practice and procedure. When a lawyer came and said something like, "This is a 497 application," I would say, "Just a moment," and take my Code of Civil Procedure and look it up. But after a few weeks I no longer had to make these daily excursions into the Code, and I am proud to say that many of my judgments dealing with civil procedure became leading cases, which proves once again my strong belief that a well-trained lawyer can become proficient in almost any area of the law.

As I said, we started with motions and then moved on to a "real" appeal, which we heard for the remainder of the morning. We broke at 12:15, as was the custom in Quebec, and Justice Rivard invited me to be his guest at lunch at the Garrison Club. In those days, all judges who were free walked together to the club from the courthouse, along rue Saint-Louis, a distance of perhaps a quarter of a mile. This was a rather solemn procession and appropriate dress was required, which meant that judges had to wear hats. I had been told about this and I was therefore properly attired for my first walk up the hill.

At the club, as with everything else we did, we proceeded by order of seniority. Justice Rivard, who was also the administrator of the province, went first, and the porter would greet him with, "Bonjour, monsieur l'administrateur." The other judges were entitled to a collective "Bonjour, messieurs les juges." We had an excellent meal, complete with wine, and returned to court for 2:15. We heard another case and then adjourned for the day.

Donna, who was with me in Quebec, was in court in the morning for my official welcome and then went back to the hotel. When I returned at the end of the day, she appeared worried and I asked why. "Well," she said, "I couldn't help but think—what if you don't like it?" I assured her that the day had gone well and that I had no concerns for the future. Her spirits improved at once and we went out and had a wonderful dinner.

◆ ◆ ◆

I spent eighteen years and five months as a judge of the Court of Appeal. During that time I heard close to 3,000 appeals and more than 5,000 motions. I wrote over 1,000 judgments—nineteen bound volumes—some short, some long, some good, some not so good. I shudder to think how many pages of evidence I must have read in those years, but since the average case has between 300 and 400 pages of printed material, the total must have exceeded one million. I do not pretend that I read every word of every case, but in fact-oriented litigation—and much of it was—it's hard to skip; one spends hour upon hour reading, underlining, highlighting, and taking notes. After that, listening to the oral argument is easy.

Life on the bench sometimes had its lighter moments, but of course legal proceedings are by their very nature serious. An occasional joke does no harm, but circumspection is called for. I remember one particular occasion, for two reasons. The first is that it was the first time I presided over a panel of the Court of Appeal. By custom, the senior judge in years of service presides. My turn came rather suddenly when the presiding judge had to recuse himself, and the judge who replaced him was junior to me. And so, for the first time, I sat in the middle, waited for everyone to be ready and then nodded to appellant's counsel to proceed.

The case concerned a Jewish businessman who had been married three times. Each time he married he changed his will. And when he died, his last will was contested by the first two wives. Appellant's counsel began in the traditional manner by telling the court that this was an appeal from a judgment of the Superior Court which held such and such. He then pointed out that there were three volumes of evidence, and he invited the court, for what he said would be a better comprehension of the case, to read volume three first, then two, and finally one. The reason for this, he said, was that the evidence was presented in such a way that the most important part came last, and that's how he wanted to present the appeal.

There was nothing wrong with the suggestion, but a thought crept into my mind, and I came within a hair's breadth of saying, "Is it because the parties are Jewish that we have to read from right to left?" Fortunately, my early warning system flashed, and I saw an imaginary sign that said, "Keep your big mouth shut." And so I did, but I felt my would-be remark was too good to be wasted, and when we adjourned I phoned Donna and told her. The first thing she said was, "I hope you resisted the temptation to say it," and when I assured her I had, we had a good laugh. Some weeks later, I met one of the lawyers involved and told him my thought, to which his reply was, "Good thing you didn't say it." All three of the deceased's wives were in court, and they would rightly have been offended.

◆◆◆

I am frequently asked about the quality of lawyers who argued their cases before us. The short answer is that some were good, even superb, while others were not so good. The problem with the latter is that judges, in order to protect the litigants, must often do the work which ought to have been done by counsel and the process is slowed as a result. There are two schools of thought about this. The first, to which I subscribe in part, is that a judge should not search the record for grounds of appeal which in his or her view might have been argued but were not. I strongly believe that it is the court's task to rule on the points raised in the Notice of Appeal (or sometimes in the course of argument) and no other. To go beyond these parameters is unfair to the respondent, who is entitled to know in advance the case he or she has to meet. For the same reason, I think it is inadvisable for judges to deal with points that were not argued. In doing so, *both* parties are deprived of a chance to present arguments, and I have never believed that sufficient wisdom resides in the breasts of the judges to "go it alone."

It happens sometimes, particularly in difficult cases where judgment is reserved at the end of the hearing, that examination of the record in the solitude of the judge's chambers will disclose a point which ought to have been explored more fully during argument. For instance, the date on a document may not make sense. A simple question by a judge might quickly have resolved the matter. Indeed, the answer may have been obvious to counsel and therefore not offered, but counsel live with a case much longer than judges, and so a hearing may close before the point is resolved. When that occurs, it is perfectly proper, indeed advisable, for the court to inform counsel of the dilemma and to hold off judgment until the answer is had, but at no time should a court speculate on what the answer might be. To ask such questions may slow the process, but fairness requires that it be done. On rare occasions, a rehearing may even have to be ordered.

The second school holds the view that an appeal puts everything in issue, and that judges must therefore search the record for any errors which may have occurred at first instance. Fortunately, this attitude is rare today, but it was very much alive when I started my practice and when procedure often took precedence over substance.

The only exception I make to my belief that judges should consider only the points advanced by counsel is in cases involving the liberty of a person, and I include in this category the custody of children. In criminal cases, when we had competent counsel, I searched no further. But where counsel was weak or ill-prepared I would do much of the work myself—before the hearing, if possible—so that an accused would have a full and fair day in court. I applied the same rule to children, and some of my most draining moments involved battles (and there is no other word for this) over which parent should have custody or access. The saddest case I had was a fight over custody where *neither* parent wanted the child. My worst moments were in my early years, when my children were young and the cases before me involved children of similar ages.

The hardest decision in a custody case involved a chambers application, heard late one afternoon. The Superior Court, after a full and lengthy hearing, had given the father custody of a child. It was known to the court that the father resided in the United States and that the child would be taken there. The judgment was declared to be executory notwithstanding appeal, a fairly rare order, not made lightly by a trial judge. The mother's lawyer inscribed an appeal at once, and a few hours later the parties appeared before me on the mother's application to overturn the judge's order so that the child could not be taken across the border before the appeal could be heard. Since the mother had had custody up to the judgment, that would have meant that the child would remain in her care for at least another few months, the very thing the trial judge saw fit to avoid.

The court normally rises at 4:30, but in exceptional cases this is waived. This was such a case, and I started the hearing at 4:00 and stayed on the bench until well after 6:00. The staff wasn't happy about this, but the matter was far too important to put over until the next day, particularly since the father had already made travel arrangements for himself and his child for later that evening. I listened to the facts and found out why the trial judge, who had seen and heard the parties, made the order he did. I concluded that the appellant had failed to demonstrate why I should change the order. I know how disappointing this must have been to the mother, but the first rule in custody cases is to do what is best for the child, and that is what I hope I did.

Unrepresented litigants—and it happens occasionally even on the level of a Court of Appeal—are another cause of concern for the judges. John Morden, the former associate chief justice of Ontario, alluded to this in an interview with the *Toronto Star*'s Tracey Tyler shortly after he retired from the bench in 2004:

> Where one side is unrepresented, it's very difficult for the lawyer on the other side, knowing how far to push. It's very hard for judges, knowing how far to go

in trying to see that the scales are evenly balanced as the trial goes on. And that's a feature of the current administration of justice that's very serious ... It's very profound because it was the unquestioned basic assumption that one of the nice things about being a judge was all you had to do was decide and the truth would come out if each side was represented by a qualified barrister. All you had to do was listen carefully. They would do their job and you would do your job. Now, it's all distorted.[154]

◆ ◆ ◆

Judgment writing is an art and courses are now offered to new judges to give them guidance on the subject. Of course, style is a personal matter, but there are some basic rules that can be taught. For instance, tell the reader early on what the case is about, state the facts clearly, set out the points of law, then deal with them in order. This may sound simple, but it isn't, and there are exceptions to the rule. For instance, there are times when a judge may wish to emphasize at the outset what the case is *not* about. A good example of this is Supreme Court Justice Brian Dickson's opening statement in a widely publicized abortion case. This is what he wrote:

> It seems to me to be of importance, at the outset, to indicate what the Court is called upon to decide in this appeal *and, equally important, what it has not been called upon to decide.* It has not been called upon to decide, or even to enter, the loud and continuous public debate on abortion which has been going on in this country between, at the two extremes: (i) those who would have abortion regarded in law as an act purely personal and private, of concern only to the woman and her physician, in which the state has no legitimate right to interfere; and (ii) those who speak in terms of moral absolutes and, for religious or other reasons, regard an induced abortion and destruction of a foetus, viable or not, as destruction of a human life and tantamount to murder. The values we must accept for the purposes of this appeal are those expressed by Parliament which holds the view that the desire of a woman to be relieved of her pregnancy is not, of itself, justification for performing an abortion.[155]

Of course, Judge Dickson was a master of clarity, and feats like this should not be attempted by those with lesser skills. But the passage illustrates well how to put an issue in focus.

I had the reputation of being a clear writer, and some of that, no doubt, can be traced to my newspaper days, when editors would mercilessly whip my copy into shape. I wasn't always convinced that the final product was better, but it certainly was shorter and that was probably all to the good.

Some judges are inclined to write too much, and I was guilty of that in the beginning. After all, there is so much to say. But must it all be said then and there? The answer is no, but it takes a while to learn this. I was lucky to have a good mentor on the court, the late Paul Casey, whose opinions were always short and to the point and steered clear of affectation or pomposity. Paul made a point of reading most of my early drafts, and he didn't hesitate to criticize both style and substance. I must admit that his comments sometimes irked me—no author likes to drop a phrase that was a long time in the making—but, on reflection, he was almost always right and I am grateful for his guidance. One of his great dislikes was the judge who tilted at windmills that didn't exist, who knocked down points that hadn't been argued, and who stressed how difficult the task had been. He hated phrases such as "it is with a great deal of hesitation ..." or "after much thought." But the worst offence in Paul's book was for a judge to say that he was *dubitante*—doubtful. I did that once, and he soon stormed into my office and said, "A judge has to decide, not express doubt. That only confuses the issue." It made me think of Sir George Jessel's famous dictum, "I may be wrong, I sometimes am, but I never doubt."[156]

While precision is essential in judgments, clarity should not be sacrificed: people other than lawyers should be able to read and understand judicial decisions. Of course, there will almost always be some technical language, particularly in appellate judgments, but even complex notions can often be expressed without recourse to legal jargon, be it English, French, or even Latin.

I recall a case in which the judgment of the Court of Appeal was eagerly awaited by the press and public, and it was clear that it would be widely reported. The principal opinion was written by Justice Rodolphe Paré and it was thorough and erudite. But it was also long, and I feared that some of the important points might be drowned in a sea of detail. So I used my prerogative and wrote a short concurring opinion that set out the substance of the decision.[157] The following day I found, somewhat to my embarrassment, that the press had picked up what I had written, with hardly a reference to my colleague's masterful judgment. Indeed, *The Globe and Mail*, in an editorial, praised the decision and quoted a sentence or two from my opinion.[158] A short time later, I met my friend Tony Lamer, who quipped: "I know what happened in that case. Judge Paré wrote the judgment of the Court. You wrote the press release." Of course, there was some truth to the statement.

This raises the matter of court reporting in general. Every once in a while a superb writer will emerge who has the knowledge, interest, and ability to analyze judgments and tell the public of their import. In Montreal, the late Leon Levinson made his mark in the field, and had the universal respect of the legal profession. He was accurate, totally fair, and utterly devoted to his job, and readers of the *Gazette* knew that they could trust his reports. Kirk Makin of *The Globe and Mail* and Tracey Tyler of the *Toronto Star* enjoy the same reputation. So does Dean Jobb in Halifax, and I am sure there are others in other parts of the country. But not everyone on the court beat has the knowledge and ability required for the job, and news stories are often garbled and frequently miss the point. This isn't always the fault of reporters. They do the best they can with a judgment, and if there is something they don't understand they can ask the lawyers, although not the judge. So what to do? The Supreme Court of Canada some years ago dealt with the problem by releasing concurrently with each judgment an official *résumé* of the case that summarizes the issues. I am told that this is helpful and I hope other courts, notably the provincial appellate tribunals, will find similar means to help in the dissemination of their judgments. Certainly, some guidance of this nature wouldn't hurt.

Lord Hewart once said in a famous case that "it is of fundamental importance that justice should not only be done, but should manifestly and undoubtedly be seen to be done."[159] I subscribe to this totally, and I abhor "secret" hearings unless there is a clearly demonstrated reason for excluding the public. Take *Treu,* the case in which I wrote the "press release." Treu was charged under the Official Secrets Act with unlawfully retaining classified documents to which he had access while employed by a government contractor. For good measure, he was also charged with failing to take reasonable care of the documents in question. The trial was heard by Judge Guy Guerin, of the Court of Sessions, a well-respected jurist with a vast knowledge of criminal law. Since the documents in question were highly classified, the crown asked that the trial be held behind closed doors, and so it was. And when, some weeks later, Judge Guerin found the accused guilty as charged, his reasons were heavily censored, and all that was released to the public were a few pages setting out the basic facts.

When the case came up for hearing in the Court of Appeal, the crown again asked that it be held *in camera.* As the presiding judge, I disliked the idea, and my two colleagues agreed that, if at all possible, we should avoid doing so. The public, we felt, had a right to know the details of the case, and we refused the application. We left the door open, however, to hold a private session should the contents of the documents become an issue. But since the accused was charged with the illegal possession of classified information, I didn't think that the contents would ever have to be disclosed. I therefore ordered the documents to be placed in a sealed envelope and told the parties that I would keep them under lock and key in my office.

That wasn't good enough for the RCMP, and within hours they appeared in my chambers with a metal filing cabinet, a heavy steel bar across the front, and a large lock to hold it in place. As two officers watched, I placed the sealed envelope into the cabinet, which they locked. When they tried to hand me the key, I said, "No, thank you. You keep the key, and should we ever need these documents I'll call you." Of course, as I had thought, the documents were never needed, and the appeal was heard in public and no classified information ever leaked out. We found that the trial judge had erred in his assessment of the accused's right to have these documents at his home, and we acquitted the accused on both charges.

In *Treu*, there had been no reason to exclude the public and hold a "secret hearing." Other cases may differ, but such requests must be scrutinized carefully, and they should be granted only in the clearest of circumstances. I use the phrase "secret hearing" on purpose, to differentiate from the prohibition in the Criminal Code against *reporting* certain proceedings until a later date. For instance, a justice of the peace holding a preliminary hearing, when so requested by the accused, must order that any evidence heard cannot be published until the accused has either been discharged or, where committed to trial, the trial has been concluded. The purpose of this is to protect the accused's right to a fair trial, which might be jeopardized if details of the crime found their way into print or broadcasts and thereby poison the minds of potential jurors. But temporary publication bans do not mean "secret trials," since the press and public can be present, and justice can therefore be seen to be done.

I have great faith in the good common sense of the public—*le gros bon sens*, as we used to say in Quebec. I feel so strongly about this that I would, subject to certain safeguards, allow television cameras in court. The Supreme Court of Canada already does so, and I see no reason that courts of appeal shouldn't do so as well. Indeed, the Court of Appeal for Ontario has taken the lead, and the first hearing to be fully televised was the federal cabinet's reference to the court in *Truscott*, which was heard at the beginning of 2007.[160] And as for trial courts, judges already have the power to regulate what can and what cannot not be broadcast. A young witness, for instance, may well feel ill at ease with a camera in the court room, as might the victim of a crime, and so discretion must be exercised.

Some years ago I was asked by the Montreal *Gazette* to write a guest editorial. The title was "Let TV Cameras Roll in Court," and my theme was that, on balance, live broadcasts were a good thing. We live in an age of instant communications, we see events as they occur, we watch astronauts walk on the moon, we see the good and the bad, and we can judge for ourselves. But when it comes to trials or appeals, we must wait. Why? The usual argument is that cameras would disturb the proceedings, and so, in some cases, they might. Also, part of the problem is human nature itself. As I wrote in the editorial:

> We are all "hams," and judges, lawyers, witnesses and jurors are not an exception. Turn on a camera and my behaviour changes: I watch what I say, I take care how I look. In short, I play to the audience. The spontaneity is gone, the actor in me takes over and things that should be said are left unsaid and vice-versa.
>
> And yet, deep down, I have the nagging feeling that justice exposed is justice well-served; that the advantages of a camera in the courtroom outweigh the disadvantages of being kept partly in the dark. If a picture is worth a thousand words, it would take many columns of print to convey all the nuances of this ongoing saga.[161]

Of course, as I said before, some safeguards are needed. For instance, the cameras must be unobtrusive, and an experienced operator must be in charge to prevent improper invasions of privacy, such as close-ups of confidential documents or audio pick-ups of private conversations. Nor must it be forgotten that the purpose of telecasts from a courtroom is to enable those who can't be there to see and hear what happens; it is not to embarrass the participants.

I had occasion to put into practice what I preached when I presided over the royal commission in *Morin*.[162] We had one camera in the hearing room, with a feed into a nearby press room. The media were free to use the broadcast either live or on tape, and the arrangements did not in any way interfere with the hearings. I truly believe that the public was better informed because of this, and I received no complaint from witnesses, lawyers, or anyone else.

The idea has now found greater acceptance, and since the Ontario Court of Appeal's decision to permit cameras in court during the hearing in *Truscott* was deemed a success, I am sure that other courts will soon follow.

◆ ◆ ◆

Since my appointment to the bench—and even before—I have met many judges in many parts of the world. Language and tradition may sometimes divide us, but there is a common bond of shared experience, the good and the bad, a genuine desire to learn and, not least, a social factor. After all, aren't we all nice people?

I have fond memories of my maternal grandparents, Markus and Gisela Mittler. My grandmother died in 1937. My grandfather was deported by the Nazis and perished in the Holocaust. This photograph was taken in happier times. Bad Ischl, Austria, 1928.

My parents on their wedding day. Zilina, Czechoslovakia, 1922.

An early look at the world around me. Vienna, 1925.

My first dog. I didn't get another dog (this time a real one)
until seventy years later. Vienna, 1927.

Wheels mean a lot to a young man! Vienna, 1928.

My first day at school. Vienna, 1930.

A work group at the New Brunswick internment camp.
I am seated at the left. Ripples, N.B., 1941.

By 1942, the designation "refugee" was substituted for "internee," and work performed in the camp was compensated at the rate of thirty cents a day. This was paid in "camp money," and a one-cent scrip would get you a cookie or some candy in the canteen. Sherbrooke, Quebec, 1942.

The Mittlemans in Sherbrooke facilitated my release from camp and warmly welcomed me into their home. From left to right in back: the rabbi's wife, Dora; their daughter, Eta; me; Rabbi Mittleman; and their son-in-law, Abe Schachter. In front: their other daughter, Gertrude Schachter, and Gertrude and Abe's son, Raphael, now a prominent lawyer in Montreal. At the time, the Mittleman's third child, Joseph, was serving overseas with the RCAF. Katevale, Quebec, 1942.

My parents, by then in New York, were able to join me
for my graduation from high school. Sherbrooke, Quebec, 1943.

A happy moment for my parents. New York, 1952.

I was proud to get my corporal's stripes in my second year in the Bishop's University Contingent of the Canadian Officers Training Corps. Lennoxville, Quebec, 1944.

Graduation day at Bishop's: a chat with the chancellor, George H. Montgomery. Lennoxville, Quebec, 1946.

An interview with the governor general, Viscount Alexander of Tunis, on his departure from Canada. From left to right: author Brian Moore, then a reporter with the Montreal *Gazette*, Grace Brynolson, a writer for *Time* magazine, me, and Lord and Lady Alexander. Montreal, 1952.

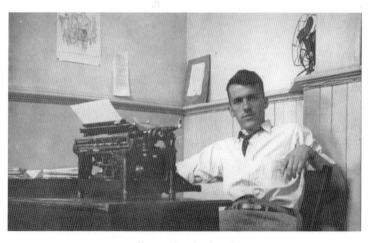

My "corner" office at the Sherbrooke *Record*, 1946.

Searching for a lost child in the Laurentian Mountains. *Montreal Star* photographer and I study a map to decide on the next move. Near Sainte-Adele, Quebec, 1948.

On assignment for *Time* magazine in Quebec's northland. Chibougamau, 1952.

The "Green Hornet," my first car, which I owned jointly with a friend. We bought it for $275 in 1952, and sold it for almost as much three years later. Montreal, 1953.

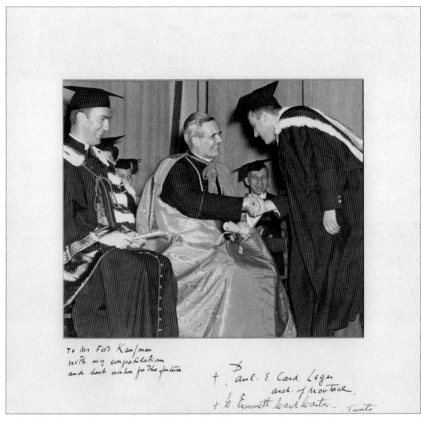

To Mr Fred Kaufman
with my congratulation
and best wishes for the future

+ Paul. E. Card. Leger
arch. of Montreal.
+ G. Emmett Card Carter. Toronto

Graduation with a Bachelor of Arts degree from the Thomas More Institute. On the left, Father G. Emmett Carter, president of the institute and later the cardinal archbishop of Toronto. In the centre, shaking hands with me, Paul-Émile Cardinal Léger, archbishop of Montreal and chancellor of the Université de Montréal, of which the institute was an affiliated college. The inscription, written in Cardinal Léger's hand, reads as follows: "To Mr. Fred Kaufman with my congratulations and best wishes for the future." It is signed "Paul E. Card. Léger Arch of Montréal," The second signature is that of Cardinal Carter. Montreal, 1953.

Graduation from law school: McGill University chancellor Bertie Gardiner confers on me the degree of Bachelor of Civil Law. Montreal, 1954. (Paul Lagace)

Le procès de Malcolm Arnold McGregor (à droite), ancien pilote commercial, accusé du meurtre qualifié de William Gunn de Brownsburg, près de Lachute, le 20 novembre 1961, a été interrompu à peine commencé, la semaine dernière. Le jury de langue anglaise a été congédié. L'homme devra subir un nouveau procès d'ici un an. Il était défendu par Me Fred Kaufman (au premier plan) tandis que la Couronne avait comme porte-parole Me Fernand Légault, c.r., de Lachute. Le procès se déroulait devant l'honorable juge Claude Prévost qui a accordé le "mistrial" à la demande de la défense après qu'un policier ontarien eut raconté que McGregor avait été arrêté et passé en procès pour effraction dans une maison privée. Le tribunal a reconnu que cette déclaration pouvait faire tort à l'accusé dans l'esprit des jurés.

(Dessin "Allô Police", par Galiana)

Le rappel de son passé vaudra un deuxième procès à l'accusé du meurtre de Brownsburg

An artist's impression of a tense moment during a cross-examination in a murder trial. On the bench, Justice Claude Prévost of the Quebec Superior Court; on the far left, the crown attorney, Férnand Légault, later Justice Légault, of the Quebec Superior Court; on the right, the accused. Saint-Jérôme, Quebec, 1963. Photo courtesy of *Allo Police*.

The day computer cards rained from the sky. Students had occupied the Computer Centre of Sir George Williams University in Montreal, and thousands of documents were destroyed and thrown into the street below. This was the scene on Bishop Street. Montreal, 1969.

Si c'est pas un Anglais on va s'en rendre compte

The trial of the "Trinidad Ten." When the panel of potential jurors was exhausted, the judge ordered the sheriff to bring in citizens from the street, with instructions that they must be fluent in English. Teams of police went to nearby Victoria Square, where the Montreal Stock Exchange was located, and brought in scores of unsuspecting English speakers, many of whom were pressed into service to complete the jury. The caption of the cartoon, loosely translated, says: "If that's not an Anglo, we've got a problem." Montreal, 1970. (*Montréal Matin*)

Become a

VOLUNTARY TAXPAYER

OF MONTREAL

Any person may pay a voluntary tax to the City of Montreal

A PAYMENT OF $2 is valid for one month and gives you the opportunity of receiving one of the 151 MONTHLY PRIZES

— ONE GRAND PRIZE —

$100,000

— IN SILVER INGOTS —

PLUS: 30 PRIZES OF $1,000 each in silver ingots
20 PRIZES OF $500 each in silver ingots
100 PRIZES OF $100 each in silver ingots

The selection of the 151 candidates whose names have been chosen for examination will be made publicly. They will be advised immediately of the time, day and place where they will have to answer, in public, questions related to the subjects printed on the reverse side of the official receipt. Having answered correctly, candidates will then be awarded their prize.

You may, if you choose, through a payment to the order of the <u>City of Montreal</u>:

1. Pay $2 for one month: you will receive an official receipt for $2.

2. Pay more than $2 for one same month: you will receive as many official receipts as there are times $2 included in your payment.

3. Pay in advance the total amount that you wish to spread out over the months to come, provided that you advise of the amount you wish to apply to each month. (Example: $2 x 6 months = $12). You will then receive receipts corresponding to your monthly payments.

4. Pay on behalf of other persons. If a child is too young to answer questions, his father, mother or the person who has made a payment on behalf of the child may answer for him.

If a candidate is not available to answer questions, the jury may set another day for such questioning or, upon acceptance of a medical certificate, allow a person duly authorized by the candidate to answer on his behalf.

No distributors, agents or intermediaries.

Fill out the included form, writing clearly the amount to be applied to each <u>particular</u> *month, and mail directly as follows:*

CITY OF MONTREAL
P.O. BOX 9999
MONTREAL 3, QUE.
CANADA

EXPO 67 WAS TOO GREAT TO LAST ONLY SIX MONTHS

VISIT "MAN AND HIS WORLD"
FROM MAY 17 TO OCTOBER 14, 1968

Same islands, same pavilions, 40 new presentations, same minirail, same express, same atmosphere, same admission price and free admission to all pavilions.

(FRANÇAIS AU VERSO)

Montreal's "Voluntary Tax" scheme was launched with great fanfare, but was held by the courts to be a disguised lottery and therefore illegal. I argued the case for the province in the Supreme Court of Canada. Montreal, 1968.

A truly memorable day. The chief justice of Quebec, Lucien Tremblay, administers my oath of office as a judge of the Quebec Court of Appeal. Behind us, Justice Marcel Crête, later chief justice of Quebec, and Justice Jules Dêschenes, later chief justice of the Quebec Superior Court. I became the acting chief justice in 1987 and remained in that post until 1988. Montreal 1973.

My family after the swearing-in. From left to right, Donna, my mother, David, Leslie, and I. Montreal, 1973.

"Here it is." I deliver the Morin Report to the public. Toronto, 1998. (*The Globe and Mail*)

Governor General Adrienne Clarkson installs me as a member of the Royal Society of Canada, a rare honour for a non-academic. Ottawa, 2002. (Government House, Rideau Hall)

The three partners of Kaufman, Yarosky, and Fish together again. From left to right: Harvey Yarosky, me, and Justice Morris Fish of the Supreme Court of Canada, on the occasion of the G. Arthur Martin Award ceremony. Toronto, 2003.

My wonderful family on my eightieth birthday. Toronto, 2004. (Jenna Muirhead-Warren)

Leslie and I. This picture appeared in the *Toronto Star* to illustrate a story about fathers and daughters in the legal profession. The title: "Law suits these offspring." Toronto, 2004. (Rick Madonik/*Toronto Star*)

Donna, David, and I with the Stanley Cup. Aurora, Ontario, 2004.

Andersenin kriisi säikäytti KPMG:n ja PWC:n Sivu 14

Talouselämä

Numero 13   5.4.2002

Perlos, Wecan
ja Scanfil kiitivät
Nokian mukana
Sivu 48

Naiset johtavat
aliarvostettuja
pörssiyhtiöitä
Sivu 63

Tuomo
Lähdesmäestä
hallitushai
ennätysajassa
Sivu 75

Talouselämän
johtajanaiset:

Donna Kaufman on
Suomen tuntemattomin
vallankäyttäjä

250 vallan naista
Sivu 22

Donna, who became the first woman director of a major corporation in Finland, was honoured by the business magazine *Talouselämä*. I love this picture of my "cover girl." Helsinki,
2002.

My wonderful granddaughter, Alexandra Rebecca Kaufman, at six months, with Donna and Rosie. Born in Birobidzhan, Russia, Ali was adopted by Leslie in 2004. Toronto, 2005.

Ali, at five years old. Toronto, 2009. (Mindy Gordy)

Over the years I enjoyed many good lunches and dinners with colleagues in Canada and abroad. But one lunch stands out because it seemed so incredible at the time. It took place in the mid-1970s in Washington, D.C. Donna and I had become friendly with David L. Bazelon, then the chief judge of the United States Circuit Court of Appeals for the District of Columbia, and his wife, Mickey. I first met David when he took part in a seminar in Toronto. He was a leading proponent of new and better ways to define insanity, and he was in great demand as a speaker. He was often controversial, which he wanted to be, and for many years he was a pivotal figure in a circle of Washington liberals that included not only lawyers and judges, but also professors, congressmen, psychiatrists, writers, and noted journalists.[163]

A year or two after our brief meeting in Toronto, Donna and I were in Washington and we made an unscheduled visit to his chambers in the federal courthouse. He received us graciously but said that he had to leave for Philadelphia in less than an hour and the visit would therefore have to be short. We soon established that we had a common friend, Justice Harry Batshaw in Montreal, the first Jewish High Court judge in Canada. I told David that I had been the first Jewish judge of the Quebec Court of Appeal, to which he replied that he was the first Jew on his court, "and this is America!" With this, the conversation took a more intimate turn, and the next thing I knew he called his assistant and told her to book him on a later flight.

A few months later, on another visit to Washington, David invited me for lunch. "Meet me at one in my chambers," he said, "and we'll go from there." At the appointed hour, David led me to the basement garage where a limousine waited. We drove through the streets of Washington for a good twenty minutes and I was beginning to wonder where we might go. Imagine my surprise when the car drove through the entrance of a liquor warehouse and came to a stop in the courtyard. David led me through a side door to the executive suite and into the office of the owner, Milton S. Kronheim, Sr. I had never heard of Kronheim, but everyone else in Washington had. He was a mover and shaker, friend of the powerful, a card-playing buddy of Harry S. Truman, and the man who controlled the wholesale liquor business in the nation's capital.[164]

Kronheim greeted me warmly, offered me a drink, and invited me to look at his collection of photographs, which covered the four walls—presidents, senators, congressmen, judges, all suitably inscribed. At about 1:30 Kronheim looked out the window and said, "Where are they?" A few minutes later, another limousine pulled up, and out stepped two Supreme Court justices, Thurgood Marshall and

William J. Brennan. The introductions made, we proceeded to the employees' lunchroom, where a corner table was set aside for Kronheim and his guests. A waiter came and asked "the usual?" to which everyone, myself included, nodded. With that out of the way, an animated conversation started. Marshall and Brennan discussed a case they had heard that morning. David made a few comments. I don't remember whether Kronheim added his views, but I listened in awe—and surprise. It was delightfully indiscreet.

The lunch ended all too soon, and on the way back to the courthouse David told me that the group met frequently. They were kindred spirits in an age when the liberalism of the 1960s was slowly being superseded by more conservative rulings from the Supreme Court, then under the leadership of Warren Burger. David and Burger were on opposite ends of the spectrum and there was no love lost between them.

In 2001 the Lillian and Albert Small Jewish Museum organized an exhibit called "Power Lunches: Milton S. Kronheim, Sr.'s Washington." It contained photographs from (and of) the lunchroom walls of Kronheim's warehouse. I didn't know it then, but I do now: I had been to a Washington power lunch. Kronheim died in 1986 at the age of ninety-eight. David stopped hearing cases in the mid-1980s and died in 1993 of Alzheimer's disease. Brennan retired from the Court after serving for almost thirty-four years. He died, at ninety-one, in 1997. Marshall served for twenty-four years and he died in 1993.

◆◆◆

In the summer of 1987 Chief Justice Crête fell ill. As the senior judge in years of service—*le juge doyen*—I took over his duties, and while it was an honour to assume this task, I quickly discovered that with the job of acting chief justice come many headaches and frustrations, caused mostly by administrative problems. Who would believe, for instance, that I once had to take a day off and travel to Quebec because a secretary was unhappy that she had to share an office with the court's chief messenger? If I hadn't found a solution we would have lost the secretary, and she was one of the best. Or what about spending two hours to convince the minister of justice that additional word processors were needed to keep up with the work, only to be told a week later that Treasury Board had refused to authorize the necessary funds? One learns to live with these irritations, but they don't help the court's morale.

Chief Justice Crête died in the spring of 1988, and it was my sad duty as acting chief justice to preside at a special session of the court to honour his memory. It was held in the court's principal courtroom where he and I had sat together so often, and friends from far and wide attended, among them the chief justice of Canada, the chief justice of Ontario, and the federal and provincial ministers of justice. It was a tribute to Marcel's great decency that there was standing room only, with an overflow into the hall.

The night before the special session, I called Herbert Marx, the provincial minister of justice, at his home, and proposed naming the room where we were to meet the next day after the late chief justice. Herb readily agreed and I was therefore able to announce the next morning that Room 17.09 of the *Palais de Justice* would henceforth be known as the *Salle Marcel-Crête*. It was a well-received gesture and much appreciated by Marcel's family and friends.

The ceremony in court was followed by a memorial Mass in Notre-Dame Basilica in Old Montreal. The Mass began at 1:30 and lasted close to an hour. Donna and I had invited Chief Justice Dickson and his wife, Barbara, and the federal minister of justice, Ray Hnatyshyn, to join us for lunch after the service, but where does one go at three in the afternoon? Clubs, hotels, and most restaurants are closed at that hour and Donna therefore suggested Moishe's steak house on the Main, which opened for lunch and didn't close until midnight. I demurred at first—was this a proper place to entertain such high-powered guests?—but in the end I said, "Why not?" As it turned out, it was an inspired idea and we had an excellent meal. Hnatyshyn had ample helpings of the chef's East European specialties, which reminded him of dishes his mother had made. When his executive assistant reminded him that he had an appointment later that day in Ottawa, he told him to phone and postpone it.

Hnatyshyn was a good minister and I was disappointed when he lost his seat in the general election later that year and I wrote and told him so. When he was appointed Governor General in 1990, he invited Donna and me to his inaugural dinner at Rideau Hall. Greeting us in the receiving line, he pointed to the beautifully set tables further on in the room and said: "That's the best I can do. Of course, it isn't Moishe's."

Chief Justice Crête's successor was appointed in May 1988 and my final act as acting chief justice was to administer his oath of office on June 2. Claude Bisson, like Crête before him, came from the *Mauricie*, the region along the St. Maurice River that flows into the St. Lawrence at Trois-Rivières. In his first remarks, Claude generously paid tribute to my leadership of the court for almost a year—a difficult year, perhaps, but a nice touch near the end of my judicial career.

I turned sixty-five on May 7, 1989, and this entitled me to elect supernumerary status, which I did. A supernumerary judge keeps his or her salary, office, and secretary, but sits less often, and I could see no downside to this status. The court, too, benefits, since it gets a new full-time judge, and every chief justice likes to have an additional body. Also, by definition, a supernumerary judge is older, and possibly wiser, and is therefore able to counsel some of the younger judges.

I carried on in this capacity until June 30, 1991, when I resigned from the court. By then I was sixty-seven and I felt that if I wanted to start another career, now was the time. It proved to be a good decision.

[24]
Return to Practice

With Donna's ever-increasing involvement in business through her law practice and corporate boards, I started to take a greater interest in business affairs, and I began to read many of the current books and journals on the subject. We were in the wild 1980s—merger mania, acquisitions, junk bonds, and more—and I realized that some formal training in the field would be of value.

Early in 1987 I saw an advertisement for an Executive M.B.A. program at Concordia University in Montreal. It was geared toward "mature" students and it sounded just right for me. I made an appointment with Steve Applebaum, dean of the Faculty of Commerce and Administration, and asked him a vital question: "Would he consider a candidate in his sixties?" He said yes without hesitation and added, "You might contribute a lot to the class." He also told me that I would, of course, like everyone else, have to meet all the normal requirements for admission.

I got busy and collected transcripts from my previous studies. I also signed up to take the GMAT, which is an aptitude test for prospective M.BA. students. I had never taken this type of test before—they didn't exist when I was in school—but I thought that with proper preparation I could get a decent score. My son David, who is a gifted teacher, volunteered to help, and every night for about three months I practised with his guidance. The day for the test finally came and I spent four hours sweating it out with two hundred other aspirants in a large lecture room at Concordia. I had a few anxious weeks before the results arrived, but they were good enough to get me a place in the class starting that fall.

Then fate intervened. After Chief Justice Crête suddenly fell ill that summer, my duties as temporary administrator of the court left no time for extra-curricular activities. I therefore asked Concordia to defer my admission, which was granted. This was a good decision because, as I later found out, the workload in an Executive M.B.A. is so heavy that I would be hard pressed to keep up even without my new administrative responsibilities.

Finally, in 1989, with fewer duties in court, the time was ideal to embark on this adventure and I started classes that fall. The going was tough. Classes were given on alternate Fridays and Saturdays, from eight in the morning until six at night, and on average a student studied at least twenty hours per week. Since almost every one of my forty-one classmates worked, evenings and weekends had to be devoted to study, much of it alone, but some in groups that we were urged to form.

I was fortunate to be part of a good group of five and we met every Tuesday evening, had a light meal, and studied late into the night. It was a diverse group: an accountant, a computer expert, a statistician, a real estate agent, and me. We each took on a subject, prepared the first draft of assignments, fine-tuned the result at our meetings, and then produced the final product. Fax machines were constantly busy and I recall one occasion when a member of the group had to take a business trip to Japan. We faxed the assignment to his hotel in Tokyo—email was not yet in common use—which he did overnight on his laptop and then faxed back the result in time for our weekly meeting. We also prepared class presentations together, and we certainly learned how to get to the "meat" of a case and make it intelligible to a very critical audience.

I completed the course in the spring of 1991 and was awarded an M.B.A. at convocation in May. My good friend Alan Gold, then chief justice of the Quebec Superior Court, was chancellor of Concordia at the time, and I received my diploma from him, which added a wonderful touch to the occasion. In fact, this was a happy week for the Kaufmans, with three degrees in three days: Leslie's Bachelor of Social Science in criminology (with first-class honours) from the University of Ottawa, David's Bachelor of Arts in North American Studies from McGill (also with first-class honours), and my M.B.A. from Concordia. Donna rightly thought that this called for a party, and we celebrated with family and friends.

I had no clear idea what I wanted to do with my new credentials, mostly because I had taken the course for pure enjoyment. But by the summer of 1991, I had served eighteen years on the court and I began to feel the time had come to leave. I was in good health, so there was still a chance to do something else, but what I didn't know. I informed the chief justice and the federal and provincial ministers of justice of my decision to retire effective July 1.

While I left many good friends at the court, I looked forward to new challenges. My friend Herb Siblin, a chartered accountant, generously offered me a *pied-à-terre* in his firm, which gave me an office with a desk and a telephone and place for some books. I got my first business assignment in the form of a consulting contract with a publisher, and quickly saw that there was indeed life after the bench.

◆◆◆

Toward the end of August, my former partner Harvey Yarosky, who now headed my old firm, called to invite me for lunch. By the time the meal was over, we had agreed that I should "come home" as counsel to the firm. I would be back in a familiar milieu with friends and former colleagues, giving legal advice, mixed, perhaps, with some business counsel as well. The arrangement was to start the day after Labour Day.

The firm, now called Yarosky, Daviault and Isaacs, is a direct descendant of a series of partnerships started by Joe Cohen in the late 1920s, beginning with Cohen, Gendron and Gauthier. When I joined in 1955, it was Cohen and Leithman, with Joe doing criminal work exclusively and his partner, Ezra Leithman, doing everything else—civil, matrimonial, and commercial. After some years, the name was changed to reflect my more senior status and three more lawyers soon joined the firm: Harvey Yarosky, Morris Fish, and Victor Glazer. Victor worked with Ezra, his father-in-law, and Harvey and Morris found their calling in criminal law.

Joe fell ill in 1969 and had to leave practice. Harvey, Morris, and I decided that this was an appropriate time to split the firm in two—the criminal lawyers and the civilians. This suited all of us and the separation was friendly: we stayed in the premises, Ezra and Victor moved to another floor in the building but kept the telephone number. The new firm was called Kaufman, Yarosky and Fish and it was a remarkable partnership. For one thing, we never got around to drafting a partnership agreement. Every major decision was made by consensus and I don't think we ever had an argument. Disagreements, perhaps, but not over anything of substance. As to the division of profits (or, God forbid, losses!), we sat down in my office on January 5, 1970, and each of us took a piece of paper. On it we wrote what we thought were the proper percentages, and when we disclosed the figures to each other, the high and the low were two per cent apart. We split the difference, wrote down the results, and initialled the paper. It was the only "contract" we ever had and I still have the original. We repeated the exercise once a year and never had a problem.

We had good people working with us. Natalie Isaacs, a classmate from McGill, joined us after raising five children. Jerry Zigman came as a *stagiaire*—an articling student—in 1969 and stayed. François Daviault was hired two years later. It was a great team. We all worked hard, but we had fun and there was never a dull moment.

After I left in 1973 to go to the bench, the firm went through a number of name changes: first to Yarosky and Fish, then to Yarosky, Fish, Zigman, Daviault and Isaacs. When Jerry was appointed to the Superior Court in 1987, his name was dropped, and two years later Morris became a judge of the Court of Appeal, and his name disappeared from the letterhead. In 1992 the firm merged with Gerry La Haye and Michael Stober, a partnership of two former crown attorneys who had established a good reputation in private practice. The new name was Yarosky, Daviault, La Haye, Stober and Isaacs, but this changed again in early 1994, when François was appointed to the Superior Court. However, he didn't like life on the the bench—I think he missed the happy atmosphere of the office—and he returned to practice six months later. Of the original six, four had become judges—a record, I believe, that I would like to think speaks well of our choice of partners and associates.

◆ ◆ ◆

Retired judges who return to practice do not appear in court, but they are free to see clients, discuss their cases, and help to plan strategy, and that is what I did. I also took on commercial arbitrations, where I put to good use not only my legal expertise, but also what I learned in business school. Alternate dispute resolution, ADR for short, is a rapidly expanding field and I enjoy the work.

But life after court didn't stop there. In the fall of 1991 Paul Fortugno, the chairman of the Quebec Securities Commission, invited me to join the commission as a part-time member. I accepted and served for two years. I was also invited to teach a course on ethics in management at McGill and an introduction to business law at Concordia. That, too, was a challenge.

In April 1992 Donna and I celebrated our twenty-fifth wedding anniversary. To mark this happy occasion, we invited Leslie and David to join us for a week's vacation in Bermuda and it was all we had hoped for. When we returned to Montreal, we found the usual bundle of mail, but since we had to go out that evening we decided not to look at it then. But one large, white envelope stood out and Donna picked it up and looked at the return address. "I think you may want to open this now," she said, and she was right. It was a letter from the secretary to the Governor General and it informed me that I had been recommended by the Advisory Council to be appointed a member of the Order of Canada. Would I accept?

I was thrilled with the honour, and I could not help but reflect that it came exactly fifty years after my admission to Canada. How much had happened since then; how wonderful to have this recognition. I turned to Donna and brought tears to her eyes when I said, "Not bad for an immigrant." The letter asked me not to spread the news until the official announcement. But of course I told my family and they were as excited as I was.

The investiture took place at Rideau Hall on October 21, 1992. It was a solemn occasion and I was delighted to have my family with me. We were particularly touched by the citation:

> Arriving in Canada as a youth displaced by war, he showed perseverance and courage, becoming a Judge of the Quebec Court of Appeal, where his judgments were models of erudition, clarity and precision. He has had a diverse career as a brilliant criminal lawyer, a teacher and a writer, dedicating his life to justice, fairness and freedom. Moreover, he has instilled in others the pursuit of these ideals.

I don't know who wrote these words, but no one could ask for a finer tribute and I was deeply moved. After the ceremony, the Governor General entertained the recipients and their guests at a banquet in the ballroom. This was the night the Blue Jays played one of their World Series games in Toronto and throughout the meal results were circulated from table to table. By the time dessert was served, an *aide-de-camp* came to the vice-regal table and whispered a few words into His Excellency's ear. The game had reached a crucial stage, and as any true baseball fan will understand, Hnatyshyn couldn't resist the temptation to go and watch. So he rose and with a big smile announced that he had to take care of "important state business." Everyone understood, no one minded, and the party went on.

Leslie flew back to Montreal and David to Toronto, but Donna and I stayed in Ottawa for the night and when we got back to the hotel we found an ice bucket with a bottle of Dom Perignon and a note from the lawyers and staff in my office wishing me well. It was the perfect end to a perfect day.

I received my second invitation to Rideau Hall in 2001, when the Royal Society of Canada elected me to be a Fellow in the Academy of Humanities and Social Sciences. Once again, my family joined me for the presentation of the certificate by the Governor General, Adrienne Clarkson. This is the citation:

> The Honourable Fred Kaufman is an outstanding Canadian, learned in the law, committed to public service and to fundamental constitutional values. He practised

criminal law for many years prior to his appointment as a Justice of the Quebec Court of Appeal. Since retiring from the court he has served on five public inquiries, reviews and investigations. He made perhaps his greatest contribution to the administration of justice as sole Commissioner of the Inquiry into Proceedings Involving Guy Paul Morin. The insight, wisdom and balance expressed in his Report have established a new standard of fairness in criminal justice procedures in Canada.

◆ ◆ ◆

A further, and much appreciated, honour came to me in 2003, when the Criminal Lawyers' Association of Ontario presented me with the G. Arthur Martin Criminal Justice Award. This award was inaugurated in 1988 to honour that great jurist, G. Arthur Martin, and it is awarded annually to "an individual in Canada who has made a significant contribution to criminal justice." Justice Martin, whom I knew well and loved dearly, was the first recipient, and I was greatly moved when the association informed me of its choice for 2003. As I said when the award was presented:

A lot of rewards have come my way, and I am grateful for every one, but the G. Arthur Martin Criminal Justice Award is very special and unique because it comes from you, my peers, my colleagues at the bar. This is a group that doesn't speak without thinking, a group which is devoted to the law, a group which doesn't make choices lightly.

So I say to you in all humility, as I did to your president when he first informed me of your choice, that I am thrilled beyond words. It is to me the ultimate recognition of a career in criminal law.

I then added this:

There is a second reason why this award is so dear to me. It was my great privilege to know Arthur Martin and to count myself a friend. We first met in the late fifties. We were both in practice at the time. We went to the same conventions, we had common interests and friends, and from time to time when I had a particularly tough problem I'd pick up the phone to discuss it with Arthur. I never failed to marvel on these occasions on the depth of his knowledge and the breadth of his interest. It seemed that Arthur not only knew every case ever reported, but also where to find it.

Arthur and I were appointed to the bench on the same day, he in Ontario and I in Quebec. A few weeks after we assumed office, Otto Lang, the minister of justice, appeared before the Justice and Legal Affairs Committee of the House of Commons. Claude Wagner, a former Quebec attorney general and judge and, at the time, a member of parliament, asked Lang what the criteria were for the nomination of judges, and he referred in particular to the "excellent appointments" of Martin and myself. "Does the government," he wanted to know, "consider, for instance, before the appointment of certain judges, what their law practice has been?" Lang said yes, the candidate's "special training" would be considered, and he added that frequently there would also be an "examination of the strength of the court at any given time as to whether it lacks criminal law expertise, relatively speaking and so on." Evidently, Arthur and I filled the bill.[165]

I kept in touch with Arthur over the years, but after he retired he became reluctant to leave home and I saw him much less frequently. I invited him for lunch one day, but he declined. However, my wife said, "Leave it to me," and she called Arthur and said "Fred and I will be in Toronto next Tuesday and we hope you will join us for lunch at the Intercontinental Hotel." Arthur, who was very fond of Donna, said at once, "I'll be there," and so he was and so were our children, who were both in law school at the time. And what a wonderful three-hour lunch it was, with Arthur regaling us with stories from his years in practice.

◆◆◆

My father, whose formal education stopped at high school but whose love for knowledge never ceased, had a great passion for geography and he instilled in me not only a good understanding of the globe but also a keen interest in people in far-distant lands. For instance, when Italy invaded Abyssinia in 1935, my father produced a map of that part of the world, spread it out on the dining-room table, and each day noted with a great deal of regret the progress of the Italian army. Our sympathies were totally with the victims, who fought a brave but ultimately futile battle, led by their emperor, Haile Selassie, also known as the Lion of Judah.

In the late 1920s, when I was four or five, my father often took me to an establishment on the Ringstrasse that showed stereoscopic pictures of different parts of the world. Mounted on a wall were binocular-like instruments, and for a small fee you could see a series of pictures depicting life in far-off countries. I watched for hours, moving from machine to machine, until it was time to go home. That was my first exposure to Africa, and while the ferocious animals (and sometimes even people!) were very scary, exaggerated, no doubt, by a child's imagination, I hoped that some day I could see them in the flesh.

That day came more than sixty years later when I got a call from a former classmate in business school. Would I be interested in an assignment in Tanzania? I said yes without a moment's hesitation, and in my haste I didn't even ask for details. This was my chance to see the pictures and impressions of my childhood brought to life.

As soon as I put down the phone I looked at my atlas. I knew of the old Tanganyka in British East Africa, and I knew something, though not very much, of the island of Zanzibar in the Indian Ocean, just off the coast of Dar es Salaam. What I didn't know was that the two had combined in 1964 to form the United Republic of Tanzania.

As in so many other countries that had recently won independence, all was not well in Tanzania. The country was poor, industry was not well developed, and the economy was in terrible shape. Determined to improve the situation, the government turned to the World Bank for help. The answer was encouraging, but the Bank said that before financial and technical support could be given, the country's infrastructure would have to be improved. High on the list was the legal system—the courts, the bar, and all that went with it.

The Bank asked nine "donor countries"—countries that, in the past, had helped emerging nations—to assist in the task, and each country was requested to supply one or more experts in specific fields. Canada was given the assignment to study the legal profession and make recommendations on how it might be improved.

In Canada, foreign assistance of this nature is channelled through the Canadian International Development Agency (CIDA), and in due course CIDA prepared terms of reference for the study. The next step was to find a consultant. Regulations required that the position be advertised, but on a second front, CIDA's East Africa desk made private inquiries in an attempt to identify persons who might be qualified but who were not likely to read the publications in which the advertisements appeared. Among the people consulted was an economist who had done work in Africa. "I might be able to help," he said. "My wife went to business school with a retired judge and he might be just the person you need.'" And so the call from my classmate. Talk about networking!

A number of weeks passed and finally I was told that the job was mine and that I should get ready to fly to Dar es Salaam. A contract, I was told, would reach me shortly. Another number of weeks passed and nothing happened, save for some urgent phone calls from the Canadian High Commission in Dar es Salaam, which wanted to know my date of arrival. I told them that I would go as soon as my contract was signed since people experienced in the field had advised me not to incur any expenses until I was officially engaged. Apparently, this type of assignment sometimes did not materialize despite initial assurances.

The delay, I later learned, was brought about by the rules of engagement. Four persons had applied as a result of the advertisements, and their names and qualifications were duly submitted to the government of Tanzania. The problem was that my name had already been informally floated by the attorney general of Tanzania, who liked my qualifications. The other applicants, I was told, whose résumés now sat on his desk, were young and inexperienced and had no particular expertise in the functioning or structure of the legal profession. The attorney general (who had never been told of the requirement to advertise and then submit to him the names of applicants) expressed his displeasure in no uncertain terms to the officials at the High Commission: he had given his blessing to the appointment of a retired judge with almost forty years' experience, and now the government of Canada wanted to send him a graduate student. He was not pleased, and neither was the *chargé d'affairs* at the high commission—there was no high commissioner at the time—who had to field increasingly angry telephone calls.

One day, with no news in sight from Ottawa, I got a call from a person who identified herself to my receptionist as Verona Edelstein. I didn't recognize the name, but she quickly told me that she had recently been appointed Canada's high commissioner to Tanzania and that she was anxious for me to begin my work. The consultants from eight or nine other countries had already begun their studies, and one or two had even completed their findings. I told the high commissioner that I had been strongly advised to make no move until I had a contract and she proposed what I considered a simple and sensible solution: I should fly to Dar es Salaam and she would sign the contract herself. On the strength of that promise, I bought a return ticket and a few days later I flew to Tanzania via Frankfurt.

Before leaving Canada, I had been in touch with the Department of Foreign Affairs in an attempt to obtain a green passport. This is not quite a diplomatic passport, but it is better than the usual blue passport; it indicates that the holder travels on government business and it facilitates travel. The request was refused: while it had been the custom to give such passports to persons travelling on this type of assignment, the privilege had been abused and the practice was stopped. In the course of my conversation with the bureaucrat in Ottawa, I asked about visa requirements for Tanzania. He assured me that a valid Canadian passport was all that I needed, so off I went. But when I arrived at Dar es Salaam late at night,

Immigration wouldn't let me into the country without a visa. I argued with the officer, who was polite but firm, and all the time the aircraft on which I had arrived was kept from returning to Frankfurt in case I was refused permission to enter.[166]

After half an hour or so, a senior immigration official arrived, but he, too, said that rules are rules: no visa, no entry. In a final desperate move—I was dirty, tired, hungry, and, by then, in a pretty bad mood—I asked the officer if he would please call the attorney general in the morning and tell him I had been turned away. (Was I trying to impress him with whom I knew, or was it a not-so-subtle threat? In retrospect, I think it was both.) He thought about this for a moment and then his face brightened and he told me he had an idea: if I was prepared to pay $50— U.S. funds, of course—he would issue a temporary landing permit, good for the length of my stay. I agreed, and to be perfectly frank I thought this was his private enterprise, intended to augment his meagre salary. To my surprise, he gave me a receipt and the next day I discovered that that was the official tariff for this kind of permit, issued at the discretion of a senior officer. *Honi soit qui mai y pense!* By the time I reached the airport exit and found a weary High Commission driver still waiting for me, I heard the roar of the departing aircraft overhead.

I met the new high commissioner the following day, and true to her word, she presented me with a very official-looking document signed by herself on behalf of Her Majesty in right of Canada and countersigned by the number two person at the commission. Many months later, when I sent my account to CIDA, the financial officer told me that a high commissioner cannot engage Her Majesty's government in this manner. To my relief, he added that the agency would honour the document anyway.

After a short night's sleep in the government-owned Hotel Kilimanjaro (which had seen better days) in downtown Dar es Salaam I walked the few blocks to the High Commission, where everyone was greatly relieved to see me. The staff gave me a lovely office with a view of the garden where peacocks marched up and down, displaying their magnificent tails. But peacock watching had to be deferred and my first order of business was to find a local assistant. With help from the CIDA officer stationed in Dar es Salaam, I was able to engage a leading local advocate, Hamida H. Sheikh, a graduate of the Faculty of Law at the University of Dar es Salaam, with a Master's degree from the London School of Economics and post-graduate studies in Geneva. Hamida knew everyone in Dar es Salaam, both in and out of government, and her guidance and advice were of great value. We argued hard, and often disagreed, but we respected each other and worked well together.

To be the last of the consultants to arrive had an advantage: I was able to avoid some of the pitfalls into which others had fallen, and I realized that my first order of business had to be to get a good grounding in Tanzania's recent history, both legal and political. What I learned quickly was that as a Canadian I carried no historical baggage. I was not a former colonial master and I would get a better hearing by that fact alone. Time and again, people I interviewed pointed to a report prepared a few months earlier by a high-powered team from England, led by a distinguished Queen's Counsel, which suggested a number of reforms to the structure of the judiciary. The recommendations were excellent, but the report was doomed from the start by an unfortunate statement in the introduction that, in effect, suggested that if the United Republic had left the English system intact, the country would not now face the problems it did. It was a needless and gratuitous insult, even if not entirely untrue.

The problems in Tanzania were neatly summarized in my terms of reference, and they pointed, in particular, to weaknesses in the legal sector, including the judiciary, various arms of government, private practitioners, and even the law school.[167]

My first item of business was a crash course on the existing structures, and Hamida was my teacher. I learned about the union of Tanganyika and Zanzibar, where executive power is exercised by two governments, the Government of the United Republic and the Revolutionary Government of Zanzibar. I also learned about the constitution of the courts, their jurisdiction, and their judges. Some of it sounded familiar to Canadian ears. For instance, of the eight judges of the Court of Appeal—the highest court in the land—two had to come from Zanzibar, which has its own legal tradition. (In Canada, three of the nine judges of the Supreme Court must come from Quebec.) Yet, as in Canada, all judges of the court will hear cases regardless of their origin. I also learned about the *kadi* courts, which decide family matters in Zanzibar, based on Islamic law.

With Hamida's help, I set up a series of meetings with judges, government officials, and members of the Bar. All were forthcoming and anxious to help, and out of these discussions came certain ideas that formed the basis of the sixteen recommendations contained in my final report. The principal problem was a great shortage of qualified lawyers—two hundred active advocates to serve a population of 28 million, a ratio of one lawyer per 140,000 people. (Canada, with a population only slightly larger, has about 75,000 practising lawyers.) This was made even worse by the fact that the greatest concentration of lawyers was in Dar es Salaam, with only a handful of practitioners in centres like Arusha.[168] Yet, despite this acknowledged shortage of advocates, it took longer to qualify for private practice in Tanzania than in almost any other country—close to nine years from the commencement of the study of law.

The Faculty of Law at Dar es Salaam turns out between fifty-five and sixty graduates a year, but most do not follow the path to private practice: many join the public service, others are enticed by business, and even those who wish to pursue a legal career may prefer to work as state attorneys or members of the Tanzania Legal Corporation (TLC), a government-owned law firm that advises public corporations but may also accept mandates from private parties. Both state attorneys and TLC members are lawyers in every sense of the word. They have law degrees and they have completed a nine to twelve-month legal internship. But they cannot switch to private practice unless they fulfil certain requirements, chief among them a five-year articling period. And even then their admission to practice is not guaranteed, because the ultimate power of admission is reserved to the chief justice who, by law, must be satisfied "of the qualification and suitability of the applicant."

It struck me, first of all, that five years is much too long an internship after law school and, second, that so serious a power should not be exercised by one person. I told the people I talked to that I would put the matter to the chief justice. Some were aghast at this proposition: it would be an insult to the chief justice to suggest that the power of admission should be shared. Nevertheless, though with some trepidation, I put my thoughts to Chief Justice Francis Nyalali. He listened intently, and even before I had finished, he told me that he had always thought that such an awesome power should not be exercised by one person; a committee, perhaps, but not the chief justice alone.

And why a five-year wait? The answer to this is more complex, but the general consensus was that it would take that long to find out about a person's "character." In other words, put bluntly, "we don't want the wrong kind of people in practice." It should not be a matter of surprise that I proposed the abolition of this rule.

While most of my research was done in Dar es Salaam, I decided to pay a courtesy call on the chief justice of Zanzibar. With Hamida's help, I managed to get an appointment on short notice, but there was a slight hitch: Zanzibar, even though part of the United Republic, has its own health requirements, and one of them was that before a person boarded the ferry for the two-hour trip, Zanzibar officials demanded to see a vaccination certificate for cholera. When I took all my "shots" at the Tropical Disease Centre at the Montreal General Hospital, I was told that they no longer vaccinated for cholera for two reasons: first, careful eating and drinking in a foreign country was just as effective, and, second, the reaction to the vaccination could be severe and not worth the risk.

Luckily, someone had told me of this requirement. My informant—a well-placed civil servant—wasn't at all surprised that I hadn't been vaccinated. But not to worry: "Give me your vaccination book," he said, "and you'll have an appropriate entry by morning." I knew better than to ask questions, and the next day, true to his promise, he returned my yellow book with a brand-new stamp attesting that I had been given the vaccine that day. It gave the manufacturer's name, the dosage, and even the lot number. With that in hand, I had no trouble boarding the ferry for which, as a non-resident, I paid about five times as much as Hamida.

The chief justice was gracious and frank. After we exchanged a few pleasantries, he motioned to his assistant, who produced a tray with soft drinks. Hamida later told me that this was a sign of acceptance: the real talk could now begin. The chief's position carried a two-year term, with reappointment possible. While this is not compatible with the notion of true independence, it at least guaranteed tenure for the term. Some of the problems faced by the Zanzibar judiciary were daunting. In 1995 only two lawyers were resident on the island. Others had to come from the mainland, but the laws of the old Tanganyika were different from the laws of Zanzibar, and few Tanzanian lawyers could practise on the island. This point is graphically brought home by the fact that the Tanzanian Bar association's official title still is the "Law Society of Tanganyika."

As a result of my research, I was able to make sixteen recommendations, among them a sharp reduction in the period of internship and official recognition for paralegals with the right of audience in lower courts. Other recommendations included compulsory malpractice insurance, the re-establishment of a system of law reporting (which had been abandoned because of lack of funds), and a revision of the official tariff, to make awards of costs more realistic. For instance, at the time I was there, an application for custody in a matrimonial suit entitled the lawyer for the winning party to collect the equivalent of $9.00 from the other side.

I decided to reward myself for ten days of hard work by a one-day trip to the hinterland of Dar es Salaam. I hired a car and driver, who assured me that his vehicle was air-conditioned. He picked me up at 6:00 a.m., and once the sun rose the car became unbearably hot. I asked him to turn on the air-conditioning, but he apologized and said that, while the car did have air-conditioning, as promised, it was out of commission. We drove westward for several hours towards a wildlife preserve. The road was fair, but the scenery was exquisite and the driver, who was quite fluent in English, turned out to be a good guide. There was little traffic either way and I was puzzled when he suddenly slowed to a crawl. Before I could ask, he pointed at the highway ahead, and in the distance I saw a family of elephants crossing the road—father, mother, and two babies, one of them quite small. They slowly lumbered over the pavement, in single file, the tallest first, the smallest last, trunk to tail. It was an awesome sight, my first view of elephants outside a zoo. We inched toward them, and by the time we got there the youngest had reached the other side of the road. I have a wonderful souvenir of the occasion—a lovely picture of a baby elephant's behind!

At the end of a long and very hot day, the driver dropped me off at the airport for a midnight flight to Frankfurt and then on to Montreal, where my wife and daughter waited for me. First the safari, then a sixteen-hour flight and no bath or shower or even change of clothes had taken their toll, but Donna and Leslie were so delighted to see me that they pretended not to notice. The first thing I did on arrival was to jump in the shower and savour the hot water for a very long time.

I returned to Tanzania in March 1995 to present my report at a public meeting to which all members of the Law Society of Tanganyika and the Bar of Zanzibar were invited. There was some discussion, but the report of the Financial and Legal Management Upgrading Project (FILMUP)—as my undertaking was known—was well received and a number of the proposals were eventually adopted. More judges were appointed, their salaries are greatly improved, and so are the working conditions. The backlog of cases has been reduced. Regrettably, other problems remain.

◆◆◆

By the mid-1990s, both our children had left for Toronto. David had finished his undergraduate degree at McGill, applied to law school at the University of Toronto, was accepted, and made the move. Leslie had decided to follow up her degree in criminology by studying law. She was accepted at McGill and graduated with degrees in civil law and common law, but left for Toronto a few days after graduation to do her articles at Crown Law Criminal in the attorney general's office.

In 1994 Donna's mother became seriously ill and it was not unusual for Donna to fly to Toronto once or twice a week. This made us realize that, if one of us became ill, we would not want our children to have to make frequent trips to Montreal. Both were at the start of their careers, and we would not have wanted to impose this burden on them. We knew that they would want to be with us if we were ill and we would certainly take comfort from their presence. Of course, illness aside, it would be wonderful to be close.

The children, too, encouraged us to move to Toronto, and they sprang into action to bring this about. I got a call one day from a real estate agent in Toronto. I was a little surprised when he said, "I understand you're are looking for a nice place to live," because at that point we hadn't discussed the idea outside the family. So I asked him how he had heard, and he said, "Well, your children engaged me." What better proof that we were wanted could we get!

We put our heads together and found that I could probably do in Toronto what I was doing in Montreal—mediations, arbitrations, consultations—and Donna could transfer to the Toronto office of her law firm. But we also loved Montreal and the Eastern Townships, where we had a weekend retreat in Knowlton on the shores of Brome Lake. The sensible solution, therefore, seemed to be a move to Toronto, with a *pied-à-terre* in Montreal. And so we started to look for a place to live. In 1996 this wasn't easy, since there was a shortage of condominiums and apartments in Toronto. But we did find exactly what we wanted—a lovely condo with a terrific view of the skyscrapers downtown—and we took possession in May. At the same time we managed to sell our condo in Montreal, which took some doing given the political situation in Quebec. And in the end we gave up the idea of keeping an apartment in Montreal. After all, there are good hotels.

I would be less than truthful if I were to say that the proximity to family was the sole reason for the move. It was, without doubt, the most important reason, but it was hard to forget the remarks of Jacques Parizeau on the night of the 1995 referendum: the *Parti Québecois* lost because of "money and the ethnic vote." True, Parizeau was gone as premier within days, but the foul taste of these comments lingered, and it made it a great deal easier for us to leave after so many very happy years in the province.

In order to practise law in Ontario, Donna had taken the necessary steps to become a member of the Law Society of Upper Canada. This was not easy. Her degree from McGill was in civil law and Ontario is a common law jurisdiction. But many of the subjects she had been taught had equal application throughout Canada. She had also written—and published—not only a book,[169] but also many articles dealing with common law topics, and after some negotiation she was "deemed" to have a common law degree, which allowed her to take the necessary Bar admission course. As it happened, our daughter, having successfully completed her articles, ended up in the same class as Donna, so mother and daughter went off to school together. It was a tough year, but both succeeded and were certified fit to practise in Ontario.

By 1997, when Donna qualified as an Ontario lawyer, she was a director of a number of important public corporations, and for some time it had been very onerous for her to carry out both functions at the same time. Her legal practice—she was an experienced and much sought-after anti-trust lawyer—was as busy as a practice can be, and so were her duties as a company director. Something had to give, and while she loved her work as a lawyer, she found new and interesting challenges in the corporate world and she resigned her partnership at Stikeman Elliott.

It was a good move and more directorships quickly followed. Corporate governance had become a major concern and she soon became an expert in the field. In 2002, TransAlta Corporation, where she chaired the Corporate Governance Committee, tied for first place in governance in *The Globe and Mail* rating, a feat that was repeated a year later. She is now the chair of the board, until recently a unique position for a woman in a publicly held, non-family corporation.

Other distinctions also came her way. Concordia University recognized her "outstanding contribution to the world of business and the community" by bestowing on her its "Award of Distinction," and the Institute of Corporate Directors gave her its "Fellowship Award" for "commitment to the highest standards of director professionalism." In the spring of 2004 the *National Post* included her in the annual listing of Canada's "Power 50 Women,"[170] and in her introduction to the feature, Deirdre McMurdy wrote:

One newcomer, Donna Soble Kaufman, exemplifies the heightened emphasis on balance. She is one of the most powerful women in corporate Canada.

Ms. Kaufman's achievements in the corporate arena tell only a small part of her story: At the centre of her life is a strong commitment to her family. After early success as a broadcaster, she stayed at home to raise her children and support her husband. She did not go to law school until her children were well established in school, and her career choices have always been predicated on putting family first.

I always knew she was good, and I am immensely proud of her, so it's nice to have others say so, too!

Our lives truly changed with the move to Toronto. At an age and stage when many are winding down, we established a new home in a new city, Donna changed professions, and I did things that I had never done before. We were made wonderfully welcome by new friends and Donna's family, and we could see our children regularly. We were thrilled and grateful that we had made such a seamless transition.

We also got a dog, Rosie. She's a bichon-shitzu cross, with the sweetest, most seductive eyes and a temperament to match. We found her at the Pooch Palace in Calgary. The only pet I ever had was a canary, and when it died I didn't want another. So I resisted the idea of a dog. But Donna thought that it would be good to have a pet, and with a public park—and lots of dogs—across the street from our condo, I agreed. Still, I wasn't at all certain how I would take to a dog, and Rosie, sensing my reservations, didn't know at first what to make of me. However, the mutual uncertainty didn't last long and now we are the best of friends.

◆ ◆ ◆

In early 2004, I was invited by Paul Martin, the prime minister of Canada, to accept an appointment as the first independent ethics commissioner of Canada. Previous office holders (then called ethics counsellors) had not been truly independent and Martin, who had been elected a few months earlier, had promised to remedy this situation. The result was new legislation,[171] which provided for the appointment of an Ethics Commissioner "to perform the duties and functions assigned by the House of Commons regarding the conduct of its members and to administer any ethical principles, rules of obligations established by the Prime Minister for public office holders."[172]

I was in Arizona when I received the call and I flew to Ottawa the next day where I had a lengthy meeting with Francis Fox, the prime minister's principal private secretary and Alex Himmelfarb, the clerk of the privy council, Canada's most senior civil servant. They explained to me what the position might entail, and we quickly came to the conclusion that it would require a move to Ottawa.

While the prospect of yet another challenge was tempting, I decided that Donna and I were now happily settled in Toronto, surrounded by family, and that I should not, therefore, consider the offer. It was the right choice, but I felt deeply honoured by the prime minister's confidence in me to assume this new and important office.

[25]
Guy Paul Morin

About a year before we moved to Toronto, my good friend Alan B. Gold, the former chief justice of the Quebec Superior Court, gave my name to the attorney general of Ontario as someone who should be considered for appointment to a royal commission that the province planned to set up. The task of the commission would be to inquire into how and why an innocent person, Guy Paul Morin, came to be convicted on a charge of first-degree murder. Alan thought that my lifelong professional involvement with criminal law well qualified me for the position. A few weeks later, I was asked if I was interested, and I said yes without hesitation.

As Alan had suggested, my practice, as well as my years on the Court of Appeal, gave me the necessary background to conduct such an inquiry. But quite beyond that, I could not help but reflect on my own past. When I was interned in England in 1940, *I* knew that I was not a spy, but how can you convey this truth to others? Morin had maintained his innocence throughout his ordeal, but he couldn't convince the police, he couldn't convince a jury, he couldn't convince the Court of Appeal, and he couldn't convince eight judges of the Supreme Court of Canada. And it wasn't even up to him to do the convincing, because it was the crown's burden to prove him guilty beyond a reasonable doubt. *He* knew that he wasn't guilty, but how to persuade someone else? It was an irresistible proposition and I hoped it would come to pass.

Months went by without any news, and I began to think that the government had abandoned the idea. But within weeks of my arrival in Toronto, I got a second call. This time, it was a firm offer, not, as suggested before, to be a member of the commission but rather to be the sole commissioner. Again, without hesitation, I said yes.

Guy Paul Morin's nightmare began in October 1984, when Christine Jessop, a nine-year-old girl who loved life, her family, school, and sports, was abducted, raped, and killed. Morin, her next-door neighbour, was charged with her murder. He was acquitted in 1986, but a new trial was ordered by the Court of Appeal for Ontario, and on his second trial he was found guilty of first-degree murder and sentenced to imprisonment for life. Throughout, he maintained his innocence, but short shrift was made of his protestations. However, in January 1995, almost ten years after his arrest, sophisticated DNA tests not previously available proved his innocence, and a formal order of acquittal was entered by the Court of Appeal.

"This course of events," as the provincial cabinet later said with some degree of understatement, "has raised certain questions about the administration of justice in Ontario," and a royal commission was set up to "inquire into the conduct of the investigation into the death of Christine Jessop, the conduct of the Centre for Forensic Sciences in relation to the maintenance, security and preservation of forensic evidence, and into the criminal proceedings involving the charge that Guy Paul Morin murdered Christine Jessop." The order-in-council—royal commissions are formal documents with lots of ribbons and gold seals—was passed by cabinet and signed by the lieutenant-governor on June 26, 1996. It appointed me to conduct the inquiry, and it directed me to make such recommendations as I saw fit concerning the administration of criminal justice in Ontario.

That Guy Paul Morin was truly innocent was not contested by the crown. Indeed, as soon as his acquittal was announced by the court, the crown attorney in charge of the case apologized in open court to Mr. Morin and went to where he sat to shake his hand. Minutes later, the deputy attorney general, speaking on behalf of Attorney General Marion Boyd, who was out of town, said this:

> The [attorney general] is deeply committed to maintaining the public's faith in the system, and to ensuring that the ministry takes whatever steps are necessary that such a situation does not reoccur. To accomplish this, Ms. Boyd [the attorney general] has decided a public airing into the justice system's handling of Mr. Morin's case is required.

These sentiments were echoed when Ms. Boyd's successor, Charles Harnick (a new government had been elected between the acquittal and the creation of the commission), made the following comment: "An inquiry cannot wipe away the years of pain and turmoil Mr. Morin suffered, but it can examine the complex circumstances surrounding the case, and allow us to learn from it and prevent any future miscarriage of justice."

Clearly, this was to be a thorough inquiry, and I eagerly looked forward to beginning my new duties. Within days I had an office and a skeleton staff. My next task was to find the most competent counsel available, and after some convincing, my friend Austin Cooper—known as the dean of the Ontario criminal bar—whom I had known since my early days in practice, accepted the assignment. His partner, Mark Sandler, another outstanding criminal lawyer, became associate counsel, and so did Mary Anne Sanderson, a highly regarded civil practitioner and now a judge of the Superior Court of Justice. It was a "dream team" and their excellent work (and that of Maureen Currie, who replaced Mary Anne when she went to the bench) contributed enormously to the success of the commission.[173]

It was a big undertaking. By the time the inquiry ended twenty-two months later, I had sat for 146 days, heard from 120 witnesses, and read, in whole or in part, more than 100,000 pages of transcripts, submissions, and reports. Twenty-five interested parties were given "standing," which meant that they could intervene in the proceedings, examine witnesses, and make final representations during the concluding arguments. It also meant that I had to orchestrate the work of at least twenty-five lawyers in addition to the three counsel that I had retained at the beginning. That, by itself, was not always easy.

What made this assignment so special was that I would have the rare opportunity to analyze a case from beginning to end, examine the proceedings, and establish the causes—there were many—of this clearly established miscarriage of justice. Moreover, I could suggest how similar errors might be prevented in future.

◆ ◆ ◆

Guy Paul Morin was twenty-five years old at the time of his arrest. He had no criminal record. He lived with his parents in Queensville, a small community fifty kilometres north of Toronto. He had a grade 12 education and had attended various courses in auto upholstery, spray painting, gas fitting, air-conditioning, and refrigeration. He worked as a finishing sander with a furniture company in Toronto.

The Jessops and the Morins were neighbours. On the afternoon of October 3, 1984, the school bus returned Christine to her home at about 3:50 in the afternoon. No one was there. Her mother, Janet, had taken Christine's older brother, Ken, to the dentist in nearby Newmarket. The precise time of their return was a major issue at trial. Morin punched out from work that day at 3:32 p.m., and police trial runs established that he could not have arrived at home before 4:14 p.m.

The Jessops' time of return therefore had an important impact on the "window of opportunity" for Morin to commit the crime. The defence submitted that he returned to Queensville well after the Jessops, but the prosecution disputed this and pointed to various statements made by him to the police that left the timing more flexible.

Christine was not in the house when the Jessops returned, but there was no immediate cause for alarm. When she failed to show up by early evening, however, her mother notified the police. A search of the area was organized and it continued for several days. No trace of Christine was found. As time passed, concerns heightened that she had been abducted and the investigation swung into high gear.

Christine's body was found on December 31 near the town of Sunderland in Durham Region, about fifty-six kilometres east of Queensville. An autopsy established that she had died from stab wounds to her chest. The presence of semen on her underpants indicated she had been sexually assaulted. Because the body was found in Durham Region, the Durham Regional Police took charge of the case.

The date of discovery of the remains is important. It was New Year's Eve. A severe snowstorm was expected. Time for a detailed ground search was limited. Sergeant Michael Michalowsky, Durham's chief identification officer, arrived at the site at 2:10 p.m. He organized a group of officers to collect and preserve whatever evidence they might find at the scene. Inspector Robert Brown, the officer in charge of Durham's Crimes Against Persons Squad, took charge. Detective Bernie Fitzpatrick, who was present, suggested that tarpaulins be obtained to cover the ground before the expected snowfall. It was a sound suggestion but it went unheeded. "Where," it was asked, "could one find on New Year's Eve enough material to do this?" The question was rhetorical and no one tried. Night at that time of year falls early, and the ground search was abandoned when it became too dark to see.

Still, in the time they had, the searchers found evidence that indicated that the perpetrator might well have been a smoker: a cigarette butt and a lighter. There might even have been a cigarette package, but the police thought that it might have been discarded by one of the officers. If the killer was a smoker, it was not Morin. At trial, however, the prosecution took the position that these items were irrelevant because even the cigarette butt and the lighter might have been dropped by careless officers. I concluded that while the items that were found may have had absolutely nothing to do with the identity of the killer, they told us a lot about the quality of the investigation. But it got worse: the crown was forced to concede that the butt that was put in evidence at the first trial was not the butt found at the scene; it was lost, so another butt was substituted. And this in a first-degree murder investigation!

♦ ♦ ♦

On February 14, 1985, six weeks after Christine's body was found, Inspector John Shephard and Detective Fitzpatrick met with Janet and Ken Jessop, who mentioned that their neighbour, Guy Paul Morin, was a "weird-type guy." This directed some suspicion toward Morin, and in notes prepared a few days later, Inspector Shephard referred to the "suspect Morin." When questioned at the inquiry, he denied that Morin was a suspect at the time and referred to his entry as "police jargon." Yet it was clear to me that both Shephard and Fitzpatrick regarded Morin as a suspect even before their first interview with him, which took place on February 22. This had a bearing on the attitude with which the two officers approached Morin that day, and it had a major impact on the inferences they drew from some of his remarks.

The interview with Morin on February 22 was tape-recorded, but the ninety-minute tape ran out after forty-five minutes because the officers didn't know that the cassette had to be turned over. So we don't know precisely what was said during the second forty-five minutes. We do know, however, that Morin said certain things that the officers found unusual. For instance, at one point, after a pause in the discussion concerning his work, he said, "Otherwise I'm innocent." An odd remark, to be sure, but much less sinister when taken in context. This was the sequence of the interview:

> *Morin:* [speaking about his place of work]: Beautiful veneer work like I've never seen ... amazing for woodworking ... like it's real super custom ... there's a long table like 12 feet long, easy. Joined together in the middle, certain beautiful anchor clips. They're far out in things today.
> *Fitzpatrick:* Ya.
> *Morin:* [A lengthy pause] Otherwise I'm innocent. But it's pretty bad how they treated the Regional. You know what they did around here. They said we're all guilty until proven otherwise.
> *Fitzpatrick:* Who said that?
> *Morin:* Well it's not exactly what they said. But we're all suspects.
> *Fitzpatrick:* Who's that, the Regional?
> *Morin:* Ya.

Fitzpatrick: That's York?

Morin: That's York Regional, yeah. Isn't that bad, eh? How they portray us all as being guilty. I mean I don't mind if I'm in Quebec, eh. But around in here. And they say "Hey we're going to be doing a door-to-door search" and you know they only did us.

This remark, coming "out of the blue," as the officers said, aroused suspicion, and it was tendered to the jury as evidence of "consciousness of guilt." But put in context, as explained by Morin, this comment is not at all sinister. He had heard on television one evening that the York Regional Police had said that everyone within the community or the surrounding area of Queensville was considered a suspect until proven otherwise. This was confirmed by a high-ranking officer. Morin said that the reason he uttered this phrase was to breach the silence, as indicated by the pause in the transcript. The lead prosecutor accepted that this was an innocent remark made in the context of York Regional's approach to the case. Yet one can well imagine that the impact of these words on the jury likely was great.

Later, during a conversation about Christine, Morin said, "All little girls are sweet and beautiful—grow up to be corrupt." Again, an odd remark, and much was made of it at trial. The judge's instruction to the jury bears this out:

> It is for you to consider that although these words, "All little girls are sweet and beautiful but grow up to be corrupt" are general, since the subject matter of this interview is the disappearance and death of Christine Jessop, did those ... words relate to Christine Jessop? If so, is that connection to Christine Jessop then transported from generalized hostility against little girls into a specific hostility against Christine Jessop? Do those words demonstrate in the accused's mind a motive in the form of hostility towards Christine Jessop as a little girl? If so, you may consider whether this utterance bears on the issue of the identity of the killer.

Unfortunately, this comment—that sweet, little girls grow up to be corrupt— was made by Morin after the tape had run out, so we don't know the precise sequence of events. But, as Morin recalled it, he said it "in relation to when [the officers] spoke to me about Christine, whether or not she was in trouble of any sort that I was aware of." And he added: "Well, I was telling them, like, she was only an innocent child. She was young and there was no way, um, and I was telling them that she was sweet and innocent and you know, it's true that some people or children eventually do become corrupt, you know, in a later portion of their life, but not at that early stage." Once again, an unfortunate utterance, but hardly an admission of guilt.

Morin also made a reference in the interview that the body was found across the Ravenshoe Road. Shephard and Fitzpatrick, working in another region, were unfamiliar with this road (which, however, is well known to local residents), and they considered this degree of precision suspicious. In addition, in the course of the interview, Morin told the investigators that he had left work on the day of Christine's disappearance at 3:30 p.m. and got home about an hour later, having stopped for groceries on the way. But later, in the unrecorded portion, he extended his time of arrival from 4:30 p.m. to between 4:30 and 5. The officers felt that Morin was now waffling, and they considered this significant.

In the face of Morin's proven innocence, his comments were innocuous, and some, like the mention of Ravenshoe Road, were insignificant. Indeed, during the entire interview with the detectives, nothing was said by Morin that even remotely constituted an admission of guilt or a demonstration of knowledge exclusive to the killer. I found that Shephard and Fitzpatrick, now the "lead" investigators because they had, in the minds of the police, a serious suspect, had fixed their sights on Morin much too early—a classic case of tunnel vision.[174] The result of this was that subsequent interviews were unduly coloured by their premature views, and this affected the quality of their work.

With Morin insisting that he did not arrive at home until 4:30 p.m. at the earliest, the time of arrival of Janet and Ken Jessop became crucial. On March 6 Shephard and Fitzpatrick interviewed both. This interview lasted two and a half hours. No formal statement was taken, nor did the officers preserve detailed notes. When first questioned by the York Regional Police about the time of their arrival at home, both Janet and Ken had said it was 4:10 p.m. They were now told by the Durham officers that they were mistaken: it must have been later. This was based in part on statements obtained from the dentist whom Ken Jessop had visited earlier that afternoon and from the dentist's receptionist.

How did the Jessops fix the time? Christine's mother said that she had looked at the kitchen clock and it said 4:10. Ken had looked at his watch, which his mother had bought him that day. The officers suggested that the clock might have been wrong, and eventually Janet and Ken agreed that this must have been so, and that they had in fact arrived later than they had originally stated. The faulty clock, Janet testified at Morin's trial, was later thrown out. This was false, and she admitted this at the inquiry.

My reconstruction of the events was that the officers believed that the timing first given by the Jessops was wrong. They suggested that the clock was at fault to give Janet an easy way out. Both Janet and Ken realized that the point was crucial, and since both were convinced that Morin was guilty, they were not prepared to say anything at the second trial that might adversely affect the prosecution's case. Inspector Shephard denied that he and his partner had pressured the Jessops, but he told the inquiry that, with hindsight, he could appreciate the Jessops' perception that they had in fact been pressured.

The prosecutors believed the core evidence—that Janet and Ken had returned home at 4:30 p.m.—and pressed their case accordingly. However, they knew by the time of the second trial that the clock had not been thrown out—it could be seen on the wall of the kitchen in a TV documentary taped many months later—and while this was put in evidence, the crown failed to advise the jury that it no longer relied on this point. Nor did the defence stress this fact, and the jury may well have been left with the impression that the clock was unreliable and that the Jessops' revised time of arrival was correct. And, as I said before, the timing was crucial.

At the inquiry, both Janet and Ken reverted to their original story that they had arrived home at 4:10 p.m. This clearly closed Morin's window of opportunity, and there was a dramatic meeting between Ken and Guy Paul Morin in a private office I had made available for that purpose. Ken apologized to Morin for having given misleading evidence that helped convict him. A few days later, the chief of the Durham Regional Police also apologized for the actions of his force. Both apologies were graciously accepted by Morin.

◆ ◆ ◆

An important task of the investigators was to collect hair and fibre samples and to submit them to the Centre of Forensic Sciences (CFS) in Toronto for analysis. This is the principal forensic laboratory for the province, and it enjoyed at the time a worldwide reputation for excellence.

When Christine's body was examined, a single dark hair was found embedded in skin tissue adhering to her necklace. This hair was not Christine's and it was presumed to have come from her killer. Three other hairs found in Morin's car were said to be dissimilar to his, but similar to Christine's. There was much work to be done on these samples.

Expert testimony at the commission hearings revealed that the hair-comparison evidence presented at the two trials had little or no probative value in proving Morin's guilt. Generally, hair-comparison evidence, absent DNA, is unlikely to have sufficient value even to justify its reception into evidence. These limitations, well known to scientists, were not clearly communicated by Stephanie Nysnyk, the analyst in charge, to Shephard and Fitzpatrick. Worse, a hasty preliminary examination conducted by the analyst in the officers' presence resulted in an ill-conceived, overstated opinion that left the investigators with the impression that important evidence implicating Morin had been found. This misinformation was subsequently relied upon by the officers to apply for a warrant to arrest Morin, which was granted on the basis of that "evidence."[175]

The forensic scientists fared even worse with their examination of fibres collected from Christine's clothing and from Morin's residence and car. Two analysts testified that several of the fibres found at the body site *could have* come from the same source as fibres found in the car and the house. I concluded that the similarities, even if they existed, proved nothing, yet at both trials the prosecutors placed heavy emphasis on several red-wool fibres purporting to link the car to Christine's body.

Shockingly, we discovered that the fibre samples—which were pivotal evidence—had been contaminated within the CFS. We could not establish the timing and origin of the contamination. However, the fact that this had occurred was known to Nyznyk and her superior, Norman Erickson, but this information was withheld from the police, the prosecution, and the defence. Indeed, had it not been for an anonymous tip received by one of the lawyers, we might never have found out about this.

The Centre had asserted that technicians and analysts always wore lab coats while at work. What the informant conveyed, however—in the proverbial manila envelope pushed under the door—was that Erickson had at one point (it wasn't clear when) asked some of the Centre's former employees if they had ever gone to work in a red sweater. If so, it might explain the source of the contamination. I don't know what answers Erickson got, but when Morin's principal lawyer, James Lockyer, put this very question to a technician who testified at the commission, she readily admitted that she had owned such a garment at the time she worked at the Centre. Once again, the public came to the commission's assistance. Someone who had read a newspaper report that red fibres may have contaminated the evidence called to say that some years before the CBC had broadcast a documentary that contained a short sequence taped at the CFS. It showed a technician doing her work wearing a red sweater. We tracked down the program, and sure enough there was the technician dressed as described.

Lockyer, quite rightly, expressed astonishment that both Erickson and Nyznyk had managed to testify at both trials while suppressing information that contamination had occurred. "I don't know about suppressing it," Erickson replied to a pointed question, "I just didn't make it available." "Interesting linguistics," Lockyer dryly observed.

I concluded that failure to disclose the contamination may have been done to avoid embarrassment to the scientists and to the Centre. It was not done out of malice toward Guy Paul Morin, nor with any desire to convict an innocent person. Yet it remains inexcusable. I also found that the Centre showed no real interest in documenting the contamination or in investigating whether it may have affected cases other than Morin. But this was not all. Evidence that might have been of help to the defence was not disclosed, samples were lost by the Centre between the first and second trials, the limitations of some of the findings were not explained, and a study published in England on fibre transference was given to the prosecution without, however, pointing out that the details had no bearing on the Morin proceedings. In short, the contribution of the Centre to Morin's wrongful arrest, prosecution, and conviction was substantial. Police and prosecutors, and ultimately the judge and the jury, relied on findings that were flawed. It was a shabby performance by an institution purportedly dedicated to impartiality and truth.

The government contritely acknowledged the Centre's shortcomings, and Dr. James Young, the assistant deputy solicitor general (and chief coroner for Ontario) publicly apologized on behalf of the institution. More important, immediate reforms were instituted, more scientists were engaged, an advisory council was established, and most of the thirty-three recommendations I made for improvements at the CFS were adopted. It gives me great satisfaction that the Centre's public humiliation, which brought me no joy, resulted in an urgent re-examination of the Centre's operations. The CFS has once again reclaimed its former fame. As Kirk Makin wrote in *The Globe and Mail*:

> No institution suffered a greater thrashing at the hands of the 1998 Kaufman inquiry than Ontario's Centre of Forensic Sciences. Hammered for dubious training methods, its lack of scientific detachment and an apparent cover-up involving fibre contamination in the Guy Paul Morin case, CFS faced a massive rebuilding job.
>
> As staff morale lay in tatters, Ontario Chief Coroner James Young said his centre elected to revamp everything from testing and reporting procedures to a relationship with police that had been repeatedly denounced as too chummy.

And rebuild they did. Besides remaking its testing and reporting procedures, the CFS added fifty-two scientists and incorporated a formal procedure for holding case conferences. It all established the CFS as the most conscientious institution ensnared in the wrongful conviction of Mr. Morin.[176]

My findings had an even wider audience than the provincial government. Subsequent commissions of inquiry have taken note of the report,[177] and so did E. James Crocker, an author and forensic scientist, who noted that "the guidance offered by Commissioner Kaufman's recommendations should be welcomed by forensic laboratories, individual examiners, counsel at trial and the trier of fact. It is an effort to make the evidence fair while at the same time understood at a proper level of significance by the jurors."[178]

♦ ♦ ♦

As part of their investigation into the Jessop killing, the detectives asked a Federal Bureau of Investigation (FBI) officer from the United States to prepare a "profile" of the killer. Criminal profiling involves the analysis of the details of a crime and of the clues left behind, in conjunction with an understanding of similar cases, to prepare a psychological profile of the killer. However, a well-trained profiler will not undertake an examination of a case in which police already have a suspect. The concern here is that, even subconsciously, the investigators will colour the information to fit the case.

When Shephard and Fitzpatrick spoke to the FBI agent, they already suspected Morin, and I found that the information provided to the profiler may therefore have been contaminated by their preconceived views. Though certain features of the profile did parallel Guy Paul Morin, it could not reasonably be said that it matched or even closely resembled him, but this caused no introspection on the part of the investigators. As Shephard candidly said at the inquiry, "if [the profile] said a female was responsible, probably we would have looked in the other direction."

The police decided to "doctor" the profile to make it correspond to Morin more closely. Similarities were left in; "facts" that did not fit were excluded or amended to conform. This modified profile was released to the press. It was intended to "spook" Morin. The net effect, however, was that by doing so, the police helped ensure that the accused could never get a fair trial in the Durham region, and a change of venue to London was ordered—a great inconvenience to all participants in the trial.

It is significant to note that the FBI, in a document entitled *Investigative Technique*, which was supplied to Shephard and Fitzpatrick along with the profile, clearly warns that "if a profile is developed by your department, the next step would be to assess the subject, giving him the benefit of the doubt that he did not perpetrate the crime." Not only did Morin fail to get the benefit of doubt, but the investigators looked to the profile for confirmation of their own strongly held views.

◆◆◆

Morin was finally put under arrest on April 22, 1985. He was questioned for over six hours and repeatedly declared his innocence. The jury, however, never heard of these protestations. They were ruled inadmissible—self-serving evidence is customarily excluded—and so the jury at the second trial never knew that, from the very beginning, Morin had loudly proclaimed that he was falsely accused of the crime.

He was lodged in the Whitby jail, and two fellow inmates later testified that he confessed to them that he had killed Christine. Commencing June 27, Morin shared a cell with Robert Dean May in the protective custody wing of the jail. On the night of June 29–30, May had a conversation with Morin about the Jessop murder. This conversation continued the following night. That night, May testified, Morin suddenly became upset and cried out, "Oh fuck, why did I do it, oh fuck man, fuck, I killed that little girl." Remarkably, this—and nothing else—was overheard by the man in the next cell, a "Mr. X," who, at the time (he said), was in bed reading the Bible: "I overheard some discussion in the cell next to me. And I heard someone weeping, and I kind of paid a little more attention. And the voice got a little louder, and I heard 'Fuck, man, fuck, I killed her, I killed that little girl.' And it's my belief that it came from Mr. Morin."

The following morning, May and Mr. X (his name was protected by a court order made in a different case) asked to see the Morin investigators and the possibility of a deal was discussed. May acknowledged at the inquiry that he was hoping to have "some charges dropped or [receive a sentence of] time served." He had a lengthy record, mostly for crimes of dishonesty involving forged documents, bounced cheques, and thefts. On April 15, 1985, he was sentenced to serve six months in jail. A few days later, he attempted to escape, assaulting a guard with two bars of soap hidden in a sock, and he was charged with assault causing bodily harm. May then asked his lawyer to have him transferred to the Whitby Psychiatric Hospital for a thirty-day mental assessment. He later admitted that he had made this request because the hospital was a minimum-security institution from which he would be able to escape, which he eventually did. He was re-arrested five days later and sent back to Whitby jail, but in June he was transferred once again to a psychiatric facility, this time the Penetanguishene Mental Health Centre. Again, the plan was to escape, but the plot was discovered and once more he was returned to Whitby. Morin's "confession" came two days later.

Mr. X, too, had a lengthy record, but his was for sexual offences against children. On June 26, he was sentenced to sixty days in jail for sexual assault. The judge had recommended him for the Temporary Absence Program, yet the correctional authorities had denied this (as they were entitled to do). Like May, X wanted out of jail "bad." He was a nervous wreck, he feared he would lose his job, lose the house he was planning to buy, and lose his wife who was threatening to leave him. He agreed at the inquiry that this was a "huge concern" for him, and it was the very thing he was thinking about when he purported to overhear Morin's confession.

Like May, X admitted that when he first spoke to the police he tried to use his information for his "own leverage." Inspector Shephard agreed that X made it abundantly clear just how desperate he was to get out of jail. In fact, again like May, X also offered to provide testimony against other inmates.

The crown placed great reliance on the reported confession. Yet it was abundantly clear that both informants—jailhouse rats in courthouse vernacular—were by any measure totally unreliable. May had a propensity for lying, and he admitted this freely at the inquiry. Dr. Glenn Cameron, a physician with the forensic assessment unit at the Penetanguishene Mental Health Centre, diagnosed May as having an anti-social personality disorder—he was a con man, a liar, a manipulator. "It was extremely difficult," he said, "to ferret out what was the truth and what was untrue." And he added: "Mr. May was an individual who... frequently interacted with others in his environment through deception, through misrepresentation, through fraudulent means. He was someone who possessed no remorse, felt no sense of guilt or moral obligation for the things he did ...." On May's claim that he heard Morin confess, the doctor said this:

> I think there are many levels of what's going on when Mr. May talks about his confession from Mr. Morin. One of the psychological explanations would be that he was trying to present himself as someone more famous or omnipotent than he was. On a very practical level, again, I think he was trying to curry favour with the police. This certainly fits into his character as I understand it. And on a completely

other level, he's a man who when I saw him just wasn't capable of telling the truth about important things that were happening in his life in his circumstances.

This assessment was confirmed by May himself. When Austin Cooper, the commission's chief counsel, asked May at the end of his examination if there was any reason anyone should ever believe anything he said, May calmly replied: "No, sir."

Mr. X's credibility fared no better with the experts. Dr. Zehenat Khan, a psychiatrist and clinical director of adult mental health at the Oshawa General Hospital, reviewed X's psychiatric history and transcripts of his evidence at the trial. He diagnosed him as suffering from a personality disorder with predominantly dependent and sociopathic characteristics. This, he explained, is a condition that is characterized by exaggeration, lying, disregard for social norms, and dependency.

Questioned about this diagnosis at the hearing, Mr. X said he could not recall a great deal about it. He did remember, however, telling various people at various times that he was losing contact with reality, that he heard voices in his head, and that the voices were so loud that he thought his head was going to explode. He explained his history of sexual misconduct by the fact that he had heard the voice of his dead uncle telling him to perform these acts.

Did May recruit X to bolster his testimony? Both May and X denied this, but there is evidence that May had offered X a loan of $5,000. To the defence, this was a bribe. To May, it was an offer that he had no intention of keeping. It was made, he said, to stop X from whining. The point remains moot.

It is significant that at the second trial the crown tried to shore up the evidence of May and X by giving them the opportunity not to testify. Why would the crown do such a thing? The reasoning was that if May and X could tell the jury that they had turned down the crown's offer and were now giving evidence out of a pure desire to help solve a crime, the jury would give greater credence to their statements. At least I believe that that was the theory. But what if May and X had accepted the offer? In the first place, the lead crown attorney, in his opening address, had already told the jury that they would hear of a confession made by the accused to fellow inmates. If this evidence failed to materialize, the judge would have been obliged to declare a mistrial. Surely that is not something the crown would have wished. Second, again if the offer had been accepted, the crown would have been deprived of what they considered a crucial piece of evidence. Would any seasoned lawyer take that chance?

The senior crown attorney, Leo McGuigan, testified at the inquiry that he was "moved by the Christmas spirit" to make the offer. X had suffered as a result of the evidence he gave at Morin's first trial. McGuigan now wished to spare him the humiliations that had been visited upon him. And, he reasoned, if the offer was made to one, it had to be made to both.

I concluded that the offers were made "for tactical reasons with the hope or expectation that their rejection would be revealed to the jury, and in the knowledge that, if revealed, it would enhance the credibility of the informants." The facts bear out this conclusion. Detective Fitzpatrick was given the task of transmitting the offer to the two informants. He told them that the crown "might" give them the option not to testify. Both said they would decline such an offer. There is no transcript of these conversations, but Fitzpatrick was able to report back that the offers would not be accepted and some time later the crown more formally repeated the offers, which were declined. And, sure enough, the offers came out into the open when May and X testified, and this was used in crown counsel's closing address to the jury:

I'm going to review the evidence of Messrs. May and X, but first, a general observation.

We heard in evidence that both Mr. May and Mr. X appeared at this trial on their own volition. They were both given the opportunity to decline to testify, to walk away from it all, no charges, no hassles, no recriminations. Both did not accept that offer and came forward at this trial, testified and placed themselves knowingly in a position where their whole life would be examined under the microscope of cross-examination.

Finally you have the offer that was made to Mr. X and May, the opportunity they were given to decline to testify in this case. Counsel ask you to believe that Robert May couldn't resist the gratification that he would get by testifying. I ask you, did Robert May look like he was having fun when he was up in that witness box? You watched him as every intimate embarrassing detail of his background was dissected over a period of six days. Do you really believe Mr. May subjected himself for his own gratification?

It is significant to note that May did not improve his ways. In 2006, he was convicted on eight counts of confining and assaulting his girlfriend and then trying to prevent her from testifying against him. The crown moved to have him declared a dangerous offender and given an indefinite sentence. As Kirk Makin noted in *The Globe and Mail*, "two decades after his fabricated evidence nearly put Guy

Paul Morin behind bars for life ... Robert Dean May now faces the same prospect."[179] On October 3, 2007, Justice Michael Brown agreed with the crown and sentenced May to at least seven years—and very possibly the rest of his life—in prison. In passing sentence, the judge described him as a psychopath and an incorrigible liar, with little prospect of rehabilitation. By a twist of fate, the sentence came on the 17th anniversary of Christine Jessop's disappearance.[180]

McGuigan referred to May's cross-examination, which lasted six days. In fact, every cross-examination at the second trial lasted longer than one might normally expect because that was the style of Morin's lead counsel on that occasion, Jack Pinkofsky. I have no doubt that there were times when the jurors grew tired of this intensive, often repetitive questioning, but Pinkofsky was convinced of his client's innocence, and in any case that was his style. Behind his back, the crown attorneys called him "the Prince of Darkness," and his demeanour and tactics sorely tested not only their but also the trial judge's patience (who, however, remained polite and courteous to him throughout the trial). At the inquiry, it was suggested that Pinkofsky's conduct of the case was detrimental to the defence and should not be ignored as a factor contributing to Morin's conviction. I dealt with this in my report:

> Having regard to all the evidence ... I have concluded that some tactical decisions taken by the defence at Mr. Morin's second trial were not the best, and it may be argued that they adversely affected the jury. However, some of the forensic skills demonstrated at that trial were exceptional. Unlike the situation in a number of notorious cases of wrongful convictions cited by some of the systemic witnesses, I do not see this as a case of defence incompetence, neglect or misconduct. Any criticisms of Mr. Pinkofsky are idiosyncratic to his style and approach and are not reflective of systemic issues or to be addressed by any systemic recommendations I may make.[181]

◆◆◆

The potential evil of using jailhouse informants has never been clearer. Dozens of cases exist in Canada and the United States where false accusations were made against innocent people in the hope of gaining some advantage, sometimes as little as an extra banana for lunch. The dangers inherent in using such evidence have been apparent for years. Yet, time and again, prosecutors would place reliance on such declarations, leaving it to judges and juries to sort it all out. In

Canada, the case law now requires judges to warn a jury in the clearest terms that it is dangerous to rely on such evidence. They *may* accept it, but if they do they must be fully aware that the potential for falseness is great.

Morin is a case in point. But even before that, others had already warned that the indiscriminate use of jailhouse informants could lead to wrongful convictions. The best demonstration of this came in "The Los Angeles Experience," which I described in the report as follows:

> In October 1988, Leslie White, a repeated jailhouse informant in Los Angeles, demonstrated for the Los Angeles County Sheriff's Department how he would impersonate public officials by telephone from inside the jail to secure information about a fellow inmate. This information would then be used to fabricate the fellow inmate's confession. Directives were issued by the Sheriff's Department and the District Attorney's Office designed to prevent unauthorized telephone access to information. Yet, notwithstanding these directives, in January, 1989, Mr. White conducted a similar demonstration in a hotel room for a television crew from the CBS program, 60 Minutes.[182] White was given the name of a defendant whose recent arrest for murder had been locally reported. Posing as a Deputy Sheriff, Deputy District Attorney, and a Los Angeles Police Department Detective, White was able to obtain [by telephone] the cause of death, date of shooting, the age and race of the victim, and the existence of multiple gunshot wounds to the victim's thighs. He then demonstrated his ability to arrange for himself and the defendant to be transported together to court so that he could demonstrate that he and his target had spent some time together.

These revelations caused the Los Angeles County Grand Jury to conduct an investigation into the involvement and use of jailhouse informants in the county's criminal justice system. One hundred and twenty witnesses were heard and hundreds of additional interviews were conducted by the Grand Jury's investigators. The result was a severe indictment of the indiscriminate use of jailhouse informants.[183]

Australia, too, had problems of this nature, and in a report issued a short time after the Los Angeles investigation, a special commissioner, Ian Tremblay, noted wryly that while there "is no reason to believe that the extreme situation that developed [in Los Angeles] has happened here ... in the absence of appropriate preventative steps it probably would."[184] The same can be said for Canada, and Morin bears out Tremblay's prediction.

In my report on the *Morin* case, I recommended caution in the use of jailhouse informants. Peter Cory, a former Justice of the Supreme Court of Canada, in his report on *Sophonow*,[185] noting that "jailhouse informants are polished and convincing liars," went even further. "As a general rule," he wrote, "jailhouse informants should be prohibited from testifying." He then laid down the strict parameters for rare exceptions to the rule. For instance, jailhouse confessions might be used in cases such as kidnapping, where jailhouse informants "have, for example, learned of the whereabouts of the victim." And even then, other factors will have to be considered.

Since my report was published, the use of jailhouse informants has been greatly curtailed. Ontario, for instance, now has rules in effect that require crown counsel who intend to use jailhouse informants to obtain permission from a panel of senior crown attorneys (known in the profession as the Kaufman Committee). Such permission, I am told, is not given lightly. Awareness of the pitfalls and potential dangers of such evidence is greater than it was before. Judges warn juries in clear terms, and so, of course, will the defence. This is all to the good.

◆ ◆ ◆

By far the most wrenching day of the inquiry came on December 16, 1997, when, at my invitation, the Association in Defence of the Wrongly Convicted (AIDWYC) presented "a panel of the innocents." Marlys Edwardh, acting for AIDWYC, explained the idea: "You have heard evidence from police officers about policing, scientists about science, and in many other areas, but have heard not that much about the human face of the effects and the pain and the tragedy of those who are wrongfully convicted. You've certainly heard from Guy Paul, but it is AIDWYC's pleasure to place before you a panel of persons who have been wrongly convicted in Canada, the United States and in England."

That said, she turned the proceedings over to Joyce Milgaard, a founding member of AIDWYC and the mother of David Milgaard, who had served almost twenty-three years in prison for a crime he did not commit and for which someone else was convicted after his release. Mrs. Milgaard had bravely fought for her son's release since the day he was convicted. At first without success, she persisted, helped gather evidence, knocked on the doors of politicians, and finally, with the aid of lawyers who volunteered their time, convinced the government to refer the case to the Supreme Court of Canada. The conviction was overturned, her son was set free, and now she was here with David and five others, all proven to have been wrongfully convicted: Rubin "Hurricane" Carter, who served twenty-eight years in prison for a triple murder he didn't commit; Rolando Cruz, who served twelve years, three months, and three weeks (as he said) for a murder of which he was later cleared; Patrick Maguire, who was in jail in England for four years before the case against him collapsed;[186] Joyce Ann Brown, wrongly imprisoned for robbery and murder; and Rick Norris, who served eight months in a Canadian jail for a sexual assault committed by someone else while he was home in bed with his wife. Donald Marshall, the first of the "three Ms"—Marshall, Milgaard, and Morin—had been invited but couldn't attend because of illness. Another potential witness, Thomas Sophonow, came to the proceedings and offered to testify, but we couldn't add him to the panel because at that point his innocence had not yet been definitively established. It was a few months later, and his sorry tale is recounted in the report of a Manitoba royal commission.[187] It is grim reading.

What these people had to say truly "put the human face," as Marlys had told us, on the pain and tragedy of the wrongly convicted. Let me give you an example. Patrick Maguire was thirteen years old when he, his mother, father, and four siblings were arrested in England and charged with the unlawful possession of nitroglycerine. All were convicted and Patrick served four years in jail before being released. But, as he told us, "my sentence started when I was released from prison." And, turning to me, he said (and how well I remember these words):

But regarding the sentencing, Judge, I don't know—I mean, I've only ever hoped someone will tell me about that. I'm sure on many occasions, you might have passed sentence on people who have done wrong, but beyond that sentence that you give, Judge, there's more sentencing waiting for them, in prison, and when they come out.

For twenty years, I have been punished. That four years in prison was easy compared to the punishment I've had since.

Maguire and his family were later exonerated. It had all been a mistake—a mistake that ruined their lives.

My overall conclusions in the inquiry were that the case had been mishandled by the police, that the initial search for clues was defective, and that "tunnel vision" caused the investigators to "zero in" on Morin much too quickly, with the result that other leads were often ignored. The crown, too, I found, suffered from tunnel vision, accepting too readily the theories of the police. The "offer" to May and

Mr. X I found to be spurious, their veracity so doubtful that their testimony should not have been used. The Centre of Forensic Sciences did not acquit itself well, nor did some of the witnesses, some of whom had been unduly coached by the police.

I concluded the report as follows:

This Report ends where it started. An innocent person was convicted of a heinous crime he did not commit. Science helped convict him. Science exonerated him. We will never know if Guy Paul Morin would ever have been exonerated had DNA results not been available. One can expect that there are other innocent persons, swept up in the criminal process, for whom DNA results are unavailable.

The case of Guy Paul Morin is not an aberration. By that, I do not mean that I can quantify the number of similar cases in Ontario or elsewhere, or that I can pass upon the frequency with which innocent persons are convicted in this province. We do not know. What I mean is that the causes of Mr. Morin's conviction are rooted in systemic problems, as well as the failing of individuals. It is no coincidence that the same systemic problems are those identified in wrongful convictions in other jurisdictions worldwide. It is these systemic issues that must be addressed in the future. As to individual failings, it is to be hoped that they can be prevented by the revelation of what happened in Guy Paul Morin's case and by education as to the causes of wrongful convictions.

◆ ◆ ◆

As several crown counsel told me during the Inquiry, prosecuting someone who turns out to be innocent is a crown attorney's "worst nightmare." I accept that. I also accept that no crown counsel involved in this case, and no police officer involved in this case, ever intended to convict an innocent person. Although I have sometimes described the human failings that led to the conviction of Guy Paul Morin in very critical language, many of the failings which I have identified represent serious errors of judgment, often resulting from lack of objectivity, rather than outright malevolence.

The challenge for all participants in the administration of justice in Ontario will be to draw upon this experience and learn from it.

The report contains 119 recommendations. I thought I had 120—a nice, round, biblically significant number—but at the last moment my staff and I decided that two recommendations were sufficiently similar that they should not bear separate numbers. So we were down to 119.

The day before the public presentation of the report, the attorney general's executive assistant called to say that the minister would like to see me prior to the publication of the report. Early morning, he said, would be best. I offered to go to the minister's office, but since this was a royal commission he explained that protocol required that the minister come to me. I suggested breakfast and so, over bagels, cream cheese, and lox, my senior staff and I received Charles Harnick.

He told me that he had read the executive summary and that he agreed with all recommendations and that he would say so at a press conference later that day. I reminded the minister that some of my recommendations were directed to the federal government and, without missing a beat, he said "of course," and that he would recommend to his federal counterpart that she do the same. True to his word, within minutes after I presented the report, he announced that he would set up a task force to implement my recommendations. I truly believe that the task force has made a difference to the administration of criminal justice not only in Ontario, but in all Canada and even abroad.

I presented the report on April 9,1998—my thirty-first wedding anniversary—at a press conference in the large hearing room that had been my "home" for almost two years. Sixteen television cameras and dozens of photographers faced me. The lights came on and I couldn't see beyond the first row. But I knew that my most ardent supporters, my wife and my children, were there. I read a short statement and left. Whatever I had to say was in the report, and I was not prepared to go beyond that. I returned to my office, where the administrator had set up a television set. As I watched the live broadcasts, I realized that this had been the most important undertaking of my career. How often is one given the chance to make a real and substantial contribution to the law? I was, and I am, grateful.

When Kirk Makin wrote his second edition of *Redrum the Innocent*,[188] he noted that betting in the legal community was divided on how I might deal with the evidence. "One school of thought," he wrote, "had it that based on his conservative evidentiary rulings throughout the inquiry, Kaufman would produce a report bearing the same traits." He added that "those adhering to this line of thought believed Kaufman was too much part of the legal establishment not to feel sympathy for the prosecutors and, to a lesser extent, the bumbling gumshoes from Durham who had been thrust in way over their heads." But the other "betting line," according to Makin, "believed Kaufman to be very much his own man, a quiet and thoughtful jurist who simply gave nothing away along the route to forming his judgments."

I can only say that it never occurred to me to be either bold or conservative, or to favour one group and be unduly harsh to another. My approach was the same as it had been throughout my entire career on the bench: hear the evidence, assess its value, and let the chips fall where they may. I have always treasured my independence—as a lawyer, as a judge, and now as head of a Royal Commission. No one has ever been able to influence my ultimate judgment, nor, I am happy to say, has anyone ever tried. Of course, lawyers appearing before me, in court or on inquiries, presented their cases with skill and thoughtful arguments. But that is how the system works, and I am free to accept or reject their submissions. The point is that no one can dictate what I should do. This is the hallmark of a free and independent judiciary, and thank God for this system. Happily, as Makin points out, my report has "belled the cat."

Public reaction was most gratifying. In its lead editorial on April 11, 1998, the *Toronto Star* described the report as "1,242 pages of calmly reasoned, concisely argued prose that describe the nightmare that Morin endured, draw the lessons to be learned and define the changes that are required." It concluded as follows:

> Kaufman's report does not prescribe quick fixes.
>
> It lays out the work for a generation.
>
> As its full implications are considered, the dimensions of the commitment required of us will become clearer and clearer.
>
> What is already clear is the debt we owe, not only to Judge Kaufman for the work he and his staff have done, but to Morin, for forcing us to the knowledge that a system that failed him can fail any of us.

The courts have also taken note. In the eleven years that followed the publication of the report, it was cited in more than two hundred decisions across Canada, including two major judgments given by the Supreme Court of Canada. I was particularly gratified when the Supreme Court saw fit to mention my work in *Morin* in *U.S.A. v. Burns*,[189] where it noted "an accelerating concern about potential wrongful convictions ... which compels increased recognition of the fact the extradition decision of a Canadian Minister could pave the way, however unintentionally, to sending an innocent individual to his or her death in a foreign jurisdiction." As a result, reversing a decision given ten years before,[190] the Court held that henceforth, in light of "these factual developments," the minister of justice should no longer authorize the extradition from Canada of persons who face the death penalty, unless assurances are given that this ultimate penalty would be neither sought nor applied. As a lifetime opponent of capital punishment, I am proud that my report helped bring about this decision.

My report was also among the materials studied by the Governor's Commission on Capital Punishment, a blue-ribbon panel of judges, lawyers, academics, and business people, charged by the governor of Illinois to examine all aspects of capital punishment in that state.[191] After two years of study, the commission concluded that there were "serious areas of concern" in many cases where the death penalty was imposed, and it made eighty-five recommendations on how the situation might be improved. In response to the commission's report, Governor George H. Ryan, in one the last acts before leaving office in 2002, commuted all sentences of those on death row at the time. His reasons were summarized in one sentence: "The legislature can't reform it, the lawmakers won't repeal it and I won't stand for it." Not surprisingly, many of the commission's recommendations echo what I had said in *Morin*.[192]

[26]
Nova Scotia

I had barely completed my report in *Morin* when I got a call from Doug Keefe, Nova Scotia's acting deputy minister of justice, to whom I had been recommended by his counterpart in Ontario. He asked me if I would undertake a review of the province's Public Prosecution Service (PPS) that, in the eyes of many, had become a dysfunctional organization. I was intrigued by the idea, and after Doug filled in some of the details, I agreed to do the review.

Three high-profile cases, laden with human interest, hadn't advanced the PPS's reputation: *Morrison, Regan,* and *Westray*. Dr. Nancy Morrison was a physician who had been accused of injecting a deadly dose of potassium chloride into the veins of a terminally ill patient. Gerald Regan was a former premier of the province who had been charged with a series of old sexual assaults. *Westray* was a mining disaster, and two of the mine managers had been indicted for manslaughter. In Dr. Morrison's case, the PPS entered a stay of proceedings. Regan was acquitted on all of the charges on which he was tried, and in *Westray*, the PPS dropped the case. Each of these cases sparked much public debate, partly because of judicial criticism of the service but, for the most part, because of decisions taken by the director of public prosecutions (the head of the service) which were unpopular (which does not mean, of course, that they were wrong). At the same time, questions arose about the involvement the attorney general had, or should have had, in these decisions, and those were some of the issues that I was called upon to resolve.

I went to Halifax and set up shop in a suite at the Maritime Centre Building on Barrington Street. From there, with the help of small but very experienced staff, I examined how the service functioned and what improvements could—and should—be made. The review took almost a year and I was able to pinpoint a number of weaknesses, many of which were subsequently corrected. A new director of public prosecutions was appointed, salaries were improved, and better management procedures were put in place. My mission, I believe, was accomplished.

◆ ◆ ◆

I presented my report on the Public Prosecution Service in Halifax in June 1999, and returned to Toronto. Little did I realize that I would be back in Nova Scotia a few months later. A provincial election had been held and the Liberal government was replaced by the Progressive Conservative opposition. Among the promises made by the new government in the course of the campaign was that, if elected, it would examine a compensation scheme for victims of abuse in provincial institutions. The former government had instituted the scheme in 1994 and it had already cost the province more than three times the estimated cost of $13.5 million.

It was a promise to be kept, and in November 1999 I got a call from Gordon Gillis, the deputy minister of justice, who told me that Michael Baker, the new minister of justice, would like me to undertake the review. I agreed, and a few days later I met with the minister in Halifax to work out the details. The government was anxious to have me start at once, and the appointment was announced at a press conference in the Red Chamber at Province House the following day.

At my initial meeting with Baker (in a steakhouse on Spring Garden Road), he suggested that what he had in mind was an inquiry into the actions of the previous government. I thought this was overly political and too narrow: while the proposed review would, of course, have to examine in detail what was done, the result would be of limited value. What was needed, I said, was a "blueprint for the future" that would be of help in dealing with similar situations in Nova Scotia and elsewhere, which I was certain were bound to arise. The minister agreed. However, at the press conference, the minister, being a seasoned politician, couldn't resist the temptation to remind his audience of the present government's promise to "investigate" the previous government's actions. So it fell to me to spell out my plans to add a further dimension, and the media accounts reflected this approach.

The official announcement, issued on the same day, said that I had been appointed "to conduct an independent review of the Government response to reports of institutional abuse in Nova Scotia." It then gave a brief history of the events:

In October 1994 Government responded to reports of physical and sexual abuse by provincial employees against former residents of provincially operated institutions with a three-pronged strategy: an investigation of the alleged abuse; an assessment of the safety of youth currently in custody; and a Compensation Program.

Subsequent to his review of the nature and extent of institutional abuse, former New Brunswick Chief Justice Stuart Stratton recommended the establishment of an alternative dispute resolution process for responding to alleged victims of institutional abuse. The Compensation Program came into effect June 17, 1996.

The Program has been adjusted twice since its inception.

The Department of Justice established an Internal Investigation Unit to investigate the allegations of abuse against current employees for disciplinary purposes. The RCMP established Operation Hope to handle the criminal investigation of alleged perpetrators.

The Program has been criticized by current and former employees who feel that their reputations have been tarnished; by claimants who believe changes made to the Program are too restrictive; and by citizens concerned about the cost and other aspects of the Program.

In response to the criticisms, the Government committed to review the Compensation Program for Victims of Institutional Abuse "to ensure the process is fair and upholds the rights of both victims and the accused."[193]

The task ahead was truly enormous. Hundreds of bankers' boxes filled with documents had to be looked at. Scores of people—ministers of the crown, administrators, past and present employees, and claimants and their lawyers—had to be interviewed. Responses to allegations of abuse in other jurisdictions had to be studied and, when that was done, a report and recommendations had to be drafted. To help me, I recruited a small but highly skilled staff. Duncan Beveridge, a well-known Halifax lawyer and now a judge of the Supreme Court of Nova Scotia, became my senior counsel. Mark Sandler, a highly respected Toronto lawyer who had been associate counsel in the *Morin* inquiry and, more recently, counsel to Sydney Robins's review of abuse in Ontario schools, agreed to become my senior policy adviser. Seetal Sunga, an Ontario lawyer who was in Halifax to work on a master's degree in law at Dalhousie University, was appointed director of research. Eventually, four more lawyers helped in the project. Together, we produced a significant and useful report[194] that, in the words of *The Globe and Mail* columnist Margaret Wente, "helped bring an end to one of the most bizarre miscarriages of justice in Canadian history."[195]

***

That things were not well in government institutions became clear in the mid-1980s, when three female residents at the Shelburne Youth Centre complained that a counsellor had made sexual advances toward them. Charges were laid, but these were later dismissed when the complainants failed to appear in court. Then, in 1991, an investigation was launched into incidents of sexual abuse of boys in the 1960s and 1970s by Patrick MacDougall, a counsellor at Shelburne at the time. Many former residents were interviewed by the RCMP, and in late 1992 eight charges were laid against MacDougall. He was convicted of indecent assault and gross indecency and sentenced to six years in prison. A short time later five additional charges were brought, to which he pleaded guilty and for which he was sentenced to a further five years.

One aspect of this case required special attention: allegations had surfaced in the mid-1970s that MacDougall had fondled a resident. As a result, he was dismissed from Shelburne, but his wife implored government officials to give him another chance—she was fearful that he would kill himself—and he was transferred to the Children's Training Centre in Sydney, where he was employed as a night watchman.[196] A notation on his record said that he was not allowed to be near children.

In 1991, the RCMP commenced an investigation into allegations of sexual abuse at the Nova Scotia School for Girls. This resulted in two convictions: Douglas Hollett, who was sentenced to two years and four months, and George Moss, who struck a plea agreement and received one year. No charges were laid against two other employees because the evidence was considered too weak. Clearly, abuses had occurred and the government was put on notice that lawsuits would be filed by some of the victims. Something had to be done.

On November 2, 1994, the provincial minister of justice, Bill Gillis, a geologist by profession, informed the House of Assembly that the government had formulated a three-pronged response to allegations of abuse at Shelburne:

1. An independent audit of current practices at Shelburne;
2. A thorough, independent investigation into the events that took place at Shelburne to determine what happened, who was involved, who knew what was happening, and what actions were taken;
3. An offer of compensation through an alternative dispute resolution "if liability was revealed" through the investigation.[197]

The minister's announcement was well received by the House. The government's intentions were good and the proposed steps seemed to be logical. Five days later, the scope of the response was widened and other government-run institutions would now be included. In short order, the minister appointed Viki Samuels-Stewart, a social worker with experience in women's shelters and a halfway house for adults, to conduct the audit of current practices at Shelburne. He also appointed the well-known and highly regarded former chief justice of New Brunswick, Stuart Stratton, to carry out the proposed investigation. Unfortunately, neither was given sufficient time or funds to accomplish these difficult tasks.

The Samuels-Stewart report was handed to the minister in March 1995. It concluded that young offenders held at Shelburne and another institution were indeed victims of abuse. Three months later, Stratton filed his report, identifying eighty-nine victims of physical or sexual abuse. Six days later, the provincial cabinet approved the compensation scheme for victims.

We know a great deal more today about schemes of this nature, but even in 1995 other provinces had already dealt with claims by former residents of institutions, and certain safeguards had been built into a variety of programs. Certainly, at least some verification of claims was required, but this was not to be in Nova Scotia: in its haste "to do the right thing," the government in effect said that compensation would be paid unless there was strong evidence to indicate that claims were false or exaggerated. However, in the beginning, at least, employees accused of misdeeds were not consulted, with the result that almost all claims succeeded, the only exception being cases where government assessors were able to demonstrate that the "victim" and the "accused" were not in the institution at the same time. The result of this was that a compensation scheme that had been expected to cost $13.5 million cost in excess of $60 million. It also left both employees and claimants angry and dissatisfied: employees because they lived under a cloud for many years, true victims of abuse—and undoubtedly there were many—because a troubled public now looked upon them as cheaters and frauds.

How could a well-intentioned effort go so wrong? There isn't a short answer—after all, my report is over six hundred pages—but it soon became clear that a combination of circumstances precipitated this well-meant but hasty and ill-conceived response.

First, the early 1990s were full of allegations of physical and sexual abuse in schools and other institutions: Mount Cashel Orphanage in Newfoundland; the

New Brunswick Training School at Kingsclear; the St. John's, St. Joseph's, and Grandview schools in Ontario; Jericho Hill School in Vancouver; and aboriginal residential schools throughout Canada. So no one was surprised when allegations of abuse surfaced in Nova Scotia.

Second, the Stratton inquiry purported to identify an alarmingly large number of victims in government-run institutions. The high reputation of the investigator as a respected former judge and astute observer lent credence to the charges, and no one at the time paid adequate attention to the caveats contained in his report. For instance, statements taken by the team of investigators were not sworn or tested by cross-examination; they described events from the distant past based on memories that could have been coloured by the self-interest of complainants and accused alike; and some complainants admitted that they were looking for financial compensation for what they had experienced.

There is nothing wrong, of course, with seeking compensation, but since the amounts awarded by courts or arbitrators or through negotiation are typically based on the extent and severity of the abuse, exaggeration is always a possibility. This was taken into account in other provinces, but with public indignation rising, and the encouragement of Mr. Stratton ("there is a high moral obligation on the Province," he wrote, "to address the present plight of the complainants"), Nova Scotia rushed into action. In fact, the government reacted so hastily that its negotiators even rejected a suggestion made by lawyers representing a large group of claimants that some degree of verification be established. The thinking was that this would slow the process and perhaps even "revictimize" the victims. As a result, those who were accused of abuse could not refute the charges and had to bear the public stigma. Their plight is detailed in my report.

Of course, hindsight is 20:20. It is easy today to say that the scheme was hopelessly flawed. But early warning signs were ignored, and even though some changes were made while the program was in progress, the basic flaws remained. For instance, Stratton spoke of eighty-nine cases. The government, quite rightly, reasoned that if his relatively quick review found eighty-nine victims, there were likely more, perhaps, over the years, as many as 200 or 300. Fair enough, but when the numbers started to escalate from 300 to 500, then to 1,000, and finally to almost 1,500, no one said, "Wait a minute, can this really be?" And so the process went on.

◆ ◆ ◆

In the course of the review, my staff and I interviewed more than one hundred persons. The most stressful and difficult interviews were those with genuine victims and also with falsely accused employees and their families. The hurt that these people felt was palpable and deep. Victims—the true "survivors"—told us that the compensation process was often humiliating and, in the words of at least one, "worse than the abuse." The retelling to government adjudicators was extremely painful, the reaction of interviewers not always sympathetic. It also was slow, increasing their level of anxiety. Then, when compensation was received, friends and neighbours sometimes told them they had done "a good thing" for themselves. In short, they were tarred with the brush of suspicion.

The impact on accused employees and their families was equally hard. It was summed up by Dr. David Sayer, a psychologist who had been asked to counsel staff. The employees felt "embattled," he wrote. Public statements by ministers, bureaucrats, media, judges, and lawyers created an atmosphere that led the public to believe that the allegations made against them were certainly true. Government apologies to claimants (they were part of the program), substantial payouts of compensation, and statements by officials that accused employees had been removed from their positions contributed to this notion. So did comments that the RCMP was involved in one of the largest investigations ever.

In Dr. Sayer's view, ordinary beliefs and faith in society's fundamental fairness were undermined, with the result that many accused employees were overwhelmed by feelings of helplessness and disillusion. Some were diagnosed with major depressive and post-traumatic stress disorders. Several were admitted to hospitals to prevent suicide. Some experienced permanent personality changes.

Many of the people we interviewed broke down completely, their anger and distress clearly genuine. I concluded my report as follows:

> Central to the Government's response to reported institutional abuse was a Compensation Program. It was seriously flawed. So flawed that it left in its wake true victims of abuse who are now assumed by many to have defrauded the Government, innocent employees who have been branded as abusers, and a public confused and unenlightened about the extent to which young people were or were not abused while in the care of the province of Nova Scotia.
>
> I was to determine if the Government response was appropriate, fair and reasonable. The simple answer is that it was not. It was commendable that the Government was concerned about the plight of abuse victims and understood its

obligation to rectify past wrongs and prevent future wrongs. However, it lost sight of its obligation to its own former and current employees. And fairness became yet another victim. And so did the credibility of the Program itself.

It would be all too easy to find malevolence in a Government response so flawed. No doubt, some affected parties have formed their own conclusions in this regard. But every tragedy does not have a villain. The issues that confronted the Government were not always free from difficulty. Nor was every Government official committed to, or equally responsible for, this flawed Program. The challenge here is to learn from the mistakes made and to avoid their repetition.

As a result, the government moved to compensate employees who had been falsely accused. This process has now been completed. "Operation Hope," the massive and costly police investigation announced by the RCMP with great fanfare, has collapsed. Despite announcements early on that "hundreds of charges" would be laid, six files were finally sent to the Public Prosecution Service for evaluation. All were found wanting. It was an ugly chapter in the history of a proud province. It was a case of good intentions gone terribly wrong.

◆ ◆ ◆

Other countries have taken note of my findings. A book published in England, where allegations of historic abuse are rampant, referred to my report as, perhaps, "the most balanced appraisal of the dilemma posed by such allegations."[198] This, in turn, led persons associated with the defence of a caregiver in South Australia to meet with me in Toronto. They, too, believed that many of the accusations of physical and sexual abuse brought by persons who had been placed in foster homes or state-run institutions were false or, at the very least, greatly exaggerated.

As a result of this meeting, I was invited to speak of my experience in Nova Scotia to a number of persons in Adelaide, including Ted Mullighan, a retired High Court judge, who had been asked by the government to head a royal commission to inquire into the mounting number of complaints.[199] I met with the commissioner, who had read my report, and he asked me to elaborate on certain aspects of my findings, which I did, informally, but in the presence of a court reporter. Mullighan, a well-known and capable barrister before his ascension to the bench, invited all potential complainants to contact him and tell their stories, and by the time I was there he had already received 780 requests from persons who were anxious to meet him. That way, he told me, he could make initial assessments of credibility, thereby avoiding the problems of the Stratton Inquiry in Nova Scotia, where the task had been relegated to investigators.

I also met with the attorney general of South Australia. I suggested that early talk of compensation might well bring on spurious claims, a proposition with which he agreed. However, he emphasized that his government (unlike the government of Nova Scotia) had not made specific promises, but he conceded that there was much talk about the subject in the air.

The third official I met with was the director of public prosecutions, and he, too, as well as his senior staff, were greatly interested in the Nova Scotia experience. In South Australia, as indeed in Nova Scotia, the prosecution service is completely independent, subject only to (again, as in Nova Scotia) the power of the attorney general to overrule the service. But, in cases where the attorney intervenes—and they are rare—he or she must answer to the legislature, with all the political consequences this might carry.

I spent a delightful week in Adelaide, leaving my last day for sight-seeing and relaxation. But this was not to be. An early-morning caller asked if I could meet with two lawyers who represented a client who, in their view, was wrongly convicted of murder.[200] They had heard of my work in the *Morin* case,[201] and they wanted to benefit from my experience. I gave them as much information as I could in the time available, and I suggested they contact James Lockyer and his associates in Toronto, who were highly knowledgeable in the field of wrongful convictions.

I had barely concluded this meeting when I was handed a message asking me if I could find the time to attend a working lunch with the Roman Catholic archbishop of Adelaide, who had learned of my presence from stories in the local press.[202] Of course, I could, and I was quickly driven to a lovely old house with a sign on the gate that said "Archbishop's House." The archbishop, a warm, intelligent, and very much "with-it" person, met me at the door. He was accompanied by his solicitor and his administrative assistant, and over an enjoyable lunch of sandwiches and coffee, prepared by his housekeeper, we discussed the implications of my report. I was greatly impressed by the forthright manner in which he discussed problems in the archdiocese, and by his determination to do the right thing and not sweep problems under the rug.

In late 2007, the case about which I was originally consulted finally came to trial before a judge and jury. The indictment contained twenty counts, seven of indecent assault and thirteen of unlawful sexual intercourse, involving eight boys between twelve and fourteen who had been under his care. Two charges were dismissed by the judge at the conclusion of the seven-week trial. After deliberating for a day and a half, the jury returned with eighteen verdicts of "not guilty."[203]

As one observer noted, cross-examination of the complainants quickly established that they were completely unreliable. Their stories were gathered by private investigators who "trawled" for victims, offering rewards and other inducements—a tactic described by a senior police official as a recipe for disaster, a path to false statements. In the face of the evidence, the prosecution's position that eight people can't all be lying was forcefully rejected by the jury. An action for substantial damages has now been filed in the Supreme Court of South Australia,[204] and a member of parliament has announced his intention to call "for a Parliamentary inquiry into how the Special Investigations Unit of the Department of Families and Communities handled child sex abuse allegations against public servant Tom Easling."[205] Further calls of the establishment of a Royal Commission to examine these matters continue, but they have so far been rejected by the government.[206]

Donna had joined me on my visit to Australia, and on the long trip home we remarked on the warmth of the people we had met and the wonderful hospitality that we had been shown at every turn. It was a privilege to have been able to help.

[27]
Four More Investigations

The first of the two Nova Scotia inquiries had barely begun when I accepted a task that took me into uncharted waters. In early 1998, the Atomic Energy Control Board of Canada (AECB) expressed concerns that poor labour/management and management/management relations in the Nuclear Division of Ontario Hydro (OHN) might ultimately affect the safety of operations in the province's three nuclear plants. The timely implementation of Ontario Hydro's nuclear-recovery plan, directed by a group of American nuclear engineers brought in for the purpose, was also put in doubt. After discussions with Hydro executives, the decision was reached to appoint an independent review panel to consider these issues. At first, it was to be a panel of three. But staffing issues arose, and in June 1998 Ontario Hydro, with the AECB's approval, established a panel of two, with me as chair and Professor Neil Todreas, a former head of nuclear engineering at the Massachusetts Institute of Technology, as a member. Dr. Hugh Arnold, an expert in organizational behaviour and the former dean of the Rotman School of Management at the University of Toronto, was appointed executive director. It turned out to be an excellent combination of talents.

With three weeks to produce a plan of action, no time could be lost. Neil joined Hugh and me in Toronto and we organized office space and a small staff. Soon, our room was filled with scores of bankers' boxes filled with background material, including copies of anonymous letters from OHN employees directed to AECB and OHN management expressing grave concerns regarding safety issues. Obviously, the situation had come to a head.

After a series of initial interviews, we realized that the focus of our work had to be safety *culture* and the labour-relations *climate*—culture and climate, not safety and labour relations—a distinction that proved to be of great value in the course of our work. Also, we determined that a combination of methods would be essential to drawing valid conclusions. This led to a two-pronged approach: structured interviews and well-designed surveys. Consultants therefore had to be found. There were some concerns about the more authoritarian, U.S. style of management, and so, while we did engage a number of U.S. consultants, we also relied on experts from Canada, the United Kingdom, France, and Spain. They were the best qualified persons we could find in a rather narrow field, and Neil's vast experience in the nuclear industry was of tremendous value. In the end, we could say with some degree of pride that we had picked not only the best, but also a group that was not wedded to the "ideological position or assumption that an authoritarian or directive style of management" was a prerequisite for the effective and safe performance of nuclear facilities.

In the course of our work, we visited all nuclear facilities in the province: Bruce, Darlington, and Pickering. What struck us most forcefully on our first visit to Pickering was a large Canadian flag hanging on a wall, visible to all who visited or worked there. There were also a number of small Canadian flags on engineers' desks. As Hugh and I explained to Neil, this was unusual for Canada. These were not symbols of patriotic pride, as might be thought. To us, with the knowledge we had acquired in earlier interviews, these were symbols of protest, aimed at the Nuclear Recovery Team that had been brought in by management from the United States. What the flags said was loud and clear: we are Canadian, we know what we're doing, and while we may need a little help now and then, we don't need a team headed by a retired U.S. naval commander. That, in essence, was the problem between the two management groups—pitting Canadians against Americans—referred to in the terms of reference. As one OHN employee told us: "They said they were going to come in and clean out the dead wood in management. All they've done is upset the fruit basket, shuffling managers all over the place, leaving us with incompetent managers who are new to their jobs and don't know the people who report to them or what they are supposed to do."

While this may have been a somewhat exaggerated view, the unprecedented level of change in the organization—and change was clearly needed—had taken a toll on many employees and managers, and they resented the new attitudes that now prevailed. For instance, in describing the general work environment, many referred to feelings of frustration, discouragement, exhaustion, and uncertainty. When asked to rate the work environment on a scale from one (negative/poor) to five (positive/good), with three as average, all three nuclear stations fell below the average. Only the head office staff came through as average—just.

We asked a lot of questions, but so did many of the employees. For instance, some managers were anxious to know if the changes introduced by the Nuclear Performance Advisory Group could be sustained "when the Americans go home?" Or, "is there sufficient talent in Canada to fill the gap?"—a reference to the 1993 reorganization of Ontario Hydro when many competent and experienced individuals left in response to enhanced severance packages offered by management as part of an initiative to reduce costs and personnel.

As these questions indicate, there was a dichotomy of thought on the part of OHN employees. On the one hand, they didn't like the Advisory Group's approach; on the other, if not them, who? It wasn't our task to resolve these issues, but we did point out the employees' concerns in the conclusions regarding overall work environment and culture:

1. While there is widespread agreement on the need for change, there is not a widely shared sense of overriding urgency for implementation of change.
2. Changes are being perceived as being forced from the top down, generating resistance on the part of employees who feel their experience and knowledge have been ignored or undervalued by the new management team.
3. The sheer volume of change implemented over the past two years has been very significant. This amount of change has been difficult for many employees to cope with and has generated feelings of tension and anxiety about the future.
4. The safety culture at OHN is not currently robust ...
5. Concerns exist among employees regarding the sustainability of the changes being implemented .... There is uncertainty whether senior management and the Board will be willing to "stay the course" with the changes initiated by the current management.

On the labour front, things weren't much better. There was a significant upward trend of formal grievances filed by the Power Workers Union, with unprecedented peaks in 1997 and 1998, which we attributed to the change in management style associated with the entry of the new team in 1997. As we were told again and again, prior years were seen as a more enlightened period of joint participation and cooperation. Probably so, but management now sought to reclaim its rights within the bounds of the collective bargaining relationship, and this caused unrest. However, we did find that by the time the survey was taken, both management and labour had made real efforts to increase the level of communication and cooperation by restarting the local joint labour–management meetings that were stopped in 1997.

One major concern to us was that "normal" adversarial labour–management relations, as suggested by some of the stakeholders, may not be good enough for the nuclear industry. Nuclear generating plants cannot be compared to auto plants and steel mills, and a comparable labour relations climate is not appropriate in the high-risk performance environment of nuclear plants. We therefore recommended that "the parties at OHN must articulate and implement a high performance mode of labour–management relations that fits this industry and their own joint interests." Yet, despite the shortcomings we found, we ultimately concluded that there was no evidence that the labour–management system currently in place prejudiced nuclear safety at Ontario Hydro. We did warn the parties, however, that "the current labour relations climate is not conducive to long-term high performance in either safety or general operations at OHN," and that it might well prejudice "the aggressive objectives of the Integrated Improvement Plan."

Our four-volume report was handed to Ontario Hydro and the AECB on March 9, 1999. Changes did occur, and ultimately the American team left. Labour relations improved, but other problems arose in the years that followed, and as I write these lines the nuclear-power plants are still not working to capacity.

◆ ◆ ◆

For almost twenty-five years, from 1967 to the end of 1991, R. Alan Eagleson could well be described as North America's Mr. Hockey. During that time, he was executive director of the National Hockey League Players' Association (NHLPA), which represented all active players employed by the clubs of the National Hockey League. His responsibilities were significant: direct the affairs of the NHLPA, appoint and supervise a director of operations (who also acted as treasurer), and ensure that the treasurer collected all monies due to the association, keeping an accurate account of all monies received and expended. He was also the spokesman for the NHLPA and his name appeared almost daily in the sports pages in Canada and the United States.

Eagleson's interests were not confined to the NHLPA. He also sat on the board of directors of Hockey Canada, which coordinates Canada's involvement in international competitions, and he served as chief negotiator and chairman of the Canada Cup Committee, which oversaw, during the years he was active, five international tournaments involving many of the finest hockey players in the world. Throughout this time, he also represented individual players, helped them negotiate their salaries, advised them on such matters as pensions and insurance, and on occasion acted for them in his capacity as a lawyer in claims arising from their activities.

But, as Russ Conway points out in his book *Game Misconduct: Alan Eagleson and the Corruption of Hockey*,[207] not all was well during those years. Conway quotes Ed Garvey, a labour lawyer hired by disgruntled players, who told his clients in 1989:

> If any other union leader did what Alan Eagleson has done over the past 22 years, the news media would be screaming for an investigation .... The conflicts of inter-est are shocking, but even more shocking is a pattern of sweetheart agreements with the NHL over all these years .... No benefits of any significance were achieved in the entire decade of the 80s through collective bargaining.[208]

Perhaps the media didn't scream, but enough players complained about their relations with Eagleson that investigations were finally launched in the United States and in Canada. In 1997 criminal charges were laid in both countries, and the Americans asked Canada to extradite Eagleson. That created a legal conundrum, since each country wanted to be the first to bring the accused to trial.

In October 1997, well-known Toronto criminal lawyer Brian Greenspan, with the assistance of an American colleague, worked out a deal: Eagleson would waive extradition and appear voluntarily in the United States District Court in Boston. There he would plead guilty to three counts of mail fraud, with an agreed-upon sentence of unsupervised probation for one year, restitution in the amount of CDN $1 million, and a "special assessment" of US$50 on each count. To trigger this arrangement, Eagleson also undertook to plead guilty to related criminal charges in Canada, where, in the words of the agreement, "he will advocate and receive a sentence of not less than eighteen (18) months of incarceration to be served in a penal institution and not in a half-way house, home confinement, or community service, such sentence to be implemented in accordance with Cana-dian law." And so it was. Eagleson flew to Boston in January 1998, pleaded guilty to the three charges, deposited a cheque for US$682,810.09, completed the nec-essary paperwork, and then returned to Toronto. There, the following day, he pleaded guilty to fraud and was sentenced to eighteen months in jail. It all went like clockwork and it was brilliant work on the part of his lawyer.

So far so good, but how was restitution to be made? The American court said only this: the amount deposited shall be paid "to a trust to be established for the benefit of members and former members of the NHLPA harmed by the defendant's conduct," with a "trustee to be designated within thirty days by the NHLPA." A few days after Eagleson's appearance in the Canadian court, I got a call from Eddie Goodman, the senior partner of Goodman, Phillips and Vineberg (now Goodmans), the lawyers for the NHLPA. Would I be interested in becoming the trustee? I said yes, and on February 6 the NHLPA entered into an agreement with me whereby I assumed the task of distributing $1 million to former and current players to compensate them for harm suffered by Eagleson's conduct.

But this wasn't as easy as it may seem. Who suffered what? And how to divide the money? I engaged counsel to help me in the task, and after many hours of looking at different possibilities, I came to the conclusion that every player who played in the NHL during Eagleson's reign was entitled to share in the distribution. The reason was that even though he had pleaded guilty in the United States to mail fraud, the underlying scheme diverted funds that properly belonged to the association for his own purposes. For instance, Air Canada was licensed by the NHLPA to advertise at hockey games. Normally, an advertiser would pay cash for this privilege. But Air Canada was asked to issue free tickets instead, and many of these were used by persons designated by Eagleson, including his law partners and members of his family. Since the NHLPA is "owned" by its members, the members had lost the benefit of these funds.

Having decided that every player was entitled to something, I then had to determine how much. With the help of NHLPA staff, we drew up a list of everyone who had ever played, even if it was one game only, during the crucial period. The number turned out to be 1,355 players—585 in the United States, 472 in Canada, 286 elsewhere (mostly in Sweden, the Czech Republic, and Finland) or with addresses unknown, and 12 deceased. We then determined how many games each player had played, since I felt that restitution should be made in proportion to a player's involvement in the NHL. I also had to calculate what each game was worth. I then decided that no one should get less than $100, since any smaller amount could rightly be considered an insult.

This work took almost five months, but on July 14, 1998, I was able to write to each potential recipient and inform him of what I proposed to do. In essence, it was this:

1. Since the wrongdoings set out in the American indictment affect all members of the NHLPA, individual claims could not be entertained.
2. Since some of Eagleson's acts were more harmful to the members following the 1983–4 season, I would allocate more money to those who played after that date.

3. The entire trust fund would be distributed to players. All fees and disbursements would be paid by the NHLPA.
4. Members could voluntarily opt out of the program, and monies so saved would be added to the pot.
5. Any player who was aware of a particular hardship case—and there were many —was, of course, entirely free to turn over his cheque to a more needy colleague.

In the weeks that followed I received hundreds of phone calls, emails, and letters from present or past NHLPA members. While most agreed with the proposed plan of distribution, some had different ideas, but usually, after discussing the matter, they were satisfied that no matter what the scheme, some inequalities were bound to arise. What was important to the players was that each should receive a tangible token of the penalty imposed on Eagleson, even if the amount had to be nominal. Indeed, some of the cheques were never cashed, and I wouldn't be surprised if quite a few were framed and now hang in some players' trophy rooms.

My staff and I spent many weeks tracking down players who had moved and could not easily be found. Ultimately, the number of "lost" players was very small and I set up a fund to hold some monies in reserve should some be located after the distribution. And some were, as much as a year later, mostly through contacts with other players.

When all calculations were complete and funds could be distributed, I faced a final hurdle—to sign 1,200 cheques. I called the bank to ask if it would accept a rubber stamp. The answer was yes, with the added information that "we never check on signatures where the amount is less than $100,000, so it doesn't matter who signs or how."

It took almost three and half years to carry out the assignment, but on July 25, 2001, I was able to report that I had distributed the money paid into court in conformity with the terms of the order. A balance of $45,860.65 remained in the account—part of the monies held back by me should further players be found (three were), as well as cheques that players failed to cash. I wrote a cheque for that amount in favour of the "Players Helping Players Fund," which, in its discretion, helps former players now in need.

◆ ◆ ◆

It is hard to imagine today that organized legal aid is a relatively recent phenomenon. In my early days of practice, judges would ask lawyers to represent impecunious accused in serious criminal cases on a *pro bono* basis. Almost no one refused. Indeed, it was a matter of pride for the Bar that no accused should have to face a judge and jury without proper representation. But what about less serious cases, where the punishment, in case of conviction, might still entail a custodial sentence? Well, the saying went, the judge will look out for the accused. And while some judges did so admirably, others did it less well, and I have no doubt that proper legal representation would have brought about more just results—not just for the accused but also for society at large.

In the 1960s I sat on a committee that helped draft a platform for the Quebec Liberal Party. "Think of the cost," people said, and that was that. But some years later the idea was adopted, and a rudimentary system of aid was established. Henceforth, in certain cases, lawyers would be compensated by the state for their time as well as their expenses connected with the cases. This was a major advance because, heretofore, not only was the work *pro bono*, but ordinary expenses such as filing fees, bailiffs' charges, the cost of transcripts, and travel expenses were borne by the lawyer who undertook this type of case.

Of course, many young lawyers established their reputation with legal aid cases, but even a good reputation does not help pay the rent! The situation was somewhat different in civil cases, in which lawyers often entered into contingency arrangements with their clients. But this was not permitted in Ontario until quite recently, although I have no doubt that arrangements of this nature did occur.

Patrick LeSage, the former chief justice of the Ontario Superior Court of Justice, in an "exit interview" with the *Toronto Star*'s Tracey Tyler, recalled the problems posed by accused without counsel:

LeSage: You don't always want to yearn for the good old days, because, I'll tell you, an accused now is much better represented in court than he was when I became a crown attorney. Because there was no legal aid when I became a crown attorney. And a lot of people who should have had lawyers didn't have lawyers.
Tyler: So you went up against unrepresented people?
LeSage: Oh, all the time. All the time. And often times, it was a medium-serious charge. I as a crown attorney would phone somebody, like (Toronto lawyer) Julian Porter ... and say, "This person needs a lawyer. Will you come over and defend them?" You know? Two hours later they were over and defended the case. But, that's not a very good way of running a system.[209]

In Ontario, the situation began to improve in 1951, when legal aid was formally established. It covered both civil and criminal proceedings, including all indictable offences punishable by imprisonment. Financial eligibility was based on annual income, the number of dependants, and a discretionary needs test. Control of the plan was vested in the Law Society. But the underlying concept of legal aid as a charitable activity remained the same: lawyers provided services on a purely voluntary basis.

The problem with the eligibility rules, then and now, is that legal aid leaves out people "in the middle." Wealthy persons can hire anyone they wish. Poor persons, who qualify, also have a choice of attorneys, but they must choose from a much smaller pool. But members of the middle class are often out of luck.

The system was refined over the years, and by 1967 it was formally recognized that legal aid should be considered a right, not a charitable gift. Lawyers were to be "reasonably" compensated for their services, and the money would come from the government. The amount suggested was a reduced rate of 75 per cent of a normal solicitor–client account. The late Arthur Martin thought this was "realistic and fair ... the fees tend to approximate the modest fees that would be charged to a client who could pay but for whom the payment of a larger fee might involve some hardship." In actual terms, this meant payment of $35 an hour for higher-court proceedings and $25 for lower-court proceedings. If this was approximately 75 per cent of the fees charged by lawyers, it meant that experienced counsel billed at $50 an hour, a long way from the fees currently charged!

The rates were increased over the years, but they kept on falling further and further behind, and by the mid-1980s a committee of the legislature pointed out that while the legal aid tariff had increased by 50 per cent in the years since its inception, the average weekly wage had risen by 350 per cent during that time. The government responded by increasing the tariff by 5 per cent!

Even though I had an early interest in legal aid, I didn't know much about the tariffs currently in force. That changed in April 2000, when the board of Legal Aid Ontario (LAO) asked me and Robert L. Holden, a lawyer of vast experience and its former chief executive officer, to carry out "an independent analysis of the legal aid tariff" and to make recommendations on three specific issues:

1. The effect of the tariff rate on the quality and accessibility of legal services in Ontario;
2. The tariff structure and alternative billing methods;
3. Modifications to improve tariff administration (including improved use of technology) for both LAO and service providers.

The board gave us eight months to accomplish the task.

With the help of Professor Michael Trebilcock, a lawyer and economist, and a team from the consulting firm of Charles River Associates, we organized a survey of the legal profession in which more than eight hundred lawyers participated. This was supplemented by "town hall" meetings that Bob and I conducted in Toronto, Cobourg, Kingston, Thunder Bay, Kenora, Windsor, London, and Ottawa. We also informed ourselves of legal aid tariffs in force in other Canadian jurisdictions, as well as in the United Kingdom, Australia, and New Zealand. We excluded evidence from the United States because legal aid delivery in that country differs substantially from the "judicare"-oriented systems generally in use in Canada and other Commonwealth countries. The "public defender" is strong south of the border, and so are other systems, including contracts between states and private law firms; clinics, primarily in the area of civil law; *pro bono* programs run by Bar associations; and prepaid legal services, again primarily in civil cases.

What we found was that almost every jurisdiction struggled with ever-increasing costs of providing legal aid services. Fees always lagged behind, often by large amounts, what practitioners could earn in private practice, and even the most public-minded lawyer had to meet the costs of maintaining an office and be left with reasonable remuneration for his or her services. Yet, with tight budgets on the part of governments, the gap could never quite be closed. It was not our mandate to restructure the system, but we could not fail to observe that in some parts of Ontario, lawyers in private practice almost never accepted legal aid mandates, with the result that LAO was obliged to hire lawyers on a full-time basis in order to provide adequate services. This, in a sense, defeated the spirit of the legislation, which emphasized that the legal aid system should resemble as closely as possible the normal solicitor–client relationship.

We produced a number of graphs that illustrated how the income of lawyers relying to a major extent on legal aid mandates compared with the income of crown attorneys (legal aid was well below) and the income of physicians paid by the Ontario Health Insurance Plan (again, legal aid was well below). The most important lesson we learned from the latter was that whenever doctors' fees were increased, something else was cut since the funds provided by the government remained the same. Indeed, LAO, in previous years, had done exactly that: increase fees but decrease the number of areas covered. This may have been the only way to meet the budget, but it made for an incomplete system.

It was therefore important to try to recommend a set of realistic tariff fees, high enough to attract a sufficiently large number of practitioners to cover all cases that qualified, yet low enough to allow LAO to provide services to everyone who qualified. Of course, no matter how well-tuned the structure, the government had to provide an adequate budget, no matter what we recommended.

We were greatly encouraged by the fact that almost all the lawyers who met with us made realistic suggestions. Legal aid is not a get-rich-quick scheme. But decent pay for decent work should not be an elusive goal, and our final recommendations reflect this: the rate, we said, should range from $105 to $140 an hour, depending on the level of experience. This was less than the approximate range of fees charged by lawyers working in practice areas served by LAO, but that could be justified by the fact that lawyers who held legal aid certificates were certain to be paid while lawyers in private practice could not always count on this.

It would be nice if I could say that these suggestions were incorporated in the law or regulations. But Ontario had recently entered a period of budget cuts, and while the province recognized that some upward adjustments had to be made, the monies set aside for this fell short of the requirements. Still, the tariff was increased, though by much less than we had recommended. But the blueprint remains, and I am content that Bob and I arrived at a formula that all concerned accepted as fair.

◆ ◆ ◆

In 1975, Leonard Peltier, a prominent member of the American Indian Movement (AIM), was invited by the traditional chiefs at the Pine Ridge reservation near Wounded Knee in South Dakota "to provide support for the political aspirations of those on the reservation." Soon after his arrival, two FBI agents were killed and Peltier and three others were charged with their murder. He fled to Canada. Six months later, at the request of U.S. authorities, the RCMP found and arrested Peltier in Hinton, Alberta. He was subsequently transferred to British Columbia, where extradition hearings were held. On June 18, 1976, Justice W.A. Schultz, in a ninety-two-page judgment, found that a *prima facie* case had been made out and he ordered Peltier to be returned to the United States for trial. Interestingly, less than two weeks before, an Iowa jury, after deliberating for five days, acquitted two of Peltier's three co-accused. Charges against the third accused were dropped.

Peltier's appeal from Justice Schultz's order was unsuccessful, and in due course, as required by the Extradition Act, the file was submitted to the federal minister of justice, whose fiat was required before the transfer could be carried out. By then, cracks had been discovered in the prosecution's case, including allegations that perjured evidence had been presented at the extradition hearing. Affidavits were filed, complaints were made to the United Nations Human Rights Commission, and Peltier's supporters urged the minister of justice to exercise his discretion and refuse extradition. But it was not to be. On December 18, Ron Basford, the minister, signed the necessary warrant and Peltier was whisked away to the United States.

He stood trial, and on April 18, 1977, he was convicted of the murder of the two FBI agents and sentenced to two consecutive life terms. A year and a half later, the United States Court of Appeals for the Eighth Circuit dismissed Peltier's appeal and confirmed the conviction. In particular, the court rejected Peltier's four principal grounds of appeal:

1. That evidence was improperly admitted;
2. That evidence designed to show that Peltier was the victim of an FBI frame-up was improperly excluded;
3. That proposed instructions to the jury concerning the frame-up theory were improperly denied; and
4. That Peltier's extradition from Canada violated the Webster-Ashburton Treaty of 1842.[210]

The first of these grounds is a standard allegation in appeals. But the frame-up theory was certainly unusual, and so was the allegation that the extradition violated an old treaty between the two nations.

That both sides—the prosecution and the defence—had strong feelings is fully understandable. Two law enforcement agents had been killed, and that alone ensured that all the powers of the state would be corralled to make the strongest possible case against the accused. That doesn't mean, of course, that evidence would be "manufactured" (although that, too, was alleged), but it does mean that the great emphasis would be placed on the evidence to paint the darkest picture of the accused. On the other hand, the defence pointed to years of oppression of aboriginal people, who, in turn, had a deep mistrust of white authority.

As Peltier's supporters later put it, the large Pine Ridge reservation had been "a natural flashpoint." A hundred years earlier, it was the site of Custer's "last stand," the massacre at Wounded Knee and the beginning of Sitting Bull's retreat, "effectively ending Indian armed resistance to Euro-American alienation of Indian land."[211] A century later, members of the reservation had been restive. The Bureau of Indian Affairs, it was said, had intervened in the politics of the reservation, setting Indian against Indian and installing a "third world-like puppet government." For those who wanted to resist these pressures, the support of the AIM was attractive, which is why Peltier and other members of the movement had been invited to the reservation.

By June 1975, the situation had reached a boiling point. Tension was high. A raid on the reservation was expected and both sides were heavily armed. On the morning of June 26, two FBI agents drove in separate cars to the reservation. Suddenly—the evidence is not clear how or why—shots were exchanged. Both agents were wounded, one of them gravely. When the shooting subsided, three or four AIM members, including Peltier, approached the two cars. Both agents were killed at point-blank range. Reinforcements then arrived and made their way onto the reservation. A number of AIM members escaped, Peltier among them.

The case against Peltier rested heavily on affidavits sworn by a native American, Myrtle Poor Bear, a member of the Oglala Sioux Nation. There were three affidavits in all. In the first, she claimed that she was Peltier's girlfriend and that even though she had not been present at Pine Ridge on that fateful day, he had confessed to her that he had committed the two murders. In the second affidavit, prepared four days later, she contradicted this story: she was indeed at Pine Ridge and saw Peltier kill the two agents. The third affidavit was of little consequence. However, at the extradition hearing, the first affidavit was not produced, and the judge was therefore unaware that Poor Bear had contradicted herself in two sworn declarations, a fact that would have suggested the need for particular caution.

During the 1960s and 1970s, Myrtle Poor Bear was arrested repeatedly for alcoholic episodes. She was hospitalized eleven times between 1963 and 1973 for a variety of disorders. In addition, she had made over one hundred outpatient visits to various clinics in the region. Her father, with whom she has lived most of her life, told investigators of an early illness, apparently typhoid fever, contracted from drinking contaminated water. "Since she was a little girl," he said, "Myrtle lived in her own fantasy world. She made up stories. She is a good girl, generous ... but ever since her fever, the one that almost killed her, her mind is like that." Still, the affidavits were powerful stuff.

As I said, the case wound its way through the courts, first in Canada, then in the United States. Peltier lost at every stage and began serving his sentence. His supporters, however, and there are many, continued the fight. In the mid-1980s, an application was brought to the United States Circuit Court of Appeals alleging that evidence favourable to the accused had been improperly withheld by the authorities. The test for the reversal of a verdict on this ground, however, is severe. As the court noted:

> There is a *possibility* that the jury would have acquitted Leonard Peltier had the records and data improperly withheld from the defence been available to him in order to better exploit and reinforce the inconsistencies casting strong doubts upon the government's case. Yet, we are bound by the *Bagley* test requiring that we be convinced, from a review of the entire record, that had the data and records withheld been made available, the jury *probably* would have reached a different result. We have not been so convinced.[212]

The court's opinion was written in 1984 by Judge Gerald W. Heaney. Seven years later, when the question of executive clemency was raised, Judge Heaney, in reply to an inquiry by Senator Daniel K. Inouye, said that "no new evidence has been called to my attention which would cause me to change the conclusion reached in that case." But he then added this:

> There are, however, other aspects of the case that the President may see fit to consider in determining whether he should take action to commute or otherwise mitigate the sentence of Leonard Peltier. My thoughts on these other aspects result from a very careful study of the records of the Peltier trial and the post-trial evidence and from a study of the record in the Robideaux-Butler trial before Judge McManus in Iowa, a trial which resulted in the acquittal of Robideaux and Butler.
>
> First, the United States government over-reacted at Wounded Knee. Instead of carefully considering the legitimate grievances of the Native Americans, the response was essentially a military one which culminated in a deadly firefight
>
> Second, the United States government must share the responsibility with the Native Americans for the June 26 firefight. While the government's role in escalating the conflict into a firefight cannot serve as a legal justification for the killing of the FBI agents at short range, it can properly be considered a mitigating circumstance.
>
> Third, the record persuades me that more than one person was involved in the shooting of the FBI agents. Again, this fact is not a legal justification for Peltier's actions, but it is a mitigating circumstance.
>
> Fourth, the FBI used improper tactics in securing Peltier's extradition from Canada and in otherwise investigating and trying the Peltier case. Although our court decided that these actions were not grounds for reversal, they are, in my mind, factors that merit consideration in any petition for lenience filed.

Fifth, Leonard Peltier was tried, found guilty, and sentenced. He has now served more than fourteen years in the federal penitentiary. At some point, a healing process must begin.

A courageous letter by an honourable person. However, no action was taken.

Many other attempts to free Leonard Peltier followed, including an application to the Supreme Court of Canada to hear an appeal from the extradition judgment. This was denied on June 22, 1989.

In 1999, Canada's minister of justice, Anne McLellan, wrote to her counterpart in the United States, informing her that a departmental review of the case, started five years before, had been completed, and that she was satisfied that "Mr. Peltier was lawfully extradited to the United States." But that did not end the matter, and later that year the Innocence Project at Osgoode Hall Law School took up the case. Myrtle Poor Bear was located and she agreed to be examined (and cross-examined) under oath. A forum was therefore required, and the late Dianne Martin, an associate professor of law at Osgoode and leader of the project, asked me if I would be prepared to preside over a hearing at which Poor Bear and others would testify. The case was of interest, perhaps another wrongful conviction, and I agreed to participate on a *pro bono* basis.

The hearing was held on October 25, 2000. Michael Code, a former assistant deputy attorney general of Ontario, and Scott Fenton, a former federal crown attorney, examined and cross-examined the witnesses, principal among them Myrtle Poor Bear, now forty-eight. It was her first public statement since signing the affidavits in 1976.

Kirk Makin, who covered the event for *The Globe and Mail*, neatly summed up what he had heard:

> Twenty-five years of pent-up fear and guilt gushed from Myrtle Poor Bear as she recanted the utterances that led to aboriginal activist Leonard Peltier being extradited to the United States in 1976 over the murder of two FBI agents.
>
> "I was forced into this, and I feel very awful," the weeping woman testified at a unique hearing held in a downtown Toronto office tower. "I just wish that Leonard Peltier would get out of prison."[213]

Poor Bear, whose evidence was corroborated in part by some of the other witnesses, told a hair-raising story of months of unrelenting harassment and threats from FBI agents: "They told me they were going to take my child away from me.

They told me they were going to get me for conspiracy, and I would face 15 years in prison if I didn't cooperate. They said they had witnesses who placed me at the scene."

The claim in her first affidavit that she was Peltier's girlfriend was utterly false. So was the claim in her second affidavit that she had seen him shoot the agents. In fact, she said, she was eighty kilometres away on the day of shooting. The horror story continued: she would face dire consequences unless she cooperated; she was taken on long drives, sometimes to neighbouring states, and confined, incommunicado, for days and weeks at a time in motels and hotel rooms. On the rare occasions when she was allowed to return to her family—her child, her father, and ten siblings—she was ordered to reveal nothing of her ordeal. The final straw was when she was told that word had leaked out that she was a police informer, and that, without protection, the AIM would kill her as a traitor. Soon afterward, she signed the first of three affidavits.

Despite her father's statement that Myrtle lived in a fantasy world, I was greatly impressed by her evidence. It had the ring of truth. Significantly, she was not called as a witness at Peltier's trial. So, until this hearing, she was never subjected to cross-examination. It did not shake her assertions.

By this time, the petition for executive clemency had recently been renewed. Bill Clinton was about to leave the White House, and Peltier's friends hoped that he would issue a pardon. Hundreds of letters were sent to the president, one of them from me. I said, in part:

> Five witnesses were heard under oath: Myrtle Poor Bear, Elaine Poor Bear Martinez, Edgar Bear Runner, Frank Dreaver and Ron George. They were examined and cross-examined by two distinguished barristers, and I believe the transcripts of their evidence are now in your hands.

> I say without hesitation that each of the witnesses appeared honest and credible. I was particularly impressed by Myrtle Poor Bear, now a grandmother .... As you can see from her evidence, she acted under duress at the time, and much of what she then said was false. I am satisfied that if this had been known when the extradition hearings took place, the request to extradite would likely have been refused.

> Myrtle Poor Bear's testimony is corroborated to the extent possible by her sister, Elaine Poor Bear Martinez. She, too, spoke before me without hesitation and with a great deal of assurance and I regard her testimony as truthful. She also spoke movingly of the "healing process" that is so necessary and which would be helped by the exercise of executive clemency to bring about Mr. Peltier's release from prison.

But it was all to no avail. As I write these lines, Peltier remains in prison. I do not know whether he is guilty or not. I do know, however, that Myrtle Poor Bear's second affidavit was largely responsible for Peltier's extradition, and this is an aspect of the case that greatly disturbs me.

[28]
"They Finally Got It Right"
—STEVEN MURRAY TRUSCOTT, ON HEARING OF HIS ACQUITTAL, AUGUST 28, 2007.

It is the case that will not go away. It has haunted the Canadian imagination for almost five decades.[214] It has been discussed in the courts, in books, by the press, in a movie, and on television. And even though Steven Truscott has finally succeeded in his long quest for justice,[215] the debate will continue. If not he, then who killed 12-year-old Lynne Harper? Why did a jury convict when we now know the evidence was flawed? Was this a rush to judgment? These and other questions remain, and while some can be answered, others cannot. I was privileged to be part of the process that led to Truscott's acquittal forty-seven years after he was sentenced to be taken to a place of execution and there to be hanged by the neck until dead.

It began in 1959. Truscott was a fourteen-year-old student at the AVM Hugh Campbell School at the Royal Canadian Air Force Base in Clinton, Ontario. So was Lynne Harper. On the evening of June 9, some time between 7:00 and 7:30, Steven was seen riding his racing bike, with Lynn on the crossbar. They were headed north along the well-travelled County Road, running between the base and Highway 8. Steven returned to the base a short time before 8:00; Lynne did not. Later that evening, with no sign of Lynne, her anxious parents called the police.

On June 10, the search intensified. And so did the investigation. Truscott, as the last person to see Lynne alive, was interviewed by police and military personnel four times that day, at 9:30 in the morning, at 12:30, at 5:00, and again at 7:00. His story didn't vary. Other children, too, were interviewed: whom did they see, where, and at what time? The following day, Steven was questioned once more. Lynne's body was found later that day, on the afternoon of June 11, in a wooded area known locally as Lawson's Bush. She had been raped and strangled with a knot made from her own blouse.

Many persons, young and old, saw Lynne and Steven ride off together. According to Steven, Lynne had asked him to give her a lift to the intersection of the County Road and Highway 8, less than a mile from the school. From there, she said, she intended to go and see some ponies at the "white house" on Highway 8. He dropped her off as requested and returned on his bike to the base. At one point he turned around, and just as he did a grey car with some yellow markings—either a license plate or possibly a bumper sticker—stopped and picked up Lynne. That, he told police, was the last time he saw Lynne.

Those who saw Steven when he returned to the base said he was calm, his usual self, and showed no sign that something untoward might have happened. His mother asked him about a tear in his jeans; he said that he had ripped them on his bicycle. Again, nothing unusual.

Various children saw Lynne and Steven on the County Road between the base and Lawson's Bush. Others testified that they did *not* see the pair north of the bush, that is to say closer to Highway 8, and this led investigators to the conclusion that Steven and Lynne never got to Highway 8; that, instead, Steven had turned into a path near the bush, where he raped and strangled Lynn. He would have had three-quarters of an hour to do this—ample time, the investigators suggested, to carry out the heinous deed.

Lynne's body was found by a search party at approximately 1:50. Dr. John Pennistan, the attorney general's regional pathologist, was called to the site, and after an initial examination he directed that the body be removed to the local funeral parlour. There, beginning at 7:15, in a crowded, ill-lit room, he conducted an autopsy. The station's chief medical officer, Dr. David Hall Brooks, was present and took notes. Also present were two police officers. Stomach contents and certain body parts were removed for later examination. In Dr. Pennistan's view, Lynne had died where her body was found and her death had occurred between 7:00 and 7:45 p.m. on June 9.

Three factors led to this conclusion: Lynne had finished her last meal at approximately 5:45. The process of digestion and emptying of the stomach is normally completed within two hours. The food had been badly chewed and very little had passed from the stomach through the duodenum into the small intestine. Had he found a normally chewed meal, digested to the slight extent found here, he would have fixed the time of death closer to her last meal. But, making allowance for the poorly chewed food, he extended this time to two hours, and hence the time-frame suggested by him. The degree to which rigor mortis had subsided, and the extent to which the body had decomposed, were also taken into consideration.

It is, of course, striking that the time fixed by the pathologist fitted exactly Steven's "window of opportunity," and early on the question was asked which had come first: determination by the police that Steven was with Lynne for at least part of that time, or the pathologist's determination that death had occurred during those hours? Or, to put it more bluntly, might Dr. Pennistan have been influenced, consciously or otherwise, by his knowledge that a possible suspect was "available" during that time? It is a question that remains unanswered.

Dr. Pennistan's findings have since been scrutinized by many of the world's leading forensic pathologists. Opinions have been divided, but if one thing is now clearly established, it is that stomach contents are a most unreliable guide to pinpointing a time of death. And the degree of putrefaction and the state of *rigor mortis* are not always of help either, since they depend on many factors, most importantly the weather. Therefore, while death *may* have occurred in the time-frame postulated by the pathologist, it may also have occurred earlier or, even more likely, later.

By then, Inspector Harold Graham, a senior investigator of the Ontario Provincial Police (OPP) had taken charge. He questioned Steven at 10:45 a.m. on the 12th—the day after Lynne's body was found—and took a written statement. Early that evening, Graham took Truscott into custody and questioned him once more. He wanted Steven examined by a doctor. Steven's father, Dan, a warrant officer in the RCAF, insisted that Dr. John Anderson, the family physician, be present. The examination started at 10:15 p.m. and was carried out jointly by Dr. Brooks and Dr. Anderson. The two doctors found lesions on Steven's penis that they believed were caused by a recent sexual adventure. At approximately 2:30 a.m., on June 13, Steven Truscott was formally charged with the murder of Lynne Harper. As Steven was under 16, the charge was laid under the Juvenile Delinquents Act.[216]

What was the basis for this accusation?

Much has been said and written on this point, but high on the list is Inspector Graham's belief that Steven made up the story about Lynne hitching a ride. He was the last person to have seen her alive, and the time of death, as found by the pathologist, fitted the picture. Graham also found inconsistencies in Truscott's various statements to the police. And, there were the lesions on his penis.

On June 30, a judge of the Juvenile Court ordered that Truscott be tried as an adult. An application for leave to appeal this order was denied ten days later.

Three days after that a preliminary hearing was held. It lasted two days and Truscott was committed for trial. Two months later, a grand jury heard evidence and returned a "true bill" of indictment.[217] The trial started the following day.

By today's standards, things moved with incredible speed, but in 1959 the short delays were not unusual. Fundamental objections were made and decided in the course of the trial, not before. Disclosure of evidence by the Crown was the exception, not the rule. All too often, the only notice of what was to come was the Crown's choice of what to present at the preliminary hearing. And with a two-day hearing, that wasn't much.

The trial lasted two weeks, Saturdays included. As the Court of Appeal saw it forty-seven years later, the Crown's case rested on four pillars: (1) Lynne's time of death, as determined by Dr. Pennistan; (2) the evidence of numerous witnesses regarding where they saw Steven and Lynne, and where they did *not* see them on the evening of June 9; (3) evidence of Truscott's post-offence conduct—lies to the police that were indicative of his guilt; and (4) the penis lesions, linked to the fact that the victim had suffered severe vaginal injuries suggestive of a sexual assault.

At 10:55 p.m. on September 30, after deliberating for almost six hours (interrupted a number of times by being recalled to hear further instructions requested by counsel), the 14-year-old accused was found guilty of murder, with a plea by the jury for mercy. But mercy is not within the judge's discretion. He had to pass the only sentence permitted by law and that was what he did: he sentenced Steven to be hanged by the neck until dead, and may the Lord have mercy upon his soul. Steven's eyes filled with tears, he gasped for breath, and he turned very pale.[218] The date of execution was set for December 8, 1959, not quite six months after the fateful bicycle ride.

Truscott's appeal was heard by a panel of five judges[219] five weeks after the verdict. It was dismissed without a dissent.[220] A day later, the federal cabinet, exercising the royal prerogative of mercy, commuted the sentence to imprisonment for life. Leave to appeal to the Supreme Court of Canada was refused. By special arrangement with the province, Steven, because of his young age, served the first part of his sentence at the Ontario Training School for Boys in Guelph. Four days before his eighteenth birthday, however, he was transferred to the federal penitentiary at Collins Bay, on the outskirts of Kingston.

Public interest in the case remained high. In 1966, Isabel LeBourdais published *The Trial of Steven Truscott*,[221] an instant bestseller, in which she concluded that "what Steven Truscott would have had to do to produce every detail of the evidence found on the victim's body or at the scene in Lawson's Bush, was factually and psychologically impossible." And she added this: "Like all democratic countries, Canada has courts, lawyers, police forces and Ministers of Government, all dedicated to upholding justice. Where was justice when Steven was convicted? Where was the evidence of his guilt beyond a reasonable doubt?"

The impact of the book was immense. Within weeks, the federal government, in an unprecedented move, not only referred the case to the Supreme Court of Canada, but also authorized the court to hear fresh evidence.[222] Truscott's legal team was headed by G. Arthur Martin, Canada's foremost criminal lawyer, assisted by E.B. Joliffe and R.J. Carter. The Crown was represented by William Bowman, Ontario's director of public prosecutions, and D.H. Scott. Five formidable lawyers.

Twenty-six witnesses were heard by the Court, including Truscott, who had not testified at his trial. He was not a good witness. As Julian Sher writes, "from the beginning, there were worrying signs that Steve's memory was fuzzy at best." When cross-examined, "Steve continued to display a dismal memory of the most basic events surrounding the crime," denying "even the most innocuous of events." The Court was not impressed. Eight of the nine judges found "many incredibilities inherent in the evidence given by Truscott before us and we do not believe his testimony."[223]

Much time was spent in the Supreme Court on the medical evidence given at trial. Could time of death be ascertained with any degree of certainty—as Dr. Pennistan had suggested—by an examination of the deceased's stomach contents? The Crown, backed by eminent forensic experts, insisted that it could. The defence, backed by equally eminent experts, insisted the opposite. Arthur Martin, in a textbook example of good cross-examination, succeeded in deflating the testimony of Dr. Keith Simpson, the United Kingdom's chief pathologist, who was called by the prosecution in an attempt to buttress Dr. Pennistan's evidence before the jury:

Q. Now you have written extensively, Dr. Simpson, in the field of forensic medicine?
A. Yes.
Q. Now, I've read a good many of your books and one of the books you have written is entitled, *Forensic Medicine* and ... it has gone through five editions now?
A. Yes.
Q. And in the last edition, indeed, you say that this edition has been combed to ensure it is abreast of the times. I notice at page 7 of the book ... you say under the heading of "Cooling" this: "This is the only real guide to the lapse of time during

the first 18 hours after death and an early measurement is often vital to the establishment of an approximate time of death."

A. Yes sir.

Q. Do you, anywhere in the book, suggest that stomach contents and the state to which digestion has proceeded following the last meal is a reliable guide to the time of death?

A. No sir. I think that is, as may be evident to you, a short book for the student.

Q. It would not have made it much bigger to put in a sentence indicating that the stomach contents were also a reliable guide?

A. No sir, I appreciate that, but it is not intended to be a comprehensive work, of course, having been only for students.

Q. It should contain the things upon which there is a greater consensus.

A. I think you may expect the next edition, sir, to contain some reference.

Q. I will throw this away and buy the next edition. You also deal with this in your 12th edition of Taylor which you have edited?

A. Yes sir.

Q. I should say you do deal with stomach contents.

A. There is a reference to the stomach contents there. It is a more comprehensive work.

Q. I think, to be fair, I should read everything that is there so I will not be taking it out of context.

A. I think I know the paragraph you are referring to.

Q. "Inference as to the time of death from the state of food. The site and state of digestion of contents of the stomach and bowels may be used as an additional means for fixing the hour of death in relation to the last meal. Most elaborate tables have been prepared of the time taken by the stomach to digest certain articles of diet but these are wholly unreliable."

Martin continued to read from the text. Simpson interrupted from time to time with explanations. Martin moved on:

Q. I will come to something that is relevant. "Gastric and intestinal activity is much retarded in cases of trauma and insensibility. Even without the paralysis of movement that is common to grave injury or deep insensibility the process of emptying the stomach may be very much delayed."

A. Yes sir.

Q. Am I talking of something that is germane?

A. Yes that's very apt.

Q. That's very apt?

A. Yes.

Q. You quote that the examination of a woman strangled about 11 P.M. one Friday night showed meat fibre, intact peas, fragments of mint leaf and potato together with some apple pits, still present in the stomach. Very little has passed into the duodenum and none into the jejunum. She had her last major meal of roast lamb, peas, boiled potatoes, mint sauce, apple tart and custard at 2:00 to 2:30 P.M. no less than nine hours previously.

A. Yes I remember that case.

Q. ... First of all the cause of death was strangling?

A. Yes.

Q. The cause of death in this case was strangling and the description of the stomach contents is remarkably like the description given by Dr. Pennistan because it is said his examination showed meat fibre, intact peas ... and fragments of mint leaf and potato ... Do you agree that the description is very much like Dr. Pennistan's?

A. Yes.

Q. Very little had passed into the duodenum. Again that is remarkably like Dr. Pennistan's?

A. Yes.

As Martin observed some years later: "Here you had in a book, edited by the witness, a case where the stomach contents, similar to those that existed in the case of Lynne Harper, were proved to have existed notwithstanding a lapse of nine hours since the last meal."[224] Nevertheless, the Supreme Court concluded that "the weight of the new evidence supports Dr. Pennistan's opinion."

On all other aspects, too, the majority of the Court found no error or doubt, and it confirmed the verdict.[225] The lone dissenter was Justice Emmett Hall, the former chief justice of Saskatchewan, the "Establishment Radical."[226] Hall was careful not to pronounce on Truscott's guilt or innocence. To him, the trial process was unfair, and the remedy for an unfair trial would be a new trial.

As Hall's two biographers point out, he believed that at least two of his colleagues, Justices Cartwright and Spence, supported his dissenting view. But a few days later he found that they had joined the majority. According to Dennis Gruendig, Justice Spence said that he was tempted by Hall's arguments. "Because I lean toward the side of the accused," he said, "I was much attracted by Hall's reasons but I couldn't be persuaded. It was a case where Emmett could not persuade us."[227] A much harsher view was expressed by Justice Abbott: "Emmett Hall never had any support on the Court for his stand in Truscott. He was grandstanding, that's all."[228]

The judgment[229] of the Supreme Court of Canada was final: Truscott was guilty. His only hope was to get an early parole. And so he did, on October 21, 1969, almost ten years to the day after being sentenced to hang. But, as I said before, this is a case that haunts the public psyche, and finality would not come for many decades.

Truscott found work after his release in the trade he had learned at Collins Bay. He was introduced to a woman who was anxious to help, and on his release they got married. He helped raise a family and made friends in the community. At first, as required by the Parole Board, he lived under an assumed identity. Later, when his children were older, he told them of his past, and the family resumed his rightful name. But, as Julian Sher says, he remained Canada's most famous convicted murderer, and at the urging of his wife and children he finally set out to try once again to remove the stain of his conviction.

In the mid-1990s, the CBC's *Fifth Estate* program began to take an interest in the case. A team of researchers tracked down and interviewed close to one hundred persons—former child witnesses, police officers, jurors, pathologists, rape specialists, and other medical experts. The program, entirely favourable to Truscott, aired on March 29, 2000. It was seen by 1.4 million viewers. As Sher, who produced the program, notes, "it touched a deep chord with Canadians who had grown up with the story, and reached out to younger citizens who had never heard the name Steven Truscott."[230]

By that time, the Association in Defence of the Wrongly Convicted had taken an interest in the case. The lead lawyer was James Lockyer, Canada's foremost advocate in defence of the wrongly convicted. He was joined by Marlys Edwardh and Philip Campbell, two distinguished criminal lawyers. By 2001, they were ready to make one more attempt to clear their client's name: an application to the federal minister of justice to use her special powers to re-examine the case.[231] The minister, if satisfied that there is "a reasonable basis to conclude that a miscarriage of justice likely occurred," may do one of two things: direct a new trial or refer the case for hearing and determination to the provincial Court of Appeal. Many applications of this nature are made but few are granted. In order to succeed, the applicant must show that new facts have come to light that, had they been known, might have affected the outcome of a case. It is not simply another appeal. Relief under this provision is an extraordinary measure; it is an exercise of the ancient royal prerogative.

To fully understand this remedy, it is important to know that the term "miscarriage of justice" does not necessarily mean that an innocent person was wrongly convicted. While the continued conviction of a person shown to be innocent is the most obvious miscarriage of justice, the finding of new evidence that could reasonably be expected to have affected the verdict also provides a basis for concluding that a miscarriage of justice likely occurred. The reason is that it would be unfair to maintain an accused's conviction without consideration of the new evidence. What the minister therefore must to do is to examine the new evidence proffered, determine if indeed it is new, weigh it, and then decide whether or not it might have affected the outcome of the trial. Only if these questions are answered in the affirmative will the minister have reason to intervene.

Until quite recently, these applications were dealt with largely by lawyers in the Department of Justice. Many still are, but the minister may also refer the application to a retired judge or senior lawyer to assess the evidence and interview witnesses, and make a recommendation as to what should be done. And that is where I came into the picture.

Truscott's application arrived in Ottawa in November 2001, when Anne McLellan was minister of justice. In January 2002, she asked me if I would undertake the investigation and I accepted at once. It was the type of assignment for which I felt uniquely qualified—eighteen years of practice, almost all of it in criminal law, eighteen years on the bench, hearing all parties to a dispute and passing judgment according to law and the evidence, followed by a detailed two-year study of the causes that brought about Guy Paul Morin's wrongful conviction.[232] By the time the engagement letter was ready, McLellan had been transferred to another ministry in a cabinet shuffle, so it was her successor, Martin Cauchon, who made the actual appointment.[233] It was well received by the press. As *The Globe and Mail* put it:

This country's justice system will avoid future miscarriages of justice only if it has the stomach to revisit and analyze its most egregious wrongs. Enough evidence has been found to suggest the system went horribly wrong in this case.

No one can doubt that all the evidence will receive close scrutiny from Fred Kaufman, a former Quebec appeal court judge who wrote a 1,400-page report in 1998 on the wrongful conviction of Guy Paul Morin. He is to advise federal Justice Minister Martin Cauchon on whether enough new and compelling information has surfaced to require another trial or more likely a hearing before an appeal court.

This process may or may not exonerate Mr. Truscott, but it should free the rest of us from the burden of wondering whether, in our name, the justice system horribly wronged an innocent boy and man. This insistence on truth is ultimately the most important line of defence against miscarriages of justice.[234]

Truscott's family was thrilled. "We're extremely happy and we're very excited about this," Truscott's wife, Marlene, told the *Toronto Star*.[235] "They've made a good choice." James Lockyer echoed the sentiment: "We think it's a very positive message .... It's happened quickly and by choosing Justice Kaufman, I think the minister's shown he is taking this application very seriously indeed."[236] A very positive start to an extremely difficult task.

My terms of reference required me to examine the application and provide advice to the minister as to whether or not he should exercise his special powers under the Criminal Code and give relief to the applicant. I asked Mark Sandler, who had worked with me not only in Morin but also in the Nova Scotia residential schools inquiry,[237] to be my counsel, and he put other assignments aside and accepted. We made a good team, and in the two years that followed we examined not only the huge amount of written material from past proceedings, but also thousands of pages of new evidence that had not previously been considered. We also interviewed twenty-six witnesses, some in person, others by telephone, some in Canada, others in the United States and the United Kingdom. All but one appeared when requested. To interview the one who did not, the minister exercised for the first time a power that he had only recently been given by parliament,[238] and authorized me to issue a subpoena. Since there was no precedent and therefore no wording I could copy, I set out to draft a subpoena in terms that I hoped would have the desired effect: "I therefore command you to appear before me." I signed this document and it was served on the witness by the RCMP. She obeyed (failure to do so could have meant punishment by the Superior Court of Justice) and Mark and I interviewed her in a hotel in Alberta.

It took me two years to complete the task and another three months to prepare the requested advice to the minister, a 705-page document, contained in four volumes, with thirty-one appendices. It was, in the words of Irwin Cotler, who by then had become minister of justice, "a monumental exercise."

What I learned in the course of my investigation satisfied me that a substantial amount of material gathered by the police during their investigation was not disclosed to the applicant prior to trial. Other material, prepared later, was not disclosed prior to the reference. Much of it was relevant, and had it been known to the defence, it might well have affected the outcome. There was also new evidence, much of it scientific, all of it helpful to the defence. As in so many other cases, tunnel vision also played its part: the police had a suspect and from that point on their minds were closed to other possibilities. For instance, when Robert Lawson (the owner of Lawson's Bush) reported to the personnel in the guardhouse that he had seen a suspicious car with two occupants near the entrance to the bush at the time of Lynne's disappearance, he was told that the case had already been solved. Other examples of disinterest in other potential perpetrators abound.

All this convinced me that there was reason to believe that a miscarriage of justice had likely occurred. That finding made, it was but a short step to recommend to the minister that relief be given. But what form should it take?

As I said before, in cases such as this, the minister has two choices: order that a new trial be held or refer the case to the Court of Appeal "as if it were an appeal by the convicted person." In my view, the appropriate remedy was a review of the new evidence by the Court of Appeal. This would enable the applicant to demonstrate to a court of law that the "new" evidence offered was indeed "fresh" evidence within the meaning of the law, that it was relevant, that it was capable of belief, and that, had it been known to the applicant at the time of his trial, it might well have affected the conduct of his case and therefore the verdict.

When I sent my report to the minister, I asked a senior member of his department if I should prepare for the minister's convenience an executive summary of my findings. The answer was that there was no need to do so: "This minister reads everything." And so he did, followed by a three-hour meeting with me at which he asked some very probing questions.

The decision to grant the application and order a review by the Court of Appeal was announced by the minister at a press conference on October 28, 2004. Truscott's wife was not happy. "It's a disgrace; I think it's a copout," she told reporters.[239] She, the lawyers, and her husband's many supporters had hoped that the minister would order a new trial and bypass the Court of Appeal. But Truscott himself was more philosophical: "They had sentenced me to death once, so anything else is a plus. I'll be vindicated. It will just take longer."[240] Prophetic words.

An editorial in *The Globe and Mail* called it "The right path for Steven Truscott."[241] George Jonas, writing in the *National Post*, agreed:

Sending the case back to an appeal court disappointed Mr. Truscott's legal team. They would have preferred that Mr. Cotler order a new trial, followed by the prosecution calling no evidence in court. Though such an outcome wouldn't specifically absolve

Mr. Truscott, it would be quick, risk-free and amount to virtual exoneration.

A tribunal re-examining everything, on the other hand, is neither quick nor risk-free. The Ontario Court of Appeal could, in theory, condemn Mr. Truscott again, just as the Supreme Court did in 1966.

It's tempting to say that, after all Mr. Truscott has been through, he shouldn't be exposed to the delay and jeopardy of yet another tribunal... Still, I'd argue that Mr. Cotler made the right decision. One mockery of justice isn't remedied by another. It would be a charade for the Minister to order a new trial, knowing that Mr. Truscott won't ever be tried.

The Ontario Court of Appeal is the forum where justice can be done, and also seen to be done. Anything else would amount to using the same cracks in the system to exonerate Mr. Truscott as were used to railroad him 45 years ago.[242]

As predicted, the proceedings in the Court of Appeal were not fast. Indeed, with the mass of evidence to be compiled, printed, and examined, even when done with all possible speed, many months had to pass before the case was ready. But on January 31, 2007, five judges, presided by the Chief Justice of Ontario, mounted the bench and listened for the next ten days to counsel's arguments. Many questions were asked and answered—it was a thorough hearing.

The court's 304-page judgment was delivered on August 28, 2007. It was unanimous: a miscarriage of justice had occurred and Truscott was acquitted of the charge he had faced as a child. With a smile on his face, he told the press later that day: "They finally got it right."[243]

What brought about the acquittal? The short answer is fresh evidence. It destroyed the "four pillars" of the Crown's case, if not completely, then at least to the point where the court felt obliged to reverse the original verdict. In clear and tightly drafted reasons, the judges examined the evidence item by item, witness by witness. And they concluded that if the defence at trial, or Truscott's legal team on the reference, had known what has since come to light, the verdict would likely have been different.

There are some striking examples of this. For instance, while Dr. Pennistan was quite firm at trial in fixing the time of death—clearly a crucial element— he sent a "clarification" of his earlier work to Inspector Graham prior to the reference to the Supreme Court of Canada. This is what it said in part:

In the review [which the Crown had requested] I have tried to clarify the facts as set out in the PM report on Lynne HARPER and the transcripts and to restate the conclusions drawn from them and expressed in the same places. I do not believe I have changed any of my essential conclusions as a result of my review (one is tempted to refer to it as an "agonizing reappraisal" in the current jargon: the adjective is probably better justified here than in most cases) but I must depend on someone else to assess whether there has been any significant change in the expression of these views. Your detailed knowledge of the transcript will enable you to do this better than most.

Dr. Pennistan then discussed in detail the various factors mentioned in his original report (stomach contents, rigor mortis, decomposition) and concluded:

1. All findings are compatible with death within 2 hours of Lynne's last meal. However—
2. The degree of *rigor* and decomposition are also compatible with death at a later time.
3. The state of the stomach contents is also compatible with death at a later hour provided that digestion and emptying were delayed by some physical or psychological episode occurring within approximately two hours of the last meal.

But this never came to light until the defence team prepared their application to the minister. It does not take great skill to imagine what Arthur Martin could have done with this had he known about this "agonizing reappraisal." As the Court of Appeal wryly noted, this document "suggests an evolution in Dr. Pennistan's description of his observations of the stomach contents. That evolution is consistent with the appellant's contention that Dr. Pennistan sought to make his evidence consistent with the Crown's theory on the time of death."

Another example of fresh evidence concerned newly discovered statements made by witnesses shortly after the homicide. Had they been known to the defence, the evidence given in court by these witnesses could have been challenged and might well have destroyed the Crown's case of when and where Truscott was seen on the County Road. This is what the Court of Appeal said on that point:

While it is impossible to fix on one reasonable version of [the County Road] evidence to the exclusion of all other versions, the archival material discovered by the appellant's counsel, combined with the other available material, would permit a formidable challenge to the Crown's theory as it relates to [this] evidence. An alternative version of that evidence which places the appellant on the County Road at a later time than argued by the Crown, and which thereby neutralizes the Crown's County Road evidence, could be constructed from the material. Even if the Crown's version of the County Road evidence remains a plausible one, there are certainly other plausible versions that could support the defence position.

All this might well have been dismissed as speculation, and the court recognized that this was so. But with the multitude of questionable incidents which Truscott's counsel managed to demonstrate, it soon became clear that there was but one just solution, and that was to acquit the appellant. To order a new trial, as a Court of Appeal would normally have done in cases where doubt was cast on the integrity and fairness of a trial, would have been an exercise in futility. Indeed, Crown counsel told the court that this could not be done: evidence had been destroyed, witnesses had died, and even those who had testified and were still living (and many of the child witnesses were) could no longer recall the events with the precision required in a court of law. The remedy, therefore, was clear.

The judgment of acquittal exonerated Truscott. But it re-opened old wounds for Lynne Harper's family. If not Truscott, then who? This we may never know. Nine potential perpetrators—known sex offenders who lived in the vicinity— who should have been investigated were not. It may now be too late. Regrettably (though not surprisingly) there is no DNA. This marker was unknown in 1959, and slides taken by the pathologist, which might disclose the killer's DNA, cannot be found. Perhaps some day they will turn up. And even though the Commissioner of the Ontario Provincial Police has indicated that the case may now be re-opened, it may well be too cold as cold cases go.

So what went wrong?

Dreadful though it sounds, the simple answer is "the usual things." That may be a cynical view, but regrettably we are all too familiar with the litany of mistakes that are made by investigators, and sometimes by the crown and even the court, which affect the integrity of a verdict. One need only look at a string of Canadian cases: Donald Marshall, Jr.,[244] Guy Paul Morin,[245] Thomas Sophonow,[246] Gregory Parsons,[247] James Driskell,[248] and, most recently, Anthony Hanemaayer.[249] And then, of course, there is David Milgaard, who served 23 years in the penitentiary for a murder he did not commit.[250]

The errors tend to repeat themselves: tunnel vision by the police, faulty eye-witness identification and testimony, ill-prepared and misleading forensic evidence, incomplete disclosure by the crown, a rush to judgment.

The final chapter in *Truscott*—if anything can ever be said to be final in this case—came in 2008, when the Ontario government accepted a recommendation made by Sydney L. Robins, a former justice of the Court of Appeal for Ontario, that Truscott receive $6.5 million by way of compensation for his ordeal. In making the announcement, Chris Bentley, the attorney general, said this:

> Given the exceptional nature of this case, Mr. Robins was asked to provide recommendations regarding compensation for Mr. Truscott, and I have accepted his advice .... I hope that Mr. Truscott and his family will now have the opportunity to move forward with their lives. My thoughts are also with the family of Lynne Harper, who will continue to live with the tragedy of their loss forever.[251]

What made this case "exceptional" is, in the words of Justice Robins, the fact

> that in all of the cases to date where compensation has been paid the innocence of the wrongfully convicted person has been established by some means—whether by DNA evidence, or by subsequent conviction of the perpetrator, or by determination following a police investigation or judicial inquiry that there was no evidence that the wrongfully convicted person committed the crime, or where there was no evidence that a crime had even be committed.[252]

However, as Justice Robins noted, a rule limiting the state's payment of compensation to those persons who can prove their factual innocence might be unduly harsh, with the further complication that it is not at all clear what standard of proof should be required—is it beyond a reasonable doubt (which generally applies only to the prosecution) or should it be the lighter burden of "balance of probabilities." These, the report suggests, are matters "for study and debate in the context of the development of a legislative scheme designed to provide a systematic basis upon which compensation for the wrongfully convicted can be determined." Be that as it may, Justice Robins concluded that, for Mr. Truscott, "vindication would not be complete without compensation," and hence his recommendation to the government that compensation be paid.

◆ ◆ ◆

In 2005, the Canadian Department of Justice published a report "on the prevention of miscarriages of justice." It dealt with the most common causes of wrongful convictions, and it urged extreme caution on the part of all participants in the process. This is what it said, in part:

> No matter how many cases are successfully prosecuted every day in our court-rooms, wrongful convictions, regardless of how infrequent, are a reminder of the fallibility of the justice system and a stain on its well-deserved positive reputation.
>
> Public confidence in the administration of justice is fostered by demonstrating that participants in the criminal justice system are willing to take action to prevent future miscarriages of justice. It is also important to foster public understanding that fair, independent and impartial police investigations and Crown prosecutions are in the public interest.
>
> Various commissions and studies, in Canada and around the world, have provided valuable insight into the systemic causes of wrongful convictions and into what has gone wrong in individual cases. What is startling, however, is that some problems, themes and mistakes arise time and time again, regardless of where the miscarriage of justice took place. These problems relate to the conduct of police, Crowns, defence lawyers, judges and forensic scientists, and they are not confined to proceedings in the courtroom.
>
> When a miscarriage of justice occurs, it is not usually the result of just one mistake, but rather a combination of events. Therefore, just as the problems and errors are multi-layered, so too must the solution also be multi-faceted.

Wise words, but will anyone heed them?

[epilogue]

I turned eighty in May 2004. My wife and children marked the occasion with a splendid black-tie dinner in Toronto. It was a moving event, an outpouring of love and affection, expressed with an eloquence that I cannot match.

Donna went first:

Fred has not always done things at what might be considered an age-appropriate time. He left home at fifteen. He married at forty-three. He earned an MBA at sixty-nine. At eighty, he is arguably more engaged and stimulated—and, perhaps, happier—than at any other time in his life.

When my father passed away, I was twenty-three and he was fifty-five. Fred was forty-three—the age at which my father had his first heart attack. I was concerned. My mother said I shouldn't be.

She said that Fred seemed like a wonderful man, that age is irrelevant, that some people have one year, others many, many more.

I followed my heart.

I did the right thing.

This is a man whose mother treated me as if I were her daughter—and Fred wasn't good enough for me.

This is a man whose mother was ecstatic that our first child was a girl. I didn't understand—Fred was a wonderful son. "You'll never have to send her to war," she said.

And, when we told her just a few months later that I was pregnant again, she was thrilled. "Leslie," she said, "will never be alone."

An unusual woman. An extraordinary son.

Leslie, David and I are the beneficiaries of what that produced—an exceptional human being whose love and friendship and availability are unwavering, whose judgment is invariably sound—and whose wonder at being eighty is truly endearing. I am immensely grateful that we have reached this milestone together. I appreciate Fred more than he can imagine and love him completely.

Can anyone ask for more?

What our children had to say also touched me deeply. Leslie went first:

As a child I always knew that, no matter what the problem, my father could convince me that everything was going to be alright. My dad continues to have an unbelievable knack for saying just the right thing at the right time to make me feel better about whatever is troubling me.

I have a vivid recollection of boarding a bus to make the big trip from Montreal to Algonquin Park to attend a sleep-away camp for the first time. I was nine and I had spent weeks persuading my parents to let me go to camp. They finally relented and as I was hugging my family goodbye it suddenly hit me that I wouldn't see them for four whole weeks—which seemed like an eternity—and I was overwhelmed with homesickness.

Big tears welled in my eyes and my dad, realizing what was going through my mind, whispered something into my ear that I will never forget: "All you need to do is make one friend and the rest will be easy." Of course, he was right and there have been many occasions in the years that followed when I have taken comfort from those same words of wisdom.

When I was seventeen and had my backpack stolen at a bus station in Australia, I called my parents—at 3 a.m. their time—in a panic. My dad answered the phone and calmly asked me what was wrong. When I told him what had transpired, he asked: "Do you still have your passport?" "Yes, dad." "And do you have your credit card?" "Yes, dad." "Then you are fine," he said. "It will be an adventure." And of course it was. There I was, literally on the other side of the world, once again reassured that I was not alone.

Leslie then recalled the day when she was in grade school and I took her and her brother to watch a criminal trial:

He left us for the morning, and when he came to pick us up I was extremely distraught. He asked me what was wrong and I began to sob—I couldn't stand to see someone in handcuffs. I felt so sorry for him I wanted to help. That is when my dad explained the role of the defence lawyer, that he or she was there to help the accused and speak for them. It was this experience that ultimately motivated me to assume that very same role.

And she concluded:

Not only am I immensely proud of my father, but I am truly inspired by him as well. As all of you already know, my dad is a person who always manages to see the good in things, something which never ceases to amaze me.

I often wondered why, after everything that he endured as an adolescent, he remains such an optimistic man. I think the answer to this question lies in the fact that he has been through so much more than many of us can even imagine. He has witnessed and been subjected to the ultimate in arbitrary unfairness, yet he has been fortunate to see goodness in people that is often only apparent in the most devastating of situations. He never dwelled on the negatives. Instead, he told us stories about the wonderful people he met along the way and who changed his life forever—the Fells in England, the Mittlemans in Sherbrooke, and others.

I am deeply honoured to be with all of you here tonight to celebrate this very special and unique man—my father.

I say again, can anyone ask for more?

David served as the master of ceremonies and he spoke last. "What makes him so special to all of us?" he asked, and these were his answers:

He is wise. In his case I use the word "wisdom" as the fusion of intelligence, industry, and knowledge. Intelligence without industry is to have capital without leverage. Knowledge without intelligence is to have a tool but no way to apply it. When hard work is coupled with knowledge and keen intelligence, the product is someone who knows it all without being a know-it-all.

He is gentle. He is the quintessential gentleman. Not only in the sense of someone who is cordial, well dressed, and generally proper (which he is), but also in the sense of being a man who possesses the qualities of being honest, fair, and generous. He is someone who cares equally about the ability of those less fortunate to improve their lot in life as he does about people of privilege maintaining their material possessions and social standing.

He is curious. While others wake each day and lounge over a cup of coffee and watch television, he is busy reading five newspapers before breakfast. And not just a casual perusal. He reads every story, covering every topic. In his world, nothing is uninteresting. He is curious about the world and even more about people. Everyone has a story, and he wants to hear it.

Finally, he is human. Having lived through the Nazi occupation of Austria and the slaughter of 30 million souls in World War II, one could understand, even expect, my father to be cynical, expecting the worst of people at every turn. Rather, he seeks out and finds the best qualities in people with whom he comes into contact. And those people are numerous because he is so engaging with everyone he meets.

I fear that my reply was most inadequate:

My road has not always been easy. There were good years in my life and there were bad years. But the good years so outnumber the bad years that I can truly say this has been a wonderful journey. And the most wonderful part of it is a wonderful marriage, now in its 37th year, and every bit as exciting today as it was on the day we said "Yes, I do," and set out together on this marvellous adventure. It is a love affair which has sustained me and kept me young in spirit and in body. Thank you, Donna.

I don't have to tell you how proud I am of the accomplishments of my wife and my children. How many men or women, already engaged in a busy career as well as raising two children, wake up one morning at the age of 38 and say, "I have decided to become a lawyer." Of course, there were obstacles to be overcome, not least among them the lack of an undergraduate degree. But Donna did it, and four years later she was indeed a lawyer, and soon became one of the best in her chosen field. And then on to corporate directorships, in Canada and abroad, and again she quickly became one of the best.

Leslie and David have done well, and I am blessed to have such wonderful and caring children. But never have I been as touched with anything they did, for me or for others, as I was last night when the four of us had a family dinner, and Leslie and David produced a small bag from Birks, with an even smaller box inside, and said "Happy Birthday." It was a lovely pair of cufflinks, but even before I could tell them how much I liked them, they said: "This is the tangible part of your present." The intangible part—and I am thrilled and excited—is that in honour of my special birthday they resolved to contribute their time and special talents—and this will be a lifelong commitment—to do good things at the Baycrest Centre for

Geriatric Care, David with the Foundation to help raise funds, and Leslie with the good work that Baycrest does to make the lives of the remaining Holocaust survivors a little more bearable. I can't begin to tell you how much this means to me and I am touched beyond words.

◆ ◆ ◆

I am now eighty-five, and I not only have a wonderful wife and two great children, but also a delightful five-year-old granddaughter, Alexandra Rebecca Kaufman, known to all as Ali. She was adopted by Leslie in 2004 from Birobidzhan in Russia[253], and she is the sweetest and most delightful young child, who brings us much joy. I don't know what the future holds but, given strength, I hope to carry on. The love and support of those around me mean more than I can say. How truly fortunate I am.

[notes]

1. Paul Hoffmann, *The Viennese: Splendor, Twilight, and Exile* (New York and London: Anchor Press/Doubleday, 1989), 172. Many books have been written about life in Vienna in the years between the two World Wars. Two others that stand out and on which I have extensively drawn are Carl E. Schorske, *Fin-du-siécle Vienna: Politics and Culture* (New York: Alfred A. Knopf 1980), and Hilde Spiel, *Vienna's Golden Autumn: 1866–1938* (London: Weidenfeld and Nicholson, 1987). Some of the historical material in this chapter comes from Robert S. Wistrich, *The Jews of Vienna in the Age of Franz Joseph* (Oxford, U.K.: Oxford University Press, 1989), and Max Grunwald, *History of the Jews of Vienna* (Philadelphia: Jewish Publication Society of America, 1936).

2. Lord Weidenfeld, *Remembering My Good Friends* (London: HarperCollins, 1995), 7.

3. An interesting account of the lives of Jews in Moravia can be found in Helen Epstein, *Where She Came From: A Daughter's Search for Her Mother's History* (Boston: Little, Brown, 1997).

4. Ibid., 49.

5. *National Post*, June 22, 2004. For the origins and meaning of Kabbalah, see David A. Cooper, *God Is a Verb: Kabbalah and the Practice of Mystical Judaism* (New York: Riverhead Books, 1997).

6. (New York: Holt, Rinehart and Winston, 1982).

7. Henry Grunwald, *One Man's America: A Journalist's Search for the Heart of His Country* (New York: Doubleday, 1997).

8. Quoted in Robert S. Wistrich, *The Jews of Vienna in the Age of Franz Joseph* (Oxford, U.K.: Oxford University Press, 1989), 625.

9. Ibid., 131 & ff.

10. The *Stadttempel*, as it was formerly called, was consecrated in 1826 by Rabbi Isaac Noah Mannheimer from Copenhagen, who had been called to Vienna the year before to be

the principal of the Israelite School of Religion. Until the formal establishment of the Jewish community twenty-six years later, this title, officially recognized by the civil authorities, covered his de facto activity as rabbi to the Jews of Vienna. A "liberal" in outlook and faith, he is generally credited with having prevented a public break between Orthodox and Reform movements and factions, such as later occurred in Germany and Hungary. Mannheimer was soon joined in Vienna by Solomon Sulzer, then twenty-one, who took charge of the liturgical music. He had an exquisite voice and became much admired not only by his congregants but also by the outside world. As Edward Rothstein recalled in the *New York Times* (December 10, 1991), when the composer Robert Schumann was in Vienna, he made a point to attend the main synagogue to hear the cantor. Franz Schubert wrote the music for a Hebrew setting of Psalm 92 ("Sing praises to the Lord") for him, and Sulzer gave one concert accompanied on the piano by Franz Liszt, who later wrote that the cantor had sounded as if he had personally heard King David's harp or had participated in the building of the pyramids. I am not sure what the pyramids had to do with it, but it was meant to be a compliment.

[11] Daniel Mendelsohn, *The Lost: A Search for Six of Six Million* (New York: Harper Perennial, 2007).

[12] Ron Chernow, *The Warburgs* (New York: Random House, 1993), 325.

[13] By most estimates, there were 180,000 Jews in Vienna in 1938. Today there are less than 10,000. Those who escaped found refuge in many parts of the world, and by way of example, at one time I had relatives in Romania, China, Japan, Australia, Israel, Argentina, and the United States—and we were a small family.

[14] David Edmonds and John Eidinow, *Wittgenstein's Poker* (New York: HarperCollins, 2001), 122.

[15] *Les Prix Nobel* (Stockholm: Norstedts Tryckeri).

[16] While the United States did admit 90,000 Jewish refugees from Germany, the director of immigration, Breckenridge Long, who "looked upon most Jews as grubby and distasteful," did his best to delay the flow. In a memorandum written in the summer of 1940, he suggested that "we can delay and stop the number of immigrants into the United States ... by simply advising our consulates to put every obstacle in the way and require additional evidence and to resort to various administrative devices which would postpone and postpone and postpone and postpone the granting of the visas." Henry L. Feingold, *The Politics of Rescue: The Roosevelt Administration and the Holocaust 1938–1945* (New Brunswick, N.J.: Rutgers University Press, 1970), quoted in Conrad Black, *Franklin Delano Roosevelt: Champion of Freedom* (New York: Public Affairs, 2003) particularly 814–16. As recently discovered documents show, even powerful connections and money were not enough to enable European Jews, including Anne Frank's father, Otto, to break through

the State Department's tightening restrictions: Patricia Cohen, "In Old Files, Fading Hopes of Anne Frank's Family," *The New York Times*, February 15, 2007.

[17] Irving Abella and Harold Troper, *None Is Too Many: Canada and the Jews of Europe 1933–1948* (Toronto: Lester and Orpen Dennys, 1982), ix. The authors attribute this phrase to an "anonymous senior Canadian official" who, in the midst of a rambling, off-the-record discussion with journalists in early 1945, was asked how many Jews would be allowed into Canada after the war. His spontaneous response was "none is too many," and that seems to have been the attitude in the pre-war years as well.

[18] See n. 7.

[19] Ruth Kluger, *Still Alive* (New York: Feminine Press at the City University of New York, 2001), 9.

[20] Mark Jonathan Harris and Deborah Oppenheimer (London: Bloomsbury Publishing 2000), 10. A documentary, by the same name, was prepared and distributed by Warner Bros. Pictures and Sabina Films. It won an Academy Award and is now available on DVD.

[21] Edith Milton, *The Tiger in the Attic* (Chicago: University of Chicago Press, 2005), 14.

[22] *Into the Arms of Strangers*, 13.

[23] Harris and Oppenheimer, *Into the Arms of Strangers*, 108.

[24] Privately published. I am indebted to her daughter, Alison Hotz de Baar, for making the above quotation available to me.

[25] Mrs. Rose's original name was Rosentrauch, but when she arrived in England the officer who processed her registration said "Nobody will be able to pronounce this" and changed it to Rose. (Communication from Mrs. Rose's granddaughter, Dr. Helen Liesl Krag.)

[26] *Into the Arms of Strangers*, 132–35.

[27] The events leading to the internment in England of enemy aliens are described in great detail by Peter and Leni Gillman in their well-researched book *Collar the Lot* (London: Quartet Books, 1980). The title comes from an order given by Churchill on June 10, 1940, when he decided that all Italian nationals living in Britain should be interned.

[28] *Collar the Lot* (London: Quartet Books, 1980), 95.

[29] May 23, 1980.

[30] *London Jewish Chronicle*, May 23, 1980.

[31] *That Was the War*, August 12, 1985. Perutz, a Cambridge Ph.D., was sent to Canada but was later returned to England and released. In 1943 he found himself back in Canada as a representative of the British Admiralty. This time, he wrote, I was "accommodated in a suite in Ottawa's luxurious Hotel Château Laurier without being searched for lice." He had been recruited by Lord Mountbatten to work on Project Habakkuk—a series of floating islands in the Atlantic that would allow planes to be flown from the United States to Britain instead of being shipped. Alas, the project failed to materialize. In

1962, Perutz received the Nobel Prize in chemistry, with John Kendrew, for their studies in the structure of globular proteins. He died in 2002. See also Georgina Ferry, *Max Perutz and the Secret of Life* (London: Chatto & Windus, 2007). Another ex-internee, Walter Kohn, also received the Nobel Prize in chemistry (in 1998). When released from internment, he applied to study chemistry at the University of Toronto, but the head of the department ruled because war work was then in progress, Kohn, as a German citizen, could not enter the building. So he took a degree in applied mathematics and then left for Cambridge to continue his studies. See Joe Fiorito, "Little Things Matter to Nobel Winner," *National Post*, April 7, 2000.

[32] Sir Michael Kerr, *As Far As I Remember* (Oxford and Portland, Oregon: Hart Publishing, 2006), 133. The Berlin-born Kerr, then a student at Cambridge, was released six months later. He served with distinction in the RAF, went to the Bar after the war, and finished a distinguished career as the Rt. Hon. Sir Michael Kerr, a Lord Justice of Her Majesty's Court of Appeal in England. He died in 2005.

[33] The Sobieski was 511 feet long and its maximum speed was 17 knots. She was designed to carry 70 first-class passengers, 270 in cabin class, and 600 in tourist class. She remained in service until 1975 when she was sold to a scrapyard in Russia.

[34] Toronto: Methuen, 1980, 55.

[35] Ibid., 66.

[36] The trials of this fateful voyage are recounted in a book published in Australia in 1979 by Benzion Patkin, who was actively involved in aiding the refugee–internees after their release from custody: *The Dunera Internees* (Melbourne: Cassel Australia).

[37] For a detailed account of the Fredericton internment camp, see Ted Jones, *Both Sides of the Wire* (Fredericton: New Ireland Press, 1988). A documentary based on the book was produced in 1993 by Neal Livingston and shown in Canada on VISION TV.

[38] Eric Koch, *Deemed Suspect: A Wartime Blunder* (Toronto: Methuen 1980), 126.

[39] Ron Csillag, in an obituary published in *The Globe and Mail* on September 27, 2003. See also Norman Doidge, "Emil Fackenheim: Thinking through Radical Evil," *National Post*, September 27, 2003. See also Eric Koch, *I Remember the Location Exactly* (Oakville, Ontario: Mosaic Press, 2006), 165 & ff.

[40] Quoted by Vernon Brooks in the *McGill News*, Winter 2001–2002. Brooks, himself a graduate of the camp school, was an assistant professor of physiology at McGill and later professor emeritus at the University of Western Ontario.

[41] Eric Koch, *Deemed Suspect: A Wartime Blunder* (Toronto: Methuen, 1980), 189.

[42] Chaim Raphael, *Memoirs of a Special Case* (London: Chatto and Windus, 1962), 204.

[43] Alfred Bader, *Alfred Bader: Adventures of a Chemist Collector* (London: Weidenfeld and Nicolson, 1995).

[44] The term "accidental immigrants" was coined by Paula Jean Draper in a paper published in the Jewish Historical Society's *Journal* in the spring of 1978. It is called "The Accidental Immigrants: Canada and the Interned Refugees." A somewhat similar term, "inadvertent immigrants," was used by Barbara Moon in an article in *Maclean's*.

[45] Order-in-Council *Re Immigration Status of Refugees*, P.C. 9140, December 10, 1943.

[46] Order-in-Council *Re Status of Refugees*, P.C. 6687, October 26, 1945.

[47] "The Welcome Enemies," February 10, 1962. In the article, Moon describes the "camp boys" who remained in Canada as "as fine an assortment of architects, artists, businessmen, chemists, dentists, engineers, economists, film-makers, geophysicists, historians, journalists, lawyers, mathematicians, musicians, novelists, philosophers, psychiatrists, research workers, religious leaders, sociologists, teachers, television executives and university professors as one could wish."

[48] Sonja Sinclair, *Maclean's*, May 15, 2000.

[49] Ibid.

[50] April 7, 2001.

[51] This was the standard National Selective Service call-up form for Military District No. 4 (Montreal and vicinity).

[52] Bishop's had a longer academic year than most universities, and so its degrees could be obtained in three years rather than the standard four.

[53] Bill Weintraub, *Why Rock the Boat?* (Toronto and Boston: Little, Brown, 1961), 5.

[54] Perhaps the *Montreal Star* was simply ahead of its time. The word "rape" was removed from the Criminal Code in 1980, and various degrees of "sexual assault" now describe offences that formerly were known as "rape" and "indecent assault."

[55] Pierre Berton, *Starting Out* (Toronto: McClelland and Stewart, 1987), 274.

[56] Many years later, when Dale Thomson interviewed St. Laurent for his biography, the former prime minister and his wife recalled the incident.

[57] Bill Weintraub, *City Unique: Montreal Days and Nights in the 1940s and '50s* (Toronto: McClelland and Stewart, 1996), 121.

[58] http://www.mcgill.ca/maritimelaw/tetley/plimsoll.

[59] Weintraub, *City Unique*, 76.

[60] The reason I kept track of my comings and goings that year was that I had been asked by the *Star*'s house organ, *The Slug*, to tell its readers about the life of a reporter.

[61] *La Grève de l'amiante* (Montreal: Éditions Cité libre, 1956). This searching and wide-ranging book was published under the direction of Pierre Elliott Trudeau, then a professor at the Université de Montreal, and it contains nine essays by such well-known thinkers as Father Gérard Dion, Gérard Pelletier, Maurice Sauvé, and Trudeau himself.

[62] Technically, there is no such thing in Canada as a Riot Act. What in fact is read is a

proclamation, set out in section 67 of the Criminal Code. Failure to obey the command to disburse may result in imprisonment for life.

[63] Four books in particular stand out in my mind: *The Autobiography of Sir Patrick Hastings* (London: William Heinemann 1948); Patricia Hastings, *The Life of Patrick Hastings* (London: Cresset Press, 1959); Gerald Rufus Isaacs, *Rufus Isaacs, First Marquess of Reading* (New York: G.P. Putnam's Sons, 1940); and idem., *Rufus Isaacs, First Marquess of Reading 1914–1935* (London: Hutchinson, 1945).

[64] See *The Trial at Large of Her Majesty Caroline Amelia Elizabeth, Queen of Great Britain; in the House of Lords, on Charges of Adulterous Intercourse* (London: T. Kelly, 1821).

[65] The point at issue was whether the wife of the heir to the throne (as Caroline was at the time of the alleged incidents) is guilty of high treason if she commits adultery in a foreign country with a foreigner who owes no allegiance to the crown of England. The lord chief justice, assisted by his colleagues, ruled that, in law, the answer is no, and Caroline was cleared of the charges. While the issue had some bearing on subsequent state trials involving foreign nationals, the case is best remembered for the ringing declaration of a lawyer's duty made by Henry Brougham, the Queen's attorney general, who said: "An advocate, in the discharge of his duty, knows but one person in all the world, and that person is his client. To save that client by all means and expedients, and at all hazards and costs to other persons, and, among them, to himself, is his first and only duty; and in performing this duty he must not regard the alarm, the torments, the destruction which he may bring upon others. Separating the duty of a patriot from that of an advocate, he must go on reckless of consequences, though it should be his unhappy fate to involve his country in confusion." Brougham went on to become lord chancellor. His words, quoted above, were cited with approval by the Supreme Court of Canada as recently as 2002 in *R. v. Neil*, [2002] 3 S.C.R. 631. More recently, in a book review in *The Economist* (December 9, 2006), the essence of the case was put as follows: "A young woman weds the Prince of Wales and finds that there are three in the marriage. She seeks solace in the arms of a foreigner, attracts intense media attention, becomes the darling of the people, and after proceedings for divorce, dies suddenly. For sheer entertainment and political theatre, the story of Caroline of Brunswick far outstrips the tale of Diana, Princess of Wales."

[66] Frank Scott and David Lewis, *Make This YOUR Canada: A Review of CCF History and Policy* (Toronto: Central Canada Publishing, 1943).

[67] *The Collected Poems of F. R. Scott* (Toronto: McClelland and Stewart, 1981).

[68] *R. V. Brodie*, [1962] S.C.R. 681.

[69] For an appreciation of Laskin's contributions to the law, see "Bora Laskin: The Legacy," *University of Toronto Law Journal*, Vol. 35, No. 4 (Fall 1985).

70 An Act to Authorize the Bar of the Province of Quebec to Admit Jean Caumartin, William Miller, Jack Shayne, Orville Frenette, Abe Shuster, François Larose, Fred Kaufman, Phil Cutler, Maurice Jacques and Abel Selick to the Practice of the Profession of Advocate, after Examination, S.Q. 1953-4, 2-3 Eliz., c. 179. All ten passed the required examinations and were called to the Bar. Three—Frenette, Cutler, and Jacques—later became judges of the Superior Court. Jacques, a former merchant marine officer, was subsequently promoted to the Court of Appeal, where he became a valued colleague of mine.

71 October 1992.

72 George D. Finlayson, *John J. Robinette: Peerless Mentor* (Toronto: Osgoode Society for Canadian Legal History, University of Toronto Press, 2003), 43.

73 The Court of Queen's Bench—the title goes back to antiquity—had two divisions, trial and appellate. However, civil trials were held in the Superior Court; the jurisdiction of the Queen's Bench trial division, known as the Court of Queen's Bench (Crown side), was limited to jury trials of indictable offences. But the appellate division, known simply as the Court of Queen's Bench, heard appeals from all jurisdictions, civil and criminal. This created a lot of confusion, and by the mid-1970s this nomenclature was changed and we now have a *chambre criminelle* of the Superior Court, which replaced the Court of Queen's Bench (Crown side), and a Court of Appeal.

74 The idea of having a student-edited law journal at McGill was first presented to the faculty by Jacques-Yvan Morin, who was a year ahead of me. Jacques knew of my experience in the newspaper world, and he invited me to work with him on the project. The faculty approved, Jacques was appointed editor-in-chief, and the first issue was published in 1953. I succeeded Jacques as editor-in-chief later that year. After postgraduate studies in Europe, Jacques taught constitutional law at the Université de Montréal. In later years, he advocated independence for Quebec, entered politics, and was elected to the legislature. He served as vice-premier under René Lévesque from 1976 to 1984.

75 Fred Kaufman, *The Admissibility of Confessions in Criminal Matters* (Toronto: Carswell, 1960). Two subsequent editions were published in 1974 and 1979.

76 (1963), 40 C.R. 90. The majority was Smith C.J., and Porter and Kane JJ.A. The dissenting judges were Johnson and Parker JJ.A. The defence was represented by the veteran Edmonton lawyer, A.W. Miller, and the crown by M.M. deWeert, later Justice deWeert of the Supreme Court of the Northwest Territories.

77 (1963), 40 C.R. 105.

78 (1980), 26 C.R. (3d) 343 at 353ff.

79 *Hansard*, 1921, 3921.

80 Section 206(2) of the Criminal Code provides that "three-card monte" means "the game commonly known as three-card monte and includes any other game that is similar to it." To induce any person "to stake or hazard any money ... on the result ... of three-card monte" is an indictable offence, punishable by imprisonment for a term not exceeding two years.

81 Montreal then had two courthouses, the Old and the New. The New was built in the 1920s, the Old a century before. They were replaced in 1970 by a new courthouse, called the *Palais de Justice*, a seventeen-storey steel structure that housed all courts, civil and criminal. The Old Court House was sold by the province to the city of Montreal, which gutted most of the interior but preserved the exterior, with its gleaming white cupola. The New Court House was turned into the provincial conservatory of music, but in 2004, with space at a premium in the *Palais*, the Court of Appeal was moved to the "old" New Court House, which at great cost was restored to its former elegance.

82 July 12, 2004.

83 The word "insanity" no longer appears in the Criminal Code. The Code now speaks of "mental disorder," and where a judge or jury finds that the accused was incapable of appreciating the nature and quality of an act or omission by reason of mental disorder, the verdict shall be that "the accused committed the act or made the omission but is not criminally responsible on account of mental disorder": section 672.34, Criminal Code.

84 Judge Sissons, *Judge of the Far North: The Memoirs of Jack Sissons* (Toronto: McClelland and Stewart, 1968).

85 In Quebec, the Bar is divided into a number of sections, each corresponding approximately to a judicial district. Each section has its own council, with a *bâtonnier* as its head. The general council of the Bar is made up of representatives from each section, and it is headed by the *bâtonnier general*.

86 See n. 81.

87 Jacques Hébert, a journalist and publisher, later became a senator. He travelled with Trudeau to China in the mid-1960s, and their adventures are chronicled in his book *Two Innocents in Red China* (Toronto: Oxford University Press, 1968).

88 April 8, 1968.

89 Pierre Trudeau, *Memoirs* (Toronto: McClelland and Stewart, 1993).

90 This is an oversimplification. A charge of murder always implied the intent to cause death. In capital (and later in first-degree) murder, the additional element was that the killing was not only intentional but also "planned and deliberate." In some cases, there could be little doubt that once the identity of the accused was established, the killing was not only intentional but also planned and deliberate. In that type of case, the judge

would likely instruct the jury that it was not open to them to reduce the charge to manslaughter. Nevertheless, despite this instruction, a jury could still return a verdict of manslaughter, and this could not be set aside by the judge. See also section 232(1) of the Criminal Code, which provides that "culpable homicide that otherwise would be murder may be reduced to manslaughter if the person who committed it did so in the heat of passion caused by sudden provocation."

[91] See chapter 28.

[92] George D. Finlayson, *John J. Robinette: Peerless Mentor* (Toronto: Osgood Society for Canadian Legal History, University of Toronto Press, 2003).

[93] *Chapdelaine v. R.* (1933), 62 C.C.C. 209. The case was Justice Rivard's greatest forensic triumph, and many years later, when we were colleagues on the Court of Appeal, I asked him one evening at a court dinner to tell us about the case. He did, in great detail, to my delight but to the groans of my colleagues who had heard the story many times before.

[94] See n. 75.

[95] Author's archives.

[96] See n. 83.

[97] All quotations are taken from the transcript of the inquest. The translations are mine.

[98] The new law provides that a coroner "shall recognize as an interested person any person, association, government department or agency requesting to be acknowledged as such and that proves his or its interest in the inquest to the satisfaction of the coroner": *An Act respecting the Determination and Circumstances of Death*, S.Q., chapter R-0.2, s. 136.

[99] Author's archives.

[100] Martha Adams, *Martha Adams* (Montreal: Editions du Jour, 1972).

[101] (1965), 46 C.R. 188. The judgment was written in French. The translation that follows is mine.

[102] Author's archives. Translation by the author.

[103] *Tamarack Construction Inc. v. The United Services Club Limited*, [1971] C.A. 334.

[104] Toronto: Carswell, 1991, 806.

[105] *R. v. Lerner and Buckley's Wholesale Tobacco Ltd.*, [1963] S.C.R. 625. State-run or licensed lotteries did not become legal in Canada until 1970, when the Criminal Code was amended to permit this activity by authorized bodies.

[106] Until the 1990s, the practice was to refer to High Court judges as "Mr. Justice" or "Madam Justice." More recently, at the suggestion of the Chief Justice of Canada, High Court judges and, in most provinces, provincial court judges as well, are simply referred to as "Justice so-and-so." Similarly, the ancient form of address of "My Lord" (and, more latterly, of "My Lady") has fallen into desuetude in many parts of the country, replaced by a more universal "Your Honour."

107 Jean-Jacques Bertrand was first elected to the Quebec legislature in 1948 at the age of thirty-four. He held a number of portfolios between 1958 and 1968 when, following the sudden death of Daniel Johnson, he assumed the leadership of the Union *nationale* and with it the office of premier. He died in 1973. The tradition of public service by the family was continued, first by his son, Jean-François, who was elected to the National Assembly in 1976, and later by his widow, Gabrielle who, in 1984, successfully contested the federal riding of Brome-Missisquoi for the Progressive Conservative Party.

108 The government of Canada may also ask for an advisory opinion, but a reference so directed is heard by the Supreme Court of Canada rather than a provincial Court of Appeal. This is what happened in the *Truscott* case (see chapter 28).

109 May 2, 1968.

110 1968-1354.

111 *Renvoie concernant la "taxe volontaire" decretée par la Ville de Montréal*, [1969] Que. Q.B. 561.

112 An Act respecting a Reference to the Court of Queen's Bench, 1968 S.Q., c.83.

113 *City of Montreal v. A.G. Que.*, [1970] S.C.R. 332.

114 The quotation is taken from a videotape of a rally held by students five days after the Computer Centre was occupied. The tape was later used in court.

115 *R. v. Frederick*, Montreal Municipal Court, No. 19-3609. The quotation is taken from the transcript.

116 *Montreal Star*, February 15, 1969.

117 *Montreal Star*, February 17, 1969. The statement is attributed to Carl Paris, identified in the report as a "West Indian and a student at McGill University."

118 Dorothy Eber, *The Computer Centre Party: Canada Meets Black Power* (Montreal: Tundra Books 1969), 95.

119 See chapter 19.

120 January 22, 1970.

121 At one point during the trial, Roosevelt (Rosie) Douglas, who attended all sessions (and whose own case was heard a few weeks later), approached Donna in the corridor, and with a big smile said: "How can a nice girl like you be married to a prosecutor?" I don't think he expected an answer, nor did he get one.

122 Dorothy Eber, *The Computer Centre Party: Canada Meets Black Power* (Montreal: Tundra Books 1969).

123 Notes on the Trial of the "Trinidad Ten," *Canadian Forum*, October 1974.

124 May 27, 2000.

125 March 26, 1969, 7192.

126 *Hansard*, March 27, 1969, 7250.

127 Advice to Vice-Principals, Senior Staff Members and Building Directors, March 28,

1969, issued by R.F. Shaw, Vice-Principal (Administration).

[128] Later a senator and, from 1974 to 1979, speaker of the Red Chamber; my translation.

[129] Many books have been written about these events. The three I found most useful for the purposes of this chapter are Ron Haggart and Aubrey E. Golden, *Rumours of War* (Toronto: New Press, 1971); Jean-Claude Trait, *FLQ 70: Offensive d'automne* (Ottawa: Les Editions de L'homme, 1970); and John Saywell, *Québec 70: A Documentary Narrative* (Toronto: University of Toronto Press, 1971).

[130] *Harrap's New Standard French and English Dictionary* (London: Harrap 1972) gives, *inter alia*, the following translations for the verb *vaincre*: "to vanquish, conquer, defeat." *The Concise Oxford French Dictionary* (London: Oxford University Press 1954) adds to these translations: "to overcome, master, subdue, surpass." I am satisfied, however, that my own translation—"we shall triumph"—best describes the spirit of the slogan.

[131] Part XI of the National Defence Act, R.S.C. 1970, c. N-4, provides, in s. 235, that "in any case where a riot or disturbance occurs, or is considered as likely to occur," the attorney general of the province may "by requisition in writing addressed to the Chief of the Defence Staff require the Canadian Forces, or such part thereof as the Chief of the Defence or such officer as he may designate considers necessary, to be called out on service in aid of the civil power." Such a request cannot be refused, and that is what happened in this instance.

[132] R.S.C. 1970, c. W-2. Note in particular s. 6(5), which reads as follows: "Any act or thing done or authorized or any order or regulation made under the authority of this Act, shall be deemed not to be an abrogation, abridgment or infringement of any right or freedom recognized by the Canadian Bill of Rights."

[133] Pt. II, Ottawa, Friday, October 16, 1970.

[134] I was surprised at the time that this point—that arrests and searches were made before the order-in-council was published—was not raised by the defendants. Certainly, the crown was prepared to argue that all actions taken were legal, but with what success remains a matter of conjecture.

[135] *Memoirs* (Toronto: McClelland and Stewart 1993), 134.

[136] That didn't come until a year later: *Public Order (Temporary Measures) Act, S.C. 1970–71–72*. This act continued in force a more limited version of the provisions previously contained in the regulations. It had a "sunset clause," and it expired on April 30, 1971.

[137] The coordinator, Stephen Cuddihy, later became a judge of the Quebec Court (the former Court of Sessions). Jacques Ducros and Jean-Guy Boilard were subsequently appointed to the Superior Court. Gabriel Lapointe and Bruno Pateras continued to have successful careers at the Bar. Yves Fortier served a term as Canadian ambassador to the United Nations.

¹³⁸ It was agreed with Choquette that "special crowns" would be paid $300 a day, a sum well below what each of us earned in private practice. No announcement was made of this arrangement, but when a reporter from *Le Devoir* asked me what I was paid, I saw no reason not to tell him. The news made a big headline and some of my colleagues were displeased with my disclosure, forgetting that these are public accounts which are published in the normal course of events. Eight months later, when estimates for the Department of Justice were discussed in the National Assembly, Choquette told the House that he had set aside $180,000 to pay the six attorneys he had hired. He added, perhaps feeling the need to justify the sum, that this was a group of "particularly competent" lawyers and that all but I were former crown attorneys, and while I lacked this experience I was "recognized as an authority on criminal law." Robert Burns, the *Parti Quebecois* justice critic, agreed and the matter ended there. In fact, Choquette was not entirely correct since Fortier had not worked for the crown, but he was an excellent lawyer with high standing at the Bar.

¹³⁹ To Montrealers, St. Lawrence Boulevard is known as "the Main." It is the street that divides the east from the west, as Yonge Street does in Toronto or Centre Street in Calgary. But, even more than that, in times gone by it was a busy centre of activity. For many delightful vignettes of the Main, see William Weintraub's *City Unique*.

¹⁴⁰ Some of the accused wanted to opt for speedy trials by a judge alone, but the case law was uncertain whether or not this could be done in cases of "preferred indictments." The crown would have been happy to oblige, but most of the judges ruled in favour of the "safe" course, that is to say trial by judge and jury. The provincial attorney general, Jérôme Choquette, tried to resolve the situation by asking the federal government to pass an appropriate amendment to the Criminal Code, and he sent me to Ottawa to present his case to John Turner, the federal minister of justice. Turner, who had been briefed on the point by officials in the federal Department of Justice, listened politely for a few minutes and then cut me off and told me that this was not the time to think of such amendments. That done, he said, "O.K., now let's talk," and we had a free-wheeling discussion about the events in Quebec.

¹⁴¹ I was a member of the Reform Club and so were some of my colleagues. My share certificate was signed by the club's secretary, Antonio Lamer, then a young lawyer, who many years later became chief justice of Canada.

¹⁴² Evan Thomas, *The Man to See: Edward Bennett Williams, Ultimate Insider; Legendary Trial Lawyer* (New York: Simon and Schuster, 1991), 44.

¹⁴³ Quentin Reynolds, *Courtroom: The Story of Samuel S. Leibowitz* (New York: Farrar, Straus, 1950), 346.

¹⁴⁴ See also, J.O. Wilson, *A Book for Judges* (Ottawa: Minister of Supply and Services, 1980), 44.

145 Author's archives.

146 *B. v. R.*, [1967] Que. Q.B. 775. The excerpt cited is taken from the judgment, not the report, which is in summary form. The translation is mine. See also the well-known statement of Lord Denning (then Denning L.J.) in *Jones v. National Coal Board*, [1957] 2 All ER. 155 at 158, where he said this (after enumerating the numerous interventions made of the judge), "all ... [made with] worthy motives on which judges daily intervene in the conduct of cases and have done so for centuries .... Nevertheless, we are quite clear that the interventions, taken together, were far more than they should have been. In the system of trial which we have evolved in this country, the judge sits to hear and determine the issues raised by the parties, not to conduct an investigation or examination on behalf of society at large ..."

147 Toronto: Carswell, 1987.

148 When Hanley was called upon to testify during the Caron "Vice Probe" (see chapter 7), he presented a picture of serene ignorance about the tough neighbourhood he represented. "On my oath, Your Honour," Hanley said at one point, "I swear there was never a brothel operated in my district." "It's your oath," said Judge Caron. "I am glad it's not mine." (Weintraub, *City Unique*, 82).

149 May 8, 1971.

150 December 4, 1971.

151 Rumours travel fast in Montreal, but not as fast as in the nation's capital. In the late 1970s, Allen M. Linden, then chairman of the Law Reform Commission of Canada, invited me to become vice-chairman of the commission. I thought about it and decided that I liked the bench too much to give it up. A few days later, I met Allen late one afternoon at the Four Seasons Hotel in Ottawa to tell him of my decision. From there, I went to the Cercle Universitaire to join my friend Jean Beetz for dinner. In another corner were Paul Martin and Senator Jack Austin. When Jean left the table for a moment, Martin came over and said, "Too bad you didn't accept Linden's offer." The total time elapsed between my meeting with Linden and the comment by Martin was less than two hours.

152 March 2, 1973. The editorial, written by Claude Ryan and entitled "Les retournements qui renforcent la justice," said, in part: "Avec la nomination recente des juges Deschênes, Gagnon, Crête, Beetz et Kaufman, il se produit a la Cour d'appel un renouveau prometteur. L'élévation à la magistrature de juristes aussi compétents sera pour le plus haut tribunal du Québec la source d'une revigoration dont plus d'un juriste eprouvait la necessite."

153 October 2, 1991.

154 April 12, 2004.

155 *Morgentaler v. The Queen* (1975), 30 C.R.N.S. 209 at 257 (emphasis added). Another good example is the opinion of Madam Justice (later Chief Justice) McLachlin in *The Competition Tribunal v. Chrysler Canada Ltd. et al.*, [1992] 2 S.C.R. 394, where she wrote: "This appeal is a simple exercise in statutory interpretation; it is subject to and determined by the principles governing the construction of federal statutes. The issue is *not* whether the Court is of the opinion that the Competition Tribunal should be given the power to punish as contempt a violation of a final order under Part VIII of the *Competition Act* ... nor whether extending this power to the Tribunal would seriously undermine the exclusive jurisdiction accorded superior courts by the common law. The issue is rather whether Parliament, in constituting the Competition Tribunal an inferior court, has clearly and expressly conferred on the Tribunal the power to punish contempt not only *in facie* (in the face of the court) but *ex facie curiae* (outside the presence of the court), a power traditionally reserved to the superior courts of record" (emphasis added).

156 This is but one variation of what Sir George Jessel, master of the rolls, supposedly said. See R.E. Megarry's delightful book, *Miscellany-at-Law* (London: Stevens and Sons 1955), 8.

157 *R. v. Treu* (1979), 49 C.C.C. (2d) 222.

158 February 21, 1979.

159 *R. v. Sussex Justices*, ex p. McCarthy, [1924] 1 K.B. 256 at 259.

160 *Re Truscott*, 2007 ONCA 575. The way for this was paved by the report of a provincial committee that recommended that proceedings in the Court of Appeal be televised, subject to certain conditions. This was endorsed by the attorney general, Michael Bryant.

161 April 2, 1995.

162 See chapter 25.

163 See the David L. Bazelon Papers, Biddle Law Library, University of Pennsylvania Law School.

164 See David McCullough, *Truman* (New York: Simon and Schuster Paperbacks, 1993). Kronheim's relationship with Truman is described in his tape-recorded reminiscences housed in the Truman Presidential Museum and Library in Independence, Missouri.

165 Minutes of Proceedings and Evidence of the Standing Committee on Justice and Legal Affairs, House of Commons, March 27, 1972, p. 1:17.

166 As a general rule, when entry is refused, carriers are responsible to take passengers back to their point of embarkation.

167 The full text read as follows: "The Government of Tanzania (GOT) has for the last several years been engaged in a far reaching economic reform program, focussing on

broadening the role of market forces in guiding economic decisions and improving or strengthening major policy instruments and institutions that would support markets and private economic activity. These reforms affect all sectors of the economy and in-volve, *inter alia*, reforms in the foreign exchange regime, the trade policy, the agricultural sector, the financial sector and the realization of the need to encourage the private sec-tor to play a greater role in the economy. It has become increasingly clear that one of the areas of weaknesses has been the legal sector which includes the Judiciary, the var-ious arms of the Government that provide legal services, private practitioners and the Law Faculty at the University of Dar es Salaam (LFUD). All these institutions and agen-cies have suffered from neglect over the last decade and are ill-equipped to meet the challenges of the evolving market economy. In addition, the legal and regulatory frame-work within which most of the commercial activities are to be conducted are too in-adequate to cater for the needs of transacting modern business."

[168] In the United States, the lawyer-to-citizen ratio is about one lawyer for 300 persons. In the United Kingdom, it is about one to 500. Canada sits in between, with more than 40 per cent of all lawyers based in Ontario. (*Law Times*, March 7, 2005.)

[169] See n. 147.

[170] March 6.

[171] *An Act to amend the Parliament of Canada Act (Ethics Commissioner and Senate Ethics Officer) and other Acts in consequence*, S.C.2004, c. 7, assented to on March 31, 2004, and proclaimed into force on May 17, 2004.

[172] Explanatory Note, published in the *Canada Gazette*, Vol. 138, No. 11, June 2, 2004.

[173] My counsel and I were ably assisted by a small staff of researchers, who worked long days, and sometimes even nights, to locate the documentation we required, read it, catalogue it, and then prepare summaries of what they had found.

[174] This is a well-known phenomenon. See, for instance, Antonio Lamer, *The Lamer Com-mission of Inquiry Pertaining to the Cases of: Ronald Dalton, Gregory Parsons, Randy Druken* (St. John's: Government of Newfoundland and Labrador, 2006) 71 & ff.

[175] For the dangers inherent in hair analysis, see, for instance, Patrick J. LeSage, *Report of the Commission of Inquiry into Certain Aspects of the Trial and Conviction of James Driskell* (Winnipeg: Government of Manitoba, 2007) 146 & ff.

[176] June 17, 2002. To help implement my recommendations, the Centre engaged Dr. James Robertson, a noted scientist from Australia, to conduct an ongoing audit. Dr. Robert-son visited Toronto a number of times, and he was so impressed with the progress that within two years he filed his final report and suggested that his services were no longer required. The ultimate proof of the Centre's rehabilitation came a short time later, when the F.B.I., having discovered problems in its own laboratory, asked the CFS to

examine the situation and make recommendations or improvements.

[177] See Patrick J. LeSage, *Report of the Commission of Inquiry into Certain Aspects of the Trial and Conviction of James Driskell* (Winnipeg: Government of Manitoba, 2007), 151 & ff.

[178] *Trace Evidence, in Forensic Evidence in Canada*, 2nd ed. (Aurora, Ont.: Canada Law Book, 1999), 277.

[179] February 20, 2007.

[180] *The Globe and Mail*, October 4, 2007.

[181] *The Commission on Proceedings Involving Guy Paul Morin* (Toronto: Ministry of the Attorney General, April 9, 1998).

[182] First aired on July 30, 1989.

[183] *Report of the 1989–90 Los Angeles County Grand Jury Investigation of the Involvement of Jailhouse Informants in the Criminal Justice System in Los Angeles County*, June 16, 1990. The report was drafted by Douglas Dalton, the grand jury's special counsel, who appeared as a witness before me.

[184] *Report on Investigation into the Use of Informers*, vol. 1, p. 37, made pursuant to the *Independent Commission against Corruption Act* 1988.

[185] Peter deC. Cory, *The Inquiry regarding Thomas Sophonow: The Investigation, Prosecution and Consideration of Entitlement to Compensation* (Winnipeg: Government of Manitoba, 2001), 69 & ff.

[186] Patrick Maguire died in 2002. He did not live to hear Prime Minister Tony Blair's apology on February 9, 2005, to members of the Guildford Four (all of whom were wrongfully convicted) and the Maguire Seven (of whom Patrick was one), in which he recognized "the trauma that the conviction caused ... and the stigma which wrongly attaches to [the families] today." The prime minister added that he was "very sorry that they were subject to such an ordeal and such an injustice ... and that's why I am making this apology today. They deserve to be completely and publicly exonerated."

[187] See n. 185.

[188] Toronto: Penguin Books, 1998.

[189] (2001), 151 C.C.C. 97.

[190] *Kindler v. Canada*, 1[991] 2 S.C.R. 779.

[191] *Report of the Governor's Commission on Capital Punishment* (State of Illinois: April 2002).

[192] In particular, the report adopted recommendations made by me concerning the training of police officers to help them recognize and understand the risks involved in using jailhouse informants, the dangers of "tunnel vision," the importance of investigating and reporting exculpatory evidence, and, in general, the risks of wrongful convictions in homicide cases.

[193] The terms of reference were as follows:

The independent review will determine if the Government response to institutional abuse has been appropriate, fair and reasonable. The review will:

- document and describe the Government response to the allegations of institutional abuse;
- assess the appropriateness of the Government response in light of the contemporary context and the public interest, the interests of claimants, staff and former staff of the institutions, other available response options; and
- assess the implementation of each element of the Government Response.

[194] *Searching for Justice: An Independent Review of Nova Scotia's Response to Reports of Institutional Abuse* (Halifax: Province of Nova Scotia, 2002). The report is available on the government's website: http://www.gov.ns.ca/just.

[195] "Counterpoint: When Redressing Abuse Becomes Abuse," February 5, 2002.

[196] Transfers of this nature still happen. In Texas, a school supervisor was transferred from one state school to another after pornography was found on his computer. Another supervisor, who had routinely awakened boys for late-night encounters, became the principal of a charter school in a different city: "Texan Calls for Takeover of State's Juvenile Schools," *New York Times*, February 28, 2007.

[197] *Hansard*, November 2, 1994.

[198] Richard Webster, *The Secret of Bryn Estin: The Making of a Modern Witch Hunt* (Oxford: The Orwell Press, 2005), 524.

[199] *Commission of Inquiry (Children in State Care) Act*, South Australia, 2004.

[200] See Robert N. Moles, *A State of Injustice* (Melbourne: Lothian Books, 2004), which deals with the case.

[201] See chapter 25.

[202] See, for instance, "Canadian Expert to Assist SA Sex Abuse Hearings," *The Independent Weekly*, August 28, 2005.

[203] *R. V. Easling*, Supreme Court of South Australia, No. 134/06.

[204] *EV, SE and K*, No. 631/07.

[205] Media release by Kris Hanna, M.P., December 11, 2007.

[206] See, for instance, questions asked in the Parliament of South Australia on July 23, 2008, by R.D. Lawson (in the Senate) and, the following day, by I.F. Evans (in the House of Assembly).

[207] Toronto: MacFarlane, Walter and Ross, 1997.

[208] Ibid., 18.

[209] April 13, 2004.

[210] 585 F. 2d 314.

[211] Author's archives.

[212] 731 F. 2d 550.

[213] November 11, 2000.

[214] Editorial, *The Globe and Mail*, October 29, 2004.

[215] *The Queen v. Steven Murray Truscott*, 2007 ONCA 575 (Ont. Court of Appeal).

[216] This act has undergone a number of changes since then. Its current successor is the Youth Criminal Justice Act, S.C. 2002, c. 1, which came into force on April 1, 2003. It is a more enlightened document, with a variety of extra-judicial measures designed to "provide an effective and timely response to offending behaviour." Among them are warnings, cautions, and referrals "to a program or agency in the community that may assist the young person not to commit offences." However, young persons charged with the most serious offences may still be referred for trial by judge and jury in the regular courts.

[217] Grand juries have since been abolished in Canada.

[218] Julian Sher, *The Globe and Mail*, Sept. 1, 2007.

[219] Porter, CJO, and Gibson, Schroeder, LeBel and Morden, JJA.

[220] (1960), 32 CR 150.

[221] Toronto: McClelland and Stewart, 1966, 256.

[222] The question referred to the Supreme Court of Canada for its determination was: "Had an appeal by Steven Murray Truscott been made to the Supreme Court of Canada, what disposition would the Court have made of such an appeal on a consideration of the existing Record and such further evidence as the Court, in its discretion, may receive and consider?"

[223] Julian Sher, *"Until You Are Dead": Steven Truscott's Long Ride into History* Toronto: Alfred A. Knopf Canada 2001), 427, 430, 468.

[224] 1992 Bernard Cohn Memorial Lecture, University of Windsor, quoted in *G. Arthur Martin: Essays on Aspects of Criminal Procedure* (Toronto: Carswell, 1997), 21.

[225] (1967). 1 CRNS 1.

[226] The term "Establishment Radical" was coined by Dennis Gruendig, who used it as a subtitle of his 1985 biography of Justice Hall: *Emmett Hall: Establishment Radical* (Toronto: Macmillan). As Gruendig explains his Prologue, Hall "is a rarity, and a study in contradictions: an Establishment man who is more interested in justice than privilege; a member of the elite, but one who has not forgotten his own humble origin or the people he has encountered on a human journey of eighty-six years; a man of intense ambition who relishes public recognition, but one who has used his fame and power for the public good rather than private gain."

[227] Ibid., 152.

[228] Quoted in Frederick Vaughan, *Aggressive in Pursuit: The Life of Justice Emmett Hall* (Toronto: Osgoode Society for Canadian Legal History/University of Toronto Press, 2004), 205.

[229] Strictly speaking, on a reference from the federal government, the Supreme Court

gives an opinion, not a judgment. In other words, it answers one or more questions put to it. But the effect is the same as that of a judgment: it is the final word on the subject.

230 Julian Sher, *"Until You Are Dead": Steven Truscott's Long Ride Into History* (Toronto: Alfred A. Knopf Canada, 2001), 538.

231 See s. 696.1 and ff. of the Criminal Code.

232 See chapter 25.

233 *The Toronto Star*, unaware that Anne McLellan had set the wheels into motion before her move to a new ministry, praised "Canada's new Justice Minister, Martin Cauchon," for having given Truscott "a chance to clear his name": Editorial, January 25, 2002.

234 Editorial, January 25, 2002.

235 Report by Tracey Tyler, January 25, 2002.

236 Ibid.

237 See chapter 26.

238 Section 696.2(2) of the Criminal Code (S.C. 2002, c.13, a. 71).

239 *The Globe and Mail*, October 29, 2004.

240 Ibid.

241 October 29, 2004.

242 November 1, 2004. Not every writer at the *National Post* showed as much understanding of the case as Jonas. On October 29, 2004, the day after the minister's announcement, a large headline on page 1 said: "Truscott 'likely' innocent." This was a total misrepresentation of what the minister had said, and the story that followed did not support the headline.

243 *Toronto Star*, August 29, 2007.

244 *Royal Commission on the Donald Marshall, Jr., Prosecution*, Nova Scotia, 1989.

245 *The Commission on Proceedings Involving Guy Paul Morin*, Ontario, 1998.

246 *The Inquiry Regarding Thomas Sophonow*, Manitoba, 2001.

247 *The Lamer Commission of Inquiry Pertaining to the Cases of: Ronald Dalton, Gregory Parsons, Randy Druken*, Newfoundland, 2006.

248 *Report of the Commission of Inquiry Into Certain Aspects of the Trial and Conviction of James Driskell*, Manitoba, 2007.

249 *The Queen v. Hanemaayer*, 2008 ONCA 580. The case is unusual because the accused, having been offered a plea bargain, pleaded guilty to two criminal charges (break and enter and assault) and was sentenced to two years less a day. In an affidavit filed with the Court of Appeal for Ontario, he explained that he had done so because he had "lost his nerve" when he found the homeowner "to be a very convincing witness and he could tell that his lawyer was not making any headway." A subsequent investigation found him to be innocent, and this was confirmed by the Court Appeal. The real culprit, it

turned out, was the notorious Paul Bernardo, now serving a life sentence for murder and other offences.

250 *Report of the Commission of Inquiry into the Wrongful Conviction of David Milgaard*, Saskatchewan, 2008.

251 News, Ministry of the Attorney General, July 7, 2008.

252 Sydney L. Robins, *In the Matter of Steven Truscott: Advisory Opinion on the Issue of Compensation*, March 28, 2008, p. 24 (references omitted).

253 Birobidzhan, a city of 75,000, is located in the far east of Russia, close to the border of China. In 1928, the Central Committee of the Supreme Soviet declared that Birobidzhan be set aside for Jewish colonization, and the area was officially proclaimed as the Jewish Autonomous Region. In the following decade, 43,000 Jews moved to the area, some coming from as far away as the United States and Argentina. But conditions were harsh, and by the late 1930s only 19,000 Jews remained. During that period, the area was hailed as a growing centre of Yiddish culture, and Yiddish and Russian became the two official languages. However, in 1936, Stalin began his infamous purges, and the NKVD, the Russian secret police, was given control of the area, intellectuals were arrested, and the idea of a self-governing Jewish region was ended, yet the name remained. In the years after World War II, Jewish immigration picked up again, and with it came a short revival of Yiddish culture—a Yiddish press, theatre, and literature. But once again, Jewish writers and politicians were arrested and charged with subversive activity, trying to create a natural culture other than the official Soviet culture. (See Arthur Rosen, *The Jewish Magazine*, February 2004.) There are now 4,000 Jews in Birobidzhan. The city has two synagogues, a Jewish National University (where Hebrew has replaced Yiddish), and Jewish traditions are taught in the city's 14 public schools. Many street signs are still in both languages, and so is the name on the railway station.

[index]

Blair, F.C., 47, 48, 52, 54
Blair, Tony, 342
Blume, Helmut, 44
Boilard, Jean-Guy, 184, 337
Boisvert, Gérald, 160
Bondi, Hermann, 48
Bourassa, Robert, 177–180, 187
Bowman, William, 309
Boyd, Marion, 254
Brennan, William J., 232
Briedl, Beatrix, 8
Broch, Hermann, 13
Bronfman, Samuel, 47
Brooks, David Hall, 306
Brooks, Vernon, 330
Brougham, Henry, 332
Brown, Joyce Ann, 271
Brown, Michael, 268
Brown, Robert, 256
Bryant, Michael, 340
Brynolson, Grace, illustration
Burger, Warren, 232
Burns, Robert, 338
Cahn, Lori, 25
Cahn, Charles, 44
Caissie, Ed, 42
Cameron, Glenn, 265
Camirand, Father, 79
Campbell, Philip, 312
Caroline, Queen, 90
Caron, François, 73, 74, 339
Carter, Emmett, 86, illustration
Carter, R.J., 309
Carter, Rubin ("Hurricane"), 271
Cartwright, John, 311
Casey, Paul, 144, 145, 147, 159, 227
Cauchon, Martin, 313, 345
Caumartin, Jean, 333
Centre of Forensic Sciences, x, 254, 260–263, 272
Cesarani, David, 21, 22
Chamberlain, Neville, 21, 31

Chambers, Egan, 213
Chapdelaine v. R., 131, 335
Charbonneau, Joseph, 73
Charbonneau, Maurice, 132
Chernow, Ron, 18, 328
Chevalier, Alexandre, 80, 81, 83
Chevrier, Lionel, 139
Choquette, Jérôme, 176–179, 184, 187, 338
Church, Howard, 59, 62
Churchill, Winston, 33, 44, 329
City of Montreal v. A.G. Que., 336
Clare, George, 9
Clarke, Gerald, 74
Clarkson, Adrienne, 239, illustration
Claxton, John, 213, 214
Clinton, Bill, 302
Code, Michael, 301
Coderre, Charles, 91
Cohen, Douglas, 121
Cohen, Joseph, 74, 83, 95–98, 104, 105, 193, 237
Cohen, Patricia, 329
Colas, Réjane Laberge, 105
Conant, Jim, 86, 87
Concordia University, 235, 236
Constantino, Dino, 214
Conway, Russ, 291
Cools, Anne, 166, 167
Cooper, Austin, 152, 255, 266
Cooper, David A., 327
Cory, Peter de C., 270, 342
Côté, Michel, 159, 171
Cotler, Irwin, 314–316
Cousineau, Maurice, 130, 163
Crankshaw, John, 83
Crête, Marcel, 218, 221, 232, 233, 235, 339, illustration
Crocker, E. James, 263
Cross, James Richard, 176–179, 188
Cruz, Rolando, 271
Csillag, Ron, 330
Cuddihy, Stephen, 184, 186, 337
Currie, Maureen, 255

Cutler, Phil, 92, 333
Dalton, Douglas, 342
Dalton, Ronald, 341
Dammers, Franz, 53
Daviault, François, 238
David, Fred, 18
Davis, Sammy Jr., 71
De Baar, Alison Hotz, 329
Dempsey, Lotta, 123
Denning, Lord, 111, 339
Deschênes, Jules, 218, 339, illustration
Deslauriers, Ignace, 185
DeWeert, M.M., 333
Diana, Princess of Wales, 332
Dickenson-Dash, Brenda, 166
Dickson, Barbara, 233
Dickson, Brian, 226, 233
Dill, Sir John, 33, 34
Dion, Gérard, 331
Dionne, Emilie, 87
Doidge, Norman, 330
Dollfuss, Engelbert, 17
Dorion, Noël, 80, 81
Dorval, C.O., 41
Douglas, Roosevelt ("Rosie"), 166, 167, 336
Drapeau, Jean, 73, 74, 80, 81, 158, 180
Draper, Paula Jean, 331
Draper, Ruth, 49
Dreaver, Frank, 302
Driskell, James, 318, 341, 342, 345
Drouin, Mark, 91
Druken, Randy, 341
Dubé, Antonio, 183
Duchess of York, 38
Ducros, Jacques, 139, 184, 337
Dufresne, Fernand, 73
Dunera, 38
Duplessis, Maurice, 72, 77, 78, 81, 92
Eagleson, R. Alan, 290–293
Easling, Tom, 286
Eber, Dorothy, 166, 336
Edelstein, Verona, 243

Edmison, J. Alex, 43
Edmonds, David, 19, 328
Edwardes, Charlotte, 5
Edwardh, Marlys, 270, 271, 312
Eidinow, John, 19, 328
Eliel, Ernest L., 54
Elizabeth, Princess, 68
Epstein, Hedy, 31
Epstein, Helen, 3, 327
Erickson, Norman, 261,262
Ettrick, 38
Evans, I.F., 343
Fackenheim, Emil, 44, 330
Falardeau, Jean-C., 77
Farouk, King, 104
Favreau, Guy, 211
Fawzia, 104
Feingold, Henry, 328
Fell, John and Mary, 22, 26–31, 34, 35
Fenton, Scott, 301
Ferguson, George, 85
Ferry, Georgina, 330
Finlayson, George D., 96, 97, 128, 333
Fiorito, Joe, 330
Fish, Morris, 183, 237, 238, illustration
Fitzpatrick, Bernie, 256–267
Flamm, Charles, 163
Forget, Toni, 219
Forrester, Maureen, 87
Fortier, Yves, 184, 187, 337, 338
Fortin, Carrier, 80, 81
Fortugno, Paul, 238
Fox, Francis, 251
Frank, Anne, 328
Frank, Otto, 328
Franz Joseph, Emperor, 13
Frenette, Orville, 333
Fuller, Sergeant-Major, 59
Gaboury, Marcel ("Hank"), 104
Gagnon, Claude, 159, 218
Gallant, Mavis, 74
Gameroff, Meyer, 219, 220

Lockyer, James, 261, 262, 285, 312, 314
Long, Breckenridge, 328
Loos, Rebecca, 5
Lunny, Adrian, 68, illustration
MacDougall, Patrick, 280
Machlovitch, Seymour, 197–200
MacKay, Kenneth C., 117, 118, 164
Macleod, A.J., 140
MacNaughton, Alan A., 210
McCrae, F.W., 59, 60
Maguire Seven, 342
Maguire, Patrick, 271, 342
Makin, Kirk, 228, 262, 267, 273, 274, 301
Mannheimer, Isaac Noah, 327
Marchand, Jean, 77, 81, 211
Marcoux, Claude, 137, 138
Marcoux, Marcel, 137, 138
Margaret, Princess, 214
Marshall, Donald Jr., 271, 318
Marshall, Thurgood, 231, 232
Martin, Dean, 71
Martin, Diane, 301
Martin, G. Arthur, 240, 241, 295, 309–311, 317
Martin, Paul, 251, 339
Martinez, Elaine Poor Bear, 302
Marx, Herbert, 233
Maxwell, Donald S., 180, 218
May, Robert Dean, 264–268, 271
McCullough, David, 340
McGill University, 44, 50, 54, 68, 84, 88–93, 169–173
McGowan, Michael, 43
McGuigan, Leo, 266–268
McKenzie, Robert, 123
McLachlin, Beverley, 340
McLean, A.T., 41
McLellan, Anne, 301, 313, 345
McMahon, Don, 64, 65
McManamy, Emmett J., 100, 101, 161
McMurdy, Deirdre, 250
Megarry, R.E., 340
Mendelsohn, Daniel, 16, 328

Meredith, W.C.J., 84
Mergler, Bernard, 164
Michalowsky, Michael, 256
Michener, Roland, 180
Milgaard, David, 270, 271, 318
Milgaard, Joyce, 270
Miller, A.W., 333
Miller, William, 333
Milton, Edith, 329
Mittleman, Abraham, 50, 51, 56, illustration
Mittleman, Dora, 55, illustration
Mittleman, Eta, 55, illustration
Mittler, Gisela, 4, 5, 15, illustration
Mittler, Markus, 4, 5, 15, 27, illustration
Moishe's, 184, 233
Moles, Robert N., 343
Montgomery, George H., illustration
Montpetit, Detective Sergeant, 121–123
Moon, Barbara, 53, 331
Moore, Brian, 74, illustration
Morden, John W., 225
Morgentaler v. The Queen, 340
Morgenstern family, 7
Morin, Guy Paul, 230, 240, 253–275, 313, 318, 342, 345
Morin, Jacques-Yvan, 333
Morrison, Nancy, 277
Morrow, William, 117
Moser, Sir Klaus, 48
Moss, George, 280
Mountain, George Jehoshaphat, 58
Mountbatten, Lord, 329
Mulligan, Ted, 284
Murphy, Ted, 67
Mydan, Carl, 87
Newmark, John, 44
Norris, Rick, 271
Nyalali, Francis, 246
Nysnyk, Stephanie, 261
O'Brady, Hertel, 80
O'Brien, John, 161, 162
O'Brien, Joseph E. ("Joe"), 88, 89